THE VISUAL GUIDE
MICROSOF
ACCESS®

THE VISUAL GUIDE TO
MICROSOFT
ACCESS®

The Pictorial Companion to Windows Database Management & Programming

Walter R. Bruce, III

Dan Madoni

Rich Wolf

VENTANA
PRESS

The Ventana Press Visual Guide™ Series

The Visual Guide to Microsoft Access: The Pictorial Companion to Windows Database Management & Programming
Copyright © 1994 by Walter R. Bruce, III, Dan Madoni & Rich Wolf

Library of Congress Cataloging-in-Publication Data

Bruce, Walter R.
        The Visual guide to Microsoft Access : the pictorial companion to Windows database management
    and programming / Walter R. Bruce, III. Dan Madoni, Rich Wolf. -- 1st ed.
        p.   cm.
    Includes index.
    ISBN 1-56604-070-1
        1. Data base management. 2. Microsoft Access. I. Madoni, Dan. II. Wolf, Rich. III. Title.
    QA76.9.D3B794 1994
    005.75'65--dc20   94-14295
                                                        CIP

Book design: Marcia Webb
Cover design: One-of-a-Kind Design; Adaptation; Robert Harris
Cover illustration: Jeff Brice
Icon design: John Cotterman
Index service: Dianne Bertsch, Answers Plus
Technical review: F. Scott Barker
Editorial staff: Eric Edstam, Diana Merelman, Pam Richardson, Jessica Ryan
Production staff: John Cotterman, Terri March, Marcia Webb, Mike Webster
Proofreader: Mike Sutton

First Edition 9 8 7 6 5 4 3 2
Printed in the United States of America

Ventana Press, Inc.
P.O. Box 2468
Chapel Hill, NC 27515   For information about our audio products, write us at
919/942-0220   Newbridge Book Clubs, 3000 Cindel Drive, Delran, NJ 08375
FAX 919/942-1140

Limits of Liability and Disclaimer of Warranty

Trademarks

Trademarked names appear throughout this book. Rather than list the names and entities that own the trademarks or insert a trademark symbol with each mention of the trademarked name, the publisher states that it is using the names only for editorial purposes and to the benefit of the trademark owner with no intention of infringing upon that trademark.

About the Authors

Walter R. Bruce, III, Executive Editor of Ventana Press, is the author of many computer books, including *Using Paradox 4.5, Special Edition, Using DataEase, Using PC Tools 8* and *Using PROCOMM PLUS*, and is coauthor of many others, including *Using MS-DOS 5, Killer Windows Utilities* and *Using PC Tools 2.0 for Windows*. Walter's books have sold more than 250,000 copies worldwide. Walter makes his home in Chapel Hill, North Carolina.

Dan Madoni is an independent contractor and author offering consulting and training services nationwide. Dan's clients include NASA's Jet Propulsion Laboratory and Microsoft, where he was previously employed as a Product Manager for Microsoft FoxPro as well as having played a key role in the original Microsoft Access beta program. Dan has also worked in Research and Development and Product Support Services at Borland International and Ashton-Tate.

Rich Wolf is President of CompuWorks, Incorporated, a consulting firm specializing in database training and development. Rich has extensive training and development experience with Fortune 500 companies and government agencies throughout the United States. He has also authored the Microsoft University Access courseware, regularly writes articles for numerous magazines and newsletters and frequently speaks at national conferences and user groups throughout the country.

Acknowledgments

My heartfelt thanks goes to everyone at Ventana Press for permitting me to neglect my duties there while finishing this book. I especially want to thank Elizabeth Woodman and Pam Richardson for their unwaivering support and understanding when I needed it most. And, as always, I owe it all to my wife and kids for putting up with my late hours and grumpy moods for the duration.

For their invaluable contributions to this project, I thank the following individuals:

○ Jude Gigliotti-Mullaney, of VisualAccess Corporation, Charlotte, North Carolina, for writing Appendix B, "Installation."

○ Michael Harding, also of VisualAccess Corporation, for writing Appendix D, "Database Administration."

○ F. Scott Barker, of Woodinville, Washington, for his excellent technical review of the manuscript and for providing the material for Appendix C, "Setting Up Multiuser Databases."

Thanks also to Jessica Ryan and Eric Edstam for wonderful editing, to John Cotterman and Mike Webster for their superb page layout and to Marcia Webb for the very attractive design. Thanks to all for not complaining (too loudly) at my many last-minute revisions.

—*Walter R. Bruce, III*

To begin with, I would like to thank the helpful staff at Ventana Press, particularly Pam Richardson and Walt Bruce.

I would also like to express how great it was to work with coauthor Rich Wolf and technical editor and close friend F. Scott Barker.

Special thanks to Steve Alboucq and all of my other friends on the Microsoft Access team who made me what I am today, although they might not want to admit it. While I'm at it, I should also congratulate them for a job well done on Access 2.0!

—*Dan Madoni*

I want to thank my coauthors Walt Bruce and Dan Madoni for their encouragement and for working together to complete this book. A special thanks to Bruce Troutman for his help with the chapter on graphs. I also want to thank my friend and business partner Lee Zuidema; I promise I'm out of "book mode" for a while. Finally, I want to thank God for giving me the ability to concentrate in spite of all of the difficulties life presents.

—*Rich Wolf*

DEDICATION

For Terry
-WB

For my wife Mary Madoni
and my son Matthew
Angelo Ciriaco Madoni
-DM

To Kevin and Kelly,
you are my inspiration
in all I do.
-RW

CONTENTS

Chapter 6　Creating Queries on the Fly 165

Chapter 7　Mastering Queries 195

Chapter 8 Designing Access Forms Quickly 227

Chapter 9 Designing Custom Forms 259

Chapter 12 **Exploring & Admiring OLE 2.0 ....375**

Chapter 13 **Presenting Your Data Graphically....................391**

Chapter 14 **Designing a "Friendly" User Interface..............411**

INTRODUCTION

Have you ever taken a course in school because your friends told you it was easy, and then barely made it out alive? Sometimes using today's crop of "easy" programs leave you with that same sense of self-doubt. It's not just you. The truth is that even the easiest computer program is far from easy. The more powerful and feature-rich they become, the more ways a user has to go wrong.

Fortunately, when it comes to Access, you have two things going for you. First, you've purchased a program that is a vast improvement over earlier generations of database management programs. And second, you purchased this book.

Access does a wonderful job of hiding much of the complexity of database management while providing tools that enable you to easily create powerful databases, as well as beautiful forms and reports. This book helps you avoid the pitfalls that remain, and in a very short time will have you creating Access databases and database applications like a pro.

TAKING THE VISUAL APPROACH

Most databases are highly text intensive. But, as a Windows-based program, Access itself is very visual in nature. Consequently, we have taken a more visual approach in this book than you will find in most computer books. As often as possible, we have illustrated discussions covered in the book with screen shots and other artwork. These illustrations enable you to work along with the text and to periodically compare the contents of your computer's screen to the screens found in the book.

Important procedures are set out clearly in numbered steps to make it easy to follow along. When you have a clear set of step-by-step instructions, as well as enough pictures to show you where you've been and where you're going, you can't go wrong!

WHAT'S INSIDE

The Visual Guide to Microsoft Access is divided into 17 chapters and four appendixes:

○ The first two chapters, "Taking a Whirlwind Tour of Access," and "Designing Your Database" orient you to database terminology and concepts in general, and Microsoft Access features and capabilities in particular.

Chapters 3 through 11 provide a hands-on tutorial to all of Access' most fundamental and most important features.

○ Chapters 3 and 4 teach you how to create Access tables, using Access' automated Table Wizards, and using Design view.

○ Chapter 5 teaches you how to enter data into your database, how to sort and arrange your data onscreen and how to easily print information from your database.

○ In Chapters 6 and 7 you discover Access' powerful *query* method of retrieving data from your database.

○ In Chapters 8 and 9 you learn how to create data-entry forms—first using Access' form generating Form Wizards, and then on your own using Design view.

○ Chapters 10 and 11 then take you through designing reports for your databases—again starting with Report Wizards and moving to Design view.

The last six chapters—Chapters 12 through 17—introduce you to Access' most powerful capabilities.

○ Chapter 12 introduces you to the Windows integration technology known as Object Linking and Embedding (OLE) and shows you how it can work for you.

○ Chapter 13 gives you a taste of the benefits of application integration by demonstrating the use of Microsoft Graph from within Access.

○ In Chapter 14 you begin to learn how to design a professional-quality database application, focusing on the visual user interface.

○ Chapter 15 then introduces you to the power of Access macros.

○ And, finally, Chapters 16 and 17 get you started with Access' programming language, Access Basic.

The four appendixes provide additional information that you will find helpful.

○ Appendix A provides guidance on deciding when it is time to consider hiring an Access professional. In addition, it provides a list of third-party resources–consultant, programmers, trainers, etc., who specialize in Microsoft Access.

○ Appendix B is a guide to installing Access. If you haven't yet installed the program, turn to Appendix B for a few pointers and tips.

○ Appendix C will be of interest to you if you plan to create Access databases that will be shared over a local area network.

○ Appendix D provides additional guidance to anyone responsible for maintaining and administering an Access database.

HOW TO USE THIS BOOK

As a hands-on tutorial, this book is most valuable to you when you work through all its examples as you read. To make it as easy as possible for you to do this, we have included all the necessary files on the companion disk, found in the back of this book. The companion disk includes all the files necessary to complete each chapter's examples. It also includes a completed version of the database discussed in this book that you can try out and explore immediately!

Just run the installation program on the disk and turn to Chapter 1–you're all set to find out just how easy and fun learning Access can be.

1

TAKING A WHIRLWIND TOUR OF ACCESS

You undoubtedly have finished installing Microsoft Access on your computer and are ready to put it through its paces. If not, take the time to do so before you start this chapter (see Appendix B for a few installation tips). As the chapter title implies, the purpose of this chapter is to take you on a quick hands-on orientation tour of Access. You'll get an idea of some of Access' fundamental capabilities and will preview some of the techniques found in this book.

The first portion of this chapter uses the Northwind Traders database distributed with Access. Using this sample database, you'll run through several exercises that show you around "Access country": you'll open the *database*; look at a few *tables*; experiment with an Access *query*; open a *form*; and view and print a *report*.

To help you focus on the topics presented here, we have developed an Access database application specifically for this book. In the latter portion of this chapter, we'll take a look at this sample application.

Finally, the last two sections of this first chapter preview Access' uniquely powerful database-building tools known as *Wizards*, and the program's special online coach known as *Cue Cards*.

WHAT IS ACCESS & WHEN SHOULD I USE IT?

Before we get started with our hands-on tour, it may be helpful to put Access into perspective. Access is computer software that fits into the broad category of software collectively known as *database management software*, or *database management systems* (sometimes abbreviated DBMS). It also fits the somewhat more narrow definition of *relational database management software*, or *relational database management systems* (sometimes abbreviated RDBMS). Software in this category is used to collect information and store it in such a way that you can easily find, retrieve and manipulate specific information, and, most often, to print the information as a *report*.

Database management software, such as Access, is not the only type of software that enables you to collect, retrieve, manipulate and report information.

○ Spreadsheet programs, such as Microsoft Excel or Lotus 1-2-3, are often used as database managers. Most people are comfortable with the row-and-column orientation of spreadsheets and like to collect information that way.

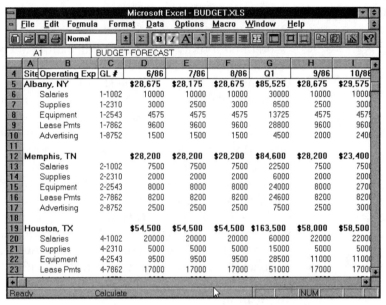

Figure 1-1: A Microsoft Excel spreadsheet.

○ Some people have special-purpose software to collect business or personal information that can also correctly be called database management programs. Such programs include check-writing programs like Quicken, accounting programs such as DacEasy and personal information management programs such as PackRat.

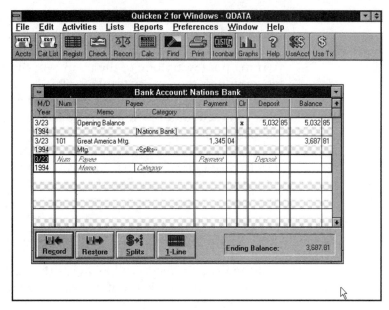

Figure 1-2: The personal financial program Quicken 2 for Windows from Intuit.

○ Many large corporations use custom-built information management systems that are tailor-made for their database management needs.

So where does Access fit into the database management landscape? In Access, Microsoft has created a program that attempts to be as easy and comfortable to use as a spreadsheet program, while providing the flexibility to create specialized applications and the power to create industrial-strength, company-wide applications. In short, it is possible to use Access to create database applications that duplicate and replace all your current information-collecting software; but, does this always make sense? Not always. The following guidelines may help you decide when to use Access and when not to:

○ If you already use a spreadsheet to keep track of a small amount of data, especially if you continually need to do a great deal of "number crunching" with the data, stick with the spreadsheet. But, if you find yourself continually sorting columns and rows of mainly text, switch to Access.

○ When you can buy a feature-rich, special-purpose program such as Quicken for less than $100, it doesn't make sense to try to use Access to duplicate its functionality. Use Quicken or one of its look-alike cousins to manage your personal or small-business finances. If your financial-management needs outstrip check-writing ponies, try one of the many workhorse, general-purpose accounting programs available for PCs before trying to develop your own system with Access. Many of the accounting programs that now sell for a few hundred dollars originally sold for thousands of dollars. If you try to develop an accounting system as rich and robust as programs such as Peach Tree Accounting, DacEasy or OneWrite Plus, you probably will spend thousands of dollars in time and effort and still not be completely satisfied.

O Use Access to build databases to collect information that is unique to your business or your life-style. If no suitable special-purpose program is available, turn to Access and develop your own. Access enables you to create screens that are just as polished and professional-looking as the best applications available on the market. But, more important, you can tailor Access databases to the special needs and requirements of the people who will have to use them. For example, if you are building a consulting business and need to collect information about your clients and the projects you are undertaking, build a database with Access. Use the database not only to collect this information, but also to track the projects, generate progress reports and do the billing. There is really no limit to what Access can do. And with the many enhancements that Microsoft has incorporated into Version 2.0, building Access databases is easier than ever.

OPENING AN ACCESS DATABASE

The remainder of this chapter is a hands-on tour of Access. Follow the steps in each section to get a quick glimpse of the things Access can do.

Microsoft
Access

To open the sample Northwind Traders database:

1. Start Access by double-clicking the Microsoft Access program item in the Microsoft Office program group. Access first displays its logo screen and then displays a welcome window (see Figure 1-3).

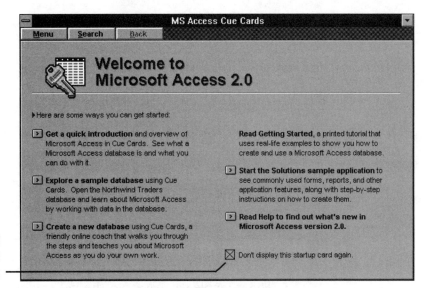

Figure 1-3: The Microsoft Access 2.0 welcome window.

Click here to prevent this screen from displaying again

2. The welcome dialog box contains five > buttons that each launch a short tutorial. The welcome window is a part of the MS Access Cue Cards system (see "Getting Help" in this chapter).

3. To close the welcome dialog window, double-click the Control-menu box in the window's upper-left corner. (**Note:** If you don't want the welcome window to display each time you start Access, click the check box in the lower-right corner of the window and then close the window.)

4. Click the Open Database button on the toolbar. Access displays the Open Database dialog box, as shown in Figure 1-4.

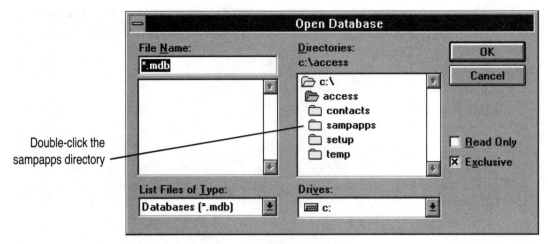

Double-click the
sampapps directory

Figure 1-4: The Open Database dialog box.

5. The example database, Northwind Traders (NWIND.MDB), is
   stored in the ACCESS\SAMPAPPS directory on your hard disk.
   To switch to the SAMPAPPS directory, double-click the
   directory name in the Directories list box, in the New Database dialog box.

6. Access lists all existing database files (NWIND.MDB,
   ORDERS.MDB and SOLUTION.MDB in the example) in the
   File Name list box. To open the Northwind Traders database,
   either double-click NWIND.MDB or type **nwind** in the File
   Name text box and press Enter. Access displays the Database
   window (see Figure 1-5).

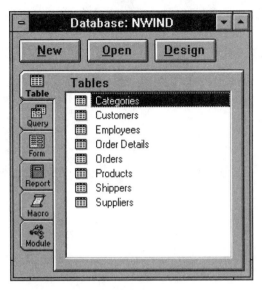

Figure 1-5: The Database window.

LOOKING AT ACCESS TABLES

The information that you collect in an Access database is stored in *tables*. Every table is composed of *fields* and *records* (columns and rows). The Northwind Traders database contains eight tables: Categories, Customers, Employees, Order Details, Orders, Products, Shippers and Suppliers.

To open the Customers table:

1. Display the Northwind Traders database (NWIND) in the Database window (see Figure 1-5). Access displays the tables list in the Database window.

2. Double-click the Customers table name in the tables list. Access displays the Customers datasheet, as shown in Figure 1-6. When you open an existing Access table from the Database window, the program displays the Table window in *Datasheet view*–a rows-and-columns format that resembles a spreadsheet. Each column represents a *field* in the table; each row represents a *record*. When the table is displayed onscreen in Datasheet view, we refer to the table as the *datasheet*. Figure 1-6 displays the Customers datasheet.

Record selector column   Field names

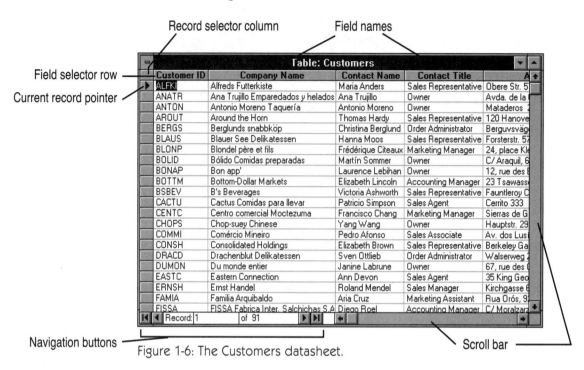

Field selector row

Current record pointer

Navigation buttons

Scroll bar

Figure 1-6: The Customers datasheet.

3. Access enables you to work in one record at a time. The record you are working in is known as the *current record*. The program places a triangular pointer in the record selector column to indicate which record is the current record. A blinking cursor indicates the current field. Try moving the cursor from field to field and record to record using the following cursor-movement keys:

Key	Move To
Enter	One field to the right
Tab	One field to the right
Shift-Tab	One field to the left
Right Arrow	One field to the right
Left Arrow	One field to the left
Up Arrow	Preceding row
Down Arrow	Next row
PgUp	Preceding window-full
PgDn	Next window-full
Home	Left-most field in the current row
End	Right-most field in the current row
Ctrl-Home	Left-most field in the first row
Ctrl-End	Right-most field in the last row

4. Also try moving through the table using the mouse. First, just click a field that is currently displayed onscreen. Access moves the cursor to that field. When there are too many rows and/or columns to display at one time, you can use the mouse and the scroll bar(s) to scroll up and down and/or left and right through the table. Use the mouse and scroll bars to scroll left and right, and up and down through the Customers table.

5. In the lower-left corner of the Table window are four *navigation buttons* that resemble the buttons on a VCR. These buttons enable you to move around the table quickly (see Figure 1-7).

Move to the preceding record

Move to the next record

Move to the last record

Move to the first record

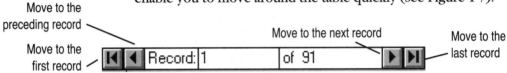

Figure 1-7: The navigation buttons.

6. After you finish perusing the Customers datasheet, close the table by double-clicking the Control-menu box in the upper-left corner of the Table window. Access closes the Table window and returns to the Database window.

On your own, open and explore the other tables in the Northwind Traders database.

Refer to Chapters 3 and 4 for a complete discussion of how to create Access tables. Then turn to Chapter 5 for full coverage of how to work with tables.

EXPERIMENTING WITH ACCESS QUERIES

In non-computereze, the term "query" means inquire or request information. In Access, a query requests information from the database. Access queries are the way you retrieve information from the tables in your Access database. For example, you may want to retrieve information as straightforward as a list of all your customers with their customer ID, or as complicated as the total sales in each product category. The understanding and mastery of queries is essential to the understanding and mastery of Access.

In the Northwind Traders database, more than 30 queries have already been designed and are ready for your use. To use a previously designed query, follow these steps:

1. Display the Northwind Traders database (NWIND) in the Database window (see Figure 1-5). Access displays the tables list in the Database window.

2. Click the Query button in the Database window. Access displays the Query list (see Figure 1-8).

Figure 1-8: The Queries list.

3. To see a list of all customers along with the identification
   number of each customer, double-click Customer List in the
   query list. Access displays the results of the query as a
   datasheet referred to as a *dynaset*. Figure 1-9 shows the
   dynaset that results from the Customer List query.

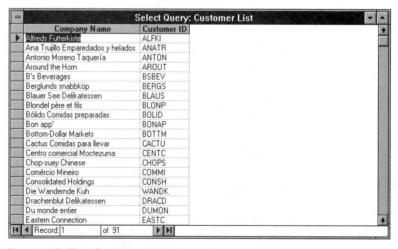

Figure 1-9: The Customer List dynaset.

4. A dynaset is a subset of a table or tables in the database. You
   can move around within the dynaset just as you can in any

datasheet. Use the cursor-movement keys and the mouse to explore the Customer List dynaset.

5. To close the dynaset, double-click the window's Control-menu box.

6. Run some of the other queries included in the Northwind Traders database. For example, the Employee Sales for 1993 query generates a dynaset that totals all the sales made by each employee during 1993.

Designing a query from scratch is quite easy. Suppose you want to see a list of all products in the Products table that have a price of less than $10. Follow these steps:

1. Display the query list for the NWIND database in the Database window (see Figure 1-8).

2. Click the New button in the Database window. Access displays the New Query dialog box (see Figure 1-10).

Figure 1-10: The New Query dialog box.

3. Click the New Query button in the New Query dialog box. Access displays the Select Query window in Design view, and then immediately displays the Add Table dialog box, which is shown in Figure 1-11, on top of the Select Query window.

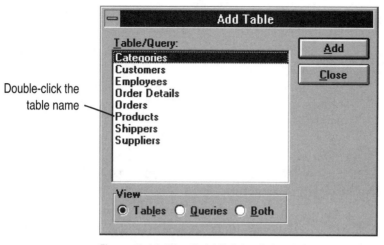

Double-click the table name

Figure 1-11: The Add Table dialog box.

4. The Table/Query list in the Add Table dialog box lists all the tables in the database (because the Tables option button is selected at the bottom of the dialog box). You want to see a subset of products, so double-click the Products table name. Access adds to the upper pane of the Select Query window a box listing all of the fields from the Products table, as shown in Figure 1-12.

5. The Add Table dialog box is still displayed on top of the Select Query window. Double-click the Control-menu box of the Add Table dialog box to return to the Select Query Design view window.

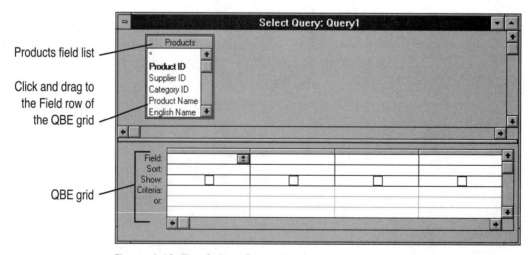

Products field list

Click and drag to the Field row of the QBE grid

QBE grid

Figure 1-12: The Select Query Design view window after adding the Products field list.

6. You are interested in only two fields from the Products table: Product Name and Unit Price. To cause only these two fields to be included in the dynaset, add the Product Name and Unit Price field names to the Field row in the grid displayed in the lower half of the Select Query window. This grid is known as the *QBE grid* (QBE stands for Query By Example, the name sometimes used to refer to the query process). To cause the Product Name field to be included in the dynaset, click Product Name in the field list and drag the field name to the Field row in the QBE grid. Access adds the field name to the QBE grid (see Figure 1-13).

7. The Unit Price field doesn't show initially in the Products field list, so use the mouse to scroll the list box. Double-click the Unit Price field name (an alternative method to the drag-and-drop methods used in step 6) in the Product field list. Access adds the field name to the QBE grid, as shown in Figure 1-13.

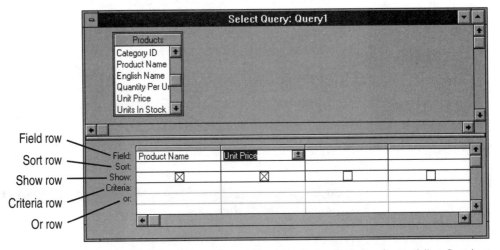

Figure 1-13: The Select Query Design view window after adding Product Name and Unit Price to the Field row of the QBE grid.

8. Before we limit the dynaset to products with prices less than $10, let's see the complete list of products. To run the query, click the Run button in the toolbar. Access displays the resulting dynaset in the Select Query window (see Figure 1-14).

Select Query: Query1	
Product Name	**Unit Price**
Chai	$18.00
Chang	$19.00
Aniseed Syrup	$10.00
Chef Anton's Cajun Seasoning	$22.00
Chef Anton's Gumbo Mix	$21.35
Grandma's Boysenberry Spread	$25.00
Uncle Bob's Organic Dried Pears	$30.00
Northwoods Cranberry Sauce	$40.00
Mishi Kobe Niku	$97.00
Ikura	$31.00
Queso Cabrales	$21.00
Queso Manchego La Pastora	$38.00
Konbu	$6.00
Tofu	$23.25
Genen Shouyu	$15.50
Pavlova	$17.45
Alice Mutton	$39.00
Carnarvon Tigers	$62.50

Record: 1   of 77

Figure 1-14: The dynaset that results from the query shown in Figure 1-13.

9. Notice that there are 77 products in the Products table. Now, let's return to Design view and modify the query. Click the Design View button in the toolbar. Access removes the dynaset from the screen and returns to the Select Query window shown in Figure 1-13.

10. Use the mouse to place the cursor in the Criteria row of the QBE grid, in the Unit Price column. To indicate that you want to see only products with a price less than $10, type **<10** in the Criteria row of the Unit Price column.

11. Click the Run button in the toolbar to run the query again. This time Access displays a list of only 11 records (see Figure 1-15).

Select Query: Query1	
Product Name	**Unit Price**
Konbu	$6.00
Teatime Chocolate Biscuits	$9.20
Tunnbröd	$9.00
Guaraná Fantástica	$4.50
Geitost	$2.50
Jack's New England Clam Chowd	$9.65
Røgede sild	$9.50
Zaanse koeken	$9.50
Filo Mix	$7.00
Tourtière	$7.45
Rhönbräu Klosterbier	$7.75

Record: 1   of 11

Figure 1-15: The dynaset that includes all products with Unit Price less than $10.

12. By default, Access assigns the name Query1 to your new query. Let's assume that you may want to run this query again, so you need to save the query with its own name. Let's use the name "Products Less Than $10." First click the Design View button to return to Design view. Then click the Save button on the toolbar. Access displays the Save As dialog box.

13. Type **Products Less Than $10** and either press Enter or click the OK button. Access saves the query to the current database. The next time you display the Queries list in the Database window, this new query will be added.

14. Double-click the Control-menu box in the upper-left corner of the Select Query window to close the window.

15. Find the new Products Less Than $10 query in the Queries list and double-click the query name to test the query. Then close the dynaset to return to the Database window.

EXPLORING ACCESS FORMS

So far this chapter has shown you two types of datasheets—the Table window in Datasheet view and a dynaset in Datasheet view. Another way to look at data from a table is through a *form*—a fill-in-the-blank screen that typically displays a database one record at a time. The Northwind Traders database contains 29 forms that can be used to input and view data.

Some forms display data from one table at a time. For example, to display the records from the Products table using the Products form, follow these steps:

1. Display the Northwind Traders database (NWIND) in the Database window (see Figure 1-5).

2. Click the Form button in the Database window. Access displays the Forms list (see Figure 1-16).

3. Use the mouse to double-click the Products form name in the Forms list. Access opens the Products form in Form view (see Figure 1-17).

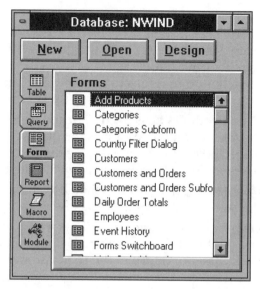

Figure 1-16: The Forms List in the Database window.

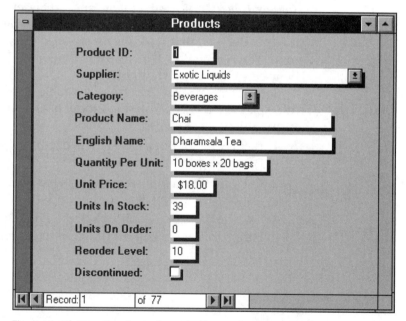

Figure 1-17: The Products form in Form view.

4. Viewing data using a form is essentially the same as viewing data in a datasheet, except that when you display a form in Form view, as shown in Figure 1-17, Access displays data from only one record. As you have seen, however, a

datasheet displays data from many records concurrently. The cursor-movement keys, therefore, work a little differently in Form view than in Datasheet view. The following table shows how cursor-movement keys work in an Access form:

Key	Move To
Enter	Next field
Tab	Next field
Shift-Tab	Preceding field
Right Arrow	Next field
Left Arrow	Preceding field
Up Arrow	Preceding field
Down Arrow	Next field
PgUp	Preceding record
PgDn	Next record
Home	First field in the current record
End	Last field in the current record
Ctrl-Home	First field in the first record
Ctrl-End	Last field in the last record

5. Use these keys and key-combinations listed in the preceding table to move around the table. You can also use the mouse and the VCR-style navigation buttons to move around the table.

6. To close the form, double-click the Control-menu box. Access removes the Form window from the screen.

Next, let's take a look at a form that uses information from two tables concurrently. The Categories form displays information from both the Categories table and the Products table. Follow these steps:

1. If it is not already displayed, open the Northwind Traders database (NWIND) in the Database window (see Figure 1-5) and display the Form list (see Figure 1-16).

2. Use the mouse and the scroll bar on the right side of the Forms list to find the Categories form name. Then double-click the Categories form name. Access opens the Categories form in Form view (see Figure 1-18).

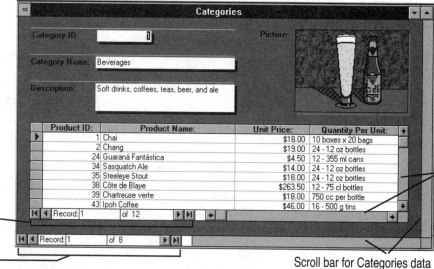

Navigation buttons
for Products data

Navigation buttons for
Categories data

Scroll
bars for
Products
data

Scroll bar for Categories data

Figure 1-18: The Categories form in Form view.

This form shows information from both the Categories table and the Products table. Each screen shows one of the categories of products sold by Northwind Traders. A scrolling region in the lower half of the window shows all the products in the displayed category. For example, the data shown in Figure 1-18 shows the Beverages category. The scrolling region—referred to as a *subform*—shows the many products that fall into that category. Notice that there are two sets of scroll bars and two sets of navigation buttons. The navigation buttons at the bottom of the Form window move through the records of the Categories table (Beverages, Condiments, Confections and so on), while the set of navigation buttons at the bottom edge of the subform move through the Products table.

3. Use the keyboard and the mouse to scroll through the categories and the products in each category.

4. Double-click the Control-menu box to close the form.

Refer to Chapter 8, Chapter 9 and subsequent chapters for more about the many powerful features you can design into Access forms.

PRINTING ACCESS REPORTS

Often the purpose of a database is to generate printouts of some kind—mailing labels, budget reports, invoices, sales analyses and catalogs are a few examples. Although Access enables you to print the contents of a form, the program's primary vehicle for creating output is the report. Let's take a quick look at a couple of the reports included in the Northwind Traders database.

Like forms, some Access reports are the product of only one table. More often than not, however, reports are based on a dynaset—the results of a query. As you will learn in Chapter 2, "Designing Your Database," a well-designed database stores its data in many different tables. For most reports, however, you need data from several of the tables in the database. A dynaset is the best way to combine data from multiple tables.

Let's take a look at the Alphabetical List of Products and the List of Products by Category reports from the Northwind Traders database, which are both based on the dynaset generated by the Product List query. Follow these steps:

1. First, take a look at the Product List query and its dynaset. Display the Northwind Traders database (NWIND) in the Database window (see Figure 1-5), choose the Query button and double-click Product List in the Queries list (see Figure 1-8). Access displays data from the Products table, as well as the Category Name field from the Categories table (see Figure 1-19). This dynaset will be the basis for the Alphabetical List of Products report and the List of Products by Category report. Double-click the Control-menu box to close the dynaset and return to the Database window.

Category Name field from Categories table ———

Fields from the Products table

Category Name	Product Name	Product ID	Units In Stock	Reorder Level	Un
Beverages	Chai	1	39	10	
Beverages	Chang	2	17	25	
Beverages	Chartreuse verte	39	69	5	
Beverages	Côte de Blaye	38	17	15	
Beverages	Ipoh Coffee	43	17	25	
Beverages	Lakkalikööri	76	57	20	
Beverages	Laughing Lumberjack Lager	67	52	10	
Beverages	Outback Lager	70	15	30	
Beverages	Rhönbräu Klosterbier	75	125	25	
Beverages	Sasquatch Ale	34	111	15	
Beverages	Steeleye Stout	35	20	15	
Condiments	Aniseed Syrup	3	13	25	
Condiments	Chef Anton's Cajun Seasoning	4	53	0	
Condiments	Genen Shouyu	15	39	5	
Condiments	Grandma's Boysenberry Spread	6	120	25	
Condiments	Gula Malacca	44	27	15	
Condiments	Louisiana Fiery Hot Pepper Sauce	65	76	0	
Condiments	Louisiana Hot Spiced Okra	66	4	20	

Select Query: Product List

Record: 1 of 69

Figure 1-19: The Product List dynaset.

2. With the Database window displayed, click the Report button. Access displays the Reports list (see Figure 1-20).

Double-click the
report name

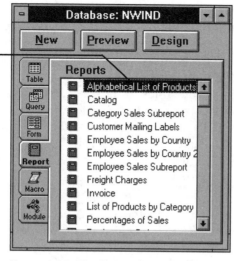

Figure 1-20: The Reports list.

3. Double-click Alphabetical List of Products. Access displays onscreen a preview of the report.

4. Click the Print button in the toolbar to display the Print dialog box. Choose the OK button to send the report to the printer (see Figure 1-21).

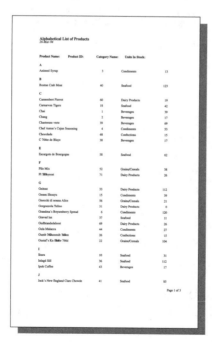

Figure 1-21: The Alphabetical List of Products report.

5. Now, on your own, preview and print the List of Products by Category report. This report, too, is based on the data included in the Product List dynaset.

TRYING OUT ACCESS APPLICATIONS

In this chapter you have explored tables, queries, forms and reports separately. An Access *application* is a collection of tables, queries, forms and/or reports tied together by a menu-like form or series of menu-like forms that make the tables, queries, forms and reports easily accessible. Later, we'll show you how to create Access applications.

So far you have explored several of the tables, forms and reports included in the Northwind Traders database. Most of the discussions in the remainder of this book, however, revolve around a database included on the companion disk that is bound in the back of this book. This companion database—the Contacts database—is a simple contact management application: a system to assist a busy salesperson in logging and following up on all the business contacts that he or she makes every day. By the end of the book, you will have developed this application yourself.

Although you will develop the Contacts database as you work through this book, a completed version of the database has been included on this disk as well. When you install the files from the companion disk on your hard disk, the sample database is stored in the \ACCESS\CONTACTS directory. You'll build from scratch the CONTACTS.MDB database file, which will eventually include the entire Contacts application. The completed version of the database application is stored under the name VENTANA.MDB.

Let's first take a quick look at the Northwind Traders database again, this time using a menu form known as the Main Switchboard. We'll then take a look at the completed Contacts application stored in the file VENTANA.MDB.

The most common way to generate an application with Access is to design a form that contains a number of command buttons. Clicking a command button takes you to a datasheet, form or report. This is how the Northwind Traders application works. The Main Switchboard form contains nothing but buttons that take you to other forms. Follow these steps to explore the Northwind Traders application:

1. If it is not already displayed, open the Northwind Traders database (NWIND) in the Database window (see Figure 1-5) and display the Form list (see Figure 1-16).

2. Use the mouse and the scroll bar on the right side of the Forms list to find the Main Switchboard form name. Then double-click the Main Switchboard form name. Access opens the form in Form view (see Figure 1-22).

Displays the Forms Switchboard form   Displays the Order Date Dialog form   Displays the Print Reports Dialog form

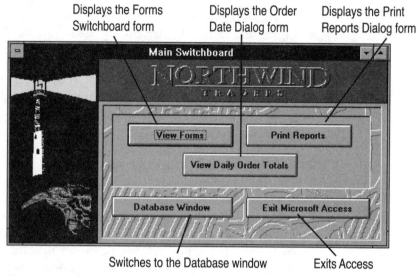

Switches to the Database window   Exits Access

Figure 1-22: The Main Switchboard form.

3. The Main Switchboard form contains five buttons. Each button opens another form. Click the View Forms button. Access opens the Forms Switchboard form, as shown in Figure 1-23.

Displays the Categories form   Displays the Products form   Displays the Sales Reps form

Displays the Customers form

Displays the Employees form

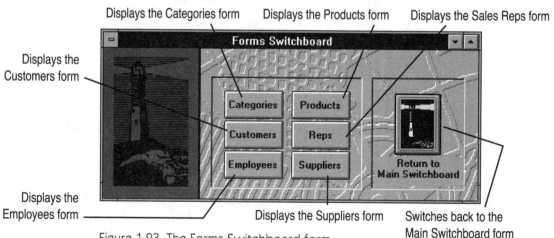

Displays the Suppliers form   Switches back to the Main Switchboard form

Figure 1-23: The Forms Switchboard form.

4. The Forms Switchboard contains seven more command buttons. Try out each of the buttons. The first six buttons display another form. After you display a form, double-click the form's Control-menu box to return to the Forms Switchboard.

5. To switch back to the Main Switchboard form, without closing the Forms Switchboard form, click the Return to Main Switchboard button in the Forms Switchboard form. Then use the View Forms button again to switch to the open Forms Switchboard.

6. When you are ready to close the Forms Switchboard, double-click the form's Control-menu box.

7. From the Main Switchboard you can switch to the Database window, without closing the Main Switchboard. Just click the Database Window button in the Main Switchboard form. To return to the Main Switchboard, double-click Main Switchboard in the Forms list.

8. Experiment on your own with the Print Reports and View Daily Order Totals buttons on the Main Switchboard. If you click the Exit Microsoft Access button, however, you will not only close the form but will exit Access as well.

9. When you are ready to close the Main Switchboard form, double-click the form's Control-menu box.

10. Now, double-click the Database window's Control-menu box to close the Northwind Traders (NWIND) database.

Next, let's get a glimpse of the Contacts application you will create during the course of working through this book. The main purpose of the Contacts application is to track your interactions with clients. Each time you talk to a client on the phone, or attend a meeting with a client, you log the interaction in the database. When a follow-up with the client is in order, you make a note of it in the database. On the day you need to contact your client again, the database reminds you.

To take a look at the Contacts application, follow these steps:

1. From the opening Microsoft Access welcome window, click the Open Database button in the toolbar to display the Open Database dialog box.

2. Use the Directories list box to open the ACCESS\CONTACTS directory. Then double-click ventana.mdb in the File Name list box. Access displays the Contact Manager Main Menu, as shown in Figure 1-24.

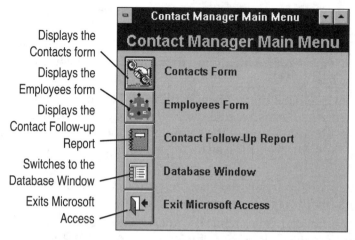

Displays the Contacts form

Displays the Employees form

Displays the Contact Follow-up Report

Switches to the Database Window

Exits Microsoft Access

Figure 1-24: The Contact Manager Main Menu.

3. Click the Contacts Form button. The application checks to see if you have any follow-up contacts to make today. Because you haven't logged any interactions with a client, the application displays a message that there are no follow-up contacts for today.

4. Click the OK button to continue. The application displays the Contacts form, as shown in Figure 1-25. (If the photographs look familiar, they are the same photos used in the Northwind Traders application. All other data in the application's tables is different.)

Displays the Interactions form

Displays only follow-up contacts

Displays the second page of the form

Displays Organization information

Scrolling Phones subform

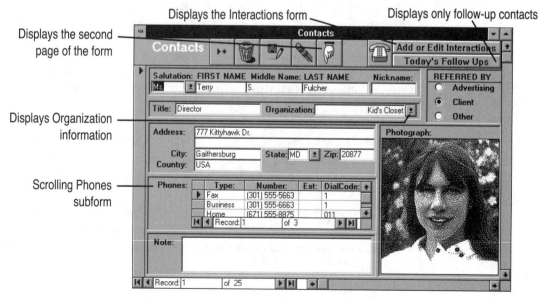

Figure 1-25: The Contacts form.

5. The Contacts form contains information about a client with whom you have dealings. The first page of the form enables you to store information such as name, address and phone numbers. To see the second page (see Figure 1-26), click the button with hand pointing down.

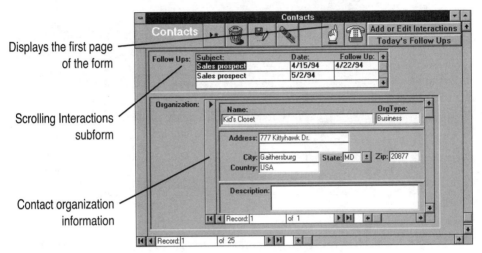

Displays the first page of the form

Scrolling Interactions subform

Contact organization information

Figure 1-26: The second page of the Contacts form.

6. The second page of the form contains information about follow ups and information about the contact's organization (usually a company), including address and phone numbers. Click the Previous Page button to return to the first page of the Contacts form.

7. The Contacts form contains three scrolling subforms—one for the contact's phone numbers (see Figure 1-25), one for logging interactions with the client whose record is currently displayed, and one for the organization's phone numbers (see Figure 1-26). First, scroll the Phone Numbers subform on the first page using the mouse and the scroll arrows on the right side of the subform. Notice that Ms. Fulcher has two phone numbers—a business number and a fax number. The form's design accommodates any number of phone numbers.

8. One interaction has been logged so far with Ms. Fulcher, and the form automatically enters the subject "Sales prospect" and today's date in the second row of the Interactions subform. If you decide to log another interaction with Ms. Fulcher, you probably want to record more information than just the subject and date. To see the Interactions form (see Figure 1-27), click the Add or Edit Interactions button in the Contacts form.

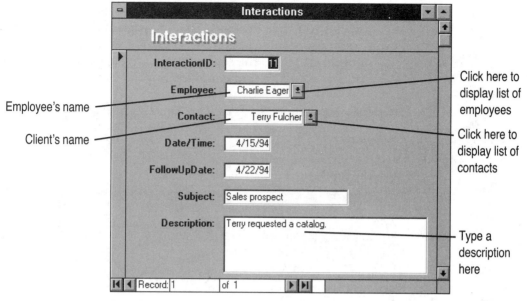

Figure 1-27: The Interactions form.

9. The Interactions form carries over the client's name to the Contact Name combo box. If you want to log in interaction information about a different contact while you are displaying the Interactions form, you can click the drop-down button at the right end of the Contact Name combo box to display a scrolling list of all contacts who have been entered into the database.

10. Let's assume you want to log a telephone call you just completed with Terry Fulcher. First, you need to move to a new record, so click the navigation button that points to the right (at the bottom of the Interactions form).

11. Assume further that your name is Charlie Eager. To add your name to the Employee Name combo box, click the drop-down button at the right end of the combo box and select your name from the list. Choose Terry Fulcher from the Contact list.

12. The application automatically enters today's date in the Date/Time text box and enters a follow-up date seven days later in the FollowUpDate text box. Let's assume you want to call Terry back tomorrow. Press the Tab key two times to move the cursor to the FollowUpDate text box. Type tomorrow's date.

13. After typing tomorrow's date, press Tab twice to move to the Description text box. Then type the following description of your conversation:

Terry inquired about prices for 500 Super Deluxe Widgets. Quoted price of $3.75 each, or $3.62 if she orders 750 or more.

After typing this note, the form should resemble Figure 1-28. Notice that as soon as you entered a name in the Employee Name combo box, Access entered a number in the Interaction ID text box. This number will be used to uniquely identify this record in the Interactions table. Access assigns the number automatically and will never reuse the number for another record in the Interactions table.

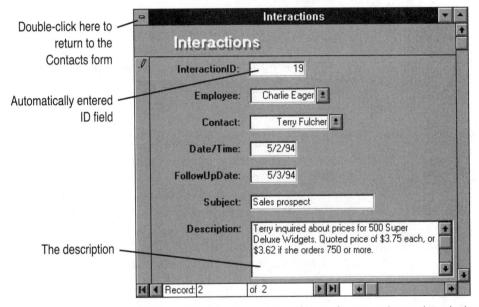

Figure 1-28: The Interactions form after entering a description.

14. Double-click the Control-menu box to close the Interactions form and return to the Contacts form. Notice that the second record in the Interactions subform in the Contacts form now lists a follow-up date of tomorrow for Ms. Fulcher.

15. Double-click the Contacts form's Control-menu box to close the form and return to the Contact Manager Main Menu.

16. Next, let's look at the Contact Follow-Up Report. From the Contact Manager Main Menu, click the Contact Follow-Up Report button. Access displays a dialog box that asks you to enter a date. To see a list of follow-ups for tomorrow, type tomorrow's date and press Enter.

17. Access displays a preview of the report (see Figure 1-29), which lists the scheduled follow up with Ms. Fulcher.

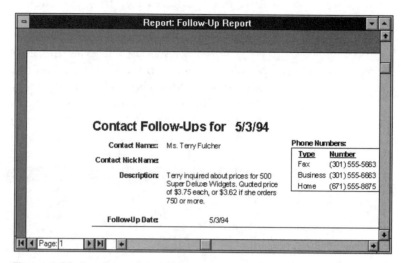

Figure 1-29: Preview of the Follow-Up Report.

18. Click the Print button in the toolbar to display the Print dialog box. Choose the OK button to send the report to the printer. Then double-click the Control-menu box of the print preview window to return to the Contact Manager Main Menu.

19. Now, take a look at the Employees form. This form contains information about the sales representatives who will be using the contact manager application. To display the Employees Form, click the Employees Form button in the Contact Manager Main Menu. The application displays the form, as shown in Figure 1-30.

Figure 1-30: The Employees form.

20. Like the Contacts form, the Employees form contains a scrolling subform for entering telephone numbers and a Notes field for recording narrative information. Use the navigation buttons in the phones subform to scroll through Sam's numbers. Then use the mouse and the navigation buttons at the bottom of the form to scroll through the four employee records.

21. Double-click the Control-menu box to close the Employees form and return to the main menu.

22. Finally, try the remaining two buttons on the Contact Manager Main Menu. First, click the Database Window button. The application displays and switches to the Database window, but does not close the Contact Manager Main Menu form. The form is still visible, but is now behind the Database window. To return to the form, choose Window, Hide from the menu bar. Access hides the Database window and returns to the open form.

23. Last, click the Exit Microsoft Access button in the Contact Manager Main Menu form. The application closes the menu form and exits Access.

WHAT ARE ACCESS WIZARDS?

As you have already seen in this chapter, even simple databases can be a bit tedious. Creating all the tables, forms, reports and so on that are part of an Access database application may seem daunting to the uninitiated. Fortunately, Microsoft has provided many automated helpers known as *Wizards* and *Builders* to assist you in building your Access database.

Access Wizards are available for nearly every database-building project you can imagine. When you need to create a table, you can use a Table Wizard. If you later need to add a field to a previously designed table, you can use the Field Builder—an abbreviated version of the Table Wizard—to add the field. After you have defined tables for your database, you'll need a few forms and reports. Quite naturally, therefore, Access includes Wizards and Builders for form building and Wizards and Builders for report building.

Earlier in this chapter you created a simple query. Most often, queries are easy enough to create that Wizards are not needed. But some types of queries are more complicated. Access Version 2.0, therefore, includes Wizards that generate certain advanced queries. As you work through this book, you'll see examples of each of these types of Wizards. It is usually the best practice to use Wizards to create a "rough-draft" of a table, form or report. Then you can use Design view to polish the Access object to your exact specifications.

GETTING HELP

Like all Windows-based programs, the online documentation supplied with Access is displayed by the Windows Help facility. If you have ever used the Help facility found in any other Windows-based program, you know how to use Access' Help facility, with one exception—Access Cue Cards.

Access Cue Cards are a feature that is unique to this Windows-based program. Cue Cards are online tutorials that walk you through various procedures in Access. Access provides a series of step-by-step Cue Cards to guide you through the following activities:

○ Learning what a database can do.

○ Building a database and creating tables.

○ Adding, viewing, editing, sorting and filtering data in forms and datasheets.

○ Creating and troubleshooting queries.

○ Creating and customizing forms.

○ Creating and customizing print reports and mailing lists.

○ Designing, running and attaching macros.

When you use Cue Cards, you don't have to work through a preexisting example. Instead, you can work through your own "real-world" problem with Cue Cards as your coach.

To use Access' Cue Cards, follow these steps:

1. Click Help on the menu bar to display the Help menu and click the Cue Cards menu command. Access displays the MS Access Cue Cards window, as shown in Figure 1-31. This screen displays a menu of available Cue Card tutorials.

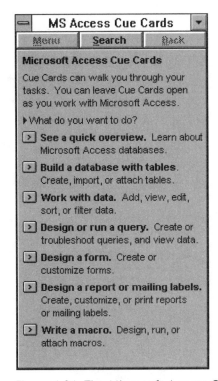

Figure 1-31: The Microsoft Access Cue Cards window.

2. Choose one of the available tutorials. For example, to see a quick overview of Access, click the first > button. Access displays another Cue Card menu screen. Click the > button located next to the topic in which you are interested.

3. Cue Card screens always remain *on top* of all other Access windows and dialog boxes but don't prevent you from carrying on with your work in Access. This allows you to see the instructions in the Cue Card while you are carrying them out in Access.

4. Use the Next and Back buttons to move between Cue Card screens. Use the Menu button to return to the most previous Cue Card menu screen. The Search button takes you to the standard Windows help Search dialog box.

5. Double-click the Control-menu box to close Cue Cards.

MOVING ON

This chapter has taken you on a quick hands-on orientation tour of Access. You should now have a good idea of some of the program's fundamental capabilities. You have explored a few forms and reports in the Northwind Traders database that is distributed with Access. And you have begun to get familiar with the sample contact management application that will be discussed at length in this book. Finally, the last two sections of this first chapter described Access' uniquely powerful database-building tools known as Wizards, and the program's special online coach known as Cue Cards.

Turn now to Chapter 2, "Designing Your Database," to begin learning how to "talk database." Then move to Chapters 3 and 4 to find out how to create tables, first using Table Wizards, and then using Design view.

2

DESIGNING YOUR DATABASE

Microsoft Access is arguably the most successful database management program to date, at least in terms of the speed at which the product has been purchased by consumers. Presumably, many of the hundreds of thousands of people who purchased Access have loaded and used the software. Access offers so many powerful tools for building and using computer databases that most users have found their experiences with the program rewarding. Just when these happy Access users least expect it, however, they realize they have to go back to the drawing board.

Most users of Access, as well as users of any other relational database product, take a serious misstep before they even turn on their computer–they don't take the time to correctly design the database before trying to build it in Access. As you have learned in Chapter 1; "Taking a Whirlwind Tour of Access," Access tempts you to just jump in and start "Accessing." But the time it takes to read this chapter and to learn how to design an Access database properly, will repay you tenfold in time you will not have to waste later redesigning your Access tables, queries, forms and reports.

THINKING DATABASE

Microsoft Access is a relational database management system for use with the Windows operating system on IBM compatible personal computers. Access can be an immensely useful tool, but first you must understand something of how to approach it, how to "think database."

Database

A database is like a clock. Most people know how to use one, but few really care to know how it works underneath. All your life you have used simple databases–telephone books, recipes, card catalogs, encyclopedias and so on–but you seldom consider how a typical database is organized.

Most databases we use every day seem pretty simple. We keep track of information about things. For each thing in the database, we collect a bunch of information. For each person or business serviced by the phone company, for example, there is at least one line in the phone book. For each dish you may want to cook, there is an entry in the cookbook, or a card in your recipe-card box. For each subject of interest, there is an article in your encyclopedia.

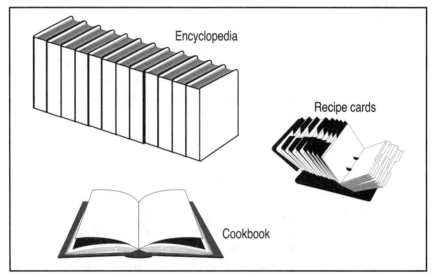

Figure 2-1: Typical "real-world" databases we use every day.

Often, however, everyday databases turn out to be more complex than they appear at first. Many businesses, for example, want several entries in a phone book: one or more in the white pages, and one or more in the yellow pages. Whenever the phone company has to change the phone number of a particular business, all of the company's entries in the phone book have to be located and changed. An article in an encyclopedia probably refers to many different topics. In a cookbook, a chicken-and-rice casserole dish could be correctly filed under chicken, rice, and/or casserole.

Figure 2-2: Many businesses want several types of entries in different locations in a phone book.

Obviously, the information we collect on a daily basis is often much more diverse and unstructured than a telephone book, encyclopedia or cookbook. As Bill Gates, the founder and chairman of Microsoft, is fond of saying, the personal computer should make such "information [available] at your fingertips." The personal computer is capable of storing vast amounts of information that, in theory, should be available for display at a moment's notice.

The trouble is, however, that in order to create out of real-world information a useful computerized database, we have to impose a structure on the information. This structure approximates or *models* the real world, but is at best very different than the real world. The most widely used method of modeling real-world data on a personal computer is based on an approach known as *relational database theory*. Microsoft Access is one of the most popular relational database management programs for personal computers.

The term *database*, when used in Access, has a broad meaning. An Access database includes *tables, forms, reports, queries, macros* and *modules* (tables, forms and reports are defined later in this chapter; queries, macros and modules are covered extensively in later chapters). Each part of a database is usually referred to as an *object*. All objects of an Access database are stored together on disk in a single file. Many other database management programs—such as dBASE IV and Paradox 4.5—store each object as a separate file.

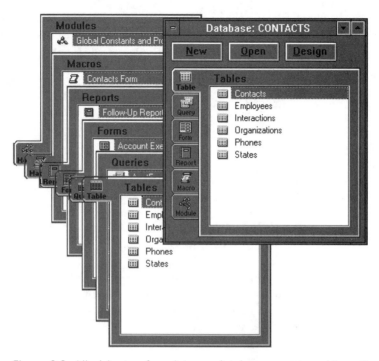

Figure 2-3: All objects of an Access database are stored together on disk in a single file.

. . . .

Note to Developers

Access is designed for ease of design and ease of use. The program's designers, therefore, chose to store tables—traditionally thought of as data—along with forms, reports, queries and modules—traditionally thought of as code. An entire database and all associated objects are stored in one convenient file on disk. This apparent design asset may, however, in fact be a liability from the point of view of someone who is developing an Access database for use by someone else. Updating or modifying any of the code objects is more cumbersome if these objects are stored in the same file as data. Using standard Access features it is possible to modify the code objects, but not as easily as it would be to modify code objects that are stored separately. Consequently, most experienced Access developers store code objects—forms, reports, queries, macros and modules—in one Access database file and store data objects—tables—in another database. These developers then *attach* the data tables (see the "Attaching Tables" section in Chapter 3) to the database that contains the code objects. For ease of use and discussion, the examples in this book store all objects in the same Access database file. In a "real" application, however, we almost certainly would store code and data in separate databases. Then, any time we need to modify the code, we would make the necessary changes to a copy of the original code database and then copy the modified version on top of the old version. The database that contains the data is never touched.

Tables

Although volumes have been written on relational database theory, the core concepts, as they relate to Microsoft Access, are relatively simple. The information that you collect in an Access database is stored in *tables*. Every table is composed of *fields* and *records* (columns and rows). Figure 2-4 shows a small table that contains data from a hypothetical phone list. This table contains three fields—Name, Address and Phone Number—and five records.

Name	Address	Phone Number
Burline S. Burke	43 Appleton Way	555-5993
Carlton S. Gump	88322 Federal Blvd.	555-4432
Sarah M. Osterman	7834 Hawk Dr.	555-7902
Paul M. Starkey	1818 Liverpool Place	555-3275
Barry C. Williamson	12045 Green Street	555-5549

Figure 2-4: A simple table containing three fields and five records.

Even without relational database theory, if you were given the task of keeping a phone list, you would probably design a table similar to the one in Figure 2-4. Many people like to use computer spreadsheets, such as Lotus 1-2-3 or Microsoft Excel, to keep track of information, because spreadsheets are arranged in rows and columns, like this table. Figure 2-5 shows a phone list stored in an Excel worksheet.

	A	B	C
1	Name	Address	Phone Number
2	Burline S. Burke	43 Appleton Way	555-5993
3	Carlton S. Gump	88322 Federal Blvd.	555-4432
4	Sarah M. Osterman	7834 Hawk Dr.	555-7902
5	Paul M. Starkey	1818 Liverpool Place	555-3275
6	Barry C. Williamson	12045 Green Street	555-5549
7			
8			

PHONES.XLS

Figure 2-5: The phone list stored as an Excel worksheet.

One of the key differences between relational databases and spreadsheets is the capability of relational database management programs to work with more than one table at the same time. This capability enables you to divide data into logical and more manageable categories.

A phone list seems simple enough, but even a simple phone list can benefit from a division into at least two tables. Many people have more than one phone number. A table design similar to the one shown in Figure 2-6 uses two tables to keep track of phone numbers. An identification number (the ID field) ties each phone number in the Phones table to an individual in the Contacts table.

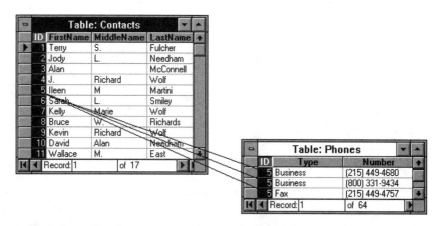

Figure 2-6: A phone list separated into two tables.

Because relational databases are usually composed of many tables, relational databases sometimes seem more complicated and confusing to design and use than data stored in a simple spreadsheet. This chapter teaches you a few simple guidelines to designing relational databases that will help you get off on the right foot in every Access database project.

FORMS

When you design an Access database, you don't stop with just tables. Tables—with rows and columns—aren't very flexible or helpful when it comes adding information to the database. Most businesses and institutions have spent a great deal of time and effort designing business forms for collecting information. Similarly, Access enables you to create beautiful forms for use with your Access tables. Figure 2-7 shows a fill-in-the blank form created with Access.

Figure 2-7: A fill-in-the-blank form created with Access.

If you completed the tour in Chapter 1, you already are familiar with the many faces of Access databases, including Access forms. Access forms can be nearly identical to the paper forms you have probably used for years, but can also be much more. In addition to the typical fill-in-the-blank-style forms that are reminiscent of paper forms, Access enables you to create powerful push-button menu forms that make it easy for any user of your database to determine what they want to do and how to do it (see Figure 2-8).

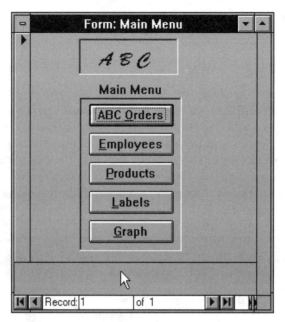

Figure 2-8: A menu form.

You can think of forms as clothing for your Access database. Using forms, you can control the way your database looks to the people who will use the database. Consequently, you need to be thinking of how the forms will look from day one. Often the forms you are already using in your business will provide a good starting point.

REPORTS

In business and in your personal life, you usually collect information for a specific purpose. If you plan to collect information in your computer, you probably plan to print some or all of the information arranged and formatted to suit your purpose. In Access, printed output from your database is known as a *report*.

In Access, reports are closely related to forms. Indeed, you can use an Access form as a report. But, more often, reports are based on summaries of your data, sliced and diced in many different ways to assist you or your customers in making personal or business decisions. Typical reports include financial statements, budgets, invoices, inventories, sales reports, form letters and mailing labels. Any printed output that you intend to produce from your database is a report.

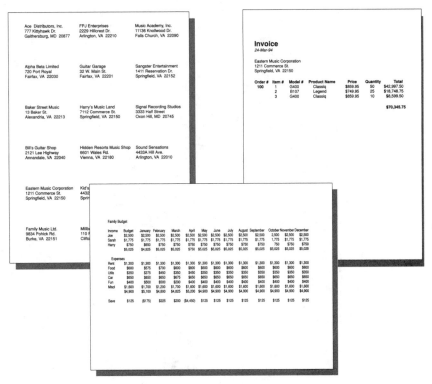

Figure 2-9: Typical "real-world" reports: a budget, an invoice and mailing labels.

The reports you create using Access are also stored as part of your Access database. Like forms, you almost certainly are already creating reports from information that you collect for use in your business. Access enables you to, at a minimum, duplicate the paper reports you already create. You can design a financial statement report, for example, that updates itself each time you update the underlying financial data in the database. But with the powerful data manipulation capabilities of Access, and the capability to incorporate graphics and data from other Windows programs, Access makes it possible to generate output that will wow even the most demanding audience.

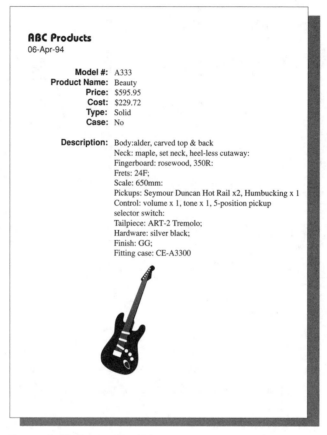

Figure 2-10: Access enables you to create reports that incorporate attractive fonts as well as informative graphics.

Although you can't generate a database report until you have collected data, you can often decrease the time needed to arrive at the optimum database design by identifying early in the design process the reports you want to produce. Be sure to collect all the information needed to create the desired report. And you don't need to waste time collecting data that will never be used.

DATABASE APPLICATIONS

A *database application* is a collection of tables, forms, reports and other related items that work together. In other words, an Access database application is just a dressed-up Access database. A typical Access database includes tables, forms and reports. Through the use of queries, macros and Access Basic modules, Access database applications present a complete package to the user. A typical database application displays an opening menu containing command buttons that each, in turn, displays a form, report or perhaps another menu. Figure 2-11 shows the opening menu of the Contacts application examined in Chapter 1.

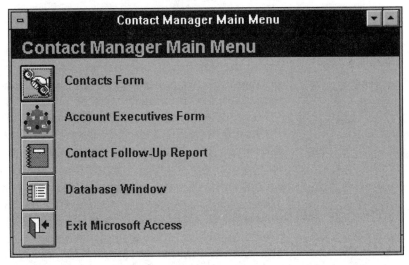

Figure 2-11: The opening menu for the Contacts database application.

Anyone creating a database application in Access is an *application developer*. Access' ease of use and many impressive features encourage application developers to create many flashy, feature-rich forms and reports. It is critical, however, that you spend the time correctly designing the underlying database before going wild designing beautiful forms and reports. Many a would-be developer has given up in frustration after realizing that the original database design was wrong and that all forms and reports must be redesigned.

DATABASE DESIGN: ASKING THE RIGHT QUESTIONS

The expression *database design* sounds like a concept you would need a degree in computer science to understand or even care about. But any time you decide what to name a table and what fields to add, you are in effect designing a database. The trick is to define tables in such a way that you don't have to redefine them over and over again. Access makes defining tables, forms and reports deceptively easy. But designing the database—deciding which tables and fields to add—is no easier or harder than it has ever been.

Before you begin designing a database, you really need to take a step back and focus on the problem you are trying to solve. Whenever possible, get the potential customer's expectations in writing BEFORE you begin designing the database. Gather enough information from your customer or on your own to be able to answer the following questions:

○ *Who is the user?* Who will be using the information collected and stored in the database? You need to know up front whom you must satisfy. What problems does the user want to solve with the database? Does the user have realistic expectations? How much "hand-holding" does the user need? How sophisticated are the individuals who will interact with the database? Who will enter data into the database? Who will view data that is stored in the database? Who will see printed output from the database? Is management already "sold" on the benefits of computerized databases, or is this database a "test case?"

○ *What computer system will host the database?* Before you start designing a database you need to be very clear on what type of computer system the database will reside. Access is designed to operate well as either a single-user database manager on a 486-based PC with at least 4MB of RAM, or as a multi-user database platform in a local network environment (see Appendix B, "Installation Tips"). An Access database can even provide desktop accessibility to minicomputer and mainframe data, through its SQL (Structured Query Language) and ODBC (Open Database Connectivity) functionality.

○ *What should be the style of the user interface?* Will the database be completely menu driven, or will the user want to work with the native Access interface to open tables, forms, reports and queries (see Chapter 14, "Designing a 'Friendly' User Interface")? Is the user more comfortable with menu bars, pull-down menus and pop-up menus, or should command buttons, check boxes and option buttons predominate?

○ *What security issues must the database address?* Does the data stored in the database need to be protected from unauthorized access (see Appendix C, "Sharing Network-Based Applications")? Should the database passively or aggressively guard against entry of invalid data, duplication of data or entry of erroneous data (see "Protecting Data" in Chapter 4, "Creating Tables in Design View")? Should users have the capability to change data in the database, or just view it?

○ *Who will provide maintenance and upgrades?* Will the database be maintained and upgraded entirely by the user, or will you be expected to provide routine maintenance and upgrades? Should periodic backup and database compacting capabilities be included (see Appendix D, "Database Administration")?

○ *What should the database do for the user?* What does the user want/need out of the database? Does the customer already have a clear idea of how they want the database output to look? Many times your customer needs you to produce form letters or reports that closely resemble form letters and reports that already exist. Collect all pertinent forms and reports. Try to weed out any forms or reports that your customer no longer uses.

○ *What information needs to be collected?* Your database design needs to account for all the information necessary to produce the output your customer wants and expects. Don't collect unnecessary information. Compile a list of information needed to generate the forms and reports you have collected. What information is currently being collected? Who collects the information now? How is it stored? What is the current information flow—how is the information routed throughout the organization? Where is information stored? Is there a central repository, or is information duplicated and stored randomly throughout the organization?

The sections that follow demonstrate how these questions can help you design your Access database.

GETTING TO KNOW THE INTENDED USER

Perhaps you have purchased Access to develop database applications for your own use. Or maybe your job duties include developing database applications for others to use. You might even be a professional programmer or developer creating Access database applications for paying customers. Whatever the case may be, the first step in designing an Access database is to get a clear picture in your mind of the person or persons who will be using the database. The last thing you want is to create a database that satisfies your tastes, but doesn't satisfy or meet the needs of the real users of the application.

Potential users of your database application may interact with the application in any of the following ways:

○ Adding information to the database.

○ Updating information in the database.

○ Viewing information from the database onscreen.

○ Receiving reports or letters generated by the application.

Often, users may fit into more than one user category. Most often the individuals who must enter data into the database will have some need to display at least a portion of the data onscreen. If you are creating a database application for your own use, you will be entering data as well as viewing the data onscreen. Whoever your customer, you need to design your tables, forms and reports accordingly.

The database that forms most of the examples presented in this book is very simple and straightforward. It is a tool for managing the countless interactions we each have during our business and personal day. Such tools are often referred to as *contact management programs*.

Our hypothetical user, Sam, is a senior account executive (sales person) with Pacific Rim Widgets, Inc. (PRWI). He has asked us to design a database to assist him in keeping track of the many contacts he has daily with customers and potential customers. He wants to be able to easily record information immediately after meetings, and even during telephone calls. He wants addresses and phone numbers immediately accessible and wants to be able to quickly list all interactions with any particular customer.

Sam is an experienced Windows user and will normally enter his own data. Two junior account executives, who work with Sam, will also use the database and enter their own data. Initially, they will all use one PC, but Sam expects to buy a small local area network within the next 6 months. Each account executive will then have his or her own workstation. Sam wants you to be prepared to set up the database on the network as soon as it is up and running.

Compiling an Information List

A key step in designing an Access database is compiling a list, on paper, of the information that needs to be collected. Sometimes the list almost writes itself, but don't be surprised if you have to make changes to the list several times before you are finished. It is usually easy to divide the list into categories or groupings as you go, but don't be too concerned at first about how the information will be separated into Access tables. The design process described in the remainder of this chapter assists in identifying tables and fields, based on your initial information list.

For example, for PRWI's contact management database, we might jot down a list that looks similar to Figure 2-12.

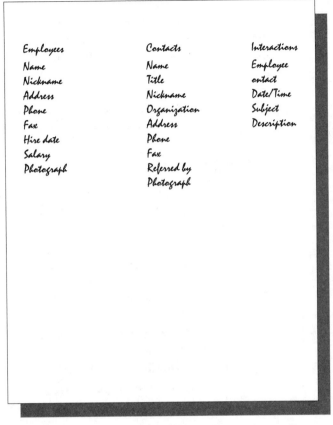

Figure 2-12: Compile an information list on paper first.

As you are compiling the information list, keep asking yourself whether all the items you are listing are really needed, and whether any needed data is missing. Often existing forms and reports will help immensely in determining the information the database has to include.

CREATING A MODEL

Computer programs cannot perfectly duplicate the complexity of the real world. But computers can manipulate large amounts of data so quickly that we can put up with certain limitations. In order to create a helpful Access database, we first have to come up with a list of tables and a list of fields for each table. These tables, when used together, form a model of the real world, at least with respect to the little real-world problem we are trying to solve.

Everyone who creates an Access database has to decide on tables and fields—the *structure* of a database—but, as you might expect, there are a few rules that can help you make the right decisions. The systematic process of refining the structure of a database is known as *data normalization* (a process championed by Edgar F. Codd in a paper published in 1970, and by many other database gurus in numerous articles, papers and books since then). The goals of this process are the following:

○ *Reduce redundancy and inconsistency.* Each time someone has to enter data into the database, there is the potential for error. If the same information, such as a phone number, is stored in multiple places in the database, there is an increased likelihood that one or more of the numbers has been entered incorrectly. In addition, any time you have to update a particular phone number, you have to change it everywhere it occurs in the database. Ideally, you want to change it only once. Finally, reducing data redundancy saves disk space.

○ *Maintain accuracy.* Many real-world databases have to keep track of mission-essential information. Accuracy is often critical. The structure of the database model can help reduce the potential for errors.

○ *Simplify information retrieval.* A database is of little use if you find it difficult to find the information you need and then to extract the information in a useful form.

The sections that follow explain the process of developing a normalized database model.

Translating the Real World Into a Database Design

At this point in your database design, you have compiled a list that includes all the information you feel should be included in your database. In beginning to design the contact management database, we have compiled the following list, which we've divided into three broad categories—employees, contacts and interactions:

Employees	Contacts	Interactions
Name	Name	Employee
Nickname	Title	Contact
Address	Nickname	Date/Time
Phone	Organization	Subject
Fax	Address	Description
Hire date	Phone	
Salary	Fax	
Photograph	Referred by	
	Photograph	

Notice that the Employee and Contact fields in the Interactions table identify the two individuals who interacted—one an account executive, and the other a customer.

You now need to begin to break the information list into Access tables. Items in the list will become fields in the tables. The following sections describe this process, sometimes known as *data normalization*.

Group Fields Into Logical Categories

Each table should have a single subject or theme. For example, in the contact management database, it seems obvious that you want people information and interaction information stored in separate tables. The account executive needs to be able to record the name of a contact, as well as the date, time and subject of each interaction. It would be very cumbersome to store all this information in the same table as the contact's address and phone number. For each interaction, you would need a Date/Time field and a Subject field. Because account executives probably have multiple interactions with any particular contact, you would need to add multiple Date/Time and Subject fields to the table. Such a table design would quickly become unwieldy. Instead, you have already split the fields into the People table and the Interactions table.

But it may not be apparent at first that you should create a third table—call it Organizations—that stores information about each organization for whom each of the account executives works. After all, the address and an individual contact at a company may change, even though the company's name and phone number don't change. In addition, if an account executive deletes a record because a contact has retired or moved on to another company, you may not want to delete the address and phone number of the organization for whom the contact worked.

The new database structure looks like this:

Employees	Contacts	Organizations	Interactions
Name	Name	Name	Employee
Nickname	Title	OrgType	Contact
Address	Nickname	Address	Date/Time
Phone	Organization	Phone	Subject
Fax	Address	Fax	Description
Hire date	Phone		
Salary	Fax		
Photograph	Referred by		
	Photograph		

Store One Value Per Field

As a general rule, store data in the smallest meaningful value possible, with one and only one value per field. For example, you can divide an individual's name into first name, middle name and last name, but dividing it any further has no useful meaning. Note also that a nickname isn't necessarily a shorter version of a person's first, middle or last name.

Computers are incredibly fast, but just as stupid. Although it's easy for you to look at someone's name and determine which is the first and last name (unless the name is like mine—three first names), the task is very difficult for Access. But if you define a table with separate fields for first name, middle name and last name, Access has no problem retrieving the correct name.

With the goal of storing data in the smallest meaningful value, we can refine the contact management database by breaking the Name and Address fields into new fields as follows:

Employees	Contacts	Organizations	Interactions
First Name	Salutation	Name	Employee
Middle Name	First Name	OrgType	Contact
Last Name	Middle Name	AddressLine1	Date/Time
Nickname	Last Name	AddressLine2	Subject
AddressLine1	Title	City	Description
AddressLine2	Nickname	State	
City	AddressLine1	ZipCode	
State	AddressLine2	Country	
ZipCode	City	Phone	
Address	State	Fax	
Phone	ZipCode		
Fax	Organization		
Hire date	Phone		
Salary	Fax		
Photograph	Referred by		
	Photograph		

Notice that Employees, Contacts and Organizations now each include AddressLine1 and AddressLine2 fields. These fields accommodate addresses that have two street address lines. The Salutation field in Contacts contains values such as Mr., Ms. and Mrs.

Assign a Primary Key to Each Table

Each table should have one field, or several fields taken together, that uniquely identify each record. If it is possible to have two identical records in a table, then you need to add at least one field that will be different in each record. The field or fields that identify each record are called the *primary key*.

Two people, for instance, can have the same name. In the Employees and Contacts tables, therefore, you need another field, an ID field, that is unique for every person in the table. The EmployeeID field becomes the Employees table's primary key. Similarly, the Contacts, Interactions and the Organizations tables should each have an ID field (ContactID, InteractionID and OrgID, respectively). None of these tables contain one field or a combination of fields that can be used to uniquely identify each record.

With primary key fields assigned, the database structure is as follows:

Employees	Contacts	Organizations	Interactions
PeopleID	ContactID	OrgID	InteractionID
First Name	Salutation	Name	Employee
Middle Name	First Name	OrgType	Contact
Last Name	Middle Name	AddressLine1	Date/Time
Nickname	Last Name	AddressLine2	Subject
AddressLine1	Title	City	Description
AddressLine2	Nickname	State	
City	AddressLine1	ZipCode	
State	AddressLine2	Country	
ZipCode	City	Phone	
Address	State	Fax	
Phone	ZipCode		
Fax	Organization		
Hire date	Phone		
Salary	Fax		
Photograph	Referred by		
	Photograph		

Don't Permit Fields to Repeat In the Same Table

Probably the most common database design mistake, especially the first time you use a relational database program, is to design a table with repeating fields. For example, most business people have at least two phone numbers—a voice number and a fax number. Many people have more than two numbers. You may be tempted to define a table with room for two or more phone numbers for each person. But if you allow for two numbers, what do you do when a customer has three numbers? If you allow for three numbers, what do you do when someone has four, and so on?

Whenever you run into repeating fields, you usually need to create a new table. The new table contains one field that identifies a record in the table that originally contained the repeating fields. A second field in the new table contains the data that was previously contained in the repeating field. With this rule in mind, we refine the design of our example database as follows:

51

Employees	Contacts	Organizations	Interactions
PeopleID	ContactID	OrgID	InteractionID
PhoneKey	PhoneKey	PhoneKey	Employee
First Name	Salutation	Name	Contact
Middle Name	First Name	OrgType	Date/Time
Last Name	Middle Name	AddressLine1	Subject
Nickname	Last Name	AddressLine2	Description
AddressLine1	Title	City	
AddressLine2	Nickname	State	
City	AddressLine1	ZipCode	
State	AddressLine2	Country	
ZipCode	City		
Address	State		
Fax	ZipCode		
Hire date	Organization		
Salary	Referred by		
Photograph	Photograph		

Phones
ForeignKey
PhoneKey
Type
Number
Extension
DialCode

In this example, the Phones table contains four fields: ForeignKey, PhoneKey, Type and Number. The first field, ForeignKey, contains the ID number of either a person (from either the Employees or Contacts table) or organization (from the Organizations table). Because there is a possibility that an employee, contact and organization could have the same ID number, we have added the PhoneKey field to the Employees, Contacts, Organizations and Phones table. The PhoneKey field in the Phones table contains the letter "E" if the phone number is for someone in the Employees table, contains the letter "C" if the phone number belongs to a contact or contains the letter "O" if the phone number belongs to an organization. The Type field stores a value of either "Business," "Home" or "Fax." The Number field contains the telephone number of the person or organization identified by the value in the ID field.

Each of the Employees, Contacts and Organizations tables also contains a PhoneKey field. Every record in the Employees table contains the value "E" in its PhoneKey field. Every record in the Contacts table contains the value "C" in its PhoneKey field. Every record in the Organizations table contains the value "O" in its PhoneKey field.

Use Foreign Keys to Define Relationships Between Tables

Primary key fields are referred to as *foreign keys* when stored in another table. Foreign keys are normally used to link tables together.

In the latest iteration of the contact management database design, shown in the preceding section, the Phones table primary key, ID, contains data that is found in either the EmployeeID field, which is the primary key for the Employees table, the ContactID field, which is the primary key for the Contacts table, or the OrgID field, which is the primary key for the Organizations table.

The Interactions table lists the fields Employee and Contact. In the design that follows, we have replaced the Employee and Contact fields with EmployeeID and ContactID. These fields each contain values from the primary key fields of the Employees and Contacts tables, respectively.

Employees	Contacts	Organizations	Interactions
EmployeeID	ContactID	OrgID	InteractionID
PhoneKey	PhoneKey	PhoneKey	Employee ID
First Name	Salutation	Name	ContactID
Middle Name	First Name	OrgType	Date/Time
Last Name	Middle Name	AddressLine1	Subject
Nickname	Last Name	AddressLine2	Description
AddressLine1	Title	City	
AddressLine2	Nickname	State	
City	AddressLine1	ZipCode	
State	AddressLine2	Country	
ZipCode	City		
Address	State		
Fax	ZipCode		
Hire date	Organization		
Salary	Referred by		
Photograph	Photograph		

Phones
ForeignKey
PhoneKey
Type
Number
Extension
DialCode

A link formed by a foreign key between the table that contains the foreign key and the foreign key's source table demonstrates a relationship between the two tables. Three types of relationships are possible between pairs of tables:

○ *One-to-one.* Any particular value of the foreign key can appear only once in the table, and each record in the table relates to only one record in the table that is the source of the foreign key. No pair of tables in the example contact management database exhibit a one-to-one relationship.

○ *One-to-many.* Any particular value of the foreign key can appear more than once in the table, but each record in the table can relate to only one record in the foreign key's source table. The Contacts table has a one-to-many relationship with the Phones table. The Phones table's ForeignKey field contains foreign key values from the Contacts table's primary key. A person listed in the Contacts table can have more than one phone number, so a particular ContactID value may appear several times in the Phones table's ForeignKey field.

○ *Many-to-many.* Any particular value of the foreign key can appear more than once in the table, and each record in the table can relate to multiple records in the foreign key's source table. Many-to-many relationships cannot be represented with only two tables. In our contact management database, the Employees table has a many-to-many relationship with the Contacts table, through the Interactions table. An account executive can interact with multiple contacts; each contact can interact with multiple account executives. The Interactions table contains two foreign keys, one from Account Execs (the EmployeeID field) and one from Contacts (the ContactID field).

Access provides a very helpful way to define and visualize the relationships between the various tables in your database. Figure 2-13 shows how the tables in the contact management database are related to one another. Refer to the "Defining Table Relationships" section of Chapter 3, "Creating Tables the Easy Way," for a discussion of the Access relationships feature. (**Note:** Figure 2-13 lists several fields that as yet have not been discussed. These fields will be discussed in Chapters 3 and 4.)

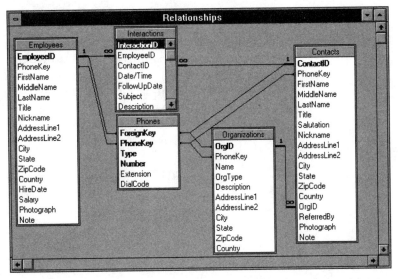

Figure 2-13: Access provides a way to visualize the relationships between tables.

Don't Include Fields That Can be Derived or Calculated From Other Fields

Any time you store a value in the database that is or can be derived from other fields in the database, you are both wasting disk space and increasing the chances that erroneous data will be introduced at some point. Whenever you need a computed result, Access can accomplish the computation, assuring up-to-the minute accuracy.

You may, for example, be tempted to define a field that uses Access operators to combine First Name, Middle Name and Last Name into a single field. It seems like this would be convenient for creating mailing labels or form letters. But by doing so, you introduce the potential that someone's name will change, rendering the computed composite name inaccurate. On the other hand, if you wait to have Access combine the three fields at the time that you need the full name, you can be certain that the full name is correct.

There are real-world situations, however, when it is desirable to store computed fields. Certain accounting practices, for example, require that you store transactions permanently.

MOVING ON

Now that you have designed your database on paper, you are ready to implement your design. You must now define each table and all its fields using Access' table creation features. Access makes this process so easy it's almost fun. Turn now to Chapter 3 to learn how to create tables the easy way.

3

CREATING TABLES THE EASY WAY

So far in this book you have taken a whirlwind tour of Access to get a quick idea of what the program can do. You've also learned how to design your database correctly the first time, so that you won't have to continually make changes (at least not big ones). You're ready now to get down to the real business of building your Access database.

This chapter first shows you how to open a new Access database. You then learn how to create Access tables in a hurry using the new Table Queries. In addition you learn how to quickly add data to your database first by attaching tables that already exist in some form, and then by importing data into your Access database from other database files, spreadsheets and word processing files.

In Chapter 1, you examined the Ventana database. In this chapter you will create a new database named Contacts and define several tables using Table Wizards. You'll then import data from the Ventana database so you will have some data to work with. When you have finished this chapter, you'll be ready to move on to Chapter 4, which covers table creation in more detail.

CREATING A NEW DATABASE

As you have already learned in Chapter 2, Access stores all related information, forms, reports and so on, in a single *database file*. Each time you solve a different real-world problem with Access, you should probably create a new database file. Don't store unrelated tables in the same database. The example we discuss most often in this book is a contact management application. We will create an Access database named Contacts. This database will contain all the tables, forms, queries, reports, macros and modules we generate in this and subsequent chapters. If we later decide to use Access to solve a different problem—say we want to create an accounting application or an order entry application—we'll create an entirely different Access database.

To create a new database, follow these steps:

1. Start Access.

2. Click the New Database button on the toolbar.

    Or, choose File, New Database from the menu bar. Access displays the New Database dialog box, as shown in Figure 3-1.

New Database

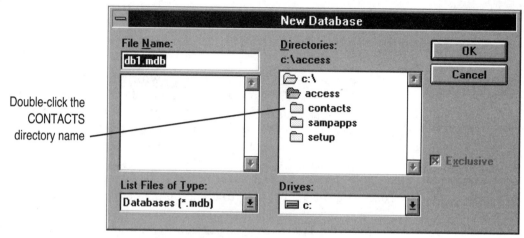

Double-click the
CONTACTS
directory name

Figure 3-1: The New Database dialog box.

3. Access enables you to store a database file anywhere on your hard disk. If you don't want to store the new database in the current directory, use the Directories list box in the New Database dialog box to select the directory in which you want Access to store the database.

    We want to store the new Contacts database in the CONTACTS directory (the program that installed the exercise files created this directory as a subdirectory of the ACCESS directory). To switch to the CONTACTS directory, double-click the directory name in the Directories list box, in the New Database dialog box.

4. Access lists all existing database files (VENTANA.MDB, in the example) in the File Name list box and suggests the name DB1.MDB for the new database. Type, in the File Name text box, the name you want Access to use for the new database. You don't need to type a file name extension, Access automatically adds the extension .mdb.

- -
Naming an Access Database

Because Access saves each database as a file on disk, database names are limited in length to 8 characters—the longest file name permitted by DOS. Access automatically adds MDB as the file name extension. You can use letters, numbers and the following special characters for the file name:

$ # & @ ! ( ) - _ ( ) ' ^

You cannot include spaces or use duplicate names in the same directory.

- -

In the example database, type **contacts** and then either press Enter or choose the OK button. Access displays the Database window for the Contacts database, as shown in **Figure 3-2**.

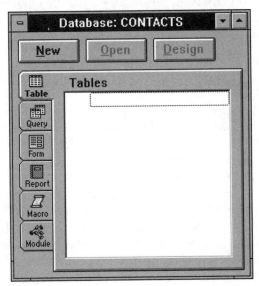

Figure 3-2: The Database window for the Contacts database.

MDB & LDB Files

Access 2.0 saves all objects of a particular database in an MDB file—a file with the MDB file name extension. If you use DOS or Windows' File Manager to look at the directory that contains the MDB file, you'll notice another file with the same file name, but with the LDB file name extension. If you are sharing the database with other users in a multiuser system, the LDB file stores information about which tables or records are locked at any particular time. The LDB file does not contain any of the database's objects. Whenever you want to make a backup copy of the database, you need only copy the MDB file, but be careful not to delete the LDB file while the MDB file is open.

When you open a new database file, the file is empty. Before you can do anything productive with the database, you have to add tables. After you add tables to the database, you can enter data and can build forms, reports, macros and modules that make use of the tables and data in the database.

CREATING TABLES

Access provides several ways to create tables for your database. The easiest way to add a table to your database is to use a Table Wizard, a feature that is new in Access 2.0. The "Using the Table Wizard" section in this chapter explains how to quickly create tables this way. You can also design tables using the table Design view discussed in Chapter 4, "Creating Tables in Design View."

In addition to designing your own tables from scratch, you can both *attach* and *import* tables from other existing databases. If you choose to *attach* a table from another database, Access gives you access to the table as if it were stored in the current database, but does not make a new copy of the table. If you make changes to the data, the changes are stored in the external database, not in the current database. Attaching tables is covered in the "Attaching Tables" section, later in this chapter. When you *import* a table from another database, you make a new copy of an existing table and store it in the current database. See "Importing Tables" later in this chapter, to learn how to import tables from other databases, as well as from spreadsheets and word processing files.

CLOSING & OPENING A DATABASE

After you finish working with your database each day, you may decide to close the database file and exit from Access. Closing a database is very similar to closing any window in a Windows program. Either double-click the Database window's Control-menu box or choose File, Close Database from the menu bar. Access saves all tables and other database's objects in the database file on disk.

To exit Access, either double-click the Microsoft Access window's Control-menu box, or choose File, Exit from the menu bar.

Later, when you are ready to work on your database again, reopen the file. To open an existing database, follow these steps:

1. Start Access.

Open Database

2. Click the Open Database button on the tool bar or, choose File, Open Database from the menu bar. Access displays the Open Database dialog box, as shown in Figure 3-3.

Double-click the CONTACTS.MDB database file name.

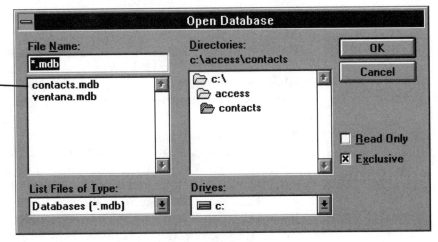

Figure 3-3: The Open Database dialog box.

3. Access enables you to store a database file anywhere on your hard disk. The database you want to open may be found in a directory other than the current directory. Use the Directories list box in the New Database dialog box to select the directory containing the Access database that you want to open.

The example database, CONTACTS.MDB, is stored in the ACCESS\CONTACTS directory on your hard disk. To switch to the CONTACTS directory, double-click the directory name in the Directories list box, in the New Database dialog box.

4. Access lists all existing database files (VENTANA.MDB and CONTACTS.MDB in the example) in the File Name list box. To open the Contacts database, either double-click CONTACTS.MDB or type **contacts** in the File Name text box and press Enter. Access displays the Database window.

CREATING TABLES USING THE TABLE WIZARD

The underlying philosophy of all Microsoft software is that programs don't have to be hard to use in order to be powerful. Whether Microsoft is always faithful to this philosophy is subject to some debate, but when it comes to creating tables, Microsoft Access' Table Wizard makes creating tables about as easy as it gets.

The next section takes you through a session with a Table Wizard. Along the way you create the Contacts table in the example Contacts database. You then have an opportunity to create several tables on your own using a Table Wizard.

Using the Table Wizard

All database management programs provide a method of defining tables. You specify the table name and then assign fields to the table. Most programs require you to come up with the table names, field names and data type for each field. Microsoft Access Version 2.0's Table Wizard enables you to benefit from the experience of previous database designers.

The Table Wizard provides a list of 26 different table designs from which you can choose. After you choose a table, the Wizard suggests a list of field names for use in the table you selected. The Wizard automatically assigns a data type to the fields. The Table Wizard also can assign a primary key field to the table for you, or, alternatively, give you the chance to assign a primary key field. Finally, after you have defined the table, with the Wizard's assistance, the Wizard takes you immediately into data-entry mode.

The remainder of this section walks you through the Table Wizard and prompts you through the creation of the Contacts table. The next section then gives you the opportunity to use the Table Wizard to create several more tables.

1. Start Access and open the Database window for the database containing the new table. For example, to create the Contacts table, from our contact management database design (see Chapter 2, "Designing Your Database"), start Access and open the Contacts database.

2. If the Tables list is not already displayed, click the Table tab in the Database window. Access displays the Tables list.

3. With the Tables list displayed, choose the New button in the Database window. Access displays the New Table dialog box, as shown in Figure 3-4.

Click the Table Wizards button →

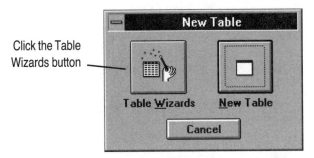

Figure 3-4: The New Table dialog box.

4. Click the Table Wizards button. Access displays the first screen of the Table Wizard dialog box (see Figure 3-5).

Fields in new table —
Sample Tables list —
Sample Fields list —
Selector buttons —

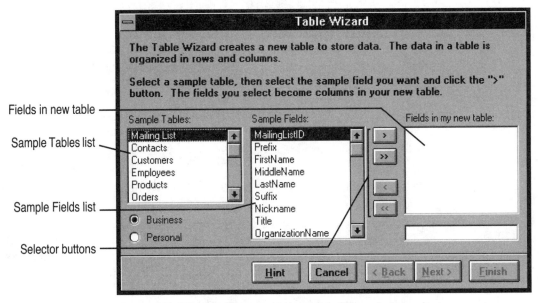

Figure 3-5: The first screen of the Table Wizard dialog box.

The screen contains three list boxes. The Sample Tables list box, on the left side of the screen, contains a list of tables that are representative of the most often used table designs. When the Table Wizard dialog box first displays, the Mailing List table name is highlighted. You can scroll through this list using the up and down arrow keys or the scroll bar.

Sample Tables

Access includes the following table designs as business-related samples in the Table Wizard dialog box:

Mailing List	Contacts	Customers
Employees	Products	Orders
Order Details	Suppliers	Category
Payments	Invoices	Invoice Details
Projects	Events	Reservations
Time Billed	Expenses	Deliveries
Fixed Assets	Service Records	Transactions
Tasks	Employees and Tasks	Students
Classes	Students and Classes	

The Wizard also lists the following personal-related sample tables (click the Personal option button to see the list):

Friends	Guests	Category
Plants	Household Inventory	Recipes
Exercise Log	Diet Log	Wine List
Rolls of Film	Photographs	Authors
Book Collection	Artists	Music Collection
Video Collection	Service Records	Accounts
Investments		

The Sample Fields list box, in the center of the dialog box, lists the fields of currently selected tables in the Sample Tables list. For example, in Figure 3-5, the Sample Fields list box shows fields from the sample Mailing List table, which is selected in the Sample Tables list box.

The right-most list box in the Table Wizard dialog box, the "Fields in my new table" list, is empty when you first open the screen. The purpose of this initial screen of the Table Wizard dialog box is to fill in this list by copying fields into the list from the Sample Fields list.

5. Select a table in the Sample Tables list box. If you are not sure which table is closest, scroll through the Sample Tables list and examine the field lists that appear in the Sample Fields list.

For example, the Contacts table in the Sample Tables list appears to be the most like our Contacts table design. Click the Contacts name in the Sample Tables list. Access lists the following fields in the Sample Fields list:

ContactID	WorkPhone
Prefix	HomePhone
FirstName	MobilePhone
LastName	FaxNumber
Suffix	EmailName
OrganizationName	Birthdate
Address	ContactType
City	LastMeetingDate
State	ActionItems
PostalCode	ReferredBy
Country	Photograph
Region	Note

6. Copy fields from the Sample Fields list to the "Fields in my new table" list in either of the following ways:

○ Double-click each field name

○ Select a field name and then choose the > selector button.

Access copies the selected field name from the Sample Fields list to the field list on the right side of the dialog box.

If you desire, you can copy fields from more than one sample table. To see a list of fields from a different table, select the table name in the Sample Tables list. Then copy the fields using the methods described in the preceding paragraph.

For example, to create fields for the Contacts table, copy the following fields from the Sample Fields list box to the "Fields in my new table" list box (see Figure 3-6).

ContactID
Suffix
Prefix
FirstName
LastName
Title (click the Employees table name first)
Address (click Contacts again)
Address1 (copy Address again)
City

State
PostalCode
Country
CustomerID (click the Customers table name first)
ReferredBy
Photograph
Note

Copy Address twice. The second time you copy the field, the Table Wizard adds the digit 1 to the new field name. We will soon modify several of the field names to match the database design from Chapter 2.

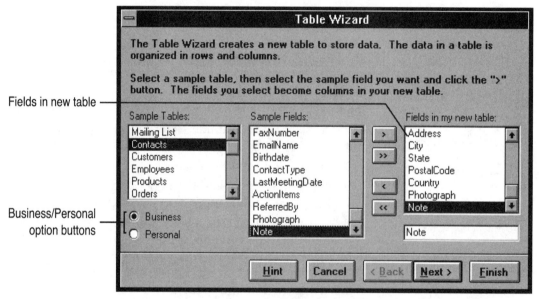

Figure 3-6: The first screen of the Table Wizard dialog box with fields copied to the "Fields in my new table" list box.

7. If you want to remove field names from the "Fields in my new table" list, double-click the field name, or select the field name and choose the < selector button.

8. To copy all fields from the Sample Fields list to the "Fields in my new table" list, choose the >> selector button. To remove all fields from the "Fields in my new table" list, choose the << selector button. If you want to use most of the sample fields in your new table, it is often easiest to first copy all fields to the "Fields in my new table" list and then use the < button to remove the unwanted fields.

9. Two option buttons near the lower-left corner of the screen (see Figure 3-6) enable you to tell Access whether you intend to use the table for business or personal use. This may seem at first to be an odd question, but you probably aren't interested in the same sort of information in a business database as you are in a personal database, and visa versa. When you choose the Personal option button, Access displays a different list of sample tables and fields than are listed when the Business button is selected.

   In the Contacts table example, choose the Personal option button and then copy the Nickname field from the Friends table's Sample Fields list to the "Fields in my new table" list.

10. After building the new field list, click the Next > button, near the lower-right corner of the dialog box. Access displays the second screen in the Table Wizard dialog box (see Figure 3-7).

. . . .

Navigating a Wizard

All Wizards share a common set of command buttons to control movement from one to the next. You tell the Wizard you are done with a window by clicking the Next > button. Clicking the < Back button takes you back to the previous Table Wizard screen. Clicking Cancel returns you to the Database window. The Finish button is available once you have answered enough questions to allow the Wizard to generate the table. Most screens have a Hint button. Clicking this button causes the Wizard to display a screen with helpful information. This information gives suggestions posed by the current screen.

. . . .

Type the name of
the new table ——

Access creates
the primary key ——

You specify
the primary key ——

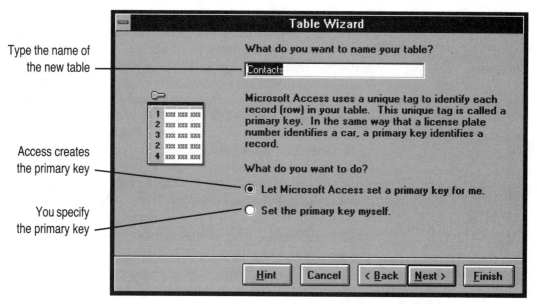

Figure 3-7: The second screen of the Table Wizard dialog box is where
you can type the name of the new table.

11. In this screen, the Wizard asks you what you want to name
    the new table and suggests the same name as the sample table
    from which you copied field names. Type the name of the
    new table in the text box that appears near the top of the
    dialog box. For the Contacts table, we'll leave the table name
    as is.

12. In the bottom half of the screen, the Wizard asks whether you
    want Access to set a primary key for you, or would you prefer
    to set the primary key yourself. As you learned in Chapter 2,
    you should always assign a primary key to each Access table.
    Choose the first option button if you want Access to create a
    field that automatically assigns a unique value to each new
    record in the table. Choose the second option to assign the
    primary key field yourself.

    In the Contacts table example, choose to assign the primary
    key yourself.

13. Choose the Next > button to move to the next screen in the
    Table Wizard dialog box. If you choose to assign the primary
    key yourself, Access displays a screen that asks what data will
    be unique for each record (see Figure 3-8). In other words,
    which field you want to use as the primary key. If you have
    chosen to have Access set the primary key, skip to step 17.

Specify the primary key field ——

Creates a counter field ——

Creates a number field ——

Creates a text field ——

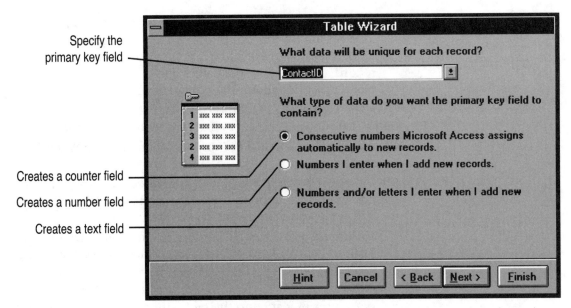

Figure 3-8: This Table Wizard screen asks you to choose the primary key field.

14. By default, the Wizard suggests as the primary key field the first field that you added to the list of fields in the first screen. If you want to select a different field, click the button at the right end of the text box to drop down a list of all fields in the table. Choose then the field you want to use for the primary key.

In the Contacts table example, we are going to use the ContactID field, which is the field suggested by the Wizard.

15. Next, you need to tell the Wizard which type of data you want to use for the primary key field. Usually, primary key fields are numbers or a combination of letters and numbers. The Wizard offers three option buttons that each select a different data type for the primary key.

○ *Consecutive numbers Microsoft Access assigns automatically to new records.* This option button makes the primary key field a counter field. Each time you add a record to this table, Access automatically places the next consecutive number into this field.

○ *Numbers I enter when I add new records.* This option button makes the primary key field a number field. For each new record in the table, you need to add a unique number value to the primary key field.

○ *Numbers and/or letters I enter when I add new records.* This option button makes the primary key field a text field. Again, you will add a unique value to each new record, but this time the values can be all text, all numbers or a combination of text and numbers.

For the ContactID field in the Contacts table, select the first option button so that Access makes ContactID a counter field.

16. Choose the Next > button to display the next Table Wizard screen.

17. This screen, shown in Figure 3-9, announces that the Wizard has enough information to create the table, and asks which of the following you want to do:

○ *Modify the table design.* Choose this option button if you want to change field names or other field properties using the Table window's Design view.

○ *Enter data directly into the table.* Choose this option to start entering data into the table using the Table window's Datasheet view.

○ *Enter data into the table using a form the Wizard creates for me.* Choose this option if you want the Wizard to build a simple data-entry form that you can use to enter data. The Wizard then enables you to start entering data using the newly built form.

Choose one of the option buttons. For the Contacts table, choose the first option button so you can modify the design to match the original design discussed in Chapter 2.

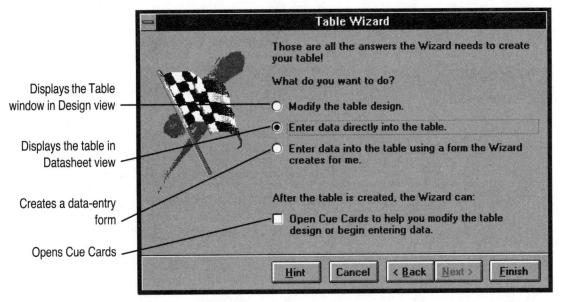

Displays the Table window in Design view

Displays the table in Datasheet view

Creates a data-entry form

Opens Cue Cards

Figure 3-9: This Table Wizard screen asks you what you want to do: modify the table design, start entering data directly into the table or start entering data using a pre-designed form.

18. This final Table Wizard screen, shown in Figure 3-9, also includes a check box that activates special *Cue Cards* for use when you either move to Design view to modify the table design or start to enter data in either Datasheet view or Form view.

Access Cue Cards

Cue Cards are a feature that is unique to Microsoft Access. They are onscreen tutorials known as *topics* (see Figure 3-11) that help you through various Access procedures, including the following:

Building a database and creating tables
Adding, viewing, editing, sorting and filtering data
Creating queries
Creating forms
Creating reports and mailing lists
Designing macros
Learning what a database can do

These tutorials are designed to coach you through your own real-world database problems. You can display Cue Cards from any Access window by choosing Help, Cue Cards from the menu bar.

· ·

Mark this check box if you want Access to display Cue Cards to coach you as you either modify the table design or begin to enter data. For the Contacts table example, mark the check box to take advantage of the additional advice provided by the Cue Cards.

19. After you have chosen an option button and decided whether to display Cue Cards, choose the Finish button to complete the Table Wizard. If you have chosen to modify the table design in Design view, Access displays the Table window in Design view, as shown in Figure 3-10.

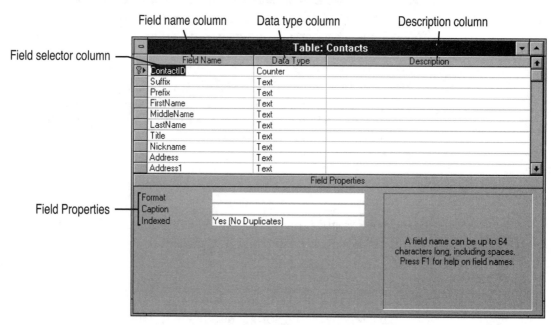

Figure 3-10: The Table window in Design view.

If you have chosen to display Cue Cards, Access displays the MS Access Cue Cards window (see Figure 3-11) on top of the Design View window or the Form view window. This Cue Card menu lists a dozen topics related to modifying a table's design. To display one of the available topics, click the button displayed to the left of the topic name. To close Cue Cards, double-click the Control-menu box.

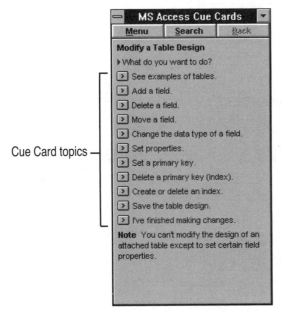

Cue Card topics

Figure 3-11: The Cue Card window.

After you choose the Finish button to complete the Table Wizard, if you have chosen to enter data directly into the table, Access displays an empty record of the new table in Datasheet view, as shown in Figure 3-12. You can begin to enter data in this screen.

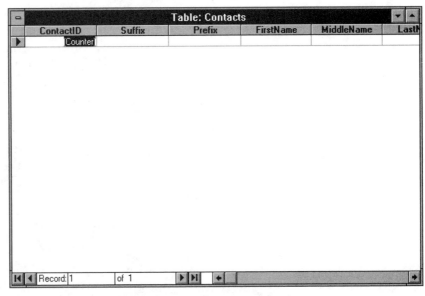

Figure 3-12: The Table window in Datasheet view.

After you choose the Finish button to complete the Table Wizard, if you have chosen to enter data using a form that the Wizard creates, Access creates a data-entry form and displays an empty record of the new table using this form in Form view, as shown in Figure 3-13. You can enter data into the table. Refer to Chapter 5, "Working With Data" for a full discussion of entering data into a table.

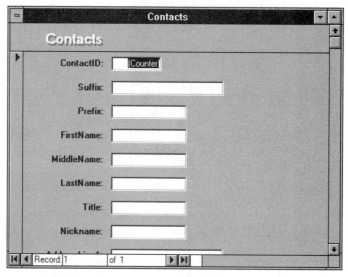

Figure 3-13: The Contacts table in Form view.

20. Most often when you use the Table Wizard to define a table, you will need to customize the field list to meet your specific needs. The Wizard therefore gives you the option of going directly to Design view after the Wizard finishes creating the table (see Figure 3-10). In Design view you can easily change field names and modify data type. You can also add new fields to the table design. Refer to Chapter 4 for a full discussion of Design view.

In the Contacts table example, use either the down arrow key or the mouse to highlight Suffix in the Field Name column and type the name PhoneKey. Using the same procedure, make the following changes:

Old Field Name	New Field Name
Prefix	Salutation
Address	AddressLine1
Address1	AddressLine2
PostalCode	ZipCode
CustomerID	OrgID

21. When you have finished modifying the table design, either click the Save button in the toolbar, or choose File, Save from the menu bar to save the changes you have made.

22. To close Design view, either double-click the Table window's Control-menu box, or choose File, Close from the menu bar.

Creating a Table On Your Own

Using the Table Wizard, create the Employees table. Follow these steps:

1. Create the Employees table with the following fields. We will define relationships later in this chapter:

> **Employees**
> EmployeeID
> Extension
> FirstName
> MiddleName
> LastName
> Title
> Address
> Address1 (Copy Address again)
> City
> State
> PostalCode
> Country
> DateHired
> Salary
> Photograph
> Note

2. Assign EmployeeID as the primary key field. Make the field a counter field.

3. When the Table Wizard asks whether the new table is related to the Contacts table, click the Next > button to skip this question.

4. Use Design view to change the field names in the new Employees table as follows:

Old Field Name	New Field Name
Extension	PhoneKey
Address	AddressLine1
Address1	AddressLine2
PostalCode	ZipCode

ATTACHING TABLES

As easy as it is to create tables using the Table Wizard, the easiest way to create tables is to use tables that someone else has already created. Access provides two ways to use existing data. You can *attach* tables or *import* tables. This section discusses when and how to attach tables and the next section discusses importing tables.

The fundamental difference between *attaching* a table to the current database and *importing* a table into the database is where the data is stored. When you import a table, Access copies the table structure and its data into the database. Data in an imported table is *internal*–stored within the open database. But when you attach a table, Access places a "shadow" of the table into the database, but leaves the data in place. Data in an attached table is *external*–stored outside the open database. In either case, you can use the table as a part of your database.

When you attach a table to the open database and then modify the data in the attached table, the data in the source table is modified. But if you import a table, changing data in the imported table does not affect the data in the source table.

There are two situations when attaching a table is preferable to importing the table:

○ *The external table is shared between two or more databases.* Perhaps the table is stored in a database that is in use by another department. By attaching the table, rather than importing it, both departments can share one copy of the table and updates by one department are immediately available to the other department.

○ *You are designing a database application for use by someone else and you expect to have to periodically update the application.* By attaching all tables, rather than storing them in the same database as forms, reports, queries and modules, you can more easily update any form, report, query or module using a copy of the database. After you make the change, copy the modified database to your customer's disk and reattach the tables. The tables containing the live data are never touched.

To attach an external table to the open database, follow these steps:

1. Open the database to which you want to attach the table.

2. Either click the Attach Table button on the toolbar, or choose File, Attach Table from the menu bar. Access displays the Attach dialog box, as shown in Figure 3-14.

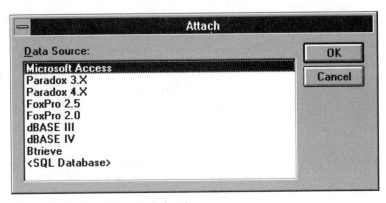

Figure 3-14: The Attach dialog box.

3. Access enables you to attach external tables that are stored in the native file format of any of the following database management programs: Microsoft Access versions 1.0, 1.1 and 2.0; Paradox or Paradox for Windows versions 3.0, 3.5, 4.0 or 4.5; FoxPro versions 2.0, 2.5 or 2.6, dBASE III or dBASE IV; as well as tables in Btrieve 5.1x or 6.0 format. Through its ODBC support, Access also enables you to attach SQL tables. From the Data Source list box, in the Attach dialog box, select the file format of the table you want to attach from the list of file formats.

4. After you select a file format, choose the OK button. If you chose the Microsoft Access format, Access displays the Select Microsoft Access Database dialog box (see Figure 3-15). Otherwise, Access displays the Select File dialog box (which is nearly identical in appearance to the Select Microsoft Access Database dialog box).

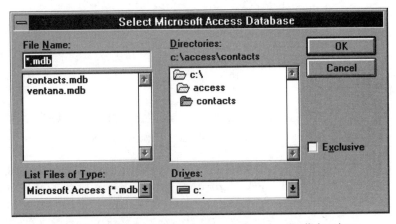

Figure 3-15: The Select Microsoft Access Database dialog box.

5. If the table to be attached is located on a different disk drive than the current database, use the Drives drop-down list box to select the drive that contains the table.

6. Use the Directories list box to select the directory containing the table you want to attach.

7. If only one user needs access to the attached table at any given point in time, mark the Exclusive check box. Access then locks the attached table each time someone opens the database to which you are attaching the table. This action results in faster performance. Conversely, do not mark the Exclusive check box if multiple users need concurrent access to the attached table.

8. When you are attaching an Access table, select from the File Name list box the database containing the table you want to attach. Then choose the OK button. Access displays the Attach Tables dialog box (see Figure 3-16), which lists all tables in the database. Select the target table from this list and choose the Attach button. Access displays a message that indicates whether it has successfully attached the table. Choose the OK button to continue. If you want to attach another table from the same database, select the table name from the Tables list in the Attach Tables dialog box and choose the Attach button again. When you are finished attaching tables, choose the Close button to return to the Database window.

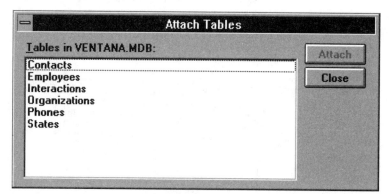

Figure 3-16: The Attach Tables dialog box.

When you are attaching non-Access tables, select from the File Name list box the name of the table you want to attach. Choose the Attach button. For Paradox, dBASE and FoxPro tables, you also select index files. Access then displays a message that indicates whether it has successfully attached the table. Choose the OK button to continue. If you want to attach another table, select the table name from the File Name list box and choose the Attach button. When you are finished attaching tables, choose the Close button to return to the Database window.

Access makes it easy to tell at a glance whether a table is an attached table by placing a pointer to the left of the table's icon in the Database window. Access also uses special icons to denote tables that are stored in a format other than Access' native format. For example, in addition to the pointer, Access lists a Px icon for tables stored in Paradox' native format, lists a dB icon for tables stored in a dBASE format and shows a fox-head-shaped icon for tables stored in a FoxPro format.

The Attachment Manager

Access 2.0 contains a special add-in utility known as the Attachment Manager. If you move the attached external table to another location, or change the structure of the attached table, you should use the Attachment Manager add-in to update the external table's database. Choose File, Add-ins, Attachment Manager to display the Attachment Manager dialog box. This dialog box displays a list of all attached tables. Mark the check box to the right of each attached table you want updated and choose the OK button. Access then updates the information stored in the database concerning the external table.

IMPORTING TABLES

The second way to use an existing table is to import the table into the open database. When you import a table—rather than attaching it—the table is stored in the open database. Changing data in the imported table does not affect the data in the source table. The preceding section describes two situations when attaching a table is preferable to importing the table. In most other situations, you should import an existing table.

Access enables you to import database tables that are stored in any of the following formats: Microsoft Access versions 1.0, 1.1 and 2.0; Paradox or Paradox for Windows versions 3.0, 3.5, 4.0 or 4.5; FoxPro versions 2.0, 2.5 or 2.6, dBASE III or dBASE IV; as well as tables in Btrieve 5.1x or 6.0 format. Through ODBC support, Access also enables you to import SQL database tables.

Data doesn't even have to be stored in a database table to be able to import the data into an Access table. In addition to providing the capability to import database tables, Access enables you to import data from an Excel worksheet, a Lotus 1-2-3 worksheet or in a text file (such as a word processing file). This section explains how to import data from Access tables as well as tables stored in other database formats.

To import a table from another database, follow these steps:

1. Open the database into which you want to import the table. Assume that you want to import from the Ventana database into the Contacts database the Organizations and Phones tables. Follow the steps described at the beginning of this chapter to open the Contacts database.

2. Either click the Import button in the toolbar, or choose File, Import from the menu bar to display the Import dialog box (see Figure 3-17).

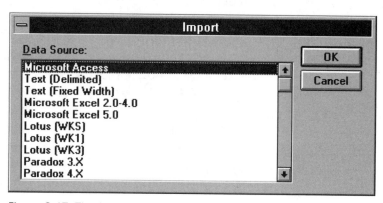

Figure 3-17: The Import dialog box.

3. Access enables you to import tables stored in the native file format of the following database management programs: Microsoft Access versions 1.0, 1.1 and 2.0; Paradox or Paradox for Windows versions 3.0, 3.5, 4.0 or 4.5; FoxPro versions 2.0, 2.5 or 2.6, dBASE III, or dBASE IV; as well as tables in Btrieve 5.1x or 6.0 format. Through its ODBC support, Access also enables you to import SQL tables. From the Data Source list box, in the Import dialog box, select the file format of the table you want to attach from the list of file formats.

4. After you select a file format, choose the OK button. If you chose the Microsoft Access format, Access displays the Select Microsoft Access Database dialog box (see Figure 3-18).

Otherwise, Access displays the Select File dialog box (which is nearly identical in appearance to the Select Microsoft Access Database dialog box).

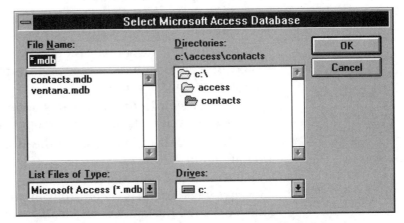

Figure 3-18: The Select Microsoft Access Database dialog box.

5. If the table to be imported is located on a different disk drive than the current database, use the Drives drop-down list box to select the drive that contains the table.

6. Use the Directories list box to select the directory that contains the table you want to import.

7. When you are importing an Access table, select from the File Name list box the database containing the table you want to import, and choose the OK button. For example, to import tables from the Ventana database, select ventana.mdb from the File Name list box and select the OK button. Access displays the Import Objects dialog box (see Figure 3-19).

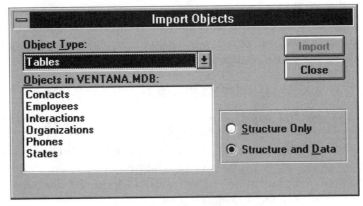

Figure 3-19: The Import Objects dialog box.

8. The Objects list box in the Import Objects dialog box lists in the Objects list box all of the tables stored in the selected Microsoft Access database. From this list box, select the name of the table you want to import.

9. The Import Objects dialog box also contains the following two option buttons:

○ *Structure Only*. Choose this option when you want to create a table with the same design as the source table, but with different data.

○ *Structure and Data*. Choose this option to copy the table design as well as its data into the open database.

For the Contacts database, select the Structure and Data option button.

10. Choose the Import button. Access displays a message that indicates whether it has successfully imported the table. Choose the OK button to continue. If you want to import another table from the same database, select the table name from the Objects list in the Import Objects dialog box and choose the Import button again.

In the Contacts database example, import the Organizations, and Phones tables—structure and data—from the Ventana database. (**Note**: You will create in Chapter 4 the Interactions table—one of the tables in the Contacts database design—so you don't need to import it now.)

11. When you finish importing tables, choose the Close button to return to the Database window.

When you are importing non-Access tables, select from the File Name list box the name of the table you want to import. Choose the Import button. Access then displays a message that indicates whether it has successfully imported the table. Choose the Close button to continue. If you want to import another table, select the table name from the File Name list box and choose the Import button again. When you are finished importing tables, choose the Close button to return to the Database window.

DEFINING TABLE RELATIONSHIPS

In Chapter 2 you learned that any two tables in an Access database can be *related* several different ways. Access tables are related if they share a field. When one table contains the primary key field of another table, we say the first table contains a *foreign key*. Using the terminology defined in Chapter 2, the tables in Contacts are related as follows:

Table Pair	Relationship
Contacts to Employees	Many-to-many
Contacts to Phones	One-to-many
Organizations to Contacts	One-to-many
Employees to Phones	One-to-many
Organizations to Phones	One-to-many

Although we have designed these relationships into the Contacts database, we also need to explicitly define these relationships in Access. Many of Access' most important features work properly only if you correctly inform the program of the relationships between the tables in the database. Fortunately, Access provides an easy way to define these table relationships.

To define table relationships, follow these steps:

1. Open the database that contains the related tables.

2. Either click the Relationships button in the toolbar, or choose Edit, Relationships to display the Relationships dialog box. Access then immediately displays the Add Table dialog box on top of the Relationships dialog box, as shown in Figure 3-20.

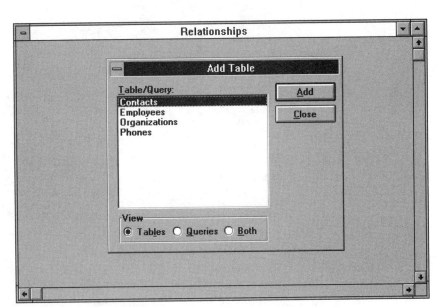

Figure 3-20: The Relationships and the Add Table dialog boxes.

3. Next, you need to add the tables to the Relationships dialog box. Double-click each table name in the Table/Query list box in the Add Table dialog box (refer to Chapters 6 and 7 for a

full discussion of Access queries). In the Contacts database example, double-click Contacts, Employees, Organizations and Phones. Each time you double-click a table name, Access adds to the Relationships dialog box a box that lists all the fields in the table.

4. After adding all the desired tables to the Relationships dialog box, choose the Close button to close the Add Table dialog box. If you find later that you forgot a table, you can reopen the Add Table dialog box either by clicking the Add Table button on the toolbar, or by choosing Relationships, Add Table from the menu bar. Figure 3-21 shows the Relationships dialog box with tables added. You can remove a table box from the Relationships dialog box by selecting the box you want to delete and either pressing the Delete key, or choosing Relationships, Remove Table from the menu bar.

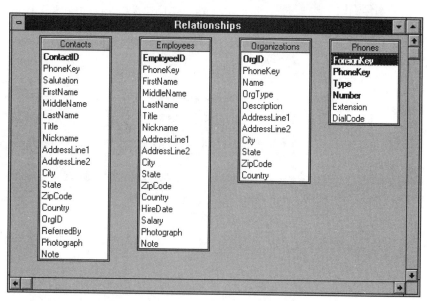

Figure 3-21: The Relationships dialog box with tables added.

5. Access makes defining the relationship between two tables very easy. First identify the fields that "link" the two tables. In one table the linking field will be the table's primary key. This table is the *primary table*. In the other table, the link will be a foreign key (refer to Chapter 2 for a discussion of primary keys and foreign keys). This table is a *related table*. Click the primary key field in the primary table and (while holding the mouse button down) drag the key field to the foreign key field in the related table. When you release the

mouse button, Access displays another Relationships dialog box (see Figure 3-22).

For example, to define the relationship between Contacts and Organizations, drag the OrgID field from Organizations (the table's primary key field) to the OrgID field in Contacts.

Primary key field in primary table ⟶

Foreign key field in related table ⟶

Enforces Referential Integrity ⟶

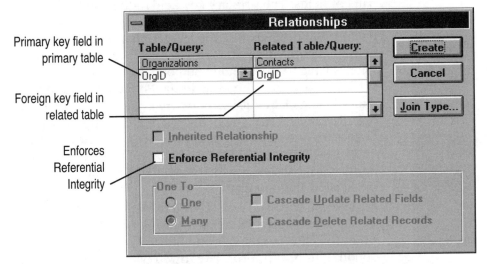

Figure 3-22: The second Relationships dialog box.

6. Check the dialog box to make sure the correct linking fields are listed. The primary key field from the primary table should be listed on the left and the foreign key field from the related table should be listed on the right. Using the drag-and-drop procedure described in the tip in step 5, you won't normally have to fill out the dialog box. In some cases, however, the primary table may have a multi-field primary key. In such a situation, you will have to complete the list of primary key fields in the left-hand column, and matching foreign key fields in the right-hand column.

 TIP It is often necessary to resize the table boxes in the Relationships dialog box in order to see all field names in each table. Use the mouse to resize these boxes the same way you resize any window in a Windows application. You can also use the mouse to drag the tables around in the dialog box. Figure 3-21 shows the table boxes after they have been resized and moved so that all field names are visible.

TIP The name of the primary key field is shown in bold in each table box.

In our Contacts database example, the relationship between the Employees table and the Phones table is defined by two pairs of fields. The primary key field in the Employees table is EmployeeID. This field links to the ForeignKey field in Phones. But in Chapter 2 you learned that the PhoneKey field is also necessary in both tables because we are using the Phones table to store phone numbers for Employees, Contacts and Organizations. The value in the PhoneKey field in the Phones table distinguishes between employees, contacts and organizations. When you define the relationship between Employees and Phones, you need to select EmployeeID and PhoneKey in the Table/Query column of the second Relationships dialog box. Select ForeignKey and PhoneKey in the Related Table/Query column.

7. If you want Access to enforce *referential integrity* rules, mark the Enforce Referential Integrity check box. Then select either the One To One option button, or the One To Many option button, as appropriate. If you want Access to update the values in the foreign key fields of the related table when you make changes in the primary key field of the primary table, then also mark the Cascade Update Related Fields check box. This is usually the best practice. On the other hand, you may want to be careful about marking the Cascade Delete Related Records. Using this option may make it too easy to delete all related records from the related table by deleting a record in the primary table. Refer to Chapters 8 and 9 for a look at how referential integrity comes into play when you use Main/Subform style forms in Access.

Referential Integrity

The concept of referential integrity, in terms of Access primary and related tables, can be summarized in the following rules:

1. You cannot add a record to a related table unless there is already a matching record in the primary table.

2. You cannot delete a record from a primary table while matching records still exist in the related table.

Access enforces these rules only if you follow the procedure described in this section to define the relationship between the tables (a) both fields have the same data type, (b) both tables are stored in the same Access database and (c) the relationship between the two tables is either a one-to-one relationship or a one-to-many relationship.

8. When you finish filling out the (second) Relationships dialog box, choose the Create button. Access draws a line in the Relationships dialog box from the primary key field in the primary table to the foreign key field in the related table. If you indicated that the relationship was one-to-many, or one-to-one, Access displays the numeral 1 above the line on the one side, and displays the infinity sign on the many side of the relationship (see Figure 3-23). Solid bars at each end of the line denote enforcement of referential integrity rules.

You may want to move the table boxes around so the lines between tables don't cross and don't go behind tables.

For the Contacts database, link the following tables in the Relationships dialog box. When you finish, the relationships should look similar to Figure 3-23.

Table Pair	Primary Table Field(s)	Related Table Field(s)
Contacts, Phones	ContactID, PhoneKey	ForeignKey, PhoneKey
Employees, Phones	EmployeeID, PhoneKey	ForeignKey, PhoneKey
Orgainizations, Phones	OrgID, PhoneKey	ForeignKey, PhoneKey
Organizations, Contacts	OrgID	OrgID

one side ⎯⎯⎯⎯⎯

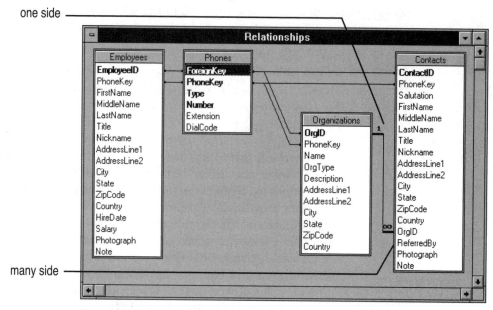

many side ⎯⎯

Figure 3-23: The Relationships dialog box for the Contacts database.

9. When you finish defining the relationships between all tables in the database, either click the Save button in the toolbar, or choose File, Save Layout from the menu bar.

10. To close the Relationships dialog box, either double-click the Control-menu box, or select File, Close from the menu bar.

MOVING ON

This chapter has introduced you to Microsoft Access' Table Wizard, which is the easiest way to create new Access tables. This chapter also described how you can easily use tables that already exist by either attaching the tables, or importing them into your open database.

Now that you are familiar with the easy ways to create tables, you are ready to look at how to design tables on your own using Access' Design view. Turn now to Chapter 4, "Creating Tables in Design View" to learn more about creating tables from scratch.

4

CREATING TABLES IN DESIGN VIEW

In Chapter 3, you learned how to create tables using the Table Wizard, and you learned how to attach and import existing tables. In the process of creating tables using the Wizard, you also took a quick look at the Table window's Design view. This chapter introduces you to all the features of Design view.

The Table Wizard of Access 2.0 provides many example tables and fields from which you can choose to build the tables in your database, but invariably you'll think of some sort of table or field that isn't provided. You will almost certainly need to make some adjustments to the design of one or more of your tables, even if you are generally satisfied with tables you created using the Wizard. And, some experienced users may just prefer to build tables from scratch, without the aid of the Table Wizard. The Table window's Design view, therefore, enables you to easily modify the design of existing tables—adding fields, deleting fields, changing field properties and so on—as well as to create tables from the ground up.

OPENING A TABLE IN DESIGN VIEW

There are two reasons to open a table in Design view. Either you are creating a brand new table for your database, or you want to modify the design of a table that already exists in your database.

In our Contacts database, we still need to add the Interactions table to the database. This table contains data about each interaction between an account executive (sales person) and a contact. From a database design point of view, the Interactions table provides a link or association between the records in the Employees table and the records in the Contacts table. Each record in the Interactions table will contain the following fields:

Interactions
InteractionID
EmployeeID
ContactID
Date/Time
FollowUpDate
Subject
Description

The InteractionID field is the primary key field for the Interactions table. Its value in each record acts as a unique identifier for the record. The EmployeeID field contains the ID number of the sales person who wants to record the interaction (meeting, phone call, etc.). The ContactID field is the ID number of the individual with whom the sales person interacted. The Date/Time field records the date when the interaction between sales person and contact occurred. And the Subject field stores a description of the subject of the meeting or phone call. The Table Wizard doesn't contain a table just like this one, so we've decided to use Design view to create the Interactions table.

To open a new table in Design view, follow these steps:

1. Open the database that will contain the new table. Access displays the Database window. If the database is already open, choose the Table button to display the list of tables (if any) already defined for the database (see Figure 4-1).

Click the New button

Figure 4-1: The list of tables in the Database window.

2. Either choose the New button in the Database window, or choose File, New, Table from the menu bar. Access displays the New Table dialog box (see Figure 4-2).

Click the
New Table button ——

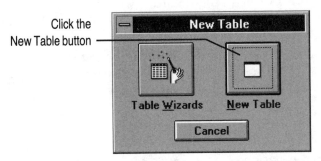

Figure 4-2: The New Table dialog box.

3. Choose the New Table button in the New Table dialog box. Access displays the Table window in Design view, as shown in Figure 4-3. You are ready to start adding fields to the table.

Field selector column   Field name column   Data type column   Description column

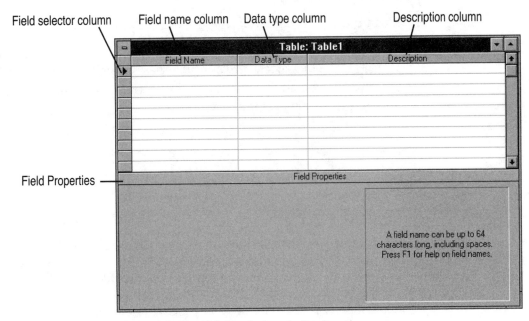

Figure 4-3: The Table window in Design view.

To open an existing table in Design view in order to modify the table's design, follow these steps:

1. Open the database that contains the table you want to modify. Access displays the Database window. If the database is already open, choose the Table button to display the list of tables already defined for the database (see Figure 4-1).

2. Select the Table you want to modify in the Database window and choose the Design button. Access displays the table's design in the Table window's Design view.

When Modifying a Table That Contains Data

Any time you modify the design of a field in a table that already contains data, you run the risk of losing some or all the data in the field. To avoid losing data, observe the following rules:

1. Don't convert a Text field to a Number field unless it contains only numbers.

2. Reduce the size of a field only if you are certain that all data will fit into the new field size.

3. Read all screen messages very carefully before proceeding. Access warns you any time you are about to delete data. Ignore these warnings at your own risk!

4. If you are unsure of yourself at this point, make a copy of the table before making changes to the table definition.

ADDING FIELDS

After you've designed your database (see Chapter 2), and opened a new Table in Design view, table creation in Access consists mainly of adding fields to the Design view. Access provides two ways to add fields. You can use the Field Builder feature—a Wizard-like tool—to add a predefined field, or you can assign field name and field type on you own. The sections that follow discuss both methods.

Using the Field Builder

Adding a field with the Field Builder is very much like using the Table Wizard. You can choose to add field definitions from the same list of sample tables that are available in the Table Wizard.

Modifying the Data Dictionary

The sample tables and sample fields that are available in the Field Builder and the Table Wizard are stored in a database. This database provides a feature that is sometimes called a *data dictionary* or *catalog*. If you intend to work on a large project that may involve many programmers, you can help insure that field definitions will be consistent between programmers by always using the Table Wizard or Field Builder to define fields. Because the default list of tables and fields may not suit your specific needs, Access enables you to modify the standard list of fields and tables or to install your own database of sample fields and tables (your own data dictionary).

To customize sample fields, or tables, or to install a different data dictionary database, choose File, Add-ins, Add-in Manager to display the Add-in Manager dialog box. Select the Table Wizard from the Available Libraries list box and choose the Customize command button. Access displays the Customize Table Wizard dialog box. From this dialog box, you can customize the sample fields and sample tables that are available in the default data dictionary, or you can choose to install a new data dictionary.

The default data dictionary is stored in a database file named WZTBLDAT.DBT. If you want to install a new dictionary, you need to create a database that contains identical tables and queries as WZTBLDAT.DBT, but different data. Then use the Install New Database button in the Customize Table Wizard dialog box to select the new database. Alternatively, you can edit the MSACC20.INI file, which is found in the \WINDOWS directory. By default the [Table Wizard Data Files] section contains the following line:

wztbldat.mdt=Standard MS Sample Fields

Replace wztlbdat.mdt in this line with the name of the new data dictionary database.

To add a field using the Field Builder, follow these steps:

1. Position the cursor in the row of the upper pane of the Table window where you want the field to be inserted. A pointer in the field selector column indicates the current row. If you use the Field Builder to add a field to a row that already contains a field, Access will insert a blank row for the new field and move the existing field(s) down one row.

2. Click the Build button in the toolbar, or right-click the Field Name column, and choose Build from the pop-up menu. Access displays the Field Builder dialog box (see Figure 4-4).

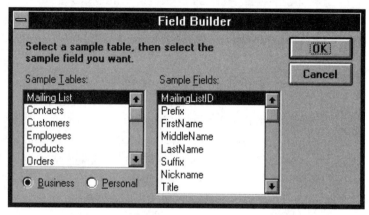

Figure 4-4: The Field Builder dialog box.

The Field Builder dialog box contains two list boxes. The Sample Tables list box, on the left side of the screen, contains a list of tables that are representative of the most often used table designs. When the Field Builder dialog box first displays, the Mailing List table name is highlighted. You can scroll through this list using the up and down arrow keys or the scroll bar. This is the same list that appears in the Table Wizard. By default, the Field Builder lists 26 business-related sample tables in the Sample Tables list box. You can switch to a list of 19 personal-related sample tables by choosing the Personal option button in the Field Builder dialog box.

The Sample Fields list box, in the center of the dialog box, lists the fields of the table that is currently selected in the Sample Tables list. For example, in Figure 4-4 the Sample Fields list box shows fields from the sample Mailing List table, which is selected in the Sample Tables list box.

3. Select a table in the Sample Tables list box. If you are not sure which table is closest, scroll through the Sample Tables list and examine the field lists that appear in the Sample Fields list.

4. To copy a field from the Sample Fields list to the Table window, either double-click the field name, or select a field name and then choose the OK button. Access closes the dialog box and copies the selected field name from the Sample Fields list to the current row in the Table window. Access fills in the Field Name and Data Type columns and fills in some of the Field Properties pane, in the bottom half of the Table window.

ASSIGNING FIELD NAMES

When you use the Field Builder to create an Access field, Access selects data type and field properties according to the values stored in Access' current *data dictionary* (see the "Modifying the Data Dictionary" sidebar in the preceding section). You can easily change data type and field properties, as explained in the remainder of this chapter, but you may just prefer to define the field name, field type and field properties yourself from the outset.

To assign a field name, position the cursor in the Field Name column and type the desired name. In Access, field names can be practically anything you want to use, up to 64 characters. You seldom should use that many characters, however. Whenever possible, follow these guidelines when naming fields:

○ Use field names that describe the contents of the data you plan to store in the field.

○ Don't use the same field name more than once in a table (Access will not permit you to violate this rule).

○ Whenever possible, use the same field name for fields used to link primary and related tables in a table relationship. In other words, the name of a foreign key field in a related table should usually match the name of the corresponding primary key field in the primary table (refer to "Defining Table Relationships" in Chapter 3 for a discussion of primary tables, related tables and table relationships).

○ Refrain from creating long field names or field names with spaces. If you think you might want to use expressions, SQL statements or Access Basic, long field names and field names with spaces are cumbersome. The most common way to make a field name descriptive, while avoiding the use of spaces, is to "squeeze" the spaces out of multi-word names, and to use uppercase letters in the middle of words. For example, instead of using the field name Address Line 1, in several of the tables in the Contacts database, we have used the field name AddressLine1. We have used FirstName rather than First Name, ZipCode rather than Zip Code and so on.

When you have decided on a field name, type the name in the Field Name column of the Table window and either press Enter or Tab. Access moves the cursor to the Data Type column.

For example, to add the InteractionID field, type **InteractionID** in the Field Name column and press either Enter or Tab. Access moves the cursor to the DataType column, as shown in Figure 4-5.

Click to display date type list

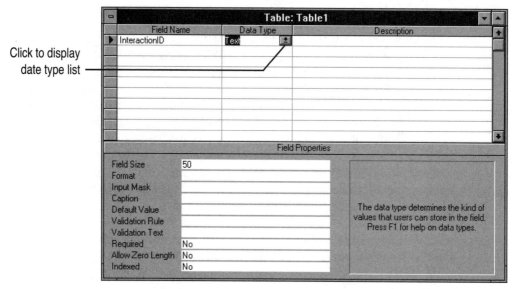

Figure 4-5: Table window in Design view after adding the InteractionID field name.

Assigning Data Type

After you specify a field name in Design view, you have to assign a data type. Access cannot determine on its own whether you intend data to be text, numeric or other. The purpose of the Data Type column, in the Table window, is to inform Access of the type of data you intend to enter in the field. To assign data type, move the cursor to the Data Type column in the Table window. Click the drop-down button to display the following list of data types (see Figure 4-6):

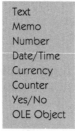

Text
Memo
Number
Date/Time
Currency
Counter
Yes/No
OLE Object

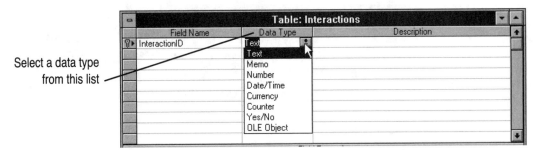

Figure 4-6: Table window in Design view after dropping down the list of data types.

Select a data type from the list. The following sections will help you decide which data type to select.

Text Fields

When you create a field on your own (rather than using the Field Builder), Access assigns the text data type to the field by default. A Text field can contain more than just text, however. A Text field can contain any combination of up to 255 letters, numbers and other keyboard characters.

The text data type is the most commonly used data type. When in doubt, assign the text data type. Very often, inexperienced database designers create a Number field when a text field is more appropriate. You can store numbers in a Text field, but you can't store text or any other non-numeric character in a Number field. The following entries are all valid in a text field:

```
Now is the time for all good men to come to the aid of their country.
ABC123456789
@#$%^&*(_)
```

When you choose the text data type, you also should specify the maximum length of the data in the FieldSize property (refer to "Setting Field Properties" later in this chapter). By default, Text fields have a maximum length of 50 characters. When you want to limit the number of characters a user will be able to type into a field, you can specify a different field length.

> Unlike many other database programs, Access does not waste storage space if Text field values do not fill the field. Access uses only as much storage space as is necessary to store the text value that has been entered into the field.

Memo Fields

The memo data type is another data type that can accommodate any combination of alphanumeric characters. Unlike Text fields, however, Memo fields are variable in length. Access only uses as much disk space as is necessary to store the values actually entered in Memo field. Each Memo field in each record in the database can potentially store up to 64,000 bytes (characters) of data.

As is suggested by the data type's name, Memo fields are most useful for storing variable length text, such as short memos or notes. When we created the Contacts and Employees tables in Chapter 3, we added the Note field to each. Each of these Note fields is a Memo field.

In the Interactions table, make the Description field a Memo field.

Although Memo fields are very flexible (they can hold data of almost any length), they are not appropriate for most fields that store alphanumeric data. Access does not enable you to sort or index Memo fields—capabilities that are available for Text fields. You can search for text in Memo fields, but not as quickly as an indexed Text field.

Number Fields

A Number field can contain any number with or without decimals. Following are all valid entries in a Number field:

```
12345
123.45
.12345
-12.345
```

As with Text fields, you can specify the size of each Number field. But, unlike a Text field, the FieldSize property of any Number field determines the storage space occupied by the field's data. Each field assigned the number data type can have any of the following FieldSize property settings (the default setting is *double*):

FieldSize	Range of Values	Decimal Places	Storage Size
Byte	0 to 255	None	1 byte
Integer	-32,768 to 32,767	None	2 bytes
Long Integer	-2,147,483,648 to 2,147,483,648	None	4 bytes
Single	-3.4×10^{38} to 3.4×10^{38}	7	4 bytes
Double	-1.797×10^{308} to $1,797 \times 10^{308}$	15	8 bytes

As a rule of thumb, you should assign the number data type to a field only when you expect to do calculations with the data you will store in the field. If you do create a Number field, assign the FieldSize property that will take the least storage space and still serve the field's intended purpose. Keep in mind that integer and long integer fields cannot contain decimal places.

In the Interactions table, assign the number data type to both the EmployeeID and ContactID fields.

Date/Time Fields

Fields of the date/time data type can be used to store dates, time or dates and time. Each date/time value in a table requires 8 bytes of storage space on the disk. Valid values for a date field include the following:

```
3/9/78
Thursday, March 09, 1978
09 Mar-78
3/9/78 9:02:00 PM
21:02
```

In the Interactions table, the Date/Time and FollowUpDate fields will have the Date/Time data type.

Currency Fields

Currency fields are a special type of Number field. It is equivalent to a Number field with the double FieldSize property and currency Format property. When you type a value in a currency field, you don't have to type either the dollar sign or commas (at the thousands place); yet, Access displays the dollar sign and commas automatically. By default, Access displays two decimal places. Access rounds to two display places the display of more than two decimal places.

The following values are valid entries in a currency field:

```
123.45
12345.678
$1234.5
$1,234.56
-$123
```

Counter Fields

When you assign the counter data type, Access automatically assigns a numeric value to this field in each new record in the database. The first record in the table receives the value of 1; the second record is 2; Access assigns the value of 3 to the third record in the table and so on.

If you delete a record in a table that has a counter field, Access does not renumber subsequent fields. And if you add another record, Access does not reuse the counter value that has been deleted. Counter fields are, therefore, frequently used as primary key fields. In each record, the counter field contains a value that doesn't appear in the same field in any other record in the table. What's more, Access assigns the values to the field automatically. For example, the primary key field for each of the Contacts, Employees and Organizations tables—ContactID, EmployeeID and OrgID—is a counter field.

In the Interactions table, assign the counter data type to the InteractionID field, as shown in Figure 4-7.

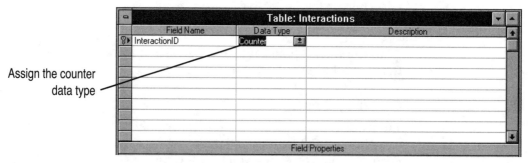

Assign the counter data type

Figure 4-7: The InteractionID field defined as counter data type.

When you assign the counter data type to a new field, you aren't given the opportunity to set the field size. Just keep in mind that counter field values are stored in the database as long integers. Each counter value occupies 4 bytes of disk space.

When you plan to define a table relationship between a table with a counter field as its primary key, define the foreign key field in the related table as a long integer Number field. For example, we want to be able to define a one-to-many relationship between the Employees and the Interactions tables. The EmployeeID field, which is the primary key field for the Employees table, is a counter field. We therefore need to define the EmployeeID field for the Interactions table, with the long integer field size. For similar reasons, we should also define the ContractID field in Interactions as a long integer field.

Yes/No Fields

Yes/No fields are appropriate when the field can have only one of two values. This type of field is often used to record true/false or on/off type data—often referred to as *boolean* data. For example, you might want a FollowUp field in the Interactions table that stores a value of Yes when the sales person needs to make a subsequent contact. The field stores a value of No when no follow up is required.

Through the Format property, you can choose to have values in Yes/No fields to display as True/False or On/Off.

OLE Object Fields

Object Linking and Embedding or OLE, in the context of an Access database, refers to the capability to store *objects* (files) created by other applications in Access fields. An OLE Object field in Access can contain OLE objects. For the user to be able to view and edit the object, however, the file must have been created by an OLE *application*, a Windows-based program that supports OLE.

Access enables you to create OLE object fields that can contain either *linked* or *embedded* OLE objects. When you are adding data to an OLE object field, Access gives you a choice between inserting (embedding) a new object, inserting the contents of an existing file (object) or linking an existing file. Each *embedded* object is stored in your database, while each *linked* object is stored only in the original file. For example, the Photograph fields in Employees and Contacts are OLE object fields (see Figure 4-8). The Photograph field in each record stores an *embedded* copy of a scanned color photograph (the same images found in the Northwind Traders application that is shipped with Access 2.0).

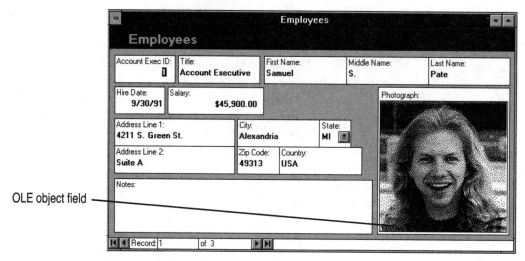

OLE object field ——————

Figure 4-8: The Photograph field in the Employees table is an OLE object field.

Embedded OLE objects can be viewed and edited without affecting the original source file. The source file doesn't need to be available to the user. If you edit a linked OLE object, however, you are modifying the source file. Linked objects must be available to the user who is trying to edit the field. In a multi-user computing environment, this means that the user has to have the necessary permissions to access the shared source files.

SETTING FIELD PROPERTIES

In addition to the FieldSize property (discussed in "Text Fields" earlier in this chapter), Access enables you to set many other field properties in the Field Properties pane of the Table window (see Figure 4.9), also sometimes known as the property sheet. By setting these properties you can determine how field data is displayed, and help ensure that invalid data is not entered into your database. You can set any of the following properties, depending on the data type of the current field:

Field Properties	
Field Size	50
Format	
Input Mask	
Caption	
Default Value	
Validation Rule	
Validation Text	
Required	No
Allow Zero Length	No
Indexed	No

The data type determines the kind of values that users can store in the field. Press F1 for help on data types.

Figure 4-9: The Field Properties pane (or property sheet) of the Table window.

Field Property	Purpose
FieldSize	Sets the maximum length for data entered in Text and Number fields.
Format	Determines how Access displays and prints data, such as whether to display Date fields in words or just numbers.
DecimalPlaces	Determines the number of decimal places displayed and printed in Number and Currency fields.
InputMask	Determines how a field looks when the user is entering data. For example, you can create an input mask for a field for entering dates that automatically display two slashes (/ /). Or you can create a field for entering phone numbers that display parentheses and a dash (( ) –).
Caption	Supplies a label for Access to use in forms and reports, instead of the field name.
DefaultValue	Assigns a value that Access inserts into the field in each new record you add to the table. You can change the value—if you desire—during data entry.
ValidationRule	Checks the data entered in the field against a set criteria to prevent entry of invalid data.
ValidationText	Defines the contents of the message that appears when a user enters data that doesn't match the criteria specified in the ValidationRule property.
Required	Indicates that some data must be entered in the field before the record can be saved (i.e., the value in the field cannot be Null). By default, Access fields are not required.
AllowZeroLength	Determines whether a *zero-length string* is a valid entry. To enter a zero-length string, type "". By default, zero-length strings are not valid entries.
Indexed	Creates an index on the field to speed up searches of the field.

Setting Field Size

As you have already learned in this chapter, for Text and Number fields you must select a field size in the FieldSize property. To set the FieldSize property, follow these steps:

1. Choose the field's data type.

2. Either press F6 to switch to the Field Properties pane of the Table window, or click the Field Size text box in the Field Properties pane.

3. For Text fields, simply type a number to indicate the maximum number of characters that will be permitted in the field. For Number fields, Access supplies several standard field sizes including Byte, Integer, Long Integer, Double and Single (refer to "Number Fields" earlier in this chapter for an explanation of these field sizes). To list the available field sizes, click the drop-down button at the end of the Field Size text box.

4. Click the field size you want in the list. For example, for both the EmployeeID and ContactID fields in the Interactions table, select the Long Integer field size (see Figure 4-10).

Choose the Long Integer field size for the EmployeeID field and InteractionID field

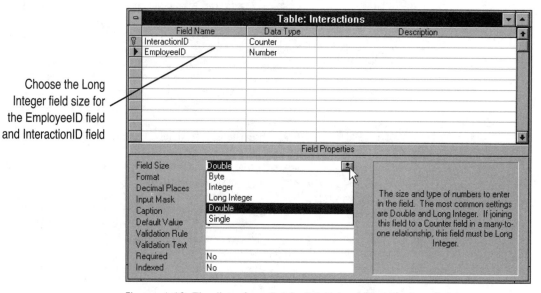

Figure 4-10: The list of available field sizes for Number fields.

Setting the Format

The Format property determines how data is displayed onscreen and when printed in reports. This property does not affect the data stored in the database, or how it is entered, just the way it looks. To set the Format property (see the following table), follow these steps:

1. Choose the field's data type.
2. Select the Format text box in the Field Properties pane of the Table window.
3. For Number, Currency, Counter, Date/Time and Yes/No data types, Access supplies several standard formats. To list the available formats (for Number, Date/Time and Yes/No data types only), click the drop-down button at the end of the Format text box. Access lists the following options, depending on the field's data type:

Format	Value Entered	Value Displayed
Number, Currency and Counter Fields		
General	1235.567	1234.567
Currency	1234.567	$1,234.57
Fixed	1234.567	1234.57
Standard	1234.567	1,234.57
Percent	.12345	12.35%
Scientific	1234.567	1.23+03
Date/Time Fields		
General Date	2/27/94 5:45 PM	2/27/94 5:45:00 PM
	February 27, 1994	2/27/94
Long Date	2/27/94	Tuesday, September 27, 1994
Medium Date	2/27/94	27-Sep-94
Short Date	2/27/94	2/27/94
Long Time	5:45:27 PM	5:45:27 PM
Medium Time	5:45:27 PM	5:45 PM
Short Time	5:45:27 PM	17:45
Yes/No Fields		
True/False	Yes, True, On, or 1	True
	No, False, Off, or 0	False
Yes/No	Yes, True, On, or 1	Yes
	No, False, Off, or 0	No
On/Off	Yes, True, On, or 1	On
	No, False, Off, or 0	Off
(none)	Yes, True, On or 1	-1
	No, False, Off or 0	0

For example, add the Date/Time field to the Interactions table. Assign the Date/Time data type, and choose the Short Date format, the default format for Date/Time fields.

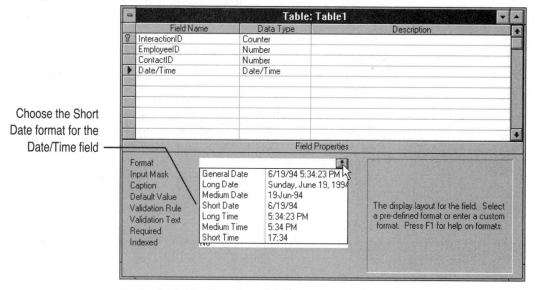

Choose the Short Date format for the Date/Time field

Figure 4-11: The list of available formats for Date/Time fields.

In the Interactions table design, also add the FollowUpDate field. Assign the Short Date format.

Creating an Input Mask

Mistakes in data entry can often be reduced by forcing the user to enter data in a predetermined format. You have seen already that the Format property affects how data is displayed, but doesn't determine how data must be entered. Access 2.0 has added the capability to define an input mask for each field. Such a mask can limit the characters the user can type in the field in the hope that data-entry errors will be reduced. For example, you can help users enter date and time correctly by requiring the entry of numbers, slashes and colons in preset positions.

Access enables you to build an input mask on your own using special characters (see the table that follows). For Text and Date/Time fields, you can also use the Input Mask Wizard. To build an input mask using the Wizard, follow these steps:

1. Choose either the Text or Date/Time data type.

2. Click the Save button on the toolbar to save the table design, as it stands up to this point in time.

3. Select the Input Mask text box in the Field Properties pane of the Table window.

4. Click the Build button at the right end of the Input Mask text box, or click the Input Mask text box and select Build from the pop-up menu. If you haven't yet saved the table design, Access prompts you to do so. Choose the Yes button to save the table design. If this is the first time you are saving a new table design, Access displays the Save As dialog box. Type a name for the table and choose the OK button to save the design under the new table name and continue with the Wizard. Access displays the initial Input Mask Wizard dialog box. Figure 4-12 shows the Input Mask Wizard dialog box for a Date/Time field.

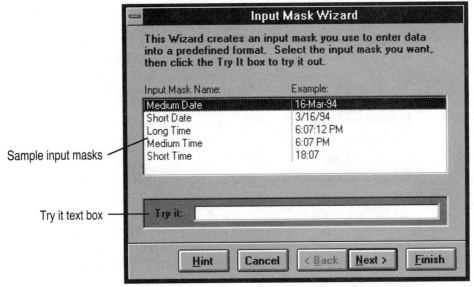

Figure 4-12: The initial Input Mask Wizard dialog box for Date/Time fields.

5. Choose an input mask from the list of sample input masks in the Input Mask Wizard dialog box. For Date/Time fields, the Wizard lists five masks that assist users in entering data. Each mask corresponds to a date/time filed Format property setting.

If you want to see the effect the input mask will have, you can try it out in the Try it text box. First, select the input mask you want to test and then select the Try it text box. The Wizard displays the same special characters the user will see during data entry. Try typing a field value in the text box.

For example, select the Short Date input mask for the Date/Time field in the Interactions table. This mask assists the user when entering data.

6. Choose the Next > button. The Wizard displays the second screen of the Input Mask Wizard dialog box. Figure 4-13 shows this screen after having selected the Short Date input mask.

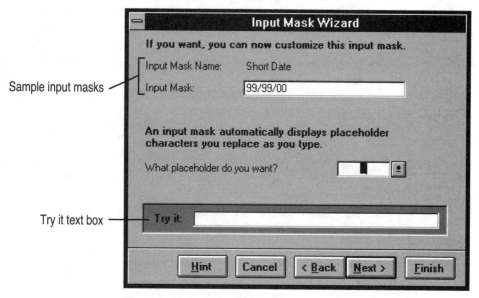

Figure 4-13: The initial Input Mask Wizard dialog box for Date/Time fields.

7. The Wizard enables you to customize the sample input mask in this second screen of the Input Mask Wizard dialog box. Use the following characters to customize the mask:

Mask Character	Meaning
0	Numerical digit; entry is required.
9	Numerical digit; no entry is required; place on the right or left side of the mask.
#	Numerical digit, plus (+), or minus (–) sign, or space; no entry is required; Access converts blanks to spaces; place on the right or left side of mask.
L	Any letter; entry is required.
?	Any letter; no entry is required.
A	Any letter or digit; entry is required.
a	Any letter or digit; no entry is required.
&	Any character or space; entry is required.
C	Any character or space; no entry is required.
. , : ; - /	Literal characters used as separators in Number fields and Date/Time fields.
<	Converts characters to the right of this character to lowercase.
>	Converts characters to the right of this character to uppercase.
!	Causes field to fill from right to left.
\	Causes character that follows this symbol to display as a literal character in the mask.

8. The second screen in the Input Mask Wizard dialog box also asks you what *placeholder* you want to use. By default, Access displays the underscore character in positions where the user is supposed to type a character. If you would prefer that Access display a different character as a placeholder, type the character in the text box provided in the Input Mask Wizard dialog box.

9. After making any desired changes to the sample input mask, and after specifying an alternative placeholder, if you desire to do so, choose the Next > button. The Wizard displays the final screen in the Input Mask Wizard dialog box (see Figure 4.14). This screen announces that you have answered all the questions necessary to create the input mask. The screen also gives you the opportunity to turn on Cue Cards.

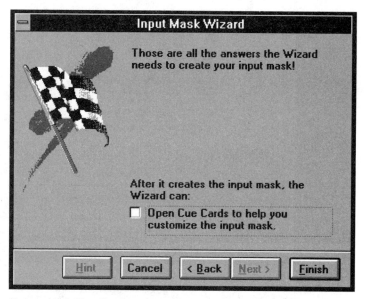

Figure 4-14: The final screen of the Input Mask Wizard dialog box.

10. Choose the Finish button to complete Wizard and generate the input mask. The Wizard adds the mask to the Input Mask text box in the Field Properties pane of the Table window. For example, after completing the Input Mask Wizard in order to create the input mask for the Date/Time field, the Wizard adds the following line to the Input Mask text box:

   99/99/00;0;_

The characters of the mask up to the first semicolon constitute the actual input mask. The 0 digit between the two semicolons is a code that causes Access to store the literal characters of the input mask in the field with the data that is actually entered in the field by the user. In the example input mask we are creating for the Date/Time field in the Interactions table, the literal characters / and / are stored with the actual data in the database. If the character after the first semicolon were the number 1, Access will not store the literal characters with the data.

The placeholder character is displayed to the right of the second semicolon.

 TIP You can cause Access to display an asterisk (*) for each character the user types in a field by typing **Password** as the InputMask property.

In the Interactions table design, add a Date/Time field named FollowUpDate, with the Short Date format, and type the following mask in the field's Input Mask text box:

99/99/00;0;_

Setting Default Values

Another way to help users enter valid data is to place an appropriate value in the field as a default entry. Access enables you to assign a default value to each field, if you desire. Often, providing default values can speed up data entry significantly because users can skip fields that contain default values that are correct for the current record.

To assign a default value, follow these steps:

1. If you haven't already done so, type a name in the Field Name column, and select a data type.

2. While the data type column is selected, type the default value in the Default Value text box in the Field Properties pane of the Table Window.

For example, create the Subject field in the Interactions table. Assign the text data type with the default field size (50). Type the following default value in the Default Value text box in the Field Properties pane of the Table window (see Figure 4-15):

Sales prospect

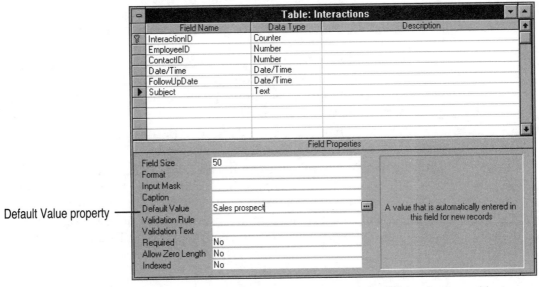

Figure 4-15: The Field Properties pane of the Table window with a default value added.

111

You can also use an Access *expression* to define a default value. An expression in Access is a combination of operators, constants, literals, functions, fields, controls and properties that evaluate to a single value. When used to define the DefaultValue property, the expression cannot refer to another field in the table.

For example, you might want to insert the current date as the default value for the Date/Time field. To do so, type the following expression as the DefaultValue property for the Date/Time field:

Date( )

If you prefer, you can use the Expression Builder to insert an expression in the DefaultValue property. Refer to the "Validating Input" section, which follows this one, for a discussion of the Expression Builder.

After you finish defining the Interactions table, you should also edit the table design of the Contacts table and assign a default value of "C" to the PhoneKey field. Similarly, assign a default value of "E" to the PhoneKey field in Employees.

Validating Input

Sometimes it is possible to define criteria that automatically eliminates invalid data. Access provides the ValidationRule property that uses validation criteria to prevent the entry of invalid data into a particular field. For example, you might want to prevent the entry of a value in the FollowUpDate field that is earlier than today's date.

To define the ValidationRule property, you can either type an expression in the Validation Rule text box in the Field Properties pane of the Table window, or use the Expression Builder. As is the case with an expression used to default the DefaultValue property, when used to define the ValidationRule property, the expression cannot refer to another field in the table.

To define the ValidationRule property using the Expression Builder, follow these steps:

1. If you haven't already done so, type a name in the Field Name column, and select a data type.

2. While the data type column is selected, click the Validation Rule text box and then click the Build button at the right end of the text box. Alternatively, right-click the Validation Rule text box and choose Build from the pop-up menu. Access displays the Expression Builder dialog box, as shown in Figure 4-16.

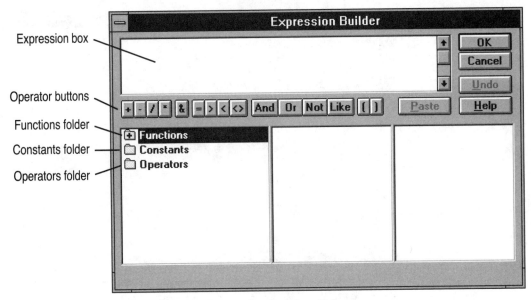

Figure 4-16: The Expression Builder dialog box.

3. Build the expression by choosing operators from the operator buttons, as well as functions, constants and operators from the folders listed in the lower half of the Expression Builder dialog box. To display the available functions, for example, double-click the Functions folder to display the Built-In Functions folder name. Then select the Built-In Functions folder to display a list of all functions in the far right column. To limit the functions listed, select a group of functions in the center column of the Expression Builder dialog box.

For example, to select date-related functions, first double-click the Functions folder in the left-most column of the lower half of the Expression Builder dialog box. Then click the Built-In Functions folder. Finally, select the Date/Time option in the center column. Access displays a list of date/time-related functions in the right-most column. Select the appropriate function and choose the OK button. Access enters the expression in the Validation Rule text box.

To establish a validation rule for the FollowUpDate field, for instance, first choose the > operator button to add this operator to the Expression box. Then double-click the Functions folder, and click the Built-In Functions folder. Choose the Date/Time option in the center column, and double-click the Date function. Finally, choose the OK button. Access enters the following expression in the Validation Rule text box (see Figure 4-17).

> Date ( )

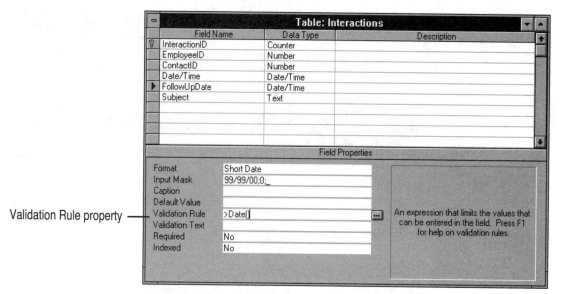

Validation Rule property

Figure 4-17: The Field Properties pane of the Table window with a validation rule added.

Requiring Fields

Not every field in every record of every table is going to store a value at all times. But some fields in some tables should always contain a value. A primary key field, for example, must always contain a value. Access enables you to specify, in the table design, which fields absolutely require data.

To indicate that a field is required, enter the value Yes in the Required property in the Field Properties pane of the Table window, or click the drop-down button at the end of the text box and select the Yes option. For example, in the Interactions table, you probably want to require an entry in the Date/Time field.

Sometimes you may want the user to be forced to consciously decide whether information is available for a particular field. But if no information is available, you want the user to be able to leave the field blank. Access 2.0 provides for this situation with *zero-length strings*—an intentionally blank field.

To use this feature, available only for Text fields, set both the Required property and the AllowZeroLength property to Yes. During data entry, Access will not permit the user to leave the field blank by accident. But if the user doesn't have any information to enter into the field, the user can type two quotation marks, back to back (" "), to indicate a *zero-length string.* Later, when the missing information is available, the user can come back and enter the data into the field.

For example, in the Interactions table, set to Yes both the Required property and the AllowZeroLength property for the Subject field.

Indexing Fields

When you assign the primary key field in a table, Access automatically builds an *index* for that field. An index, in Access, is analogous to the index of a book. An index keeps track of the location of the values in the indexed field. Like the index of a book, Access sorts each index in order by the values stored in the indexed field. Indeed, when you display a table in Datasheet view, Access uses the primary key field's index to display the records in order by the primary key field.

You can cause Access to build an index for any field or a combination of fields in a table. Indexes make searching indexed fields and sorting on indexed fields much faster. For example, you may frequently want to sort the information stored in the Interactions table by the values in either the EmployeeID field or the ContactID field. You'll certainly want to be able to search quickly for the interactions with a particular contact. Both EmployeeID and ContactID are, therefore, good candidates for indexes.

 In general, it's a good idea to index all foreign key fields in a table. The performance of queries, forms and reports based on multiple tables will benefit from indexes on the fields that link the related tables to the primary table.

You cause Access to index a field by changing the Indexed property in the Field Properties pane of the Table window. Follow these steps:

1. If you haven't already done so, type a name in the Field Name column and select a data type.

2. While the data type column is selected, click the Indexed text box and then click the drop-down button at the right end of the text box. Access displays a drop-down list of the following options (see Figure 4-18):

Indexed Setting	Results
No	No index.
Yes (Duplicates OK)	Speeds searches and sorts but does not prevent duplicates.
Yes (No Duplicates)	Speeds searches and sorts and prevents duplicates.

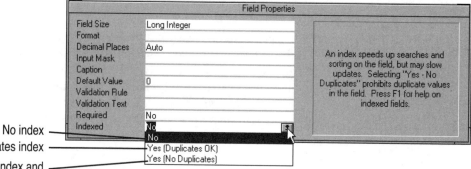

No index
Creates index
Creates index and
prevents duplicates

Figure 4-18: The Indexed property determines whether Access creates an index for the field.

3. Select the Yes (Duplicates OK) option to create an index that does not prevent the entry of duplicates. This setting is appropriate when the values in the indexed field should be permitted to repeat in the table. For example, in the Interactions table, the values in both the EmployeeID field and the ContactID field will repeat in the table. Each sales person (employee) will have many interactions recorded in the table. Similarly, each contact person will likely have multiple records in Interactions. So, for both EmployeeID and ContactID you should choose the Yes (Duplicates OK) setting for the Indexed property.

If you prevent duplicates in a field other than the primary key field (which is automatically indexed), select the Yes (No Duplicates) setting for the Indexed property. The index created by this setting is known as a *unique index*. Access automatically creates a unique index for every primary key field(s).

In addition to the Indexed property, Access enables you to modify and delete indexes, and to assign multi-field indexes using the Indexes dialog box. To use the Indexes dialog box for a table, follow these steps:

1. While a table is displayed in Design view, either click the Indexes button on the toolbar, or choose View, Indexes from the menu bar. Access displays the Indexes dialog box for the current table (see Figure 4-19).

Field indexed —

Index name —

Sort order —

Index properties —

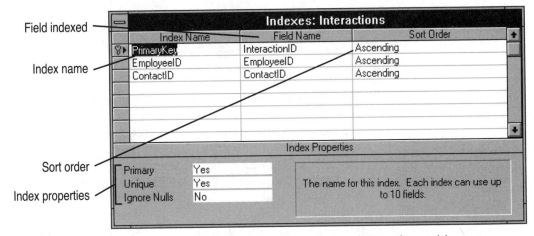

Figure 4-19: The Indexes dialog box for the Interactions table.

2. The Indexes dialog box contains three columns: Index Name, Field Name and Sort Order. The Index Name column contains a name for each index that Access maintains for the current table. The Field Name lists the fields indexed by the named index. The Sort Order column indicates whether Access maintains the index in ascending order or in descending order.

   Access automatically assigns index names when it indexes the primary key field(s) and when you index a field using the Indexed property. The index for the primary key gets the name PrimaryKey, and indexes generated by the Indexed property have the same name as the field they index. To create another index, first type a name in the Index Name column.

3. After you type an index name in the Index Name column, move the cursor to the Field Name column and click the drop-down button at the end of the text box. Access displays a list of all the fields in the table. Select the field you want to index.

4. Next, move the cursor to the Sort Order column and click the drop-down button at the end of the text box. Choose Ascending from the drop-down list (the default) to cause the index to be stored in ascending (A to Z, or 0 to 9) order. Choose Descending from the drop-down list to cause the index to be stored in descending order. The order you choose depends on whether you are more likely to need to search or sort the indexed field in ascending or descending order.

5. The lower pane of the Indexes dialog box, the Index Properties pane, enables you to set each of the following three properties to a value of Yes or No (all have a default value of No):

Property	Results When Yes
Primary	Adds the field to the primary key.
Unique	Prevents duplicates in the named field.
Ignore Nulls	Doesn't include null values in the index.

6. Sometimes you will be routinely searching tables based on the values in two or more fields concurrently. In the Interactions table, for example, you may frequently need to retrieve records based on the values in both the EmployeeID field and the ContactID field. Access, therefore, enables you to assign an index to multiple fields together, referred to as a *multi-field index*.

To assign a multi-field index, complete steps 1–5 for the first field, and then move the cursor to the Field Name column of the next row in the Indexes grid, leaving the Index Name column blank. Using the procedures described in steps 3 and 4, select the name of the second field you want to index, and specify a sort order. Repeat for each additional field you want to add.

For example, create an index named EmployeeContactIDs for the Interactions table. Index on both the EmployeeID field and the ContactID field, both in ascending order (see Figure 4-20).

Index name   Fields indexed

Indexes: Interactions		
Index Name	Field Name	Sort Order
PrimaryKey	InteractionID	Ascending
EmployeeID	EmployeeID	Ascending
ContactID	ContactID	Ascending
EmployeeContactIDs	EmployeeID	Ascending
	ContactID	Ascending

Index Properties
Records can be sorted in ascending or descending order.

Figure 4-20: The Indexes dialog box for the Interactions table showing the EmployeeContactIDs multi-field index.

7. If you want to delete an index, click the field selector in the row you want to delete and press the Delete button.

8. After you are finished adding, modifying or deleting indexes in the Indexes dialog box, double-click the dialog box's Control-menu box to return to the Table window.

9. Click the Save button in the toolbar or choose File, Save from the menu bar to save all changes you have made to the table design. If this is the first time you are saving a new table design, Access displays the Save As dialog box. Type a name for the table and choose the OK button to save the design under the new table name.

10. Double-click the Table window's Control-menu box to close Design view and return to the Database window.

DEFINING ADDITIONAL RELATIONSHIPS

In Chapter 3, you specified the relationships between the various tables in the Contacts database. Now that you have added the Interactions table to the database, you need to specify how the new table is related to the tables already in the database. Follow these steps:

1. With the Contacts database open, and the Database window displayed, either click the Relationships button in the toolbar, or choose Edit, Relationships to display the Relationships dialog box.

Add Table

2. Either click the Add Table button in the toolbar, or choose Relationships, Add Table from the menu bar. Access displays the Add Table dialog box.

3. Either double-click Interactions in the Add Table dialog box, or select Interations and choose the Add button. Access adds the Interactions fields list to the Relationships dialog box.

4. Create a one-to-many relationship between Contacts and Interactions using the ContactID field in each table as the linking field.

5. Create a one-to-many relationship between Employess and Interactions using the EmployeeID field in each table as the linking field. The completed Relationships dialog box should look similar to Figure 4-21.

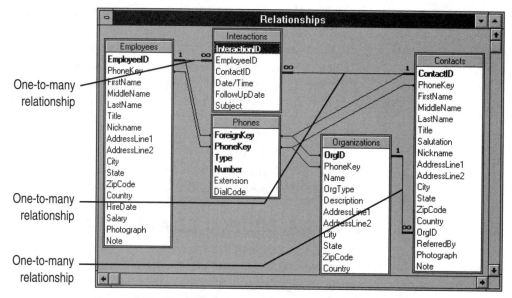

Figure 4-21: The Relationships dialog box after adding the Interactions table and defining relationships to Contacts and Employees.

6. Click the Save button in the toolbar to save the changes, and double-click the Control-menu box to close the dialog box.

MOVING ON

In this chapter you have learned how to create and modify tables in Design view. You have seen how to create fields, assign data type and set field properties. Now that you are comfortable with the Table window's Design view, you should begin to concentrate on the particulars of adding data to and working with data in your Access tables. Turn now to Chapter 5 to learn how to add data to a table in Datasheet view and use a form. In Chapter 5, you'll also learn how to import and export data, sort and filter records, and how to easily print data from an Access table.

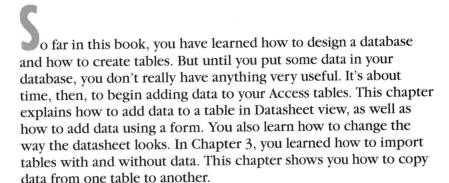

5 WORKING WITH DATA

So far in this book, you have learned how to design a database and how to create tables. But until you put some data in your database, you don't really have anything very useful. It's about time, then, to begin adding data to your Access tables. This chapter explains how to add data to a table in Datasheet view, as well as how to add data using a form. You also learn how to change the way the datasheet looks. In Chapter 3, you learned how to import tables with and without data. This chapter shows you how to copy data from one table to another.

After you know how to add data to your database, you still need to know how to work with the data. Sections in this chapter teach you how to find records and how to sort records in the database using the quick sort method. You also learn how to use filters to limit the records Access displays and prints. Finally, this chapter teaches you how to print records quickly from the database without loading a report.

OPENING & CLOSING A TABLE IN DATASHEET VIEW

In Chapters 3 and 4, you have seen the Design view of Access' Table window. But you can't add data to a table while it is displayed in Design view. There are two views, however, in which you can enter data: Datasheet view and Form view. The first part of Chapter 3 and Chapter 4 discusses how to enter data using Datasheet view. Refer to "Adding Data Using a Form" later in this chapter for a discussion of entering data in Form view (refer also to Chapters 8 and 9 for a discussion of how to create powerful Access forms).

Accountants and bookkeepers traditionally keep track of financial data in a grid known as a *spreadsheet*. If you have ever kept a mailing list, or prepared a budget, you probably used a similar format. Most people are very comfortable with this arrangement. As a result, many PC users employ spreadsheet programs such as Lotus 1-2-3 or Microsoft Excel to collect data. Spreadsheet programs, however, are poor substitutes for full-featured database management programs such as Access.

An Access datasheet (a table displayed in Datasheet view) is similar in appearance to a spreadsheet. Each field in the table is displayed in its own column; and each record in the table is a separate row in the grid. In fact, when you think of the term *table*, you probably envision just such a *tabular* format.

When you want to add data to a table in Datasheet view, you can open the Table window in Datasheet view. To open a table in Datasheet view, follow these steps:

1. If you haven't already done so, open the database that contains the table to which you want to add data. Access displays the Database window.

2. If it is not already selected, choose the Table object button in the Database window. Access lists all available tables in the Tables list box. Figure 5-1 shows the Database window for the Contacts database.

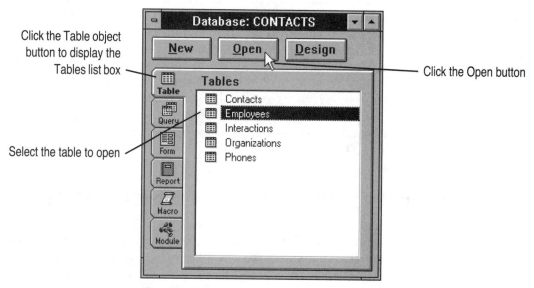

Click the Table object button to display the Tables list box

Click the Open button

Select the table to open

Figure 5-1: The list of tables in the Database window.

3. Either double-click the name of the table you want to open, or select the table name and choose the Open button in the Database window. Access displays the Table window in Datasheet view. For example, to open the Employees table you created in Chapter 3, select Employees in the Database window and choose the Open button. Figure 5-2 shows the Employees table in Datasheet view.

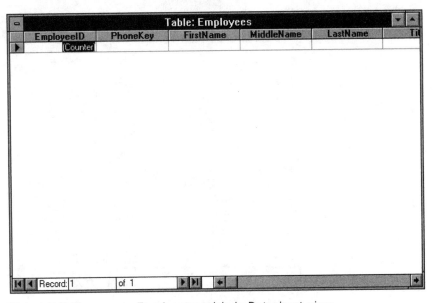

Figure 5-2: The empty Employees table in Datasheet view.

After you have finished working with a datasheet, double-click the Control-menu box to close the Table window.

Navigating the Datasheet

Before you add records to a table, the datasheet includes one empty row, as shown in Figure 5-2. Figure 5-3 shows the Organizations table, which you imported from the Ventana database, in Datasheet view. It contains 26 records. Even when the table contains data, the datasheet always contains one empty row at the bottom, indicated by an asterisk in the *record selector column*, the gray column at the left edge of the datasheet.

Record selector column

Field selector row

Current record pointer

Field names

Scroll bar

Navigation buttons

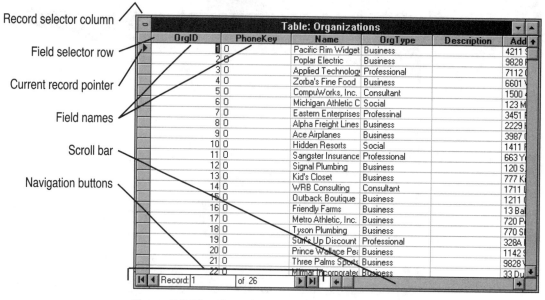

OrgID	PhoneKey	Name	OrgType	Description	Add
1	0	Pacific Rim Widget	Business		4211
2	8	Poplar Electric	Business		9828
3	0	Applied Technolog	Professional		7112
4	0	Zorba's Fine Food	Business		6601
5	0	CompuWorks, Inc.	Consultant		1500
6	0	Michigan Athletic C	Social		123 M
7	0	Eastern Enterprises	Professinal		3451
8	0	Alpha Freight Lines	Business		2229
9	0	Ace Airplanes	Business		3987
10	0	Hidden Resorts	Social		1411
11	0	Sangster Insurance	Professional		663 Y
12	0	Signal Plumbing	Business		120 S
13	0	Kid's Closet	Business		777 Ki
14	0	WRB Consulting	Consultant		1711
15	0	Outback Boutique	Business		1211
16	0	Friendly Farms	Business		13 Ba
17	0	Metro Athletic, Inc.	Business		720 P
18	0	Tyson Plumbing	Business		770 S
19	0	Surf's Up Discount	Professional		328A
20	0	Prince Wallace Pe	Business		1142
21	0	Three Palms Sport	Business		9828
22	0	Miramar Incorporated	Business		33 Du

Record: 1   of 26

Figure 5-3: The Organizations table in Datasheet view.

Most of the datasheet consists of a grid of rows and columns. Each field in the table is assigned a column. By default, the field name appears as a heading at the top of this column. Each record in the table occupies one row in the grid.

Unlike some older-style databases, Access does not maintain a record number field. As you have learned already, however, you should always include a primary key field in each table. In many cases the primary key field may be a *counter field*. The OrgID field, the first column in the table shown in Figure 5-3, is a counter field–not a record number field.

Access enables you to work in one record at a time. The record you are working in is known as the *current record*. The program places a triangular pointer in the record selector column to indicate which record is the current record.

From time to time, other symbols appear in the record selector. For example, a pencil icon appears in the record selector column when you change a value in the current record, but haven't yet saved the change. A locked icon (a circle with a slash through it) appears in the record selector column when another user, on a local area network, locks a record.

Note to Developers

Microsoft Access does not use true Record Locking. They actually use a scheme referred to as *Page Locking*. Your data is actually locked in 2k pages. This has a different effect than true record locking in that when you edit a record with Lock Edited Record enabled, you are actually locking the group of records surrounding the edited record. The number of records affected depends on the size of the records. This will also affect you if you are editing a record at the end of the record set and somebody tries to add a new record at the same time.

You can work in only one field at a time. A blinking cursor indicates the current field. You can move the cursor from field to field and record to record using the cursor-movement keys. Some cursor-movement keys include:

Key	Move To
Enter	One field to the right
Tab	One field to the right
Shift-Tab	One field to the left
Right Arrow	One field to the right
Left Arrow	One field to the left
Up Arrow	Preceding row
Down Arrow	Next row
PgUp	Preceding window-full
PgDn	Next window-full
Home	Left-most field in the current row
End	Right-most field in the current row
Ctrl-Home	Left-most field in the first row
Ctrl-End	Right-most field in the last row

You can also move through the table using the mouse. When all the rows and columns fit on one screen, click the field you want to work with. More often than not, however, your table will not fit in one screen. When this occurs, Access adds a vertical scroll bar on the right side of the Table window. You can then use the mouse and the scroll bar to scroll up and down through the table. Similarly, if all the fields in the table won't fit into the Table window, Access adds a horizontal scroll bar at the bottom of the screen. Use the mouse and the horizontal scroll bar to scroll left and right in the table.

In the lower-left corner of the datasheet window are four *navigation buttons* that resemble the buttons on a VCR. These buttons enable you to move around the table quickly (see Figure 5-4).

Move to the first record   Move to the last record

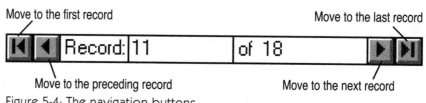

Move to the preceding record   Move to the next record

Figure 5-4: The navigation buttons.

Between the navigation buttons, a text box (to the right of the word Record) indicates the number of the current record (see Figure 5-4). Although this number is not the record number per se, since Access does not maintain a constant record number value for each record in the table, this text box is known as the *record number box*. The number in the record number box denotes the position of the current record in relation to all the records included in the current view of the table. Nevertheless, you can use the "record number" listed in this text box to move directly to a particular record in the Table window:

1. Either double-click the record number box or press F5.
2. Type the "record number" of the record to which you want to move and press Enter.

Keep in mind, however, that the record number of any particular record in the table may change each time you display a table.

Understanding the Datasheet View

Whenever you are working in Datasheet view, you should be aware that Access provides several ways to limit how much data is included in the active window. In database lingo, it is common to use the term *view* to refer to a subset of data from a table or collection of tables. Using the term *view* in this special sense, the datasheet displays a view of a table or collection of tables that may or may not include all the data stored on disk. For example, when you use the New button in Datasheet view to add data to a table, the number of records indicated in the record number box is the same as the number of records stored on disk. But if you use the Data Entry command to display a blank record, the record number box indicates only one record, even if there are actually hundreds or thousands of records already in the table. Similarly, you can use filters (covered later in this chapter), and queries (covered in Chapters 7 and 8), to define additional views of the same underlying data. Regardless of the view of the data Access currently is displaying in the datasheet, any changes, additions or subtractions you make to the information onscreen is reflected in the table or tables stored on disk.

. . . .

ADDING DATA TO A TABLE IN DATASHEET VIEW

The primary purpose of most database management systems is to store information in such a way that you can easily retrieve and display selected portions of the information on demand. The Access Datasheet view is one of several mechanisms though which you can enter information into your database.

When you are adding data using Datasheet view, Access offers you a choice to either display existing records while you add new records or hide existing data. Whether you hide or display existing data depends on several sometimes competing factors. The following factors suggest hiding existing records:

○ You are concerned about accidentally changing existing data.

○ Each record is completely different from the preceding records.

○ The table is very large and/or is stored on a local area network so that moving to the blank record at the end of the table is relatively slow.

The following factors suggest displaying existing data:

○ You are entering data that is similar to or related to existing records so that viewing existing records would speed data entry or improve its accuracy.

○ Data in the database is updated frequently by many users on a network and you want to be able to view the changes immediately.

To add data to a table with existing records displayed in Datasheet view, follow these steps:

1. Open the table in Datasheet view. Access displays as many existing records from the table as will fit in the Table window.

2. Choose the New button in the toolbar or choose Records, Go To, New from the menu bar. Access moves directly to the new record, the one with the asterisk in the record selector column. You are ready to start adding data to the empty row.

To add data to the current table with existing records hidden, follow these steps:

1. Open the table in Datasheet view.

2. Choose Records, Data Entry from the menu bar. Access hides all existing records and displays only an empty row. You are ready to start adding data to the empty row (see Figure 5-5).

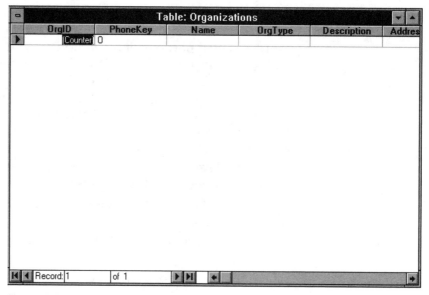

Figure 5-5: The Organizations table after executing the Data Entry command.

Entering Data in Text, Memo, Number, Currency, Date & Yes/No Fields

To enter data in text, memo, number, currency, date or Yes/No fields, follow these steps:

1. When you move to a new record using either the New button or the Data Entry command, Access places the cursor in the first (left-most) field in the new record. To enter data into most fields, all you have to do is type. You cannot type an entry in counter fields, however. Access automatically assigns a value to a counter field when you save the new record. Refer to the following table for examples of valid and invalid entries in text, memo, number, currency, date and Yes/No fields (subject to any validation rules you have defined in the table's design—see "Validating Input" in Chapter 4):

Data Type	Valid Entries	Invalid Entries
Text	Any text or numbers !@#$%^&*()	None
Memo	Any text or numbers !@#$%^&*()	None
Number	12345 12.345 −123.45 1,234.5	Any text 1/2 2+3
Date/Time	8/26/72 August 26, 1972 5:25 pm 5:25:03 26 Aug 72	26/8/72 August 26 '72 5 5:25:61 26.8.72
Currency	$1,234.567 1234.567 (1234) −1234	Any text 1/2 2+3
Yes/No	Yes No True False On Off 1 0	Y N T F

2. When you finish typing in a field, press Enter or Tab to move to the next field in the record. When you press Enter or Tab after the last field in the record, Access adds another blank record and moves the cursor to its first field.

For example, enter the following information in the Employees table. Remember to skip the EmployeeID and PhoneKey fields. EmployeeID is a counter field and Access assigns a default value of "E" to the PhoneKey field. This default value should not be changed. For now, leave the Photograph field and Note field blank:

Name:	Samuel S. Pate
Title:	Account Executive
Nickname:	Sam
AddressLine1:	411 S. Green St.
AddressLine2:	Suite A
	Alexandria, MI 49313
Country:	USA
HireDate:	9/30/91
Salary:	$45,900

When you are finished adding this data, but before you move to the next record, your Employees table should resemble Figure 5-6. The pencil-shaped symbol in the record selector column indicates that Access hasn't yet saved the data you have entered in the record.

Indicates changes
not yet saved

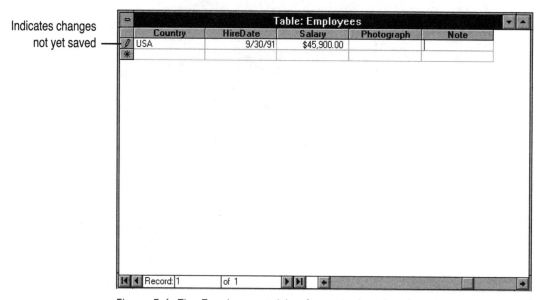

Figure 5-6: The Employees table after entering data in one record.

Any time you make a long entry in a field, you may want to expand the size of the data-entry area. This is particularly true with memo files, which can be virtually unlimited in length. To expand a field's data-entry area, do the following:

1. Either press Shift+F2, or right-click the field and choose Zoom from the pop-up menu. Access displays the Zoom dialog box, as shown in Figure 5-7.

2. Make the desired entry and choose the OK button to return to the datasheet.

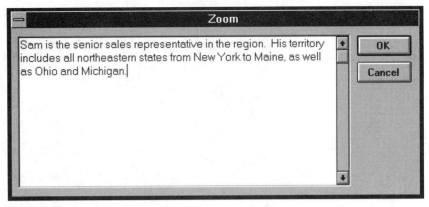

Figure 5-7: The Zoom dialog box.

When you are working in the Zoom dialog box, you can type multiple lines of information. If you just type a continuous paragraph, Access automatically word-wraps text from one line to the next. If you want to cause Access to start a new line in the data-entry area of the dialog box, position the cursor just to the left of the character you want to begin the next line with and press Ctrl+Enter. Access moves all the text to the right of the cursor to the next line.

Adding OLE Objects

As you learned in Chapter 4, an OLE object is any file that was created by a Windows program that complies with the Object Linking and Embedding standard. Access enables you to store (embed) OLE objects in, or to link OLE objects to, OLE object fields in Access tables. Access even enables you to display and edit the OLE objects. The Photograph fields in our Employees and Contacts tables are examples of OLE object fields.

Adding OLE objects in an Access table is a bit different from adding other types of data. To embed or link an OLE object in an OLE object field in an Access table, follow these steps:

1. Move the cursor to the OLE object field. For example, in Samuel Pate's record in the Employees table, move the cursor to the Photograph field.

2. Either right-click the field and choose Insert Object from the pop-up menu, or choose Edit, Insert Object from the menu bar to display the Insert Object dialog box (see Figure 5-8).

List of object types

Creates a new object

Inserts an existing file

Displays object
as an icon

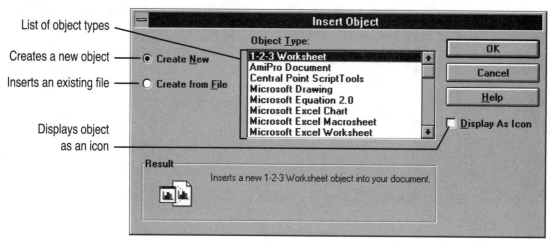

Figure 5-8: The Insert Object dialog box.

3. If you want to create a new object, select the type of object that you want to insert from the Object Type list box. The objects listed in the Object Type list box vary from computer to computer, depending on which OLE server applications are installed on the machine. For example, to create a picture using the Paintbrush program that comes with every copy of Microsoft Windows, choose Paintbrush Picture from the Object Type list box (you may have to scroll the box). **Note:** if you are going to embed or link an existing file, you don't need to make a selection from the Object Type list box.

4. To create a new object, choose the Create New option button (the default). When you choose the OK button, Access opens the Windows application you selected in the Object Type list box so you can create a new object.

To use an existing file, choose the Create from File. We're going to insert an existing file in the Employees table's Photograph field, so choose the Create from File option button.

5. When you choose the Create from File option button, Access changes the Object Type list box to a text box and adds the Browse button and Link check box (see Figure 5-9). Either type the name of the object file in the File text box, or choose the Browse button and select the object file using the Browse dialog box. In the Photograph field example, choose Browse and select the file named **sam.bmp** from the Browse dialog box. Choose OK in the Browse dialog box to return to the Insert Object dialog box.

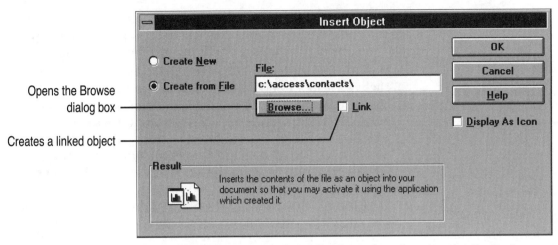

Opens the Browse dialog box ——

Creates a linked object ——

Figure 5-9: The Insert Object dialog box after choosing the Create from File option button.

6. If you want Access to store a copy of the OLE object in the table, leave the Link check box empty. But if you want to link the existing file to the table so subsequent changes to the original file will automatically be reflected in the Access table, mark the Link check box.

7. The last decision to make is whether you want Access to display the object as an icon. This option is irrelevant to the datasheet, but is important when you display table data using an Access form. (**Note:** this option is available only for objects created by applications that comply with the OLE 2.0 specification.) When the OLE object is large or complex, performance may suffer if Access has to display the object in a form. Moving around a record, and moving between records, may be slowed significantly if Access has to continually redisplay a complex object. By choosing to have Access display an OLE object as an icon, performance is improved, and the object is still only a mouse click away. In this form, you'll be able to display the object by double-clicking the icon.

8. After selecting an object type and the desired options in the Insert Object dialog box, choose the OK button. Access embeds or links the OLE object in or to the table. In the datasheet, Access displays the object type in the field. For example, Access displays the words Paintbrush Picture in the Photograph field in the Employees table.

After you have added an OLE object to a table, Access doesn't make the object visible in the datasheet itself, but you can easily display the object for viewing or editing by following these steps:

1. Move the cursor to the OLE object field, and either double-click the field, or choose the Edit from the menu bar and then choose the object type from the Edit menu (the menu command differs depending on which type of object you have added to the table). For example, to view Sam's picture, double-click the Photograph field in the first row of the Employees table, or select the field and choose Edit, Paint-brush Picture Object,
EDIT from the menu bar. Access opens the Paintbrush application and displays the picture (see Figure 5-10).

Figure 5-10: The Paintbrush application with picture displayed, ready for editing.

2. View and/or edit the object as desired. When you are ready to return to the datasheet, double-click the application window's Control-menu box. If you have changed an embedded object in any way, Access displays a message that asks whether you want to update the open embedded object. If you have changed a linked object, Access displays a message asking if you want to save the changes. In either case, choose the Yes button to save the changes, or choose the No button to abandon the changes. Access returns to the datasheet.

Access also offers the option of converting certain types of OLE objects to pictures. When you convert an object to a picture, you can no longer open the OLE server application from the OLE object field that contains the picture, and can no longer edit the object. To convert a Paintbrush Picture object to a picture, follow these steps:

1. Move the cursor to the OLE object field.

2. Either right-click the field and select Paintbrush Picture Object, Change to Picture from the pop-up menu, or choose Edit, Paintbrush Picture Object, Change to Picture from the menu bar.

3. Access displays a message indicating that you can't undo this command and you won't be able to edit the object after executing the command. Choose the Yes button to continue or the No button to abort the command. If you choose the Yes button, Access changes the object type in the OLE object field to Picture.

After you have converted OLE objects to pictures, you cannot display the pictures from the datasheet. You can, however, display pictures in forms and reports. Refer to Chapters 9 through 11 for a full discussion of forms and reports.

Saving Records

As you enter data in a record, the data does not go directly into the table on disk. As you have learned, a pencil-shaped symbol in the record selector column indicates that you have made changes to the record that haven't yet been saved. To save the entries in the record, either move the cursor to another record and press Shift+Enter, or choose File, Save Record from the menu bar.

For example, in the Employee table, move the cursor to the next record in the table. Access saves the first record to disk. Add the following information as the second, third and fourth records in the table. After entering the data in each record, move to the next record to save the data.

Name:	Charlie Y. Eager
Title:	Account Executive
Nickname:	
AddressLine1:	411 S. Green St.
AddressLine2:	Suite A
	Alexandria, MI 49313
Country:	USA
HireDate:	3/9/92
Salary:	$33,750
Photograph:	(embed the file CHARLIE.PCX)
Name:	Timothy Ronald Alan
Title:	Account Executive
Nickname:	Tim
AddressLine1:	411 S. Green St.
AddressLine2:	Suite A
	Alexandria, MI 49313
Country:	USA
HireDate:	11/15/93
Salary:	$28,400
Photograph:	(embed the file TIM.BMP)
Name:	Steven A. Bunch
Title:	Account Executive
Nickname:	Steve
AddressLine1:	5506 E. 25th Street
AddressLine2:	Suite 201
	Agana 55210
Country:	Guam
HireDate:	1/22/91
Salary:	$38,000
Photograph:	(embed the file STEVE.PCX)

Editing Records

So far we have looked primarily at entering data in new records.
You may often also need to modify data that is already stored in the
database. When you open an existing table, Access highlights the
first field in the first record in the table. If you start typing, the
program erases the original contents of the field and replaces its
contents with your typing.

If you want to change the contents of a field in the table, without completely replacing it, follow these steps:

1. Highlight the field you want to edit using either the cursor-
   movement keys or the mouse.

2. Either click the mouse within the field, or press F2 to switch
   to editing mode.

3. Use the arrow key, Home or End keys to move around within the field. Use any other keyboard characters as well as the space bar, Ins and Del keys to make the needed changes.

4. When you move to another record, Access saves the changes.

Access also provides the following special editing shortcuts for use while editing a field:

Shortcut	Purpose
Ctrl+Enter	Starts a new line.
Ctr+"	Replaces the current field value with the value found in the same field in the preceding record.
Ctrl+Alt+Space bar	Replaces the current field value with the default value.
Shift+F2	Opens the Zoom box.
Shift+Enter	Saves changes to current record.
F9	Refreshes the records that are currently displayed.

Deleting Records

Just as you certainly will have to make changes to the data in existing tables, so too will you occasionally have to delete records from a table in the database. To delete a record in the database, follow these steps:

1. Click the record selector column to the left of the record you want to delete. Access highlights the entire record.

2. Press the Delete key or choose Edit, Delete.

3. Access displays a dialog box asking you to save or cancel your changes. Choose the OK button to confirm the deletion, or choose Cancel to restore the deleted record. Be careful! Access cannot undo a record deletion after you choose OK.

UNDOING MISTAKES

Unless you're perfect, you'll occasionally make a mistake while entering information into an Access table. Sometimes the mistake can be as simple as accidentally pressing the space bar. Fortunately, Access helps you undo some mistakes:

○ To undo all your most recent typing in the current field, either click the Undo button in the toolbar, or choose Edit, Undo Typing from the menu bar. Access reverts to the contents of the current field before you started typing. To reinstate the typing that the Undo Typing command just removed, either click the Undo button in the toolbar again, or choose Edit, Redo Typing from the menu bar. After you move the cursor to another field in the record, or to another record in the table, and after you save the current record, the Undo Typing command (or Undo button) is no longer available to undo the changes in previous fields. The command is effective only for changes in the current field and before the changes are saved.

○ To undo all changes to the current field, either press Esc, click the Undo Current Field/Record button in the toolbar, or choose Edit, Undo Current Field from the menu bar. Access reverts to the field's value when the cursor entered the field. After you move the cursor to another field in the record or to another record in the table, or save the current record, the Undo Current Field command is no longer available to undo the changes in previous fields. Like the Undo Typing command, the Undo Current Field command is effective only for changes in the current field before these changes are saved.

○ Even after you have moved the cursor to another field in the record, you can still undo changes, but you have to undo *all* changes to the current record. To undo all the changes you've made to the current record, since the record was last saved, either click the Undo Current Field/Record button or choose Edit, Undo Current Record from the menu bar. Access returns the value stored in each field to its value when you started editing the current record.

○ Even after you save a record's changes by moving to another field, or by executing the Save Record command on the File menu, you still have one more chance to undo the changes. Before you begin typing again, you can undo the last record saved. Either click the Undo button in the toolbar, press Ctrl+Z or choose Edit, Undo Saved Record from the menu bar. Access restores the record that was last saved to its contents before you made any changes to that record. After you begin typing in another record, or even in the same record, you can no longer use the Undo Saved Record command to restore the original contents of the record.

CHANGING THE WAY THE DATASHEET LOOKS

When you display a table for the first time in Datasheet view, Access displays all fields and records in columns and rows. Every field gets its own column, and all columns are the same size. The order of the fields, from left to right, corresponds to the order of the fields in Design view. Obviously, however, the data contained in the various fields of a table are not all the same size. Some fields may be of little interest onscreen. At times you may prefer to have certain fields displayed side by side that aren't listed together in

Design view. Fortunately, Access makes it easy to change the way the datasheet looks.

Access allows you to change the look of the datasheet in several respects. You can change the order of the columns, change column width, change row height, hide columns, freeze columns and change the font used to display text in the datasheet. The following sections explain each of these techniques.

Rearranging Columns

When you are working with an Access table, you may occasionally want to display two columns of data side by side. By default, Access displays columns in the same order as the fields are listed in the table design in Design view. For example, in the Organizations table's datasheet, two columns separate the Name column from the AddressLine1 and AddressLine2 columns. It would be convenient, at times, to display these columns side by side.

It is easy to rearrange the column order. If you've ever worked with any Windows-based program, you probably already know how to rearrange columns in Access. All you have to do is drag the columns where you want them to be.

Follow these steps:

1. Move the mouse to the field selector row (the gray-colored row that contains the field names) in the column you want to move. Notice that the mouse pointer becomes a downward-pointing arrow.

2. Click the field name to select the column. Access highlights the selected column. To select a group of side-by-side columns, hold the Shift key while you click each field name, or click the first field name and drag the pointer to the last field name in the group (see Figure 5-11). Now release the mouse button. To unselect columns, click a field outside the selected columns.

The selected columns ————

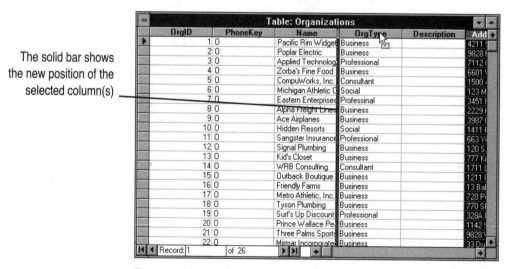

Figure 5-11: The Organizations datasheet with 5 columns selected.

3. Click and drag the highlighted column to its new position. Notice that as you drag the mouse pointer, the column itself doesn't move onscreen. Instead, a solid vertical bar moves from one column boundary to another, in the direction you are dragging the mouse (see Figure 5-12). When the solid bar is at the desired position, release the mouse button. Access moves the entire column to that position. Click outside the highlighted columns to turn off the highlight.

The solid bar shows the new position of the selected column(s) ————

Figure 5-12: Moving columns in the Organizations datasheet.

For example, Figure 5-13 shows the Organizations table after moving the AddressLine1, AddressLine2, City, State and ZipCode fields next to the Name field.

Name	AddressLine1	AddressLine2	City	State	Z
Pacific Rim Widget	4211 S. Green St.	Suite A	Alexandria	MI	49313
Poplar Electric	9828 Rocky Ridge	Suite 400	Centreville	MI	49020
Applied Technolog	7112 Commerce St		Springfield	MI	49150
Zorba's Fine Food	6601 Wales Rd.	Dept. 33	Vienna	Mi	49180
CompuWorks, Inc.	1500 44th St. SE		Grand Rapids	MI	49508
Michigan Athletic C	123 Main Street		Hometown	MI	49000
Eastern Enterprises	3451 Fox Lane		Arlington	MI	49210
Alpha Freight Lines	2229 Hillcrest Dr.	Suite 102	Arlington	MI	49210
Ace Airplanes	3987 Glendale Dr.		Springfield	VA	22152
Hidden Resorts	1411 Reservation D		Springfield	VA	22152
Sangster Insurance	663 Yuppie Lane	Mail Stop #800	McLean	VA	22101
Signal Plumbing	120 S. 2nd	Suite B	Springfield	VA	22152
Kid's Closet	777 Kittyhawk Dr.		Gaithersburg	MD	20877
WRB Consulting	1711 Lakeview Dr.		Chapel Hill	NC	27514
Outback Boutique	1211 Commerce St		Springfield	VA	22150
Friendly Farms	13 Baker St.	Suite 1700	Alexandria	VA	22213
Metro Athletic, Inc.	720 Port Royal	Building 33, Suite 4	Fairfax	VA	22030
Tyson Plumbing	770 Shaw Rd.	Suite 701	Alexandria	MI	49313
Surf's Up Discount	328A Front St.	Suite 100	Maui	HI	61010
Prince Wallace Pea	1142 S. Orange Blv		Sinajana		55523
Three Palms Sports	9828 White Sands		Toto		55523
Mirmar Incorporated	33 Duke St		Honolulu	HI	61016

Table: Organizations

Record: 1   of 26

Figure 5-13: The Organizations datasheet after moving fields.

Adjusting Column Width & Row Height

Regardless of actual field size, Access, by default, displays all columns of a table with the same width in Datasheet view. Some columns don't need to be that wide to display their data. Other columns truncate data because they are not wide enough. For example, in the Organizations table, the OrgID field is much wider than necessary; while, the Name, AddressLine1, and AddressLine2 are too narrow.

Because of the occasional need to change column width, Access enables you to easily adjust up or down the width of columns in Datasheet view.

To change the width of a datasheet column, follow these steps:

1. Move the mouse pointer to either the left or right side of the field selector for the column you want to make wider or narrower. The mouse pointer changes in shape to a double vertical line flanked by two arrow heads (see Figure 5-14).

Drag to adjust column width

OrgID	PhoneKey	Name	AddressLine1	AddressLine2	
1	0	Pacific Rim Widget	4211 S. Green St.	Suite A	Alexar
2	0	Poplar Electric	9828 Rocky Ridge	Suite 400	Centre
3	0	Applied Technolog	7112 Commerce St		Spring
4	0	Zorba's Fine Food	6601 Wales Rd.	Dept. 33	Vienna
5	0	CompuWorks, Inc.	1500 44th St. SE		Grand
6	0	Michigan Athletic C	123 Main Street		Homel
7	0	Eastern Enterprises	3451 Fox Lane		Arlingt
8	0	Alpha Freight Lines	2229 Hillcrest Dr.	Suite 102	Arlingt
9	0	Ace Airplanes	3987 Glendale Dr.		Spring
10	0	Hidden Resorts	1411 Reservation [		Spring
11	0	Sangster Insurance	663 Yuppie Lane	Mail Stop #800	McLea
12	0	Signal Plumbing	120 S. 2nd	Suite B	Spring
13	0	Kid's Closet	777 Kittyhawk Dr.		Gaithe
14	0	WRB Consulting	1711 Lakeview Dr.		Chape
15	0	Outback Boutique	1211 Commerce St		Spring
16	0	Friendly Farms	13 Baker St.	Suite 1700	Alexar
17	0	Metro Athletic, Inc.	720 Port Royal	Building 33, Suite 4	Fairfax
18	0	Tyson Plumbing	770 Shaw Rd.	Suite 701	Alexar
19	0	Surf's Up Discount	328A Front St.	Suite 100	Maui
20	0	Prince Wallace Pe:	1142 S. Orange Bl\		Sinaja
21	0	Three Palms Sports	9828 White Sands		Toto
22	0	Mirmar Incorporated	33 Duke St		Honol

Record: 1 of 26

Figure 5-14: Adjusting column width in Datasheet view.

2. Click and drag the border line of the column to the left or right. When the border line is in the desired position, release the mouse button. Figure 5-15 shows the Organizations datasheet after adjusting the column widths of the Name, AddressLine1 and AddressLine2 columns.

You can adjust the width of multiple columns concurrently by first selecting the columns using the field selector and then adjusting the width of one of the selected columns.

To return one or more columns to the default width, select the columns and either right-click the field selector and choose Column Width from the pop-up menu, or choose Format, Column Width from the menu bar. Click the Standard Width check box and choose the OK button.

OrgID	PhoneKey	Name	AddressLine1	AddressLine2	Cit
1	0	Pacific Rim Widgets, Inc.	4211 S. Green St.	Suite A	Alexandria
2	0	Poplar Electric	9828 Rocky Ridge	Suite 400	Centreville
3	0	Applied Technology Center	7112 Commerce St		Springfield
4	0	Zorba's Fine Food	6601 Wales Rd.	Dept. 33	Vienna
5	0	CompuWorks, Inc.	1500 44th St. SE		Grand Rap
6	0	Michigan Athletic Club	123 Main Street		Hometown
7	0	Eastern Enterprises	3451 Fox Lane		Arlington
8	0	Alpha Freight Lines	2229 Hillcrest Dr.	Suite 102	Arlington
9	0	Ace Airplanes	3987 Glendale Dr.		Springfield
10	0	Hidden Resorts	1411 Reservation Dr.		Springfield
11	0	Sangster Insurance	663 Yuppie Lane	Mail Stop #800	McLean
12	0	Signal Plumbing	120 S. 2nd	Suite B	Springfield
13	0	Kid's Closet	777 Kittyhawk Dr.		Gaithersbu
14	0	WRB Consulting	1711 Lakeview Dr.		Chapel Hil
15	0	Outback Boutique	1211 Commerce St.		Springfield
16	0	Friendly Farms	13 Baker St.	Suite 1700	Alexandria
17	0	Metro Athletic, Inc.	720 Port Royal	Building 33, Suite 4	Fairfax
18	0	Tyson Plumbing	770 Shaw Rd.	Suite 701	Alexandria
19	0	Surf's Up Discount	328A Front St.	Suite 100	Maui
20	0	Prince Wallace Pearls, Inc.	1142 S. Orange Blvd.		Sinajana
21	0	Three Palms Sports	9828 White Sands Dr.		Toto
22	0	Mirmar Incorporated	33 Duke St		Honolulu

Record: 1 of 26

Figure 5-15: The Organizations datasheet after adjusting column widths.

It is possible in Access to adjust row height. If you increase row height a sufficient amount, Access word wraps long fields, rather than truncating them at the column boundary. Alternatively, if you decrease row height, you can display more records in the Table window at one time. Any row height change applies to all rows in the datasheet.

To change row height, follow these steps:

1. Move the mouse pointer to one of the lines between record selectors. The mouse pointer's shape becomes a dark horizontal line with opposing arrow heads pointing up and down.

2. Click and drag this row border up or down to make the row height shorter or taller. Release the mouse button when the row border is at the desired position. Access adjusts the height of all rows in the datasheet.

To return all rows to the standard height, either right-click a record selector and choose Row Height from the pop-up menu, or choose Format, Row Height from the menu bar. When Access displays the Row Height dialog box, choose the Standard Height check box and then choose the OK button.

Access also provides a quick way to adjust column width to fit the widest data currently contained in a particular column. Select the column or columns using the field selector row. Then right-click the selected column(s) and choose Column Width from the pop-up menu (or choose Format, Column Width from the menu bar). When Access displays the Column Width dialog box, choose the Best Fit button. Access adjusts the width of each column so that the widest value in each column just fits. You can, if you like, adjust all columns in the datasheet at once.

Hiding & Freezing Columns

Some columns in a datasheet contain data that needs to be stored in the table, but is of little value when viewed onscreen. For instance, the Organizations table's PhoneKey field is necessary to link records in the Phones table, but is of no value when you are simply displaying the Organizations datasheet. It would be beneficial, therefore, to hide this column from view whenever you display the datasheet.

There are two ways to hide columns in Datasheet view:

1. Use the procedure described in the preceding section to give the column zero (0) width—just drag the right side of the column to the left side, or visa versa.

2. Click the field selector of the column you want to hide and then either right-click the highlighted column and choose Hide Columns from the pop-up menu, or choose Format, Hide Columns from the menu bar.

Figure 5-16 shows the Organizations table after hiding the PhoneKey column.

OrgID	Name	AddressLine1	AddressLine2	City	
1	Pacific Rim Widgets, Inc.	4211 S. Green St.	Suite A	Alexandria	MI
2	Poplar Electric	9828 Rocky Ridge	Suite 400	Centreville	MI
3	Applied Technology Center	7112 Commerce St		Springfield	MI
4	Zorba's Fine Food	6601 Wales Rd.	Dept. 33	Vienna	Mi
5	CompuWorks, Inc.	1500 44th St. SE		Grand Rapids	MI
6	Michigan Athletic Club	123 Main Street		Hometown	MI
7	Eastern Enterprises	3451 Fox Lane		Arlington	MI
8	Alpha Freight Lines	2229 Hillcrest Dr.	Suite 102	Arlington	MI
9	Ace Airplanes	3987 Glendale Dr.		Springfield	VA
10	Hidden Resorts	1411 Reservation Dr.		Springfield	VA
11	Sangster Insurance	663 Yuppie Lane	Mail Stop #800	McLean	VA
12	Signal Plumbing	120 S. 2nd	Suite B	Springfield	VA
13	Kid's Closet	777 Kittyhawk Dr.		Gaithersburg	MD
14	WRB Consulting	1711 Lakeview Dr.		Chapel Hill	NC
15	Outback Boutique	1211 Commerce St.		Springfield	VA
16	Friendly Farms	13 Baker St.	Suite 1700	Alexandria	VA
17	Metro Athletic, Inc.	720 Port Royal	Building 33, Suite 4	Fairfax	VA
18	Tyson Plumbing	770 Shaw Rd.	Suite 701	Alexandria	MI
19	Surf's Up Discount	328A Front St.	Suite 100	Maui	HI
20	Prince Wallace Pearls, Inc.	1142 S. Orange Blvd.		Sinajana	
21	Three Palms Sports	9828 White Sands Dr.		Toto	
22	Mirmar Incorporated	33 Duke St.		Honolulu	HI

Record: 1   of 26

Figure 5-16: The Organizations datasheet after hiding the PhoneKey column.

To restore the hidden column to view in the datasheet, follow these steps:

1. Choose Format, Show Columns from the menu bar to display the Show Columns dialog box.

2. The Column list box in the Show Columns dialog box lists all the columns in the datasheet. Columns that have not been hidden show a check mark. Hidden columns are not checked. Scroll the Column list box until you find the name of the hidden column.

3. Either double-click the name of the hidden column or select the name of the hidden column and choose the Show button.

4. Repeat steps 2 and 3 for any other hidden columns you want to show and then choose the Close button in the Show Columns dialog box to return to the datasheet.

You probably have noticed that scrolling horizontally (left or right) in the table causes columns to temporarily disappear from view. Often this is not a problem, but sometimes it is difficult to know which records you are viewing when the columns that identify the records are out of view. In the Organizations datasheet, for example, if the Name column isn't visible, there's no way to determine whose address you are viewing. Access, therefore, enables you to *freeze* columns so that they do not scroll off screen.

To *freeze* a column or columns in a datasheet, follow these steps:

1. Using the field selector row, select the column or columns you want to prevent from scrolling off screen (selecting columns is described in "Rearranging Columns" earlier in this chapter).

2. Either right-click one of the selected columns and choose Freeze Columns from the pop-up menu, or choose Format, Freeze Columns from the menu bar. If the selected columns are not already positioned at the left side of the datasheet, Access moves them there. Now, as you scroll horizontally through the columns of the datasheet, the frozen columns always remain visible, at the left side of the window. A black border line on the right side of the right-most frozen column denotes the boundary of the frozen area (see Figure 5-17).

	OrgID	Name	ZipCode	OrgType	Description	Country
	1	Pacific Rim Widgets, Inc.	49313	Business		USA
	2	Poplar Electric	49020	Business		USA
	3	Applied Technology Center	49150	Professional		USA
	4	Zorba's Fine Food	49180	Business		USA
	5	CompuWorks, Inc.	49508	Consultant		USA
	6	Michigan Athletic Club	49000	Social		USA
	7	Eastern Enterprises	49210	Professinal		USA
	8	Alpha Freight Lines	49210	Business		USA
	9	Ace Airplanes	22152	Business		USA
	10	Hidden Resorts	22152	Social		USA
	11	Sangster Insurance	22101	Professional		USA
	12	Signal Plumbing	22152	Business		USA
	13	Kid's Closet	20877	Business		USA
	14	WRB Consulting	27514	Consultant		USA
	15	Outback Boutique	22150	Business		USA
	16	Friendly Farms	22213	Business		USA
	17	Metro Athletic, Inc.	22030	Business		USA
	18	Tyson Plumbing	49313	Business		USA
	19	Surf's Up Discount	61010	Professional		USA
	20	Prince Wallace Pearls, Inc.	55523	Business		Guam
	21	Three Palms Sports	55523	Business		Guam
	22	Mirmar Incorporated	61016	Business		USA

Table: Organizations

Record: 1 of 26

Boundary of the *frozen* area

Figure 5-17: The Organizations datasheet after freezing the OrgID and Name columns.

To *unfreeze* all columns, choose Format, Unfreeze All Columns from the menu bar. The columns return to normal. If Access had to move the frozen columns to the left side of the datasheet, however, it does not automatically move them back when you unfreeze the columns.

Changing the Font

Finally, if you don't like the standard font Windows uses to display text onscreen (by default, MS Sans Serif), Access enables you to choose from other fonts currently installed in Windows on your computer.

To change the font, follow these steps:

1. Choose Format, Font from the menu bar. Access displays the Font dialog box (see Figure 5-18).

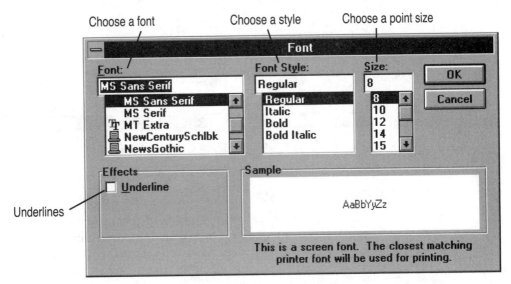

Figure 5-18: The Font dialog box.

2. In the Font dialog box, choose the new font from the Font list box. If you desire, you can also choose a different style (regular, italic, bold or bold and italic; the default style is regular) from the Font Style text box. You can also choose a different point size (default is 8) from the Size list box. If you want all text to be underlined, mark the Underline check box.

3. When you have made all your selections in the Font dialog box, choose the OK button. Access displays all text in the datasheet using the newly selected font, font style and point size. For example, Figure 5-19 shows the Organizations datasheet displayed in the Times New Roman font.

OrgID	Name	AddressLine1	AddressLine2	City	State	Zi
1	Pacific Rim Widgets, Inc.	4211 S. Green St.	Suite A	Alexandria	MI	491
2	Poplar Electric	9828 Rocky Ridge	Suite 400	Centreville	MI	490
3	Applied Technology Center	7112 Commerce St		Springfield	MI	49:
4	Zorba's Fine Food	6601 Wales Rd.	Dept. 33	Vienna	Mi	491
5	CompuWorks, Inc.	1500 44th St. SE		Grand Rapids	MI	49:
6	Michigan Athletic Club	123 Main Street		Hometown	MI	490
7	Eastern Enterprises	3451 Fox Lane		Arlington	MI	491
8	Alpha Freight Lines	2229 Hillcrest Dr.	Suite 102	Arlington	MI	491
9	Ace Airplanes	3987 Glendale Dr.		Springfield	VA	22:
10	Hidden Resorts	1411 Reservation Dr.		Springfield	VA	22:
11	Sangster Insurance	663 Yuppie Lane	Mail Stop #800	McLean	VA	22:
12	Signal Plumbing	120 S. 2nd	Suite B	Springfield	VA	22:
13	Kid's Closet	777 Kittyhawk Dr.		Gaithersburg	MD	208
14	WRB Consulting	1711 Lakeview Dr.		Chapel Hill	NC	27:
15	Outback Boutique	1211 Commerce St.		Springfield	VA	22:
16	Friendly Farms	13 Baker St.	Suite 1700	Alexandria	VA	22:
17	Metro Athletic, Inc.	720 Port Royal	Building 33, Suite 4a	Fairfax	VA	220
18	Tyson Plumbing	770 Shaw Rd.	Suite 701	Alexandria	MI	491
19	Surf's Up Discount	328A Front St.	Suite 100	Maui	HI	610
20	Prince Wallace Pearls, Inc.	1142 S. Orange Blvd.		Sinajana		55:

Table: Organizations

Record: 1 of 26

Figure 5-19: The Organizations datasheet displayed in Times New Roman.

Closing the Datasheet & Saving the Layout

After you have gone to the trouble of rearranging, hiding and freezing columns, changing row height and selecting different fonts, you probably want to save the datasheet's new *layout*. To close the datasheet and save the layout, follow these steps:

1. Double-click the Control-menu box. Access displays a message that asks whether you want to save the layout changes to the table you have been working on.

2. Choose the Yes button in the dialog box to save the layout. Access saves the layout changes and closes the datasheet. The next time you display the same datasheet, Access applies all the layout changes.

ADDING DATA USING A FORM

Although you can enter all data into your database through a datasheet, Access enables you to design powerful and very "user-friendly" data-entry forms. Chapter 8 explains how to design forms quickly using Form Wizards, and Chapter 9 covers how to create custom forms using the Form window's Design view.

Entering data using a form is essentially the same as entering data in a datasheet, with one major difference. When you display a form in Form view, as shown in Figure 5-20, Access displays data from one and only one record. As you have seen, however, a datasheet displays data from many records concurrently. The cursor-movement keys, therefore, work a little differently in Form view than in Datasheet view:

Figure 5-20: An Employee table record displayed in a form.

The following table shows how cursor-movement keys work in an Access form:

Key	Move To
Enter	Next field
Tab	Next field
Shift-Tab	Preceding field
Right Arrow	Next field
Left Arrow	Preceding field
Up Arrow	Preceding field
Down Arrow	Next field
PgUp	Preceding record
PgDn	Next record
Home	First field in the current record
End	Last field in the current record
Ctrl-Home	First field in the first record
Ctrl-End	Last field in the last record

Refer to Chapters 8, 9 and subsequent chapters for more about the many powerful features you can design into Access forms.

COPYING DATA BETWEEN TABLES

In Chapter 3 you learned how to create tables quickly by importing them from existing databases. So why create a table from scratch when you can import one that has already been created.

Many times the tables in your database have a somewhat different design than existing tables. But the existing tables contain data you would like to be able to use without having to retype it into the new tables. In such cases you'll need to use the Table Wizard or the Table window's Design view to design your tables and then use a *copy* procedure to insert the existing data into your new tables.

For example, assume that your client Sam has been keeping track of his contacts in a dBASE database file named CUSTOMER.DBF. Most of the data you now need for your Contacts table in the new Contacts database is in there. If the design of the dBASE file is exactly like your new Contacts table design, the easiest way to use the dBASE data would be to convert the table to an Access table using the Import command (see "Importing Tables" in Chapter 3). But as is more often the case, the field names of the dBASE file do not match up exactly to the fields of the Contacts table. The easiest way to get the dBASE data into your Contacts table is to use the Copy command to copy the data from one table to another.

Before you can copy data into the Contacts table, you should import the dBASE file to an Access table. It will then be easy to copy data from the imported table to Contacts. Import the CUSTOMER.DBF database file into a new Access table named CUSTOMER. See "Importing Tables" in Chapter 3 for instructions.

CUSTID	PHONEKEY	FNAME	MNAME	LTNAME	
1	C	Terry	S.	Fulcher	Direct
2	C	Jody	L.	Needham	Owner
3	C	Alan		McConnell	Head
4	C	J.	Richard	Wolf	Owner
5	C	Ileen	M	Martini	Order
6	C	Sarah	L.	Smiley	Order
7	C	Kelly	Marie	Wolf	Marke
8	C	Bruce	W.	Richards	Office
9	C	Kevin	Richard	Wolf	Owner
10	C	David	Alan	Needham	Owner
11	C	Wallace	M.	East	Owner
12	C	Alfred	H.	Long	Accou
13	C	Francis	P.	Jones	Sales
14	C	Rex	T.	Comfort	Sales
15	C	Roberta	M.	Sangster	Marke
16	C	Wynona	R.	Brown	Owner
17	C	Helen	H.	Harrison	Sales
18	C	Richard	B.	Walters	Buyer
19	C	Toni	S.	Fulcher	Owner
20	C	Jane	N.	Smith	Order
21	C	Alan		Moonie	Owner
22	C	Richard	B.	Walters	Buyer

Table: CUSTOMER

Record: 1 of 25

Figure 5-21: The imported CUSTOMER table.

The fields of CUSTOMER and Contacts match up in the following way:

CUSTOMER Field	Contacts Field
CUSTID	ContactID
PHONEKEY	PhoneKey
FNAME	FirstName
MNAME	MiddleName
LTNAME	LastName
TITLE	Title
GREETING	Salutation
NNAME	Nickname
ADDR1	AddressLine1
ADDR2	AddressLine2
CITY	City
STATE	State
ZIPCODE	ZipCode
COUNTRY	Country
ORGID	OrgID
REFERREDBY	ReferredBy
(none)	Photograph
(none)	Note

To copy data from CUSTOMER to Contacts, follow these steps:

1. Display the CUSTOMER table in Datasheet view, as shown in Figure 5-21. Make note of the column order.

2. Use the field selector row to select all columns in the table. Alternatively, click the gray box just below the Control-menu button. Access highlights the entire datasheet.

3. Either right-click the selected columns and choose Copy from the pop-up menu, or choose Edit, Copy from the menu bar.

4. Close the CUSTOMER table. Access may inform you that there is a large amount of data in the Clipboard and ask whether you want to keep the data on the Clipboard. Respond affirmatively by choosing the Yes button.

5. Open the Contacts table you created in Chapter 3, "Designing Your Database."

6. With the cursor in the first column of the first field, choose Edit, Paste Append from the menu bar. Access pastes the 25 records from the CUSTOMER table into the new Contacts table.

7. Access displays a message indicating that you have pasted 25 records into the datasheet and asks you if you want to save the changes. Choose the OK button. Access saves the data to the Contacts table (see Figure 5-22).

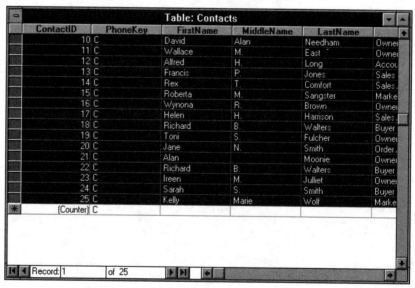

Figure 5-22: The Contacts table with records copied from the imported CUSTOMER table.

In Chapter 4 you created the Interactions table in the Contacts database, but so far there is no data in this table. Use the Copy procedure described in the preceding steps to copy all records from the Interactions table in the Ventana database (installed to your hard disk from the companion disk) to the Interactions table in the Contacts database.

The preceding steps used the Copy Append command to copy data and create new records at the same time. Access also enables you to copy data into existing records as well. For example, the CUSTOMER table did not include the Photograph and Note fields that are included in Contacts. To practice copying data into existing records, try copying the Photograph and Note field values from the Contacts table in the Ventana database to the Photograph and Note fields in the Contacts table in the Contacts database. Follow these steps:

1. Open the Ventana database (that you installed from the companion disk to your hard disk) and display the Contacts table in Datasheet view.

2. Select the Photograph and Note columns using the field selector row.

3. Either right-click the selected columns and choose Copy from the pop-up menu, or choose Edit, Copy from the menu bar.

4. Close the Contacts table and the Ventana database. Access may inform you that there is a large amount of data in the Clipboard and ask whether you want to keep the data on the Clipboard. Respond affirmatively by choosing the Yes button.

5. Open the Contacts table you created in Chapter 3.

6. Select the empty Photograph and Note columns using the field selector row.

7. Choose Edit, Paste from the menu bar. Access pastes the Photograph and Note field values from the 25 records in the Ventana database into the existing rows of the Contacts datasheet in the Contacts database.

8. Access displays a message indicating that you have pasted 25 records into the datasheet and asks you whether you want to save the changes. Choose the OK button. Access saves the data to the Contacts table.

FINDING RECORDS

When you are working in an Access table, you may want to edit one particular record out of hundreds, or even thousands, in your table. Access provides a number of ways to help you find the record quickly, but the easiest way is to use the Find command. Find works best if Access is searching through the table using a single primary key field. You can use this technique whether working in Datasheet view or Form view.

To use the Find command, follow these steps:

1. Place the cursor in the field you want Access to search, in any record in the table.

2. Either click the Find button in the toolbar, or choose Edit, Find from the menu bar. Access displays the Find in field dialog box (see Figure 5-23).

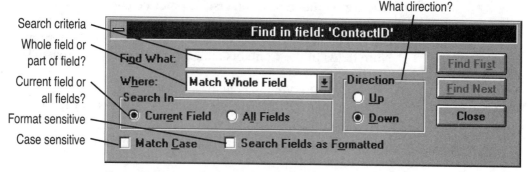

Figure 5-23: The Find in field dialog box for the ContactID field.

3. Type the *search criteria*—the text you want Access to find—in the Find What text box. This criteria can be a specific value such as a word, name or number, or can include *wildcard characters* (?, * or #), *alternative characters* enclosed in square brackets and *character ranges* separated by hyphens (see the "Search Criteria" sidebar below). You can exclude characters with the exclamation point.

. . . .

Search Criteria

Search criteria in the Find in field dialog box can contain either or all of three wildcard characters: the question mark (?), the asterisk (*) or the number sign (#). In a search criteria, a question mark represents any single alphanumeric character; an asterisk represents any number of alphanumeric characters; and the number sign represents a single numeric digit.

To specify alternative characters, enclose the alternatives together in brackets ([ ]). For example, the criteria J[au]ne would find both June and Jane. To exclude characters, insert an exclamation point after the opening bracket. To specify a range of alternative characters, specify the upper and lower limits of the range, separated by a hyphen.

. . . .

Following are examples of valid search criteria:

Criteria	Finds	But Not
Jo*	Jones	Mr. Jones
	Johnson	
	Jolliet	
	Jo Jo	
J??n	Jean	jeans
	John	Johnson
J[eo]an	Jean	Jan
	Joan	
j[a-o]g	jag	jug
	jig	
	jog	
q	quick	
	aquatic	
	WMZQ FM	
@q	aquatic	quick
*th*r	Mother	Mother's day
	path finder	
	Fifth of October	
??other	brother	other
	another	
12/??/94	12/25/94	12/5/94
	December 25, 1994	
21*	21.000	.21
	210.45	2.1
	21.3	
*21	13,018.21	130,182.1

4. By default, the Find command tries to match the contents of the Find What text box to entire contents of each field value. For example, searching for *mother* would not return *mothers* as a match. If you want Access to search for a match anywhere in the field, choose Any Part of Field from the Where drop-down list box in the Find in field dialog box. Alternatively, if you want Access to return a match only if the search criteria appears at the beginning of the field—for example, to match *mothers* but not *smothers*—choose Start of Field from the Where drop-down list box in the Find in field dialog box.

5. The Find command, by default, ignores the case of the characters in the search criteria. If you want Access to return a match only when the case of the characters in the field value is exactly the same as the case of the letters in the search criteria, mark the Match Case check box in the Find in field dialog box.

6. You learned in Chapter 4 how to set field formats and input masks. The Format property and input masks cause Access to

display data in a different form than it is stored on disk. By default, the Find command tries to match the search criteria to the values stored on disk, rather than the values displayed onscreen. If you want to match the field values displayed onscreen, mark the Search Fields as Formatted check box in the Find in field dialog box.

7. Finally, the Find command by default searches through the datasheet or form from top to bottom. (Access normally displays records in order by the primary key field, but see "Sorting & Filtering Records" later in this chapter.) To search from bottom to top, choose the Up option button from the Find in field dialog box.

8. After you have specified a search criteria, and selected any other of the options in the Find in field dialog box, choose the Find First button. Access searches through the table and displays the first record in which there is a match. If you are working in Datasheet view, Access scrolls to the matching record and highlights the matching field.

9. Depending on the criteria, there may be more than one matching record in the table. To find the next match, if any, choose the Find Next button. Access displays the next match, if one exists.

When Access reaches the end of the records, the program displays a note to that effect and asks whether you want to continue searching from the beginning. If you didn't start searching in the first record, choose Yes to continue from the top of the table.

When Access has searched all records without finding another match, it displays a message indicating it has reached the end of the records. Choose OK to continue.

From time to time, you may have a need to make a global change in a table. For example, an area code may have changed, or you have decided to replace every occurrence of Miss with Ms. Access enables you to use the Replace command for this purpose. The Replace command is just a variation of the Find command.

To use the Replace command, follow these steps:

1. Place the cursor in the field that contains the values you want to replace.

2. Choose Edit, Replace from the menu bar. Access displays the Replace dialog box (see Figure 5-24).

Figure 5-24: The Replace in field dialog box for the Salutation field.

3. Type the *search criteria*—the text you want Access to re-place—in the Find What text box.

4. Type the replacement value in the Replace With text box.

5. Choose the Find Next button to find the first match, and then choose Replace to replace the contents of the field with the replacement value.

   To replace all matching fields, without displaying them one by one, choose the Replace All button.

6. When you are finished, choose the Close button to close the Replace in field dialog box.

SORTING & FILTERING RECORDS

When you display a table in Datasheet view, Access lists records in order by the value in the primary key field, unless you didn't assign a primary key field. (As you learned in Chapter 2, you should *always* assign a primary key field.) Access provides several ways for you to temporarily change the order records are displayed in the datasheet. For example, in the Contacts table, you may want to occasionally display records in alphabetical order by the LastName field, instead of in order by the primary key field, ContactID.

The following sections explain how to use the Quick Sort command and the Filter dialog box to sort records in the datasheet.

Using Quick Sort

As you might guess, the quickest way to sort records in Datasheet view is the Quick Sort command. To sort records using this command, follow these steps:

1. Select the column or columns by which you want to sort the datasheet. (**Note:** To sort by multiple columns, you first have to arrange these columns side by side with the primary sort field on the left, and secondary sort field on the right—see "Rearranging Columns" earlier in this chapter.)

For example, if you want to sort Contacts by the values in the LastName column, select LastName column. If you suspect that several contacts may have the same last name, you may want to sort by LastName and then by FirstName. Rearrange columns so that LastName is just to the left of FirstName and then select both columns (see Figure 5-25).

Selected columns ————

ContactID	PhoneKey	LastName	FirstName	MiddleName	
1	C	Fulcher	Terry	S.	Direct
2	C	Needham	Jody	L.	Owner
3	C	McConnell	Alan		Head
4	C	Wolf	J.	Richard	Owner
5	C	Martini	Ileen	M	Order
6	C	Smiley	Sarah	L.	Order
7	C	Wolf	Kelly	Marie	Marke
8	C	Richards	Bruce	W.	Office
9	C	Wolf	Kevin	Richard	Owner
10	C	Needham	David	Alan	Owner
11	C	East	Wallace	M.	Owner
12	C	Long	Alfred	H.	Accou
13	C	Jones	Francis	P.	Sales
14	C	Comfort	Rex	T.	Sales
15	C	Sangster	Roberta	M.	Marke
16	C	Brown	Wynona	R.	Owner
17	C	Harrison	Helen	H.	Sales
18	C	Walters	Richard	B.	Buyer
19	C	Fulcher	Toni	S.	Owner
20	C	Smith	Jane	N.	Order
21	C	Moonie	Alan		Owner
22	C	Walters	Richard	B.	Buyer

Record: 1 of 25

Figure 5-25: The Contacts datasheet with LastName and FirstName columns selected.

2. To sort by the selected column in ascending (A-Z) order, either click the Sort Ascending button in the toolbar, or right-click the selected column(s) and choose Quick Sort Ascending from the pop-up menu, or choose Records, Quick Sort, Ascending from the menu bar. Access sorts the records by the values in the selected column(s). Figure 5-26, for example, shows the Contacts datasheet with records sorted by the LastName and FirstName fields. Notice that the ContactID column is no longer in order.

ContactID	PhoneKey	LastName	FirstName	MiddleName	
16	C	Brown	Wynona	R.	Owner
14	C	Comfort	Rex	T.	Sales
11	C	East	Wallace	M.	Owner
1	C	Fulcher	Terry	S.	Direct
19	C	Fulcher	Toni	S.	Owner
17	C	Harrison	Helen	H.	Sales
13	C	Jones	Francis	P.	Sales
23	C	Julliet	Ireen	M.	Owner
12	C	Long	Alfred	H.	Accou
5	C	Martini	Ileen	M	Order
3	C	McConnell	Alan		Head
21	C	Moonie	Alan		Owner
10	C	Needham	David	Alan	Owner
2	C	Needham	Jody	L.	Owner
8	C	Richards	Bruce	W.	Office
15	C	Sangster	Roberta	M.	Marke
6	C	Smiley	Sarah	L.	Order
20	C	Smith	Jane	N.	Order
24	C	Smith	Sarah	S.	Buyer
22	C	Walters	Richard	B.	Buyer
18	C	Walters	Richard	B.	Buyer
4	C	Wolf	J.	Richard	Owner

Record: 1 of 25

Figure 5-26: The Contacts datasheet sorted by the LastName and FirstName columns.

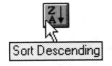
Sort Descending

To sort in descending order, either click the Sort Descending button in the toolbar, or right-click the selected column(s) and choose Quick Sort Descending from the pop-up menu, or choose Records, Quick Sort, Descending from the menu bar.

Filtering Records

Sometimes you want to not only sort the datasheet differently, but you want to display only a subset of the entire table. For instance, you might want to see a list of only contacts from a single state. Or perhaps you want to search for a record based on the contents in more than one field. The most powerful way to display subsets of your data, or to search for data based on values in multiple fields, is to use Access queries. Refer to Chapters 6 and 7 for a full discussion of queries.

A somewhat more limited version of an Access query is called a *filter*. Using an Access filter you can *filter* the datasheet—display a subset of records based on the values in one or more fields in the datasheet. You can also sort records in the datasheet.

To create a filter that determines which records display in the datasheet, or that sorts the datasheet, follow these steps:

1. From the Datasheet window (or from the Form window in Form view—when viewing records in a form), either click the Edit Filter/Sort button on the toolbar, or right-click the datasheet's title bar and choose Edit Filter/Sort from the pop-up menu, or choose Records, Edit Filter/Sort from the menu bar. Access displays the Filter window (see Figure 5-27).

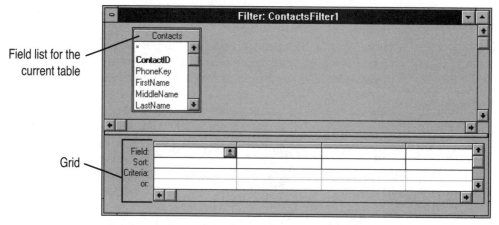

Field list for the current table

Grid

Figure 5-27: The Contacts datasheet sorted by the LastName and FirstName columns.

The upper pane in the Filter window contains a field list from the current table. The lower pane of the window contains a *grid* with rows labeled Field, Sort, Criteria and or. In this grid you can specify criteria that limits which records display in the window or how the records should be sorted.

2. Decide on which field(s) you want to base the filter criteria. Click the field name(s) in the field list, and drag the field name(s) to the Field row of the grid. For example, to begin building a filter for the Contacts table that will display only contacts from Michigan, drag the State field name from the field list to the Field column in the grid.

3. Type a criteria in the Criteria row of the grid column where you placed the field name (refer to Chapter 7, "Mastering Queries," for a full discussion of how to use expressions in queries and filters). For example, to display only contacts from Michigan, type = **MI** in the Criteria row (see Figure 5-28).

4. If you want Access to sort the records based on the values in one or more fields, click the field name(s) in the field list, and drag the field name(s) to the Field row of the grid.

5. Click the Sort row and select Ascending or Descending from the drop-down list box. Figure 5-28 shows a filter for the Contacts table that will sort the records in ascending order by last and first names.

Sort fields

Criteria

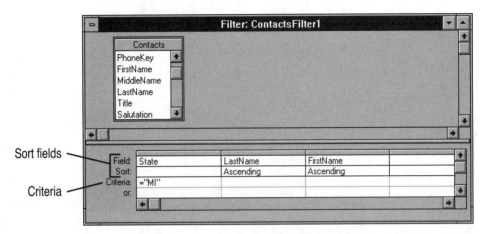

Figure 5-28: A filter for the Contacts table that limits records to Michigan contacts and sorts records by the LastName and FirstName fields.

6. Either click the Apply Filter/Sort button in the toolbar, or right-click the window title bar and choose Apply Filter/Sort from the pop-up menu, or choose Records, Apply Filter/Sort from the menu bar. Access applies the filter to the table and displays the filtered records. Figure 5-29, for example, shows the Contracts datasheet, filtered by the filter shown in Figure 5-28.

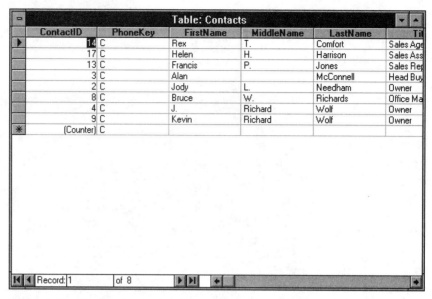

Table: Contacts					
ContactID	**PhoneKey**	**FirstName**	**MiddleName**	**LastName**	**Tit**
14	C	Rex	T.	Comfort	Sales Age
17	C	Helen	H.	Harrison	Sales Ass
13	C	Francis	P.	Jones	Sales Rep
3	C	Alan		McConnell	Head Buy
2	C	Jody	L.	Needham	Owner
8	C	Bruce	W.	Richards	Office Ma
4	C	J.	Richard	Wolf	Owner
9	C	Kevin	Richard	Wolf	Owner
(Counter)	C				

Record: 1   of 8

Figure 5-29: The Contacts datasheet filtered by the filter shown in Figure 5-28.

Show All Records

To turn off the filter, either click the Show All Records button in the toolbar, or right-click the window title bar and choose Show All Records from the pop-up menu, or choose Records, Show All Records from the menu bar.

When you close the window after applying a filter, Access does not save the filter or ask whether you want to save the layout. The filter is lost. You can, however, save the filter as a query. To save the filter as a query:

1. Use the Edit Filter/Sort command to display the current filter.

2. Choose File, Save As Query from the menu bar. Access displays the Save As Query dialog box.

3. Type a name for the query and choose the OK button. Access saves the filter as a query.

To use a previously saved query as a filter:

1. Use the Edit Filter/Sort command to display the Filter window.

2. Choose File, Load From Query from the menu bar. Access displays the Applicable Filter dialog box.

3. Select the query from the Filter list box and choose the OK button. Access loads the previously saved query as a filter in the Filter window.

4. Either click the Apply Filter/Sort button in the toolbar, or right-click the window title bar and choose Apply Filter/Sort from the pop-up menu, or choose Records, Apply Filter/Sort from the menu bar. Access applies the filter to the table and displays the filtered records.

PRINTING RECORDS

The best way to print data from a table is to use an Access report. Using Access reports, you can create nicely designed professional-looking output quickly and easily (see Chapters 10 and 11). Sometimes, however, it is convenient to just dump records from the datasheet to the printer—a sort-of "quick-and-dirty" report.

To print a copy of the records currently included in the active datasheet, follow these steps:

1. Either click the Print button on the toolbar, or choose File, Print from the menu bar. Access displays the Print dialog box.

2. To print all records in the current datasheet, choose the OK button. You can, optionally, limit the output by specifying which pages to print in the From and To text boxes before choosing the OK button.

MOVING ON

In this chapter you've learned how to add data to a table in Datasheet view, as well as how to add data using a form. You also learned how to change the way the datasheet looks and how to copy data from one table to another. Next, you learned how to find records and how to sort records in the database using the quick sort method. In this chapter you also learned how to use filters to limit the records that Access displays and prints. Finally, this chapter taught you how to quickly print records from the database without needing to load a report.

The next chapter, Chapter 6, "Creating Queries on the Fly," introduces you to the fundamentals of Access' querying capabilities. Using Access queries you can retrieve data from one table, or many tables. Queries even make it possible to analyze and summarize your data without the need for any programming or complex formulas. Turn now to Chapter 6 and create queries quickly using Access' Query Wizards.

6

CREATING QUERIES ON THE FLY

In this chapter we will discuss the types of queries available in Access and how we can put them to use. We'll also look at the Query Wizards, and see how they help us create some fairly advanced queries.

We will begin with a discussion of what queries are and how you will find them useful when developing applications. We'll explain some terms used when discussing queries so you can talk with the pros when you're done. And finally, we'll take a look at Query Wizards, powerful tools that walk you through the steps necessary to create queries.

There are four Query Wizards included in Access 2.0. Each generates a query capable of performing some fairly sophisticated tasks. The query generated by the Find Duplicates Wizard locates records in your database containing redundant information. The query generated by the Find Unmatched Wizard locates incomplete data. The query generated by the Crosstab Wizard summarizes the data in your database. And the query generated by the Archive Wizard can be used to copy records from one table to another.

TAKING A LOOK AT QUERIES & DYNASETS

Access *queries* provide a way to view or manipulate data in one or more tables. You can use queries to perform many common tasks, from retrieving specific records from a table, to manipulating data contained in multiple tables. Not only is it easier to create a query than to write a program, queries perform many functions more efficiently than programs. The ability to quickly create queries to perform these functions is one of the many features that make Access such a revolutionary PC database product.

There are several different types of queries available, and each performs a specialized function. To help understand the many types of queries, they can be grouped into three categories: *select queries*, *crosstab queries* and *action queries*.

Select Queries

Select queries do just what their name implies: they select, or retrieve, data from tables. Often you will want to look at just a few of the records a table contains. For example, you might want to see just the organizations from a certain state. Or maybe you want to see the interactions you've had with a particular person in the last six months. Figure 6-1 shows what a typical select query looks like.

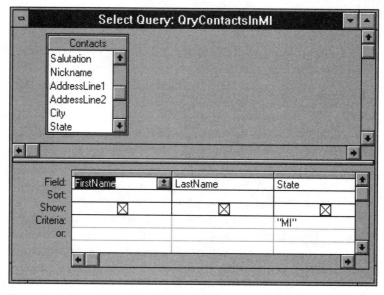

Figure 6-1: Example select query design.

Select queries give you a way of looking at just the records you are interested in using. When a select query is executed, it looks at the tables you specify and retrieves data from the fields you want. You limit the records retrieved by defining selection criteria. The result of the query is a set of records, called a *dynaset*.

A *dynaset* is an updatable view of the records requested from the query. The term *view* describes the set of records looked at separately from the table itself. You may add new records, delete existing records or change the data contained in any record in the dynaset. When you make changes to the data in a dynaset, the changes are written to the underlying tables. Figure 6-2 shows what the dynaset display looks like when you execute the query shown in Figure 6-1.

Select Query: QryContactsInMI

FirstName	LastName	State
Jody	Needham	MI
Alan	McConnell	MI
J.	Wolf	MI
Bruce	Richards	MI
Kevin	Wolf	MI
Francis	Jones	MI
Rex	Comfort	MI
Helen	Harrison	MI

Record: 1 of 8

Figure 6-2: Example dynaset produced by running the query in Figure 6-1.

Crosstab Queries

Crosstab queries are used to summarize data by row and column. This might sound a little confusing at first, but once you understand the basic concept, the rest is easy. Let's look at an example to help explain the idea behind crosstabs. In our sample application, we track interactions between account executives and contacts. To see how many interactions occur between any two people, you could use a crosstab query to look up each interaction record and count the number of records returned. This would require a spreadsheet-like setup to track the data. Each row would show a person's name, and a column would be created for each person with whom he or she interacted. The number of interactions between two given people will be shown in the appropriate row and column. Figure 6-3 shows how this might look.

Crosstab Query: QryInteractionNames_Crosstab1

EmpName	RowSummary	Alan	Alfred	Bruce	Helen	Ileen	J_	Jane	Jody
Charlie Eager	6		1						2
Samuel Pate	4			1	1	1			
Steven Bunch	6	1						1	
Timothy Alan	3						1		

Record: 1 of 4

Figure 6-3: Example crosstab query result display.

Action Queries

A select query is used to retrieve a set of records meeting specific criteria. To change the data, you make a change to the returned dynaset record. An *action query*, on the other hand, is used to make in-place changes to data in a table. Action queries do not return dynasets. You must look at the table to see the results of an action query.

There are four types of action queries: make table, append, update and delete.

A *make table* query creates a new table whenever the query is executed. Make table queries can perform all of the same functions as select queries. The records selected are placed in a new table; no dynaset is created. The new table may be located in either the current database or in a separate database. Changing data in this new table does not affect the data in the original table. For example, you might use a make table query to copy records for last year's interactions to a separate table for historical purposes.

An *append query* is similar to a make table query, the difference being that the append query places the results of the query in an existing table rather than creating a new table. This table may be located in the current database or in a separate database. Append queries can perform all of the same functions as select queries. For example, you might use an append query to add data collected from a regional office to the headquarters table.

An *update query* changes data in an existing table. Update queries are useful for making similar changes to several records at once. For example, suppose, because of the great job they've been doing, you want to give all employees a ten percent pay increase. You could change all the employee payroll records at once by using an update query. An update query can only change existing records. You cannot add or delete records with an update query.

A *delete query* deletes records from an existing table. Delete queries are useful for deleting several records at a time. For example, you might want to delete records containing data more than a year old. You can create a delete query to perform all the steps necessary to identify the records and delete them. For example, you might use a delete query to remove records for interactions you no longer need to track.

We will discuss action queries in more detail in the next chapter.

CREATING QUERIES WITH QUERY WIZARDS

Query Wizards provide an easy way to create a few types of queries. A Query Wizard guides you through the process of creating a query a step at a time. In each step you answer a few questions about how you want the query to work. Once the questions are answered, a Wizard generates the query. A Query Wizard will even execute the query after it is generated if you want.

To start creating a query using a Query Wizard, follow these steps:

1. Open the database containing the data that you want to query.

2. Choose the Query button in the Database window to view a list of the queries, if any, that have already been defined in the database.

3. Next, choose the New button in the Database window to start creating a new query. Access displays the New Query dialog box, as shown in Figure 6-4.

Figure 6-4: The New Query dialog box.

4. You have two options from which to select in the New Query dialog box. You can select the Query Wizards option to walk you through the process of creating a new query. Or you can select the New Query option to take you into Design view and build the query yourself. We will discuss creating queries yourself in the next chapter. For now, let's select the Query Wizards option. Access displays the Query Wizards dialog box.

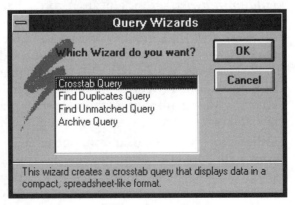

Figure 6-5: The Query Wizards dialog box.

5. Choose one of the query types listed in the Query Wizards dialog box. Either select the query type and click the OK button, or double-click the query type. Access displays the Query Wizard dialog box for whichever query you have chosen.

The dialog box in turn displays several screens as it gathers information from you in order to build the query. The additional steps to complete each Query Wizard are described in the remaining sections of this chapter, depending on which type of query you are creating.

Figure 6-5 shows the four types of Query Wizards supported in Access 2.0. Let's take a quick look at the queries generated by these Wizards and at what they can do for you:

○ *Crosstab queries* provide a two-tier summary of data. Crosstab queries are an excellent way of grouping data together based upon common values in one field, and then breaking the data into individual columns (fields) based upon common values in another field.

For example, suppose your application keeps track of sales information. You will probably want to see the total dollar purchases made by each of your customers. You can group all of the sales data by customer and arrive at the total dollar purchases. A crosstab query will let you break down the sales figures into smaller groups. You can separate the total amount into amount by month or year.

○ *Find duplicates queries* locate two or more records containing the same information. You can compare one or several fields in the record to help decide if it is a duplicate record.

For example, you can use this type of query to determine if there are multiple records on file for the same person.

○ *Find unmatched queries* locate records that don't have related records in another table. Related data is typically needed when there are a variable number of associated pieces of information required to show a complete picture of the data.

For example, you can use this type of query to locate organizations without any corresponding contacts with whom you interact. An organization without contact people isn't of much use, unless you want to talk to the building itself.

○ *Archive queries* copy data from one table to another. You can copy a single record or many records. You create selection criteria to determine the records to be copied. Once a record is copied, the archive query can optionally delete it from the original table. Copying and deleting a record is how you move a record from one table to another.

For example, you could use an archive query to move records containing information more than a year old to a history table.

We will discuss each of these types of queries in more detail in the remainder of this chapter.

CREATING A FIND DUPLICATES QUERY

We discussed in the previous chapters the importance of good table design. We discussed how to design your tables so there is only one occurrence of any given piece of information. Good table design only insures that you won't have to enter data in more than one place. But what happens when you enter information more than one time in the same table? Unless you prevent this from happening (which we'll discuss how to do in later chapters dealing with form design), you'll end up with multiple records containing the same data.

You can use the Find Duplicates Query Wizard to help you find records containing redundant data in a table. This Wizard constructs a query to search tables for records containing identical data in selected fields. When the query is executed it will show the contents of the duplicate records. Remember, data in the resultant dynaset can be changed; deleting a duplicate record from the dynaset actually deletes the record from the table.

The next few pages describe the screens you'll see when using the Find Duplicates Query Wizard. You will need to answer several questions to let the Wizard know exactly what to do.

Let's assume an account executive, Steve, has just transferred in from our office in Guam (there's a real good market for widgets in Guam). Being a good account executive, he brought along a table containing information regarding the organizations he did business with. The first thing he did when he got settled into the office was to append his table to our existing Organizations table. Because this office may have done business with some of the same organizations as the Guam office, we already may have records on file for some of these organizations. In the query we are creating in this example, we will attempt to locate any redundant organization data.

To create a find duplicates query, select Find Duplicates Query from the list in the Query Wizards dialog box, then follow these additional steps:

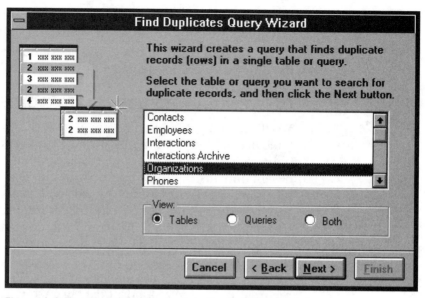

Figure 6-6: The first Find Duplicates Query Wizard dialog box.

1. The first screen you'll see is the table selection screen (see Figure 6-6). On this screen you identify the table or query you want to examine for duplicate records. The option buttons on the lower part of the dialog box tell the Wizard what to show in the list of entries to select from. You can see a list containing just the tables in the database by choosing the Tables button, just the queries in the database by choosing the Queries button, or both the tables and queries in the database by choosing the Both option button. You may select only a single entry from the list. If you want to look at more than one table for duplicate data, you must create a select query that joins the tables and then choose that query from the list of queries. In the example shown in Figure 6-6, we've selected the Organizations table, since that is the table containing information describing our client organizations.

2. After you have selected the table or query to examine, click the Next > button to move to the next dialog box (see Figure 6-7).

. . . .

Navigating a Wizard

All Wizards share a common set of command buttons to control movement from one window to the next. You tell the Wizard you are done with a window by clicking the Next > button.

Clicking the < Back button takes you back to the Query Wizards screen. Clicking Cancel returns you to the Database window. The Finish button is available once you have answered enough questions to allow the Wizard to generate the query. Some windows have a Hint button; pressing this button causes the Wizard to display a screen with helpful information about how to answer the questions posed by the current screen.

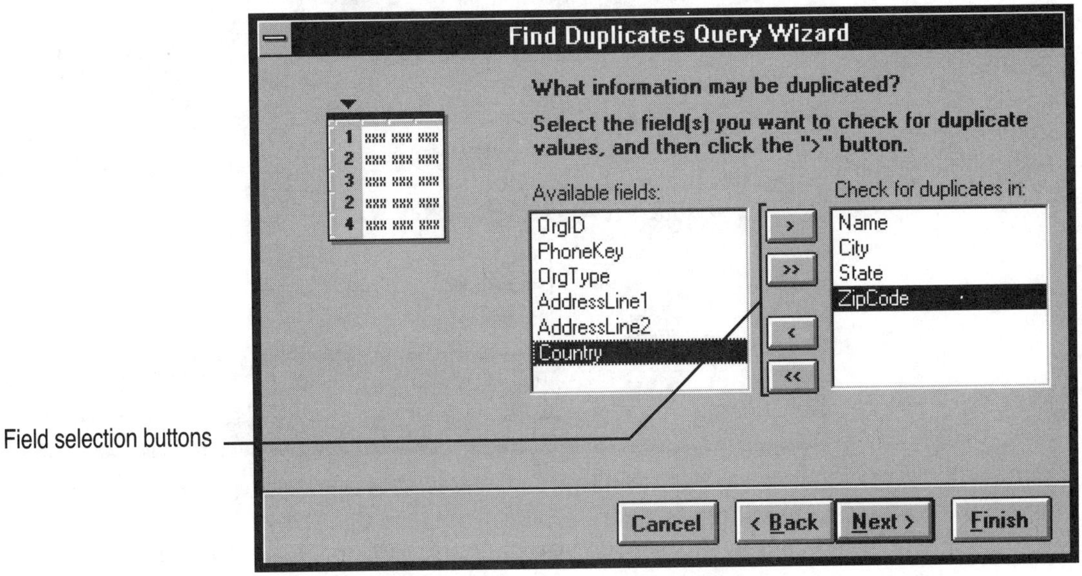

Field selection buttons —

Figure 6-7: The second Find Duplicates Query Wizard dialog box.

3. After you've selected the table or query to examine, you need to tell the Wizard what fields to use. The field selection screen contains two lists. The Available fields list, on the left, contains all the fields in the table or query you specified in the previous screen. The "Check for duplicates in" list, on the right, shows the fields you want the query to use to determine record duplication.

Use the field selection buttons to build the list of fields to be checked for duplicate values. To move a field from the list on the left to the list on the right, highlight the desired field and click the > button. To select all fields, click the >> button. If you want to remove a field from the list on the right, highlight the field and click the < button. To remove all fields, click the << button. You may double-click the mouse pointer on a field in either list to move it to the other list.

In Figure 6-7, we are looking for records containing duplicated Name, City, State and ZipCode data. If two or more
records contain redundant data in the selected fields they will
be considered duplicate records.

4. After you have selected the fields to examine, click the Next >
button to move to the third dialog box (see Figure 6-8).

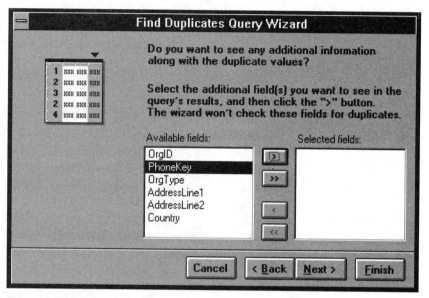

Figure 6-8: The third Find Duplicates Query Wizard dialog box.

5. On this screen you have the option of identifying any additional fields you would like to display in the event a duplicate
record is found. Fields selected in this screen are not used to
determine record duplication, but displaying these fields
gives additional information that might be useful in determining what to do with the duplicated records. The screen works
in the same manner as the field selection screen, discussed
above. The Available fields list contains the remaining fields
from the table or query you selected in the first screen of this
Wizard. The Selected fields list contains the list of any additional fields you want to see. The fields we selected on the
previous screen give us the information we need to identify
any duplicate records, so we haven't selected any additional
fields on this screen.

6. After selecting the desired fields, click the Next > button to
move to the final screen (see Figure 6-9).

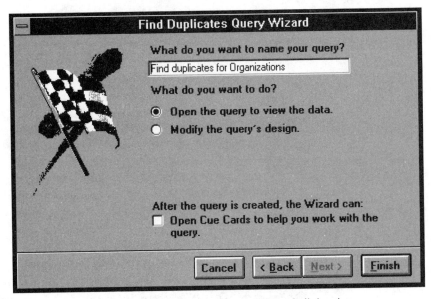

Figure 6-9: The final Find Duplicates Query Wizard dialog box.

7. You have now specified all of the information necessary to determine if there are duplicated records in a table or query. You use the screen shown in Figure 6-9 to give the query a name, and to choose to either execute the query at this time or look at the design in the query design window. Type the name you want to give this query in the text box. The query name must be unique, and it cannot be the same as any table in the database. The query generated in the example will be named Find duplicates for Organizations.

8. Select one of the following two options to determine how to proceed:

○ *Open the query to view the data.* Selecting this option tells the Wizard to generate the query and immediately execute it, displaying the results in a window, when the Finish button is pressed. This is the default option.

○ *Modify the query's design.* This option will generate the query and then open the query in the design window, allowing you to modify the design before executing.

9. The final entry on this screen is a check box. Select this check box to open the Access Cue Cards for additional assistance.

10. After you have named the query and selected the option informing the Wizard how to proceed, you are done. Choose the Finish button to enjoy the fruits of your labor. Figure 6-10 shows the results we get when we execute the

query. We see there is one organization containing duplicate information. The first few columns show you the fields we decided to use to determine duplicate records. The last column tells you how many records were found in the table containing the same data, in this case two.

Name Field	City Field	State Field	ZipCode Field	NumberOfDups
Surf's Up Discount	Maui	HI	61010	2

Figure 6-10: Example results of find duplicates query.

Creating a Find Unmatched Query

As we discussed when we looked at the Find Duplicates Query Wizard, good table design eliminates the need to enter data more than once. This is done by isolating data into tables, each table storing only information relating to a single subject.

There are times when you will break up data relating to a single subject into multiple tables. But when data is broken up in this way, you will have to retrieve records from more than one table to get all the information you need to make the data useful. In a situation such as this, you typically create a single record in one table, usually referred to as the *parent* (or *primary*) tables, and you create one or more related records in additional tables, usually referred to as *child* (or *related*) tables.

The Find Unmatched Query Wizard generates a query that returns a set of primary table records that do not have matching records in a child table. For example, in our Contacts database it is possible to have individuals listed in the Contacts table (the *primary* table) with whom there has been no recent interaction (Interactions is the *related* table). Perhaps these people need to be contacted, or maybe they just need to be removed from the database. The Find Unmatched Query Wizard generates queries to check for this type of situation.

To complete this Query Wizard, you'll need to provide four pieces of information: the name of the primary table, the name of the related table, the common fields between the two tables and the data from the primary table to display in the event an unmatched record is found.

We'll discuss the screens you'll see in the Find Unmatched Query Wizard in the next few pages. The example we'll use will locate any records in the Contacts table that don't have matching records in the Interactions table.

The first thing you need to do is to follow the general procedure we discussed earlier to invoke a Query Wizard. Select the Find Unmatched Query Wizard, and then follow these steps:

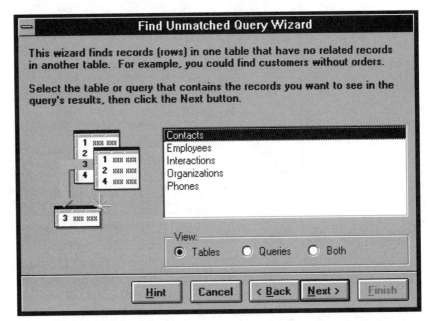

Figure 6-11: The initial Find Unmatched Query Wizard dialog box.

1. The first screen you see is shown in Figure 6-11. When you run the query, all of the data in the table or query you choose will be read. For each record that is read, the query will attempt to find any associated child table data.

   Select the table or query to use. The option buttons on the lower part of the dialog box tell the Query Wizard what to show in the list of entries to select from. You can see a list containing just the tables in the database by choosing the Tables button, just the queries in the database by choosing the Queries button, or both the tables and queries in the database by choosing the Both option button.

   In Figure 6-11, we have selected the Contacts table. We are looking for Contacts without Organizations, so the primary table is the Contacts table.

2. Once you have selected the table or query to examine, click the Next > button to move to the second dialog box (see Figure 6-12).

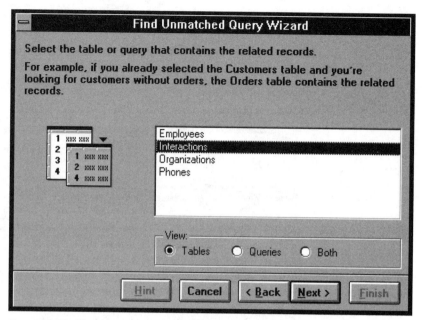

Figure 6-12: The second Find Unmatched Query Wizard dialog box.

3. This screen asks for the name of the table or query to use to locate the related data associated with the first table or query specified. The data in this table represents additional information relating to the data in the first table.

   Tell the Wizard what related table or query to use in the same manner as on the primary table selection screen. In Figure 6-12, we have selected the Interactions table.

4. Click the Next > button to move to the next dialog box (see Figure 6-13).

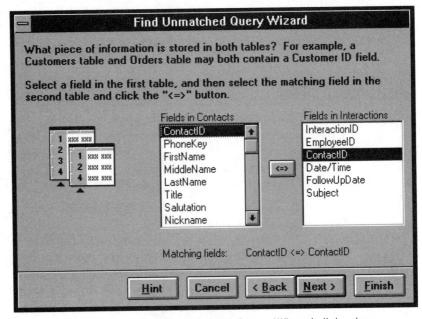

Figure 6-13: The third Find Unmatched Query Wizard dialog box.

5. In this screen the Wizard asks you what fields in each table contain the common data. To answer this question, highlight the entry in the list on the left containing the data that uniquely identifies each record. This is typically the primary key field. In Figure 6-13, we identify the ContactID field.

6. The list on the right, called Fields in Interactions in this example, shows the fields in the related table. Because this table contains data related to the first table, it includes a foreign key field containing the primary key value of a record in the first table. You want to highlight this foreign key field from the list on the right. In Figure 6-13, we identify the ContactIDfield.

   For a match to be found, the fields do not need to have the same name; they just need to contain the same value.

7. After you identify and highlight the fields in the two tables containing common data, you must tell the Wizard to "relate" the two lists. To relate the lists, press the <=> button.

8. Click the Next > button to move to the next dialog box (see Figure 6-14).

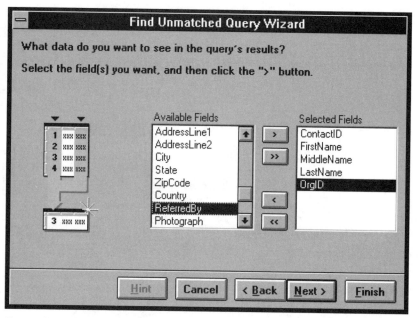

Figure 6-14: The fourth Find Unmatched Query Wizard dialog box.

9. This fourth screen asks you what data from the first table you want to see for unmatched records. When an unmatched record is found, you will want some of its data displayed in the dynaset. Move the fields you want displayed from the Available Fields list on the left to the Selected Fields list on the right. To move a field from the list on the left to the list on the right, highlight the desired field and click the > button. To select all fields, click the >> button. If you want to remove a field from the list on the right, highlight the field and click the < button. To remove all fields, click the << button. You may double-click the mouse pointer on a field in either list to move it to the other list.

10. Click the Next > button to move to the next and final screen (see Figure 6-15).

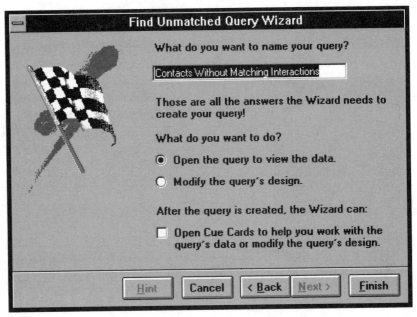

Figure 6-15: The final Find Unmatched Query Wizard dialog box.

11. This is the last screen in the Find Unmatched Query Wizard set. After this screen is completed, the query will be generated and optionally executed. There are just a couple of things the Wizard needs to know before it can complete its work. The first thing is what you want to call the query you are creating.

Enter the name in the text box under the "What do you want to name your query?" prompt. The name you enter must be unique within this database. No other table or query can have the same name. The query we've generated in the example is named Contacts Without Matching Interactions.

12. Your last step is to tell the Wizard what you want it to do after it completes the generation process. Select one of the options under the "What do you want to do?" prompt.

○ *Open the query to view the data*. Selecting this option tells the Wizard to generate the query, and when done, to run it.

○ *Modify the query's design*. Selecting this option tells the Wizard to generate the query, and when done, to open the query in Design view.

13. Of course, nothing happens until you choose the Finish button; this tells the Wizard you are done answering questions.

Figure 6-16 shows an example of the resulting dynaset generated when you run this query. You see a datasheet view containing the fields you selected for display. If all of the records in the first table have matching records in the second table, the datasheet is shown without any data.

ContactID	FirstName	MiddleName	LastName	OrgID
8	Alan		McConnell	2
9	Kevin	Richard	Wolf	18
10	David	Alan	Needham	11
13	Francis	P.	Jones	8
14	Rex	T.	Comfort	4
15	Roberta	M.	Sangster	10
16	Wynona	R.	Brown	14
23	Ireen	M.	Julliet	23
(Counter)				0

Select Query: Contacts Without Matching Interactions

Record: 1 of 8

Figure 6-16: Example results of a find unmatched query.

Creating a Crosstab Query

Crosstab queries are useful for getting a summary of data from a table. For example, suppose you want to see how each of your sales staff is performing on a monthly basis. A crosstab query can perform all of the tasks necessary to summarize the sales data and also display it by month. Crosstab data is often used as the source for graphs and printed reports.

When you execute a crosstab query, you are returned a set of records or rows. These records contain a summarization of the data in a table you specify. There is a single row created for the group of records containing a common value in the field you identify as the row header. In the example above, one row will be created per salesperson. Within each record, there is a field or column created containing a summary value for each group of records containing a common value in the field you identify as the column header. In the example above, one column will be created in each row for each month of sales.

Here is another example. Suppose you want to see how many interactions have occurred between a salesperson and his or her contacts. This data is stored in the Interactions table. You would like to see one row per salesperson. Within each row you'd want a column representing each contact interacted with, and in each column the number of interactions between this contact person and the salesperson this record represents. Figure 6-3 shows what the results of this query might look like.

Because a crosstab returns a summary of the data in a table, the data returned by a crosstab query cannot be changed by editing the resulting dynaset.

Creating a crosstab query is fairly straightforward. There are only a few questions you need to answer. Where is the data coming from? What are the fields that you want to use? And what do you want to know about the data?

The example we'll use in the following pages will give us a summary of the interactions our account executives have had. We will see the names of the people they recorded interactions with and the number of times they were contacted.

Note: Before trying this example, import the query named QryInteractionNames from the Vantana database.

First follow the general procedure we discussed earlier to invoke a Query Wizard. Select the Crosstab Query Wizard, and then follow these steps:

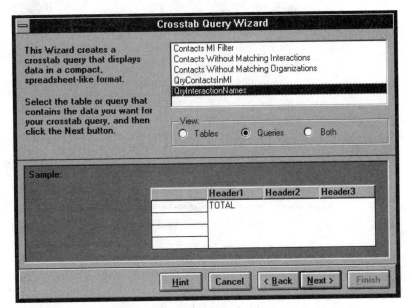

Figure 6-17: The initial Crosstab Query Wizard dialog box.

1. The first thing you must do is select the table or query containing the data to summarize. Highlight the entry in the list containing the name of the table or query you want used. The option buttons on the lower part of the dialog box tell the Wizard what to show in the list of entries to select from. You can see a list containing just the tables in the database by choosing the Tables button, just the queries in the database

by choosing the Queries button, or both the tables and queries in the database by choosing the Both option button.

In the example shown in Figure 6-17, we have selected the query called QryInteractionNames. We are going to create a crosstab query listing the number of interactions occurring between any two people on file. The query selected contains four fields: the interaction id, the date of the interaction, the contact name and the salesperson's name.

2. Click the Next > button to move to the second dialog box (see Figure 6-18).

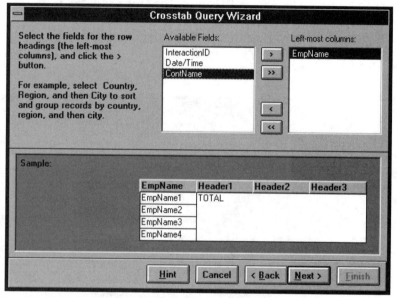

Figure 6-18: The second Crosstab Query Wizard dialog box.

3. The second dialog box in this Wizard asks the name of the field, or fields, containing the value you want to group together to create rows. These fields are called the row heading fields. The descriptive text on the Wizard screen calls this the "left-most column(s)"; that's because this data will be displayed in the first column of the datasheet. There will be one row created for each group of records containing common values in the fields you select on this screen.

You select fields to use as row headers by moving the field name from the Available Fields list on the left to the Left-most columns list on the right. To move a field from the list on the left to the list on the right, highlight the desired field and click the > button. To select all fields, click the >> button. If you want to remove a field from the list on the right, highlight the field and click the < button. To remove all fields, click the << button. You may double-click the mouse pointer on a field in either list to move it to the other list.

In the example, we'll get one row for each EmpName value. In other words, one row per salesperson.

4. Click the Next > button to move to the third dialog box (see Figure 6-19).

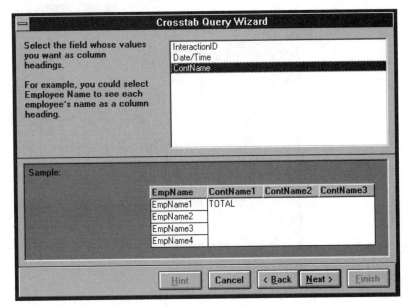

Figure 6-19: The third Crosstab Query Wizard dialog box.

5. This screen asks for the names of the fields you want to group together to create a column header. This works just like the row header except instead of creating a new row for each common value, a new column is created.

You select fields to use as column headers by highlighting the field in the list shown at the top of the screen. The sample shown on the lower portion of the screen is updated to show the field you select.

To identify the data presented, each column will be identified with a unique name. The name assigned to each column is the value contained in the fields selected as the column header fields.

In the example, we are going to get one column for each ContName value. In other words, one column per person contacted.

6. Click the Next > button to move to the fourth dialog box (see Figure 6-20).

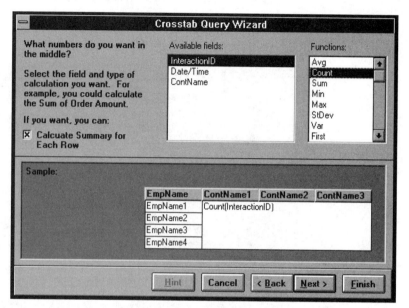

Figure 6-20: The fourth Crosstab Query Wizard dialog box.

7. On this screen the Wizard needs to know what you want to do with the data you've asked for. To answer the question you must select two things: a field to calculate, and the type of calculation to perform on the field you select.

The list on the left contains the names of the available fields from the table you are summarizing. The list on the right contains the functions that can operate on the selected field.

In the example shown in Figure 6-20, we are going to count the number of interactions occurring between people, so we highlight the InteractionID field and the Count function. The results of the calculation will be placed in the appropriate row and column.

8. There is one more item on this screen worth noting: the check box to the left of the Available fields list. Checking this box will generate an additional column in each row. This column will contain a value showing the results of the selected function performed on all of the columns in the row. In the example, we'll get a total count of all of the interactions for this row.

9. After you've identified the function and field, click the Next > button to move to the next and final screen (see Figure 6-21).

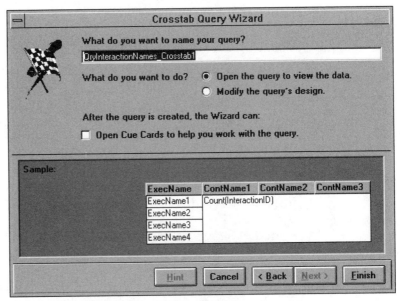

Figure 6-21: The final Crosstab Query Wizard dialog box.

10. As with all the other Wizards we've looked at in this chapter, you need to tell the Crosstab Wizard what to name the query it will generate, and how to proceed once the generation is completed. The query generated in this example will be called QryInteractionNames_Crosstab1.

11. After you have named the query and selected the option informing the Wizard how to proceed, you are done. Choose the Finish button to tell the Wizard to generate the query and proceed.

EmpName	RowSummary	Alan	Alfred	Bruce	Helen	Ileen	J_	Jane	Jody	I
Charlie Eager	6		1						2	
Samuel Pate	4			1	1	1				
Steven Bunch	6	1						1		
Timothy Alan	3						1			

Crosstab Query: QryInteractionNames_Crosstab1 — Record: 1 of 4

Figure 6-22: Example crosstab query results.

Figure 6-22 shows an example of the results of the crosstab query we just created. Notice, a row was created for each account

executive. In each row, a column was created for each person the
account executive contacted. The number of contacts made is
listed under each contact name, and the total number of contacts is
shown in the RowTotal column.

Creating an Archive Query

Archive queries copy data from one table to another. There are
many reasons why you might want to archive data. For example,
you might want to save a copy of historical data, such as the previous year's sales activity, in a separate table. Or you might want to
copy all of the data for a particular topic, such as all of the interactions for a specific salesperson, to a new table. Or you might want
to copy old data you don't use on a regular basis to a history table
and then delete it from the original table. The Archive Wizard will
help you create queries to perform these as well as many other
useful tasks.

In the following example we'll create an archive query to copy
the records from the Interactions table containing information
prior to May 1, 1994.

First, select Archive Query from the Query Wizards dialog box,
and then follow these steps:

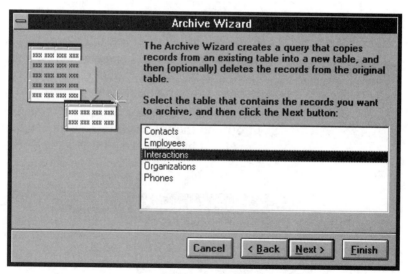

Figure 6-23: The initial Archive Wizard dialog box.

1. The first thing you must specify when creating an archive
   query is where you want to copy the data from.

   You'll notice a slight difference between this screen and the
   other initial Wizard screens. While the other Wizards allowed

operation on either tables or queries, an archive query only works with a table. The reason for this is that at the end of an archive query, the data that's been copied can be deleted, but there are certain types of queries where you won't be able to delete data. For example, a query that summarizes data cannot modify the original data. Because of the possibility of selecting a query returning non-modifiable data, the list contains only the tables available in the database.

To tell the Wizard the name of the table to use, highlight the correct name. We've selected the Interactions table in the example shown in Figure 6-23.

2. Click the Next > button to proceed to the second dialog box (see Figure 6-24).

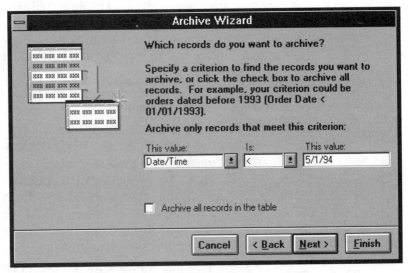

Figure 6-24: The second Archive Wizard dialog box.

3. In this screen the Wizard asks you which records you want to archive. To answer this question you need to create the criteria to be used to select records. Records in the table meeting the specified criteria will be written to the archive table.

This screen makes it easy to specify criteria by breaking the criteria statement into three parts: comparator, operator and comparison value. We'll discuss the three parts individually in the next three steps.

4. *This value:* In this first text box you select the *comparator*, the field in the table to be evaluated. When the query is run, the query will look at the value this field contains to determine if the record should be written to the archive table. In Figure 6-24,

we've identified the Date/Timefield as the field to look at to determine if a record should be archived.

5. *Is:* Here you specify the *operator*, which determines how the field is to be compared. The list of operators you may choose from consists of the common comparison operators along with the Like and Between operators.

○ *Like* is used to search the field for an occurrence of the comparison value. For example, if you were to enter the criteria "LastName Like Sm," any record containing a LastName beginning with *Sm* will be selected, such as Small, Smiley, Smith, Smithers, etc.

○ *Between* is used to locate ranges of values. When you use the Between operator, you will be prompted for two comparison values. (An additional comparison value text box will appear on the screen, identified by the word *And* appearing to its left.) The Between operator is inclusive; values equal to the start and end comparison values are included.

In Figure 6-24 we've selected the less than operator; we want to find records with dates before (or less than) a given date.

6. *This value:* In the rightmost text box you enter the *comparison value*, which is used in conjunction with the *Is* operator and the first *This value* entry (the comparator) to select records from the input table. This is the check value used to compare the input data. In Figure 6-24 we've entered the date 5/1/94: this value is used together with the operator to identify the records to be archived.

7. If you check the "Archive all records in the table" check box, the criteria statement is ignored. All the records in the specified table will be written to the archive table. In the example shown in Figure 6-24 we have left this check box blank; we want to see only those records that meet the defined criteria.

8. Once you have specified the three components to the criteria statement, you are ready to see the results of what you've done so far. Click the Next > button to proceed to the third dialog box (see Figure 6-25).

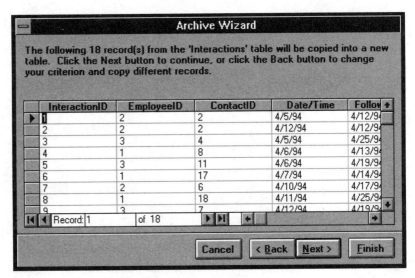

Figure 6-25: The third Archive Wizard dialog box.

9. This screen lists records meeting the criteria specified in the previous screen. This is a preview of the data that will be written to the archive table if you choose to proceed.

   Scroll through the list to determine if the data displayed is what you want archived. If the data displayed isn't what you want, you must go back to the selection criteria screen and change the specifications. In Figure 6-25 you see 18 records.

10. After you are satisfied with the record selection, click the Next > button to proceed to the next dialog box (see Figure 6-26).

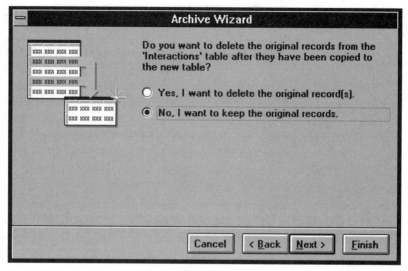

Figure 6-26: The fourth Archive Wizard dialog box.

11. This screen is where you tell the Wizard what you want done with the data in the original table. You may select one of the two options presented.

○ *Yes, I want to delete the original record(s)*. Select this option if you want to delete the original data. When you run the query the data will be copied to the archive table and deleted from the original table. This in effect moves the data to the archive table.

○ *No, I want to keep the original record(s)*. Select this option if you want the original data left in the original table. When you run the query the data is just copied to the archive table. This is the option chosen in the example in Figure 6-26.

12. After you decide what to do with the original data, you are just about done. Click the Next > button to proceed to the next and final screen in this Wizard (see Figure 6-27).

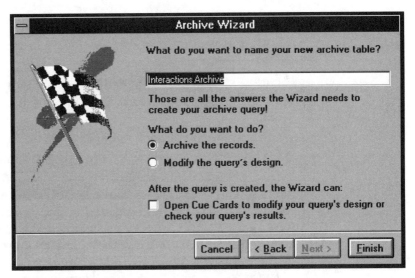

Figure 6-27: Archive Wizard completion screen.

13. All that's left to do is name the archive table and save your work. Enter a name for the archive table in the text box area at the top of the screen. This name must be unique; no two tables or queries can have the same name.

14. You also need to tell the Wizard what to do after it generates the query.

   ○ *Archive the records.* If you select this option, the query will be generated and executed.

   ○ *Modify the query's design.* If you select this option, the query will be generated and opened in design mode.

   In Figure 6-27 we've selected the first option, Archive the records.

15. Click the Finish button to generate the query. If you have chosen to run the query, Access displays a message asking whether you want to copy the records into the archive table. Choose the Yes button to complete the archive operation.

Each time an archive query is run, the records meeting the criteria are added to the table you specified in the Archive Wizard completion screen (see Figure 6-27). The selected records are deleted from the original table depending upon your choice of options on the record disposition screen (see Figure 6-26). The only way you can actually see the results of an archive query is to look at the tables. The archive table will contain the recently added records, and the records in the original table will be deleted, if you choose the appropriate option.

MOVING ON

The Wizards we just looked at will help you create a few types of queries. We saw that

○ Find Duplicates queries help you locate redundant data.

○ Find Unmatched queries help you locate records missing related data.

○ Crosstab queries summarize data.

○ Archive queries save old data to separate tables.

Once you get comfortable with one type of Query Wizard the others should be fairly easy to use. After you use a Wizard to create a query, you never have to create that query again. At the completion of each Wizard, a query was generated and saved with the name you specified. To execute the task again you simply locate the query in the Database window and run it.

There will be times when your application will require a query not supported by the Wizards. In the next chapter we will take a look at some of the other types of queries you can create.

7 MASTERING QUERIES

In this chapter, we'll discuss how to build your own queries. In the previous chapter, we looked at how to use the built-in Query Wizards to create some very powerful queries. There are times when you'll need to either change a generated query or create a query the Wizard doesn't handle. The basic concept of queries and dynasets are discussed in Chapter 6, "Creating Queries on the Fly." As we discussed in that chapter, there are three types of queries: *select queries*, *crosstab queries* and *action queries*. In this chapter, we'll look at how to create each of these types of queries.

UNDERSTANDING QUERY TYPES

Each of the following types of queries performs a particular action on one or more tables or queries. The queries work on a set of records in the targeted tables or queries. The set of records is determined by the tables identified when creating the query and by comparing the records in the tables to the selection criteria you specify:

○ *Select Queries*. You use a select query when you want to look at, and possibly change, the data in your database. Select queries are very flexible. You can look at any part of the data in one table, or in several tables at once, and have the data presented in a sorted order. A select query can even summarize data. For example, using the example application on the companion disk, you could use a select query to get a list of organizations you haven't heard from in the last six months.

Select queries return a set of records called a *dynaset*. In many cases the dynaset is a modifiable set of records. Any changes you make to the data in the dynaset are written to the tables where the data was found. A dynaset is not modifiable if the data it contains represents a summary of the data in the tables.

○ *Crosstab Queries*. Crosstab queries are a specialized type of select query. A crosstab query presents data in a table in a highly summarized form. For example, you could use a crosstab query to summarize the interactions data to show how many interactions each account executive had with his or her customers.

Each group of records containing similar data is used to create either a row or column of data. The tasks performed by a crosstab query are quite difficult to do without the power of the query language. The data returned by a crosstab query is not modifiable.

○ *Action Queries.* Action queries have many uses. Action queries, unlike select queries, don't return a dynaset. Instead, they work with the data in the tables directly. Because of this difference, you must look at the table the query manipulates to see the results. Using an action query to perform a task greatly reduces the amount of work you, as an application developer, must do to get a job done.

There are four types of action queries:

○ A *make table query* can be used any time you need to copy data from one table into another. For example, a make table query would be helpful when you need to make a backup copy of a table prior to changing the data contained in that table. When you run a make table query, it creates a new table and copies the data you specify into the new table. If the table you tell the query to copy to exists prior to running the query, you will be prompted whether or not to delete and re-create it.

○ An *append query* is similar to a make table query in that it copies data from one table to another. The append query differs from the make table query in that the table you are copying data to must exist. With an append query, you are adding data to a table. For example, you might use an append query to merge tables from multiple locations for year-end processing.

○ An *update query* is useful when you want to modify the contents of a table. Update queries can make changes to several records simultaneously. For example, if you were writing a payroll application, you might use an update query to change the salaries of people in a particular division.

○ You can use a *delete query* to remove records that meet a particular set of criteria you specify. For example, you could use a delete query to delete any record for an interaction that occurred more than three years ago.

The programming code underlying the queries in Access is a language called *Structured Query Language (SQL)*. SQL is a database query language supported on a wide variety of computer platforms, from personal computers to large mainframe computers. We won't go into the details of SQL here; there are, however, complete texts available on this subject.

By using SQL as the query language, Access can communicate with other computers and retrieve the data you need. Like any language, SQL has its own local dialects. The syntax of Access SQL isn't the same as that on some other computer platforms. You don't need to worry about that right now, however. As long as you can Attach to a table (see Chapter 3), you can use a query to retrieve its data.

Before you can create any type of query, you need to understand its tools. The main tool you'll be using is the Query window in Design view (see Figure 7-1). This window is divided into two major parts. The top portion of the window shows the field lists where the data is coming from in this query. The lower portion of the window shows the fields you want to use in this query.

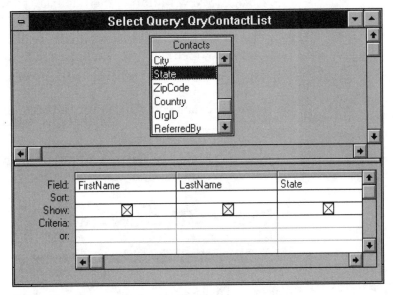

Figure 7-1: Query window in Design view.

The Query window is a graphical tool. You *draw* the design of the query in this window. Once you draw the picture of the query you want, you're done. Access interprets the images you place in the window and creates the programming code to execute the query.

CREATING A NEW QUERY

The following procedure walks you through the process of creating a query without the assistance of a Query Wizard. The queries generated by the Wizards supplied with Access 2.0 perform specific tasks. If you need to perform one of the tasks supported by a Wizard, you can save yourself time by generating your query with the appropriate Wizard. For this discussion, we'll create our own query for a task not supported by a Wizard.

There are a few steps common to creating any type of query. Let's walk through these steps one at a time.

1. Open the database where you want to create your query.

2. Click the Query button on the Database window to see a list of the queries defined in the database. Remember, queries are database objects.

3. Click the New button in the Database window to begin creating a new query.

4. The New Query dialog box appears. Click the New Query button to open the Query window in Design view.

5. You need to identify where the data you are going to use is stored. A Query can look at either tables or other queries to locate the data you want to use. Figure 7-2 shows the Add Table dialog box that appears when you start creating a new query. In this dialog box, you identify the tables and/or queries containing the data you want to use in the query. We have selected the Contacts table in Figure 7-2.

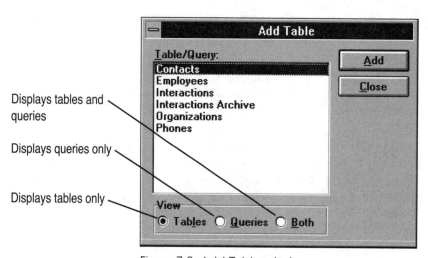

Figure 7-2: Add Table window.

The Table/Query list box lists the available tables and/or queries. The contents of the Table/Query list box are determined by the option you choose in the View option group. You can only select one of the three options at a time. Selecting the Table option lists the Tables in the database. Selecting the Queries option lists the Queries in the database. Selecting the Both option lists both the Tables and Queries in the database.

To add a table or query, highlight the entry you want to use, and either click the Add button or double-click on the name with the left mouse button. Once you've identified all of the tables and queries you need, you're done with the Add Table window. Click the Close button to remove this window.

6. Once you've added the tables you want to use in the query, you need to define the relationships they have to one another. For now, we will limit our discussion to queries involving one table. We will discuss the process of defining the relationships between tables later in this chapter.

7. Once you identify what tables and/or queries to use, you need to select the fields to include in the query. The lower portion of the Query design window shows a grid containing the fields used in the query. These fields can come from the tables/queries in the top portion of the window. Or you can create new fields by defining calculated fields. Calculated fields display the results of *expressions*. We will discuss calculated fields and expressions in more detail later in this chapter.

There are several ways to select the fields you want to use in the query.

○ *Drag and drop* fields from the Table lists in the top portion of the window into empty columns in the field grid.

○ *Double-click* on a field name in the top half of the design window.

○ *Select a field from the drop-down list* in the field row of an empty grid column.

8. After you finish defining the query, you need to save it so that you can use it again. To save the query, either click the Save button on the toolbar, or choose File, Save from the menu bar. Access displays the Save As dialog box. Type a name for the query and choose the OK button.

Run

9. To run the query and display the resulting dynaset, either click the Run button in the toolbar, or choose Query, Run from the menu bar. Access runs the query and displays the dynaset in Datasheet view.

Design View

10. If you want to return to Design view in order to modify the query, either click the Design View button in the toolbar, or choose Query, Design view from the menu bar.

11. When you are finished using the query, double-click the Control-menu box. Access closes the Query window and returns to the Database window (see steps 8–11).

Now that you know the basics of how to use the design window, it's time we talked about what you want the query to do. We'll begin our discussion with select queries. They are the most common type of query. By understanding how they are created, we'll lay a good foundation to build upon.

USING SELECT QUERIES TO RETRIEVE DATA

There are many tasks you can perform with a select query. The most common use is to retrieve some or all of the data from a table. However, there are many instances when you'll need just one or two fields from a table. Or, you might want data spread over several tables to give a complete picture of a subject. Or, maybe you just want to see the records containing information about a particular activity. You can perform these tasks very easily with a select query.

For example, suppose you want a list of the contacts you have on file. You can create a select query to give you the information you want, presented in a manner most helpful to you. Figure 7-3 shows what the completed design of this query looks like. Figure 7-4 shows the dynaset that results when you run this query.

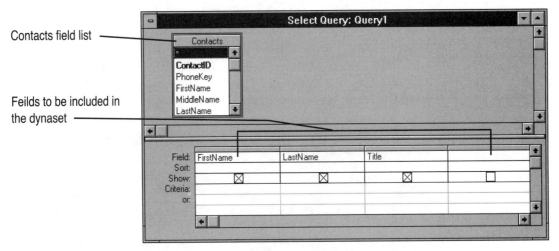

Contacts field list

Feilds to be included in the dynaset

Figure 7-3: Example select query design.

Figure 7-4: The dynaset that results from running the query in Figure 7-3.

Create this query and save it as Contact List.

Selecting Records Using Simple Criteria

You won't always want all the records from a table included in the dynaset. You can limit the records to be included by entering a comparison value in the field grid. Figure 7-5 shows a query with selection criteria specified. In the QBE grid, you see the Criteria row. The Criteria row is where you enter the comparison values you are attempting to locate in the table. The value you type is what the query will look for when you run the query. The query, in turn, looks for the value you enter in the field matching the column where you typed the value. The dynaset contains only the records with the value you entered.

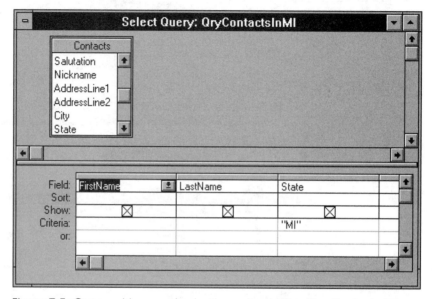

Figure 7-5: Query with record selection criteria. The Qry Contacts MI.

Entering selection criteria is very straightforward; there are only two steps.

1. Locate the column in the field grid containing the field you want to use.

2. Enter the value you want to find. For example, the QryContactsMI query, shown in Figure 7-5 contains the value "MI" in the State field. This criteria limits the data returned to MI (Michigan) data (see Figure 7-5). Figure 7-6 shows the dynaset that results from running this query.

Select Query: QryContactsInMI		
FirstName	**LastName**	**State**
Jody	Needham	MI
Alan	McConnell	MI
J.	Wolf	MI
Bruce	Richards	MI
Kevin	Wolf	MI
Francis	Jones	MI
Rex	Comfort	MI
Helen	Harrison	MI

Record: 1   of 8

Figure 7-6: The dynaset that results from running the query shown in Figure 7-5.

Values of this type are called *literals*. The data is compared to the exact value you enter. You must enter one of three types of literals, depending upon the data type of the field you are comparing.

○ A *string literal* is used for Text and Memo and Yes/No data type fields.

○ A *date literal* is used for Date/Time data type fields.

○ A *number literal* is used for Number, Currency, Counter and Yes/No data type fields.

If the field you are comparing is a Text, Memo or Yes/No type field, the query uses a string literal as a comparison value. You create a string literal by enclosing the value you enter in the Criteria row in quotation marks. The query design tool places quotation marks around literals not containing spaces. You must supply the quotation marks if the literal contains spaces.

If you are comparing a Yes/No type field, you can search for the string literals "Yes", "No", "On", "Off", "True" or "False".

If the field you are comparing to is a Date/Time type field, the query expects to see a date literal. Date literals are similar to string literals, except they are enclosed in pound signs (#). The query design tool adds pound signs if you enter a valid date literal. Date literals are displayed in the MM/DD/YY format.

If the field you are comparing to is a Number, Currency, Counter or Yes/No type field, the query uses a number literal as a comparison value. You create a number literal by entering a number value. Number literals are not enclosed in quotation marks or pound signs. If you are comparing a Yes/No type field, you can search for a number literal zero (0) for No or negative one (-1) for Yes.

Looking for an exact numerical value in a field limits the data returned to a very specific set of records. At times, you will want to find records containing the exact number you enter. In many cases, you will want to use the number literal entered along with a *comparison operator*. Comparison operators modify the criteria to act as a base value. The comparison operator tells the query what to look for compared to the base.

(**Note**: Before trying the next example, import the All Employees table from the Ventana database. This table lists all employees in the company.)

Suppose you want to locate the employee records in the All Employees table for all employees whose salary is more than $40,000. If you enter the number **40000** in the Criteria row in the Salary column, in the QBE grid, the query will retrieve the records for employees earning exactly $40,000. To see the records of employees whose salary is greater than $40,000, add the greater than operator (>) to the citeria. The criteria should be >40000, as in the QryEmployeesSalaries query shown in Figure 7-7. Figure 7-8 shows the dynaset that results.

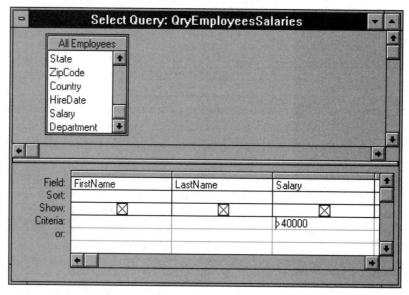

Figure 7-7: The QryEmployeesSalaries query.

Select Query: QryEmployeesSalaries		
FirstName	**LastName**	**Salary**
Samuel	Pate	$45,900.00
Samantha	Jones	$78,936.00
Tim	Bronson	$43,056.00
Steven	Harrison	$44,616.00
Stanley	Harrell	$51,558.00
Hercule	Plum	$44,887.50
George	Green	$51,312.56
Angel	Smith	$46,280.00
Christopher	Harvey	$44,935.00
Joseph	Quick	$55,120.00

Record: 1   of 10

Figure 7-8: The QryEmployeesSalaries dynaset.

Using Expressions in Queries

You use *expressions* when a simple value won't give you the data you're looking for. A single literal value is an expression. For our use here, to differentiate between simple literal values and more complex criteria, we will define the term expressions as follows. An expression is a comparison value used in conjunction with one or more *operators*. An operator is a symbol or word you enter that performs an action or somehow modifies a value. There are several types of operators we can use when we create a criteria expression.

- ○ *Comparison* operators use the value entered as a base value; the comparison operators tell how the data is to be compared to the base value.
- ○ The *Like* string operator performs pattern matching.
- ○ The *Between...And* operator returns records containing data within a range of values.
- ○ The *In* operator checks for data matching a list of supplied values.
- ○ The *Is* operator is used together with the *Null* keyword to locate fields that contain no data.

  Let's take a look at these operators in more detail.

Comparison

You use comparison operators when you want to compare the data in a field to a value. The following table lists the comparison operators and their meaning.

Operator	Meaning
=	Equal
>	Greater than
<	Less than
<>	Not equal
>=	Greater than or equal
<=	Less than or equal

Creating an expression using a comparison operator is easy. Enter the comparison operator and then enter the value to compare. For example, the expression "> 40000" will be true if the data in the table is greater than one thousand (see Figures 7-7 and 7-8).

Like

The Like operator checks fields for data matching a pattern you supply. The pattern can be a literal value, as we have been discussing, or, you can use wildcard characters to represent a range of values. Wildcard characters represent one or more characters of data in a field. The table below lists the wildcards available.

Wildcard	Description
?	The *question mark wildcard* represents a single character of any type in the position entered. This works just like the DOS question mark wildcard. For example, the pattern "?BC" is interpreted as any character in the first position, followed by the letters "B" and "C" in the second and third positions.
*	The *asterisk wildcard* represents any number of characters in the position. This works just like the DOS asterisk wildcard. For example, the pattern "*Inc." is interpreted as any number of characters with an "Inc.".
#	The *pound sign wildcard* represents a number in the position entered. For example, the pattern "#*" is interpreted as any number in the first position, followed by any number of any characters.
[charlist]	The *square brackets wildcard* is used to represent a list of valid characters in the position entered. You can enter a series of ANSI characters separated with commas, or a range of ANSI characters separated with a hyphen between the high and low values. For example, the pattern "[A-F]*" is interpreted as the letters A through F in the first position, followed by any number of any characters.

| [!charlist] | The *exclamation mark wildcard* in the charlist represents a list of characters *not* in the position entered. |
| | For example, the patterns "[!A-F]*" is interpreted as not the letters A through F in the first position, followed by any number of any characters. |

Using the Like operator gives you a way to create very sophisticated selection criteria. An important thing to keep in mind is that while the Like operator is very flexible, it also has an effect on the performance of the query. Because of the work done in processing the Like operator, queries using it run slower than those without. In many cases, it is more efficient, from an execution performance standpoint, to use a series of criteria together to perform the function of a Like operator. For more on this, see "Multiple Selection Criteria" later in this chapter.

Between...And

You can locate records containing data between two values with the Between...And operator. The Between...And operator identifies starting and ending values to act as high and low water marks. Any data equal to or between these values is accepted. The values can be entered in any order you prefer, low then high or high then low. This is useful when comparing negative numbers. For example, you can enter the values as Zero (0) and Negative one hundred (-100) or vice versa.

You're not limited to using the Between...And operator on number type data.

Figure 7-9 shows the QryInteractionsByDate query, which is an example of how you create an expression using the Between...And operator. In the example shown, the dynaset contains records for the first five months of 1994. To retrieve those records, we look for dates between 4/3/94 and 4/9/94. Remember, the Between...And operator is inclusive; that is, it includes records with values equal to the values specified. Figure 7-10 shows the dynaset that results from the query.

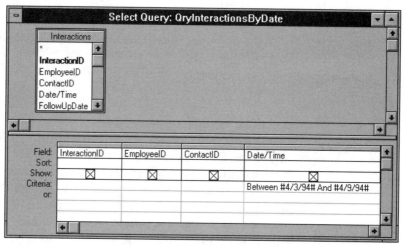

Figure 7-9: The QryInteractionsByDate query.

Figure 7-10: The QryInteractionsByDate dynaset.

In

The In operator is easy to understand if you read it as "Look for values In the list." You use the In operator to check a list of values you supply for matching data. The list must contain literal values separated with commas.

You enter the values to use with the In operators in a slightly different manner than with the other operators. To use the In operator, type the word **In** immediately followed by an open parenthesis. Next, enter the list of values you want to check for as described earlier in the chapter. Enter a comma between each value in the list. To finish the list, enter a close parenthesis. The list of values must be literal values. Pattern matching is not available from within the In operator.

Figure 7-11 shows an example of an In operator expression. In this example, we're looking for contacts in California, North Carolina, Michigan or Hawaii. Figure 7-12 shows the resulting dynaset.

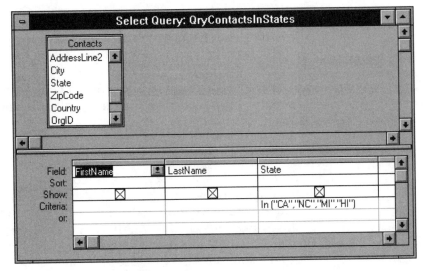

Figure 7-11: The QryContacsInStates query.

Figure 7-12: The QryContactsInStates query.

The In operator is useful for creating lists of values to compare. However, they become difficult to manage when you enter a large number of values. They are also inefficient performers when they get too large. If you have a large list of comparison values, you might consider creating another table to store the possible values. As we will see later in this chapter, you can retrieve records in one table based upon the values in records in another table.

Is

The Is operator is used with the Null keyword to check for fields that contain no data. Null is not the same as spaces or zero. It implies that the field contains no value at all. You can also use the Is operator with the *Not* operator to check for a field that doesn't contain specified data. For example, "Is Not Null" checks for a field that is not empty.

Multiple Selection Criteria

At times, you will need to look at more than one field to determine if a record should be selected. To do this, enter an expression in more than one column in the field grid. When you run a query, all the expressions entered will be used to select records. How the query combines the criteria entered is determined by where you enter them.

When you enter more than one criteria expression on the same criteria row, they will be used together to select a record. For a record to be selected, it must match all of the criteria in the row. Figures 7-13 and 7-14 show a query using multiple selection criteria in the same row. Only records containing "MI" in the State field and "Business" in the OrgType field are selected.

Chapter 7: Mastering Queries

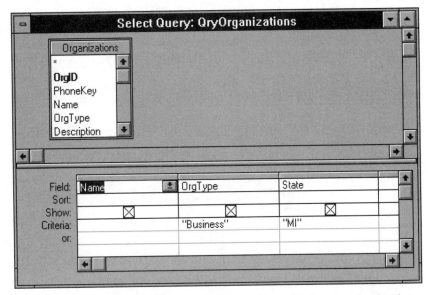

Figure 7-13: The QryOrganizations query with multiple record selection criteria on same line.

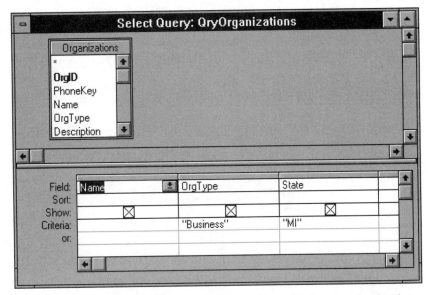

Figure 7-14: The dynaset resulting from the query in Figure 7-13.

When you place the criteria in different rows, the records selected will match one criteria *Or* the other. This gives you the ability to look for records meeting one set of criteria or another. When you run the query, records in the table are compared to each row of the selection criteria. If a record matches all the criteria in any row, it is included on the dynaset. Figures 7-15 and 7-16 show a query using multiple selection criterion in different rows. In this example, records containing "MI" in the State field or records containing "NC" in the State field are be selected.

211

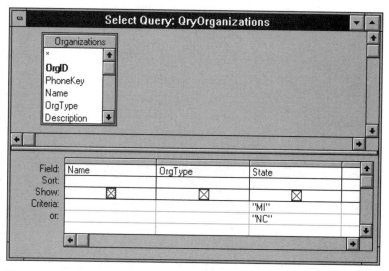

Figure 7-15: The QryOrganizations query with multiple record selection criteria on different lines.

Name	OrgType	State
Pacific Rim Widget	Business	MI
Poplar Electric	Business	MI
Applied Technolog	Professional	MI
Zorba's Fine Food	Business	Mi
CompuWorks, Inc.	Consultant	MI
Michigan Athletic C	Social	MI
Eastern Enterprises	Professinal	MI
Alpha Freight Lines	Business	MI
WRB Consulting	Consultant	NC
Tyson Plumbing	Business	MI

Record: 1 of 10

Figure 7-16: The dynaset resulting from the query in Figure 7-15.

When you want each criteria row to check for the same criteria, you must enter the criteria expression in each row. For example, suppose you want to locate records for businesses in Michigan or Virginia. Using the Or row is one way to find these records. Figures 7-17 and 7-18 show an example of how you might construct this query. Notice the selection criteria for OrgType is repeated in each criteria row.

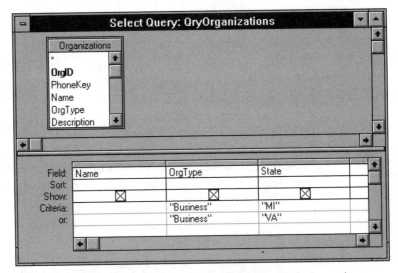

Figure 7-17: Query with redundant selection criteria in each row.

Figure 7-18: The dynaset resulting from the query in Figure 7-17.

Take time to test the query when you are using multiple selection criteria. Keep in mind the few simple guidelines we've discussed here and you'll be on your way to developing queries like a pro.

Creating Parameter Queries

In all the criteria we've created so far, we've entered the value to look for explicitly. This restricts the flexibility of the query quite a bit. Wouldn't it be more flexible if you let the user enter a value to look for when the query is run? Allowing the user to enter the value to compare to when they run the query makes the application easier to use. And, it reduces the work you must perform. You'll only have to create one query to check for multiple values instead of creating a separate query for each value. A query that allows the user to enter the value to search for is called a *parameter query*. A parameter query accepts a value to use as selection criteria when it is run.

You create a parameter query the same way you do a select query. Instead of entering a value to search for, you enter a phrase within square brackets ([ ]). Figure 7-19 shows how a parameter is entered into the criteria row. When you run the query, a window appears prompting the user for input. The phrase you entered between the square brackets is displayed in the input window. Figure 7-20 shows the input window you see when this query is executed.

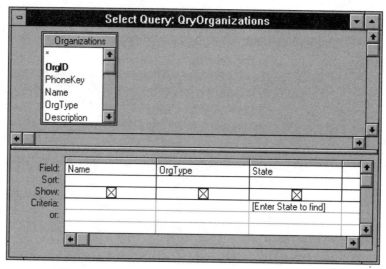

Figure 7-19: Example parameter criteria.

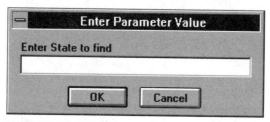

Figure 7-20: Enter Parameter Value dialog box.

When the query is run, the records are compared to the value the user enters.

Calculated Fields

So far, all the data displayed in the dynaset represent fields as they appear in the input tables. However, suppose you want to manipulate the data before it is displayed. In a spreadsheet application, you would use a formula to accomplish this task. In Access, this type of field is called a *calculated field*.

Calculated fields display the results of an expression as a field in the dynaset. There are two parts to a calculated field.

1. The *name* of the field you are creating.

2. The *expression* used to calculate the value placed in the field.

There are two steps you must follow to create a calculated field.

1. Enter a name that identifies the field, followed by a colon (:). The name must be unique: it cannot be the same as any field in the query.

2. Enter the expression to execute. When you run the query, the results of the expression will be placed in the field.

Figures 7-21 and 7-22 show a calculated field. The name of the field is "FullName." It contains the FirstName data, a space and the LastName data from the table. The ampersand character (&) is used to combine text values. To add a space between the names, we inserted a string literal containing a space between the field names. Notice we entered the field names in square brackets. Access performs more efficiently if we enter names this way.

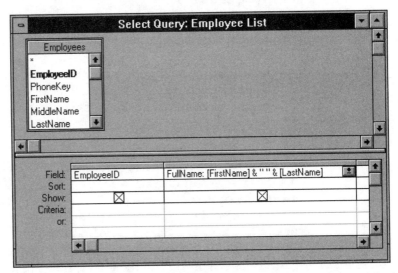

Figure 7-21: The employee List query containing the FullName calculated field.

□	Select Query: Employee	▼	▲
	EmployeeID	FullName	
▶	1	Samuel Pate	
	2	Charlie Eager	
	3	Timothy Alan	
	4	Steven Bunch	
*	(Counter)		
|◄ ◄	Record: 1	of 4	

Figure 7-22: The dynaset that results from the query in Figure 7-21.

The expressions used in calculated fields can get more complicated than the expressions we used as selection criteria. Calculated field expressions can use *mathematical operators* as well as many of the functions built into Access. Here's a list of the mathematical operators:

Operator	Meaning
+	Addition
-	Subtraction
*	Multiplication
\	Integer division
/	Floating-point division
^	Exponentiation
Mod	Modulo (Remainder)

Notice there are two division operators, each performing its own type of division.

○ The *floating-point division operator* divides the operands and returns the results as a floating-point number, a number including decimal value.

○ The *integer division operator* returns the integer portion of dividing one integer by another. This operator converts either operand to an integer prior to executing the operation.

Sorting Data

You can sort the data in the dynaset by identifying the fields you want to use as sort criteria. You can sort up to 10 fields in either ascending or descending sequence. You identify the fields to sort by selecting either Ascending or Descending in the Sort row of the field grid.

In Figure 7-13, the output data will be sorted by FirstName and LastName. When you run the query, the data meeting the selection criteria is selected; this data is then sorted into the order you specify. If you specify a sort on more than one field, the leftmost field is processed first.

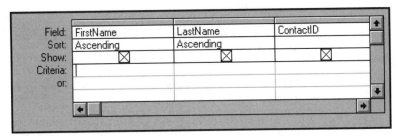

Figure 7-23: Select query with sort.

Creating Queries That Include Data From Multiple Tables

At times, you may need to include data from more than one table in your query. When your query contains more than one table, you must tell the query how the tables are related to one another. This relationship is called a *join condition.* You join tables by identifying the fields containing common values. These fields are typically the primary and foreign key values in the tables. See Chapters 2 and 3 for a complete discussion of key values and relationships.

Figure 7-24 shows a query using two tables. Notice the line between the tables. This line is called the *join line*. The join line represents the relationship between the tables.

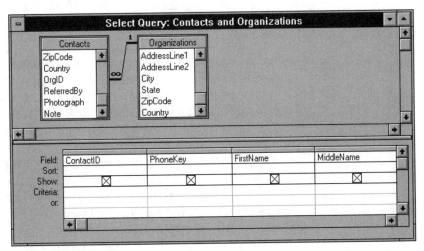

Figure 7-24: The Contacts and Organizations query with joined tables.

To add an additional table to your query, click on the Add Tables button on the toolbar. This is the same dialog box you get when you initially create a query (see Figure 7-2). Choose the tables and/or queries you want to add to the query design in the same manner described earlier in the chapter.

In "Defining Table Relationships," in Chapter 3, we discussed how to define the relationship between tables. You will see a visual indication of the relationships created with a *join line* between the table field lists. If you haven't defined the table relationships, you will have to join them manually. Joining tables is a simple procedure.

1. Identify the fields in the tables containing common values.
2. Drag the field name from one table and drop on the common field in the other table.

A join line appears between the tables, once you drop the field on the second table.

Once you have added and joined all the tables containing the data you need, you can select fields from any of them.

There are three types of joins you can create in a query.

○ Equi-joins

○ Outer joins

○ Self-joins

Let's look at each of these types of joins. The type of join used determines the records returned from *both* tables. Changing the type of join between tables can have a significant effect on what records are retrieved.

Equi-joins

The default type of join created when you drag and drop a field is called an *equi-join*. Equi comes from the word equal. An equi-join looks for records containing the same (equal) value in both tables. This type of join is used when you want to retrieve data *only when matching data is found* in both tables. If data exists in one table and no records are found with a matching value in the joined field, no records are retrieved from either table.

For example, suppose you want to get a list of all the organizations you have on file along with the contact person. Furthermore, you have decided you don't want to see any organizations you don't have a contact on file for. The query design shown in Figure 7-24 gives you just what you are looking for.

Figure 7-25 shows the Join Properties dialog box. This is where you specify the type of join to use. To get to this box, double-click on the join line between two tables. Option 1 in the Join Properties dialog box describes an equi-join condition.

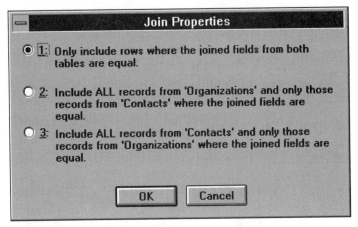

Figure 7-25: Query Join Properties dialog box.

Outer Join

An *outer join* retrieves *all* the records from one table *and* records containing matching data in the other table. There are two types of outer joins. Options 2 and 3 in the Join Properties dialog box, shown in Figure 7-25, describe the two possible outer join conditions. As you can see, option 2 retrieves *all* the records from one table, whereas option 3 retrieves *all* the records for the other. Select the option that describes the way you want data retrieved from the tables. Remember, an outer join gives you all of the records from one table, and any matching records from the other.

Again, suppose you wanted to look at information about *all* the records on file for organizations *along with* any associated contact information. If you use an equi-join condition, option 1 in the Join Properties dialog box, you won't see any information for organizations who don't have associated contact records. Remember, an equi-join retrieves records with matching data in both tables. If you use an outer join, you get the data you expected. Select the option that says "Include ALL records from 'Organizations' and only those from 'Contacts' where the joined fields are equal." The key to look for is the phrase "ALL records from 'Organizations'." In the dialog box shown in Figure 7-25, that is option 2. The dynaset may contain some records showing just the data from the Organizations table, and some records containing data from both tables.

Self-join

A *self-join* joins a table to itself. But why in the world would you want to do that? To locate records in the same table containing related data.

For example, suppose some of the organizations in your database have parent organizations. If you had a field in the Organization table containing the key value of the parent organizations, you could look up the parent data by relating the table to itself. To create a self-join, you must include the table twice in the table list. Figure 7-26 shows what a self-join looks like in the Query design window. Notice, the table name in the second list has a "_1" appended. This is necessary to identify which occurrence of the table was used in the field grid.

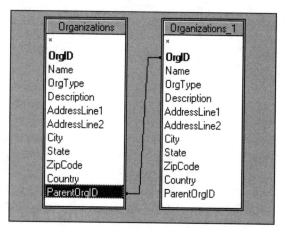

Figure 7-26: Example query design showing a self-join.

USING QUERIES TO APPEND DATA

When you want to add data from one table to another, use an *append query*. An append query copies data from one or more *source* tables into another table. The table where the data is being copied is called the *target* table. An append query cannot create a new table; it can only copy data into an existing table. The target table must exist prior to running an append query or the query will fail to execute. If you want to copy data to a new table, you must use a make table query.

There are many uses for append queries. Suppose your company has locations throughout the world. Each location is using a copy of the same Access application you created. The president of your company comes up to you one day and asks to see a report showing the activity from all the offices. "No problem," you say, except of course the president probably wants to see it in 15 minutes! You get a copy of the database containing your applications data from all the offices by having them run an archive query. They send you a copy of the table containing the data you need. You run an append query to copy the data from the copy they sent into a central table, and you now have a single table containing data from all the offices to run your report against.

To create an append query, click the append query button on the Query design toolbar. Then, follow the procedure listed below.

Append Query

1. Identify the source table(s).

2. Identify the target table.

3. Select the fields to copy.

4. Enter any necessary selection criteria, including parameters and sorts required.

5. Save and name the query

The only difference between an append query and a select query is that you must specify the name of the target table. Figure 7-27 shows the Append To box in the Query Properties dialog box where you enter the name of the target table. The table you append the data to must exist. However, it doesn't have to be in the same database as the append query. If you want to write the data to a table in another database, click the Another Database option button and enter the name of the database in the File Name text box. If the database name you enter is not in the same subdirectory as the database containing the query, you must enter the pathname as well as the database name.

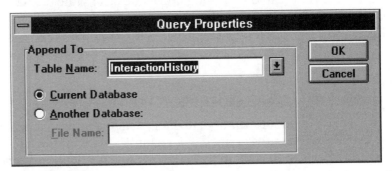

Figure 7-27: Query Properties dialog box with an example Append To query dialog box.

USING QUERIES TO CREATE A TABLE

When you want to copy data into a new table, you can use a make table query. In Chapter 6, "Creating Queries on the Fly," we discussed the Archive Wizard. The query generated by the Archive Wizard is a make table query.

Make table queries are often used when you want to save a copy of data at a given point in time. For example, the interactions that have taken place with a particular business within the last six months.

Using a make table query as the basis for your reports can actually improve the performance of your application. When you're going to run several reports using the same data, usually it is faster to first run a make table query and have the reports use the table created.

On a more advanced level, you can significantly improve the performance of many applications that use tables attached from an SQL database server with make table queries. Many times there are tables that contain data that doesn't change very often. For example, a table containing a list of your company's remote offices. For most companies, this list is not subject to change on a daily basis. If the table containing this information is stored on a SQL database server, you could periodically run a make table query to retrieve this data, rather than requesting it every time you want to use it. Your application will run more efficiently, because it doesn't have to contend with all the other applications using the same SQL database.

When you run a make table query, the retrieved data will be written to a new table with the name you specify. If a table with the same name already exists, it will be deleted and a new table created with the same name. The same dialog box is used to enter the name as the append query.

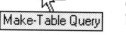
Make-Table Query

You create a make table query the same way as the append query we just discussed. Click the make table query design toolbar button.

USING QUERIES TO UPDATE TABLES

You use an update query when you want to change data in several records at once. For example, many of the large metropolitan areas of the country are receiving new telephone area codes. An update query can simplify the task of changing the phone records to reflect the new area code. You can look up each customer and change the area code manually. Or, you can write an update query to locate all the records that need to be changed and change them in a single step.

Update Query

Update queries can only change data in existing records; they can't add or delete records. Remember, action queries change the data stored in the tables directly. It's a good idea to make a backup of the data you're going to change before you run an update query. A make table query is an excellent way of backing up the data to be changed. Click on the update query design toolbar button to identify the query you are creating as an update query.

In the example shown in Figure 7-28, we are giving all our employees a 10% pay raise. This query changes the value stored in the Salary field, updating the value stored in each record to the current value times 1.1 (a 10%) increase.

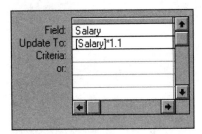

Figure 7-28: Example update query design.

The Update To row is where you enter the expression that determines what is written in the field being changed.

Fields are only included in the field grid of an update query for one of two reasons.

1. The value the fields contain is being changed in the record.

2. They are being used as record selection criteria.

USING QUERIES TO DELETE DATA

Delete Query

When you want to delete a set of records containing specific data, you can use a delete query. Delete queries are great for removing groups of records from a table. A delete query removes records, not data stored in individual fields. An update query can be used to clear the contents of a field.

For example, suppose you want to remove any record pertaining to an interaction with a client that occurred prior to 1992. Figure 7-29 shows what the design of this query would look like.

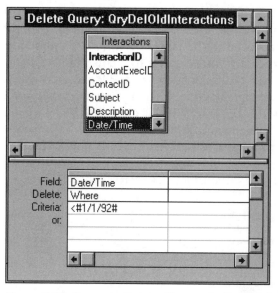

Figure 7-29: Example Delete Query design field grid.

When you create a delete query, the only fields you need to include in the QBE grid are those used as selection criteria. Any record containing data meeting the criteria you specify will be deleted.

Under certain circumstances, deleting a record can cause Access to delete related records in other tables. This occurs when you delete a record from the "one" side of a one-to-many relationship and if the "Cascade Delete Related Records" option was selected when the relationship was defined. For example, in the Contacts database, deleting a record from the Contacts table causes the related records in the Phones table to be deleted. Without the record in the Contacts table, the Phones records aren't of any use.

CREATING CROSSTAB QUERIES

As discussed in Chapter 6, "Creating Queries on the Fly," Access provides a Crosstab Query Wizard capable of generating crosstab queries. A crosstab query returns a highly summarized image of the data on file. You can use a crosstab query when you want to see an overall picture of the data. Crosstabs are a great way to gather the information you need to generate a graph. Management can use crosstab queries to see trends in business or to view how certain products are performing.

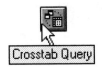

The easiest way to create a crosstab query is to use the Crosstab Wizard. You can create a crosstab without the Wizard, in the same way as any select query. Click on the crosstab query button on the query design toolbar to identify the query you are creating as a crosstab query.

In addition to identifying the tables and fields, a crosstab query needs to know how to summarize the data. You must select three fields to create a crosstab query.

○ The *row heading* is the field used to summarize the data into rows, or records.

○ The *column heading* is the file used to summarize the data into columns, or fields.

○ The *value* is the field you want to total to see a summary for.

Crosstab queries have two rows in the field grid we haven't discussed yet.

○ The *crosstab row* is where you identify the row heading, column heading and value fields. Select the appropriate option from the drop-down list in the crosstab row to tell the query the role the field plays in the query.

○ Set the *total row* to group data for the row heading and column heading fields. This tells the query you want one row or column for each group of records containing the same value in this field. Set the total row to the calululation you want to perform on the field you identify as the value field.

Figure 7-30 shows an example of a Crosstab Query design. This query returns a summary showing the number of interactions occuring between account executives and customers. The Account Executive field is identified as the row heading. One row will be created for each account executive. The customer name is identified as the column heading. One column will be created for each customer name. The InteractionID is identified as the Value, the Total row shows this field will contain the count of the number of records read. An example of the dyanset generated when you run this query is shown in Figure 7-31.

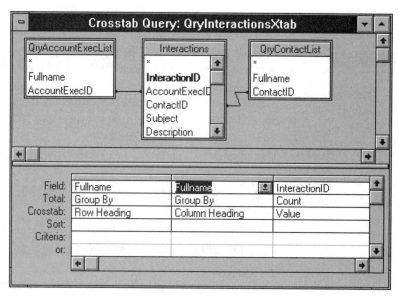

Figure 7-30: Example Crosstab Query design.

Fullname	Francis	Ileen	Jody	Kelly	Kevin	Lee	Roberta	Sarah	Terry	Wallace
Charlie Eager		1	3		2	1			1	
Samuel Pate		1	1	3	1	1			1	
Timothy Alan	1	3	2	2	3		1			1

Figure 7-31: Example output from a Crosstab Query.

MOVING ON

In this chapter, we discussed how to extend the power of your application by using queries. In many cases, queries can perform tasks much more efficiently than any other means available. We also discussed each of the types of queries available, along with many options available when designing them.

In the next chapter, we'll look at how you can quickly create Forms to maintain data.

8

DESIGNING ACCESS FORMS QUICKLY

In this chapter, we will look at *forms*. You use forms to display and modify information in your database. You can design a form to look like a printed form you might use in your business. Or you can come up with a design of your own. The purpose of a form is to make your application easier to use, by presenting information to the user in a consistent, logical manner.

This chapter shows you how to create forms quickly. First you learn how to use Form Wizards to create several types of forms, including single-column, main/subform and tabular forms. Then you learn how to use the Form window's Design view to easily customize forms that you created using Form Wizards. When you finish with this chapter, you'll be ready to move on to the more advanced form-design topics that are presented in Chapter 9.

TAKING A LOOK AT ACCESS FORMS

Figure 8-1 shows the datasheet window for the Employees table. In this window, you can add records, delete records and change data in existing records. It looks similar to a spreadsheet, and the data is organized in a logical manner. So, why create a form when you already have a datasheet available?

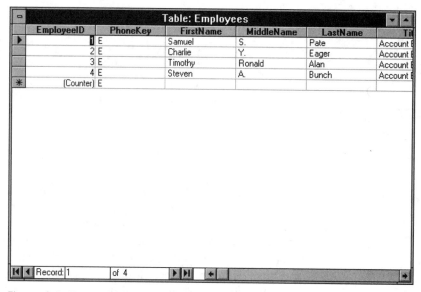

Figure 8-1: Example Employees datasheet window.

Let's create a form for the Employees table and compare it to the datasheet:

1. With the datasheet displayed, click the AutoForm button on the toolbar. Access generates the form shown in Figure 8-2.

2. Double-click the Control-menu box to close the form. Click Yes when asked if you want to save the changes to Form1. Access displays the Same As dialog box.

3. Type **Employees** in the Form Name text box of the Save As dialog box and click OK. Access saves the form using the name Employees.

To use the form again, double-click Employees in the Forms list in the Database window.

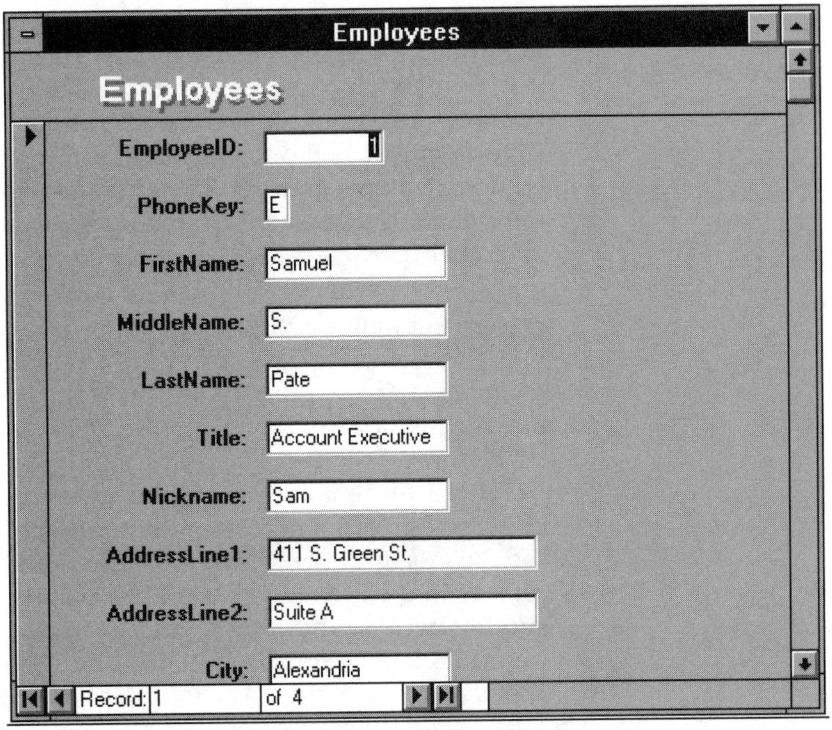

Figure 8-2: Example Employees form generated by the AutoForm button (or the AutoForm Form Wizard).

The form in Figure 8-2 not only looks better than the datasheet, it's also easier to use. All the information about the employee is available at a glance. If you want to change a particular item of information about an employee, you just click on the field containing the information.

To maintain information in a datasheet, you need to scroll through the fields to find the one you want to change. Datasheets are useful if you want to display more than one record at a time—though you can also use a *tabular form* to display multiple records.

Let's take a quick look at the types of forms available.

UNDERSTANDING FORM TYPES

There are several types of forms you can use in your applications. Each type has its own advantages.

○ *Single-column.* A single-column form displays data one record at a time using an arrangement of fields that you design. Single-column forms generated with a Wizard show the fields in a single vertical column with the name of each field on the left.

Single-column forms are the most common type of form used in most applications. The example form shown in Figure 8-2 is a single-column form that has been customized. Choose a single-column form when the records in your table or query don't have any relationship to one another. For example, a single-column form is a good choice for contact information, since the information for one contact doesn't have a direct relationship to any other contact.

○ *Tabular.* A tabular form displays data using an arrangement you design. But unlike a single-column form, a tabular form enables multiple records to be displayed in the window at once. Tabular forms generated with a Wizard show the fields from each record in a single horizontal row with the name of each field at the top of the form.

Tabular forms are a good choice when you want to display data from several records at a time. Choose a tabular form when the records in a query relate to one another. For example, records in the Interactions table are indirectly related to one another because they may describe interactions with the same person. A tabular form could be used to display information about several interactions in a single window.

○ *Main/subform.* The main/subform design displays data from two or more related tables at once. The most common use of main/subform design is to maintain data with a one-to-many relationship. For example, a form showing information about a particular contact (one) and all of the interactions you had with him or her (many). Main/subform design is actually two forms used together. The main form displays data from the table on the one side of the relationship. The subform displays data from the table on the many side of the relationship.

Main/subform forms, in most cases, combine a single-column form and a tabular form. The main form is a single-column form displaying one record at a time. And the subform is a tabular form displaying several related records. Suppose you wanted to see information from the Contacts and Interactions tables at the same time. A main/subform form is the best choice. The main form would show the information about the contact. The subform would show information about the interactions with the contact shown on the main form.

○ *Graph.* A graph form uses Microsoft Graph to display your data in a graphical manner. You can use graph forms by themselves or as subforms. We will discuss graph forms in Chapter 13, "Putting Pizzazz in Your Forms & Reports."

USING FORM WIZARDS

You can generate forms quickly and easily using the Form Wizards supplied with Access. Each Wizard asks questions about how you want the generated form to look, and produces a fully functional form based on your answers. You can use the form as generated or you can customize the form to meet your exact specifications.

Let's create a form for entering data in the Organizations table. To create a new form using a Wizard, follow these steps:

1. Start Access.
2. Click the Open Database button on the toolbar.
3. Highlight the name of the database to open and click the OK button on the Open dialog box. Or click on the Forms tab in the Database window to display the current forms objects, and click the New button to begin building a new form.

4. In the Database window, select the name of the table for which you are creating the form and then click the New Form button on the toolbar. For example, to create a form for entering data in the Organizations table, select Contacts in the Tables list and click the New Form button on the toolbar.

Figure 8-3: New Form dialog box.

Alternatively, click the Forms tab in the Database window to display the Forms list and check the New button in the Database window to begin a new form.

In the New Form dialog box, shown in Figure 8-3, choose the name of the table or query containing the data for the form from the list under the Select A Table/Query prompt. For example, select the Organizations table.

5. Click the Form Wizards button. Access displays the Form Wizards dialog box.

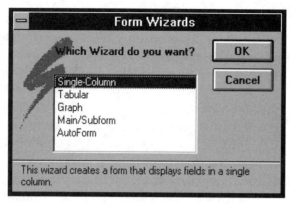

Figure 8-4: Form Wizards dialog box.

After you have completed these steps, you need to decide what type of form to create, based upon your intended use. We'll take the rest of the chapter to discuss the process of creating each of the types of forms available.

AutoForm

The fastest way to generate a form is with the *AutoForm* Wizard. The AutoForm Wizard creates a single-column form containing all the fields from the table or query you identified in the New Form dialog box.

To generate a form using the AutoForm Wizard (this Wizard option creates the same result as the AutoForm button on the toolbar), either double-click AutoForm or select the AutoForm option in the Form Wizards dialog box (see Figure 8-4), and click the OK button.

That's all there is to it! Figure 8-2 shows an example of a form generated by the AutoForm Wizard. While the AutoForm Wizard is simple to use, it lacks flexibility. If you need a little more control over the design or your form, you probably will want to use one of the other Form Wizards.

Single-Column

Single-column forms are the most common type of form used in most applications. They give you a way to display information from a single record at a time. With the Single-Column Wizard you have some choices about how the generated form will look. You can show all or a few of the fields from a table or query. You can specify the order in which the fields appear on the form. And you can dress up the form by choosing a layout style. This is the Form Wizard we're going to use to create a form for the Organizations table.

Follow these steps to generate a form using the Single-Column Wizard:

1. Either double-click the Single-Column option in the Form Wizards dialog box (see Figure 8-4) or select and click the OK button.

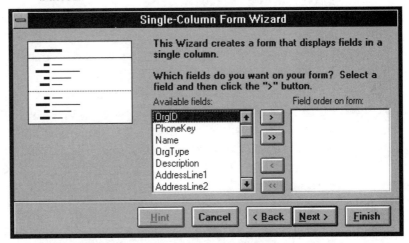

Figure 8-5: Sample Single-Column Form Wizard field selection dialog box.

2. Access displays the first screen in the Single-Column Wizard, as shown in Figure 8-5. You use this screen to select the fields to include on the generated form. The Available fields list box, on the left, contains a list of the fields from the table or query selected. The Field order on form list box, on the right, contains the fields you've chosen to include on the form. Identify the fields to include on the form in one of the following ways:

○ Double-click on any field name to move it to the opposite list.

○ Click on a field name in the list on the left, and choose the > button to move it to the list on the right.

○ Choose on the >> button to move all fields from the list on the left to the list on the right.

○ Click on a field name in the list on the right, and choose the < button to move it to the list on the left.

○ Choose the << button to move all fields from the list on the right to the list on the left.

In the Organizations example, click>> to include all fields.

3. After you have identified all the fields to include on the form, choose the Next > button to move to the next screen. Access displays the second Single-Column Form Wizard dialog box (see Figure 8-6).

Navigating a Wizard

All Wizards share a common set of command buttons to control movement from one screen to the next. You tell the Wizard you are done with a screen by clicking the Next > button. Clicking the < Back button takes you back to the previous screen. Clicking Cancel returns you to the Database window. The Finish button is available once you have answered enough questions to allow the Wizard to generate the form. Most screens have a Hint button. Clicking this button causes the Wizard to display a screen with helpful information about questions posed by the current screen.

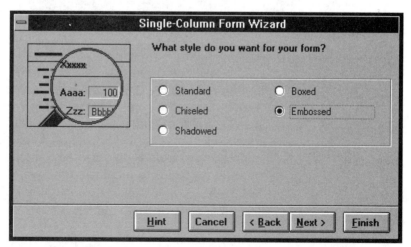

Figure 8-6: The second Single-Column Form Wizard dialog box.

4. In the second Single-Column Form Wizard dialog box, select the layout style to apply to the generated form. For the Organizations example, choose the embossed style.

Form Layout Styles

There are five layout styles you can choose when creating a form with a Wizard. You can see an example of each of the styles by clicking on the option buttons. An example of the chosen style is shown in the image displayed to the left of the buttons.

○ *Standard.* The standard style displays the data in black text on a white back color with a clear border. The field name prompts are shown in black text on a clear back color. The form back color is gray.

○ *Chiseled.* The chiseled style displays the data in black text on a gray back color with a clear border. Below each field is a rectangle with a white back color and a sunken border attribute. The field name prompts are shown in black text on a clear back color. The form back color is gray.

○ *Shadowed.* The shadowed style displays the data in black text on a white back color with a clear border. Offset below and to the right is a gray rectangle that looks like the shadow of the text box. The field name prompts are shown in black text on a clear back color. The form back color is gray.

○ *Boxed.* The boxed style displays the data in black letters on white back color with a clear border. The field name prompts are shown in blue text on a white back color with a clear border. Both the field and prompt are enclosed in a single rectangle with a white back color and a black border.

○ *Embossed.* The embossed style displays the data in black text on gray back color with a sunken border. The field name prompts are shown in black text on a clear back color. The form back color is gray.

5. Choose the Next > button to move to the third Single-Column Form Wizard screen (see Figure 8-7).

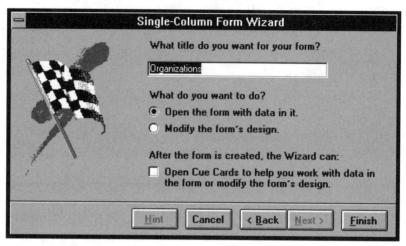

Figure 8-7: The third Single-Column Form Wizard dialog box.

6. Enter a title you'd like to appear at the top of the generated form. For example, accept the default **Organizations** for our data-entry form.

7. Choose the option button to indicate what the Wizard should do after it generates the form. You can choose to have the Wizard do either of the following:

   ○ Open the form showing data from the source specified.

   ○ Display the generated form in the Form design window.

   In the Organizations example, choose the first option (the default).

   You also have the option of looking at the Cue Cards for additional help.

8. Choose the Finish button to generate the form. Figure 8-8 shows the new form for the Organizations table.

9. Double-click the Control-menu box to close the form. When Access asks whether you want to save the changes to Form1, click Yes.

10. When Access displays the Save As dialog box type the name you want to give to the form. In the Organizations example, type **Organizations** in the Form Name text box. Click OK to save the from with the new name and to return to the Database window.

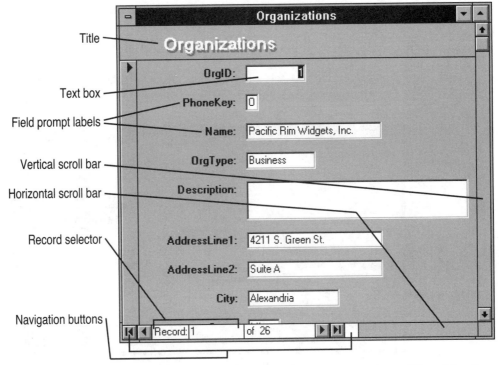

Figure 8-8: Form generated by Single-Column Form Wizard for the Organizations table.

Figure 8-8 shows data from one record in the Organizations table. The embossed layout style was selected so the data is displayed in black text with white back color and sunken borders. The field prompt labels are to the left of each text box in black text with clear fill and borders. The form has a gray back color. The title "Organizations" is shown at the top of the form in white letters.

The form has both horizontal and vertical scroll bars. The Record Selector bar is on the left of the form; in Figure 8-8 it displays an arrow, indicating that no changes have been made to the data in the form. Navigation buttons are displayed on the bottom of the form to enable movement through the records in the table.

Tabular

Tabular forms are a good choice when you want to display several records in a window at a time. You can choose the fields you want displayed from a table or query. You can specify the order the fields appear on the form. And you can choose a layout style for the form to improve the appearance. Let's create a tabular form for the Interactions table.

The steps you follow to generate a tabular form are similar to those just described for a single-column form.

1. Either double-click the Tabular option in the Form Wizards dialog box (see Figure 8-4), or select the option and click the OK button. Access displays the first Tabular Form Wizard dialog box (see Figure 8-9).

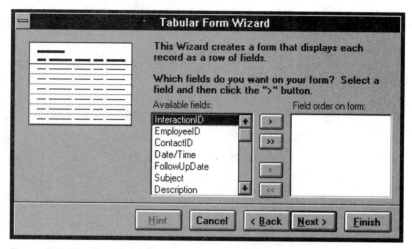

Figure 8-9: The first Tabular Form Wizard dialog box.

2. The first screen in the Tabular Wizard is shown in Figure 8-9. You use it to select the fields to include on the generated form. The Available fields list box, on the left, contains a list of the fields from the table or query selected. The Field order on form list box, on the right, contains the fields you've chosen to include on the form. Identify the fields to include on the form in one of the following ways:

O Double-click on any field name to move it to the opposite list.

O Click on a field name in the list on the left, and choose the > button to move it to the list on the right.

O Choose on the >> button to move all fields from the list on the left to the list on the right.

O Click on a field name in the list on the right, and choose the < button to move it to the list on the left.

O Choose the << button to move all fields from the list on the right to the list on the left. For the Interactions form, click the >> button to move all fields to the list on the right.

3. After you have identified all the fields to include on the generated form, choose the Next > button to move to the next screen, the second Tabular Form Wizard dialog box (see Figure 8-10).

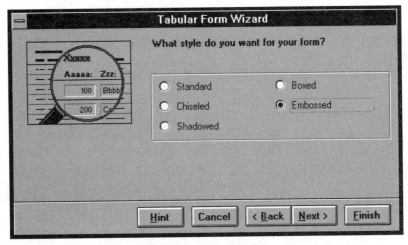

Figure 8-10: The second Tabular Form Wizard dialog box.

4. Select the layout style to apply to the generated form. In the Interactions example, select the standard style.

5. Choose the Next > button to move to the next screen. Access displays the third Tabular Form Wizard dialog box (see Figure 8-11).

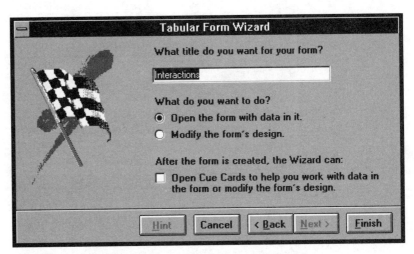

Figure 8-11: The third Tabular Form Wizard dialog box.

6. Enter a title you'd like to appear at the top of the generated form. The Wizard suggests the table or query name as a title. In the Interactions example, accept the default name (Interactions).

7. Choose an option button to indicate what the Wizard should do after it generates the form. You can choose to have the Wizard do either of the following:

   ○ Open the form showing data from the data source specified.

   ○ Display the generated form in the Form design window.

   In the Interactions example, accept the first option (the default). You also have the option of looking at the Cue Cards for additional help.

8. Choose the Finish button to generate the form (see Figure 8-12).

9. When you are ready to close the form, double-click the Control-menu box. Click the Yes button when Access asks whether you want to save the changes to Form1.

10. In the Save As dialog box, type a name for the form in the Form Name text box. In the Interactions example, type **Interactions** and click the OK button. Access saves the form and returns to the Database window.

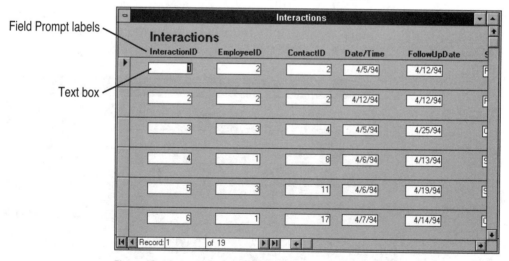

Figure 8-12: Interactions form generated by the Tabular Form Wizard.

Figure 8-12 shows the Interactions form generated by the Tabular Form Wizard. What you see is data from several records in the Interactions table. The standard layout style was selected so the data is displayed in black text with white back color and black borders. The field prompt labels are at the top of the columns of data in black text on a gray back color. The form has a gray back color. The title Interactions is shown at the top of the form in black.

Navigation buttons are displayed on the bottom of the form to allow movement through the records in the table. The vertical scroll bar can be used to display data from other records. However, you must click on a field in order to select a record for processing. Use the horizontal scroll bar to see other fields from the table.

Main/Subform

Main/subform forms are the most complex type of form you can generate with a Form Wizard. They are complicated because you are actually creating two forms at once. The main form displays data from one table or query and the subform displays data from a second table or query.

In the example that follows, we will create a form to display information about our contacts. The Contacts table contains some of the information about our contacts, but not all of the information we need. The Phones table contains the phone numbers for these people. Many of our contacts have more than one phone number. As we discussed in Chapter 2, we store the phone numbers in a separate table so we can keep track of a variable number of phone numbers for each contact. The form we'll create will show the Contacts information in the main form and the Phones information for that contact in the subform.

Follow these steps to generate a form using the Main/Subform Wizard:

1. Either double-click the Main/Subform option in the Form Wizards dialog box (see Figure 8-4), or select the option and click the OK button. Access displays the first Main/Subform Wizard dialog box (see Figure 8-13).

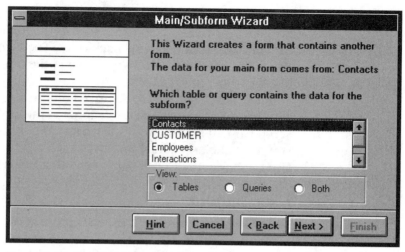

Figure 8-13: The first Main/Subform Wizard dialog box.

2. Highlight the name of the table containing the data to display in the generated subform. In the New Form dialog box (see Figure 8-3), you selected the table containing the data to display on the main form (the Contacts table, in this example). So on this screen you're specifying where the data for the *subform* is coming from. Specify the Phones table, as shown in Figure 8-13.

3. Click the Next > button to move to the next screen, the second Main/Subform Wizard dialog box (see Figure 8-14).

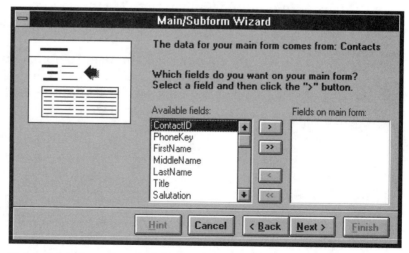

Figure 8-14: The second Main/Subform Wizard dialog box.

4. There are two list boxes on this screen. The Available fields list box, on the left, contains a list of the fields from the table or query selected for the main form. The Field on main form list box, on the right, contains the fields you've chosen to include on the main form. Identify the fields to include on the main form in one of the following ways:

   ○ Double-click any field name to move it to the opposite list.

   ○ Click a field name in the list on the left, and choose the > button to move it to the list on the right.

   ○ Choose the >> button to move all fields from the list on the left to the list on the right.

   ○ Click a field name in the list on the right, and choose the < button to move it to the list on the left.

   ○ Choose the << button to move all fields from the list on the right to the list on the left.

Since we will use this form to maintain our contact information, in the Contacts/Phones example, click the >> button to include all fields from the Contacts table.

5. After you have identified all the fields to include on the main form, choose the Next > button to move to the third Main/Subform dialog box.

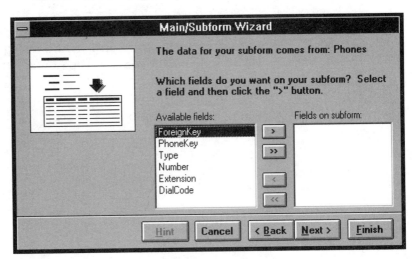

Figure 8-15: The third Main/Subform Wizard dialog box.

6. In the third Main/Subform dialog box, identify the fields to include on the subform in the same way you identified the main form fields. In the Contacts/Phones example include the

following fields from the Phones table: Type, Number, Extension and DialCode. These are the fields we need in order to identify the phone numbers for our contacts.

7. After you have identified all the fields to include on the generated form, choose the Next > button to move to the next screen, the fourth Main/Subform dialog box (see Figure 8-16).

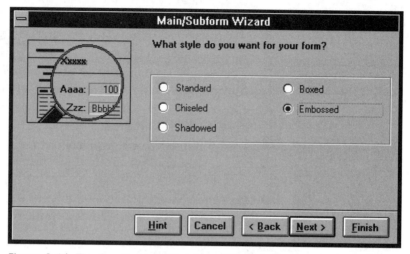

Figure 8-16: The fourth Main/Subform Wizard dialog box.

8. In the fourth Main/Subform Wizard dialog box, select the layout style for the form. In the Contacts/Phones example, choose the Embossed style.

9. Choose the Next > button to move to the next screen (see Figure 8-17).

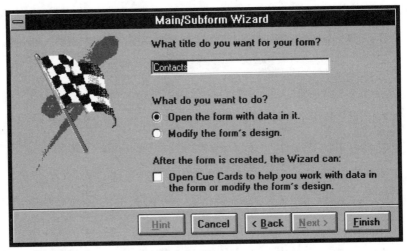

Figure 8-17: The fifth Main/Subform Wizard dialog box.

10. Enter a title you'd like to appear at the top of the main form. In the example, accept the default, Contacts.

11. Choose an option button to indicate what the Wizard should do after it generates the form. You can choose to have the Wizard:

   ○ Open the form showing data from the underlying tables or queries.

   ○ Display the form in Design view so that you can modify the form design.

   You also have the option of looking at Cue Cards for additional help.

12. Choose the Finish button to generate the form.

13. Figure 8-18 shows the informational message displayed at this point in the Main/Subform Wizard. The Wizard will generate two forms when you are done answering the necessary questions, and it actually generates the subform before it generates the main form. In order to reference the generated subform, the Wizard needs to know the name you want to give the subform. Click the OK button display the Save As dialog box.

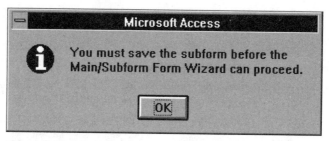

Figure 8-18: Message indicating that you must save the subform before preceding.

14. Type in the Form Name text box, the name you want to give the generated subform. In our example, use the name Phone/Subform.

15. Click the OK button to save the form. Access continues to generate the new form.

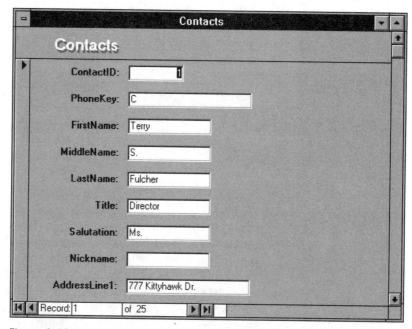

Figure 8-19: Sample Main/Subform form for the Contacts and Phones tables.

16. When you are finished viewing the form, double-click the Control-menu box. When Access displays a message asking whether you want to save the changes to Form1, click the Yes button.

17. In the Save As dialog box, type a name for the form in the Form Names text box. In the Contacts/Phones example, type **Contacts** and click the OK button. Access saves the form and returns to the Database window.

Figure 8-19 shows an example of the Contacts form generated by the Wizard.

CUSTOMIZING THE GENERATED FORM DESIGN

After you've generated a form using a Wizard, you'll probably want to make a few minor changes to the design. In this section, we will discuss a few of the things you typically might want to change on a form, including

○ The arrangement of the fields.

○ The size of the fields.

○ The order in which the fields are processed.

○ The prompts.

○ Text justification.

○ The colors used on the form.

The first thing you need to do to customize a form is to open the form in Design view with the following steps:

1. Start Access and open the database that contains the form you want to open.

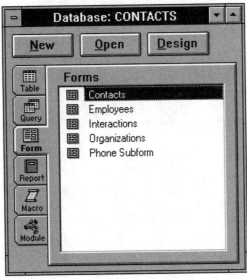

Figure 8-20: Database window showing available forms in the Forms list.

2. Click the Form button in the Database window to display the Forms list (see Figure 8-20).

3. Locate and highlight the form you want to change and click the Design button in the Database window. For example, to open the Contacts form, generated by the Main/Subform Wizard, click Contacts in the Forms list and click the Design button. Access displays the form in Design view (see Figure 8-21).

The Form Design Window

The Form design window is like a canvas on which you *paint* the form design. Figure 8-21 shows in Design view the Contact form we generated in the previous section. Now changing the form design is easy.

The Design window is divided into several sections. We will discuss what each of these sections is in the next chapter. For now, let's focus our attention on the detail section.

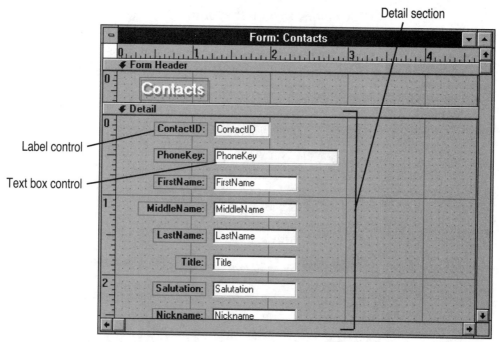

Figure 8-21: Form design window showing Contacts form.

All the fields you included in the Wizard screens appear in the detail section along with the appropriate prompts. The areas where the data will be displayed are called *text box controls*. They will display the text contained in the fields in the table. The areas where prompts are displayed are called *label controls*. They identify or label the corresponding text box objects.

There are three rather large areas on the form, above the subform control, that have special functions. The area at the bottom of the form that says "Phone Subform" inside is where the phone data will be displayed. (You'll have to scroll the form to see this area). Remember, when we used the Main/Subform Wizard, we said we wanted to see the phone data in a subform on the main form. This area is called a *subform control*. A subform control defines an area on the main form in which to display another form. You are, in essence, creating a window inside the main form.

The other large area on the form, above the subform control, is where we'll display the contact photograph, if we have one. We use a special control called a *bound object frame* to display fields that contain graphic images.

A somewhat smaller area, between the Photograph control and the subform, is an area labeled "Note." This is a text box containing the Note field, which has the memo data type.

Let's see how we can change the design of the form. We will look at a few of the basics here, and save the more advanced topics for the next chapter.

Moving & Resizing Controls

The first thing you'll probably want to do with a form generated by a Wizard is to move the controls into a design that you like. Moving a control takes a little practice—stick with it until you get comfortable. When you click on a control in the Form design window, a set of *handles* appears around the control. You use these handles to move and resize the control. Figure 8-22 shows these handles.

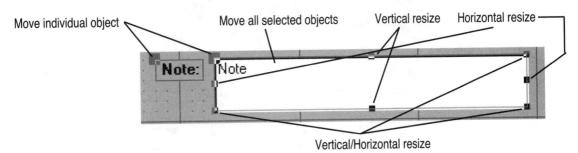

Figure 8-22: Handles for moving and resizng controls.

When you move a control that has an associated label, you have the option of moving the controls either together or individually.

There are two mouse pointers you can use to move a control. The hand pointer moves all selected controls as a group and the pointing finger moves an individual control.

To see the hand pointer, position the mouse pointer over a line anywhere except over one of the handles. When you see the hand pointer, click and drag the controls into the desired location.

You will see the pointing finger when you position the mouse pointer over the handle in the upper left corner of a selected control. When you see the pointing finger, click and drag the individual control into the desired location.

In addition to moving the controls on the form, you can change their size. The Wizard does a pretty good job at estimating the size of a control when it generates the form. But you might want to alter the size based upon the design you have in mind.

You resize a control with a double-headed arrow pointer. You get a double-headed arrow pointer by positioning the mouse pointer over any handle *except* the handle in the upper left corner. You can resize the control in the direction of the arrow by clicking and dragging the control to the desired size.

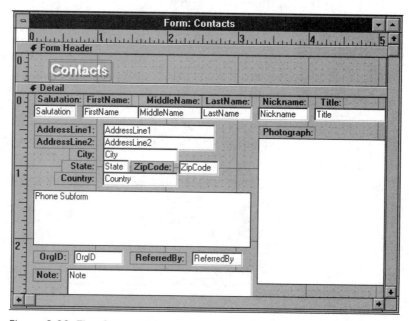

Figure 8-23: The Contacts form after resizing and moving controls.

Figure 8-23 shows the Contacts form after moving and resizing controls so that they all fit on one screen. To gain experience, try to duplicate the figure. (**Note:** The ContactID and PhoneKey fields have been deleted because Access automatically assigns values to these fields.)

To switch from Design view to Form view, to see how the form looks with "live" data, click the Form View button in the toolbar, or choose View, Form from the menu bar. Access displays the form in Form view with data from the current record in the underlying table or query displayed. Figure 8-24 shows the revised Contacts form in Form view.

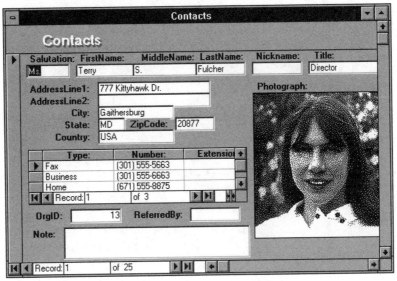

Figure 8-24: The first Contacts form in Form view.

To switch back to Design view, click the Design view button on the toolbar, or choose View, Form Design from the menu bar.

To save your changes to the form design, click the Save button on the toolbar, or choose File, Save from the menu bar.

Layout Finishing Touches

The Form and Report design windows have several features you can use to help put the finishing touches on the layout of your form or report. You get at these features through the Format menu.

(**Note**: To select multiple controls, "draw" a box around the controls you want to select by clicking and dragging the mouse.)

○ *Snap to Grid*. When this option is selected, selected controls position themselves at the nearest grid intersection when moved.

○ *Align*. This option causes the selected controls to move with respect to one another.

Left	Aligns the left edge of the selected controls to match the left edge of the control currently in the leftmost position on the form.
Right	Aligns the right edge of the selected controls to match the right edge of the control currently in the rightmost position on the form.
Top	Aligns the top of the selected controls with the selected control located at the highest position on the form.
Bottom	Aligns the bottom of the selected controls with the selected control located at the lowest position on the form.
To Grid	Aligns the selected controls at the nearest grid intersection.

○ *Size*. This option adjusts the size of the selected controls.

To Fit	Matches the dimensions of a label to the caption text.
To Grid	Adjusts the dimension of the control to match the grid size.
To Tallest	Adjusts the height of the selected controls to match the tallest selected control.
To Shortest	Adjusts the height of the selected controls to match the shortest selected control.
To Widest	Adjusts the width of the selected controls to match the selected control with the greatest width.
To Narrowest	Adjusts the width of the selected controls to match the selected control with the least width.

○ *Horizontal Spacing*. This option adjusts the spacing to the left and right between selected controls.

Make Equal	Moves the controls to the left or right to equalize the space between controls.
Increase	Moves the controls to the left or right to increase the space between controls.

Decrease	Moves the controls to the left or right to decrease the space between controls.

○ *Vertical Spacing*. This option adjusts the spacing above and below the selected controls.

Make Equal	Moves the controls up or down to equalize the space between controls.
Increase	Moves the controls up or down to increase the space between controls.
Decrease	Moves the controls up or down to decrease the space between controls. ·

Changing Prompts

The prompts displayed in the label controls are determined by the field definitions in the table. As you'll remember from our discussion in Chapter 3, the Caption property determines the text in a field's associated label. If the Caption property is empty, the field name is used as the label text value.

The first thing you have to do to change a label is to select the label control by clicking it. Changing the text displayed in a label can be done a couple of ways:

Properties

○ Click inside the selected label to place the cursor in the control. Enter the text you want displayed in the label.

○ Click on the Properties button on the toolbar. Change the Caption property to the text you want displayed in the label.

After you've changed the label text, remember to resize the control to the proper size to hold the text.

Changing Text Appearance

The toolbar in Design view contains several buttons you can use to change how text appears in the controls on your form.

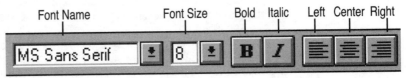

Figure 8-25: Appearance buttons on the toolbar in Design view.

You can change the font or size used to display the text in a control. To change the typeface, select the control and choose the desired font from the Font Name drop-down list on the toolbar. To change the size of the text, select the control and choose the size from the Font Size drop-down list on the toolbar. You can cause the text displayed within a control to appear in a boldface or italics by selecting the control and clicking on the Bold or Italic button on the toolbar.

You can cause the text in a control to be left aligned, centered or right aligned within a control by selecting the control and clicking on the appropriate alignment button on the toolbar.

Changing Colors

Palette

You can really get fancy when you start changing the colors used on your form. But a word of caution: using too many colors can cause a form to become confusing. Consistent use of color will make your forms more understandable and easier to use.

We will discuss colors in more detail in Chapter 14. But let's take a brief look at how to set colors here. If the Palette is not already displayed, click the palette button in the toolbar.

Figure 8-26 shows the Palette. Click on the Palette button on the toolbar to see this window.

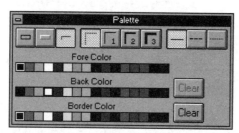

Figure 8-26: The Palette.

There are several settings you can choose using the Palette.

O *Fore Color*. The fore color determines the color of the text displayed in a control.

O *Back Color*. The back color determines the background color of an object.

O *Border Color*. The border color determines the color of the border around an object. This setting is only used when the border appearance is set to normal.

○ *Border Appearance*.

Normal	The border is shown as a line around the object. The color of the line is determined by the Border Color setting.
Raised	The border shown causes the object to look as though it is raised above the surface of the form. This is done by changing the color of the lines to suggest a shadow below and to the right of the object.
Sunken	The border shown causes the object to look as though it is slightly indented into the surface of the form. This is done by changing the color of the lines to suggest a shadow at the top and at the inside left edge of the object.

○ *Border Line Width*. This setting is ignored for Raised and Sunken borders.

Hairline	A very fine border line is used.
1, 2 or 3 point line	A 1, 2 or 3 point border is used.

○ *Border Line Type*. This setting is ignored for Raised and Sunken borders.

Solid	The border line is drawn as a solid line.
Dashes	The border line is drawn using a series of dashes.
Dots	The border line is drawn using a series of dots.

Both the Back Color and Border Color can be set to clear. When you set a color to clear, the color of the object behind shows through.

Setting the Tab Order

After you've arranged the controls on the form into a design you're happy with, you need to tell the form the order in which to process the controls.

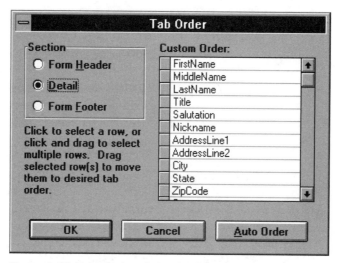

Figure 8-27: Tab Order dialog box.

Follow these steps to change the tab order for your form:

1. Click on the Edit Menu.

2. Choose the Tab Order menu option. Arrange the fields into the sequence you desire. Access displays the Tab Order dialog box in Figure 8-27.

3. In the Tab Order dialog box, shown in Figure 8-27, you specify the sequence in which the user will advance through the form controls as he or she presses the Tab key. On the right of the Tab Order dialog box, you see a list of the controls in one of the form sections. You choose the section of the form you want to look at by clicking the appropriate option button in the group on the left.

 To quickly reorder the tab order to match the order of the fields onscreen, click the Auto Order button in the Tab Order dialog box.

4. Choose a field by clicking the Record Selector located beside the name in the list you want to move.

5. Click and drag the field into the desired sequence position.

6. Click the OK button to save the new tab order and return to the Form window.

MOVING ON

In this chapter, we discussed the reasons why you would want to use forms in your applications. We walked through creating several types of forms using a Wizard. Then, we discussed how you can modify the generated form to meet your design requirements.

In the next chapter, we'll continue our discussion of forms by looking at some of the more advanced features you can use.

9

DESIGNING CUSTOM FORMS

In the previous chapter, we discussed how to create forms using a Form Wizard and how to modify the generated forms design. We'll continue our discussion of forms in this chapter by taking a closer look at how Design view works.

On our tour through this chapter, we'll discuss the tools you'll be using when designing forms; along the way, you'll have the opportunity to design a form. Figure 9-1 shows an example of the completed Contacts form we will create in this chapter by modifying the Contacts form we created in Chapter 8. Take time to work through this form as you read through the chapter and see how easy creating a form can be.

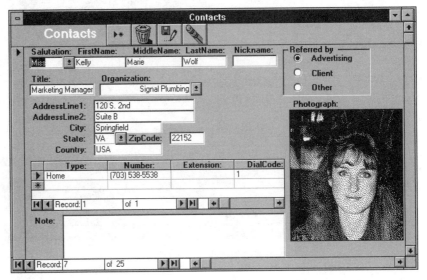

Figure 9-1: Contacts form.

CREATING OR MODIFYING A FORM IN DESIGN VIEW

There are four ways you can view a form.

○ *Form view* displays the form for interactive use.

○ *Datasheet view* displays the content of the form in a spread-sheet-like manner.

○ *Print Preview* previews how the form will look when directed to the designated print device.

○ *Design view* modifies the layout of the form.

OPENING DESIGN VIEW

To build a new form, open the database you are going to use. Select the table on which the form is based and click the New Form button on the toolbar.

In the New Form dialog box, identify the data source by selecting the table or query containing the data to maintain, and click the Blank Form button. You will see a blank form displayed in the design window, as shown in Figure 9-2.

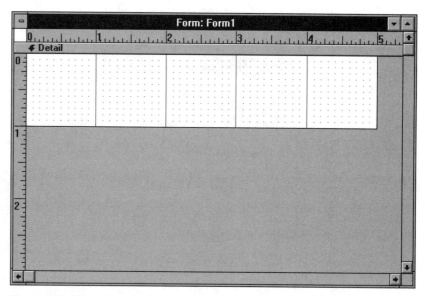

Figure 9-2: Blank form in Design view.

To open an existing form in Design view, display the Forms list in the Database window and either double-click the form name, or select the form name and chose File, Open from the menu bar. Access displays the existing form design in Design view (see Figure 9-3).

GETTING COMFORTABLE WITH DESIGN VIEW

When you work with a form in Design view, you have several tools you can use to help you create the design you want. Just click the button on the toolbar representing the tool you need, and it appears onscreen. As you can see in Figure 9-3, a form in Design view looks like it does in Form view, without any data. It's sort of like looking at an X-ray of your form—you see how everything's put together.

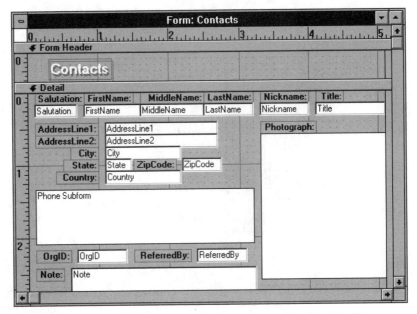

Figure 9-3: Contacts form in Design view created in Chapter 8.

Before we jump right into creating our form, let's take a little time to get to know the tools we'll be using.

Controls

The term *control* is used to identify an object on a form or report, such as a text box or a label. There are 16 controls available in the toolbox supplied with Access 2.0. In addition, other controls are available as OLE 2.0 objects. An easy way to add controls to a form is using the toolbox. Figure 9-4 shows the toolbox. If the toolbox is not already displayed in the Form window, click the Toolbox button on the toolbar; this is where you'll find the controls.

The toolbox contains the set of controls you can use on your form to display data and to create an effective visual design. Use one of these controls whenever you want to put something on the form—from a text box that displays the data contained in a field to a rectangle drawn around several other controls, giving a visual indication that the data they contain has a logical relationship.

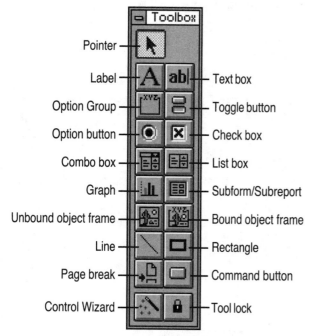

Figure 9-4: The toolbox.

Each button on the toolbox represents a control you can use on your form, or a setting that affects how controls are created.

Pointer

The pointer is selected by default whenever you open the toolbox. Use the pointer to select and change the controls currently on the form. Clicking the pointer button causes the default mouse pointer to appear.

Label

Use the label control to place text on a form. The most common use for a label is as a prompt placed next to a data-entry area, such as a text box.

Text Box

A text box control is the most common type of control on most forms. Text box controls are used as areas to display and maintain data contained in the fields in the record source. For example, you'd use a text box control to maintain a person's name.

They are also used as areas to display the results of calculations performed while using the form. For example, you'd use a text box to display the sum of the sales for an account executive to date.

You can also use text box controls for storing values to be used by other controls or procedures in the form. You'd use this type of text box control if you wanted the user to enter a value to search for in the data. Once the user enters the value, you could execute a procedure you've created to search the table for a match.

Option Group

An option group control is used when you want the users of your form to select one of a group of options representing a condition. For example, you would use an option group to select either Male or Female for the sex of an individual.

Toggle Button

Toggle buttons are used to indicate the status of a value in a visual manner. If a toggle button appears to be pressed, the associated value is in an active or true state. Toggle buttons are used extensively on the toolbar. For example, if the Bold button appears pressed, the selected object uses a bold typeface.

Option Button

An option button is placed inside an option group control to represent one of the available options. In the example given in the option group description, there would be two option buttons inside the option group. One representing a Male selection and another representing a Female selection.

Check Box

Check boxes are used to indicate that something is either true/false, on/off or yes/no. You would use a check box if you wanted to select one or more options for processing the data. The difference between a check box and an option button is that only one option button may be selected at a time. Whereas you may select several check boxes. For example, you could create a form that shows the reports available in your application. Next to each report name you could place a check box control. When you want to run a report, open your form and check the boxes for the reports you want.

Combo Box

A combo box drops down a list of possible values to select from. The list can be created in one of three ways.

○ *Table/Query.* The data in the list can come from the records in a table or query you specify.

○ *Value List.* You can enter the possible selection values when you create the combo box control.

○ *Field List.* You can choose to have the list show the names of the fields in a table or query you specify.

Combo boxes are a very good way to make your application easier to use. Instead of typing in a value, the user selects from a list of valid values, thus reducing the amount of invalid data entered into your database.

The size of the drop-down list varies upon the number of possible selections. If the number of possible selections is larger than the drop-down list the combo box can display, a scroll bar is shown on the right side of the list. The user can scroll through the list to find the value to select.

List Box

A list box is very similar to a combo box. The main difference is that a list box occupies a set amount of space on your form. When you create a list box, you determine the size of box to display the number of selections. If the number of possible selections exceeds the size of the list box, a scroll bar is shown on the right side of the list. The user can scroll through the list to find the value to select.

Graph

A graph control displays a graph on your form.

Subform

A subform control displays a form within a form. The most common use of a subform control is to display related data from another table. You'd use a subform control to display a form showing the associated Phones records for a contact.

Unbound Object Frame

An unbound object frame control displays data from a source outside of Access that doesn't have a direct correlation to the data on the form. For example, you'd use an unbound object frame to display your company logo on your form.

Bound Object Frame

A bound object frame control displays data from an OLE data-type field. The Photograph field in the Contacts table would be displayed in a bound object frame control.

Lines

The line control is used to draw lines on your form. In many cases, placing a line between objects on the form helps the design become more understandable. For example, placing a line between groups of controls sends the visual clue that the information is arranged in logical groups.

Rectangles

The rectangle control appears as a box on the form. You can place other controls within a rectangle control. Placing controls in a rectangle control gives a strong visual clue that the data contained is related. Forms containing a lot of information can, in many cases, appear less cluttered by grouping the controls in rectangles. When you look at the form, your eyes move from rectangle to rectangle rather than looking at each control.

For example, placing all the text boxes containing address information within a rectangle sends the visual clue that all of the controls deal with the address.

Page Break

The page break control identifies the location, within the form, to move to when a new page is requested. A form can contain multiple pages of information. A page is the area of the form you want to display at one time. In many cases, forms containing large numbers of controls can be made more useable by separating the data into logical pages of information. Using lines, rectangles and page breaks can significantly affect the look of your forms.

Command Button

A command button control invokes an action when you click it. Command buttons are common in all Windows applications. They are the OK and Cancel buttons you click when you finish a form. The actions the buttons perform are accomplished through macros or Access Basic procedures.

Control Wizard

The Control Wizard button toggles to identify when a Control Wizard is to be used to create certain types of new controls on the form. The Control Wizard asks a series of question about how you want the control to function. Once you answer these questions, the Wizard creates and places the control on the form.

Tool Lock

By default, once you place a control on a form, the pointer button is automatically selected. If you want to add several of the same types of controls to a form, you must re-choose the control button prior to creating each control. Clicking the tool lock button causes the toolbox button chosen to stay selected. You must click another toolbox button to select another tool.

Form Sections

A form in divided into areas called sections. A form section groups controls by the function they perform. Placing a control in a section determines when it is used. The sections fall into three basic groups.

○ *Form Header and Footer.* The form header and footer sections appear at the top and bottom of the window when in Form view. They are a good place to locate controls you want available at all times during the processing of your form.

○ *Page Header and Footer.* The page header and footer sections appear at the top and bottom of each page when a form is printed. These sections are where you place controls you want to use only on a printed form.

○ *Detail.* The detail section is used both with a printed and displayed form. You'll use the detail section on almost every form you create. As its name implies, the detail section is where most of the actual data, or detail, is located on a form.

A detail section is automatically created on each form. To add form or page sections, choose the Form Header/Footer or Page Header/Footer options from the Format menu. Figure 9-5 shows a new form once the Form Header/Footer option was chosen.

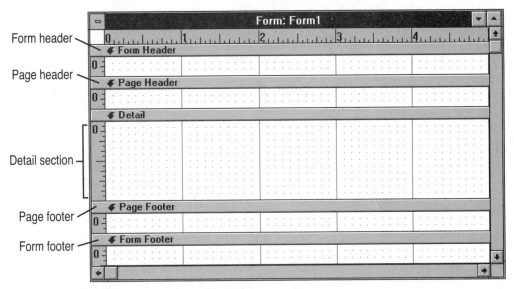

Form header

Page header

Detail section

Page footer

Form footer

Figure 9-5: New form with Form Header/Footer sections.

The Palette

The Palette is used to modify the appearance of the selected object. Click the Palette button on the toolbar when you want to change how an object looks on the form. Figure 9-6 shows the Palette.

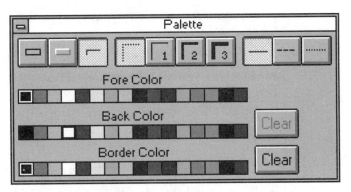

Figure 9-6: The Palette.

To change a property setting, click one of the following attributes or color, and the associated property changes to reflect your choice. There are several settings you can choose using the Palette.

○ *Fore Color.* The fore color determines the color of the text displayed in a control.

○ *Back Color.* The back color determines the background color of an object.

○ *Border Color.* The border color determines the color of the border around an object. This setting is only used when the border appearance is set to normal.

○ *Border Appearance.*

Normal	The border is shown as a line around the object. The color of the line is determined by the border color setting.
Raised	The border shown causes the object to look as though it is raised above the surface of the form. This is done by changing the color of the lines around the object to look as though a shadow is below and to the right of the object.
Sunken	The border shown causes the object to look as though it is slightly indented into the surface of the form. This is done by changing the color of the lines around the object to look as though a shadow is cast at the top and at the inside left edge of the object.

○ *Border Line Width.* This setting is ignored for raised and sunken borders.

Hairline	A very fine border line is used.
1, 2 or 3 point line	A 1, 2 or 3 point border is used.

○ *Border Line Type.* This setting is ignored for Raised and Sunken borders.

Solid	The border line is drawn as a solid line.
Dashes	The border line is drawn using a series of dashes.
Dots	The border line is drawn using a series of dots.

Both the Back Color and Border Color can be set to Clear. When you set a color to Clear, the color of the object behind is shown.

ADDING CONTROLS USING WIZARDS

Adding a control to a form couldn't be easier. Just click the type of control you want to create in the toolbox, position the pointer on the form and click. The following controls have Wizards available to step you through the creation process:

○ Option Groups

○ Combo Boxes

○ List Boxes

○ Graphs

○ Command Buttons

Each of these types of controls performs actions requiring additional information beyond that of other controls. Option groups need option or toggle buttons; combo and list boxes need the list of valid choices; graphs need to know where to get the data to graph; and command buttons need to know the action to perform when clicked. The Wizards make it easier to create these types of controls.

Let's take a look at how to add controls to a form using a Control Wizard.

Option Groups

The first control we'll add will be an option group to update the ReferredBy field. There are three types of referrals we track in our system: Advertising, Client and Other. An option group is a good choice for this type of situation.

Option Group

1. Click the Toolbox button on the Forms Design toolbar to open the toolbox.

2. Click the option group tool in the toolbox.

3. Position the mouse pointer at the place on the form where you want to create the option group and click. Figure 9-7 shows the first dialog box for the Option Group Wizard.

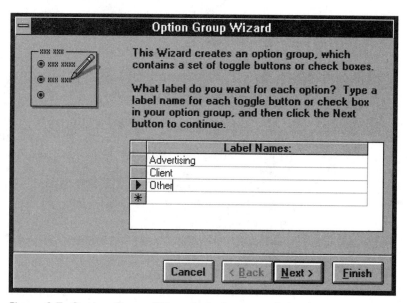

Figure 9-7: Option Group Wizard label names dialog box.

4. Enter the text describing the options users can select in the option group. Try and keep the text as brief as possible. In the example in Figure 9-7, we've entered three single-word option buttons describing the ways we receive referrals at Pacific Rim Widgets.

5. Click the Next > button to move to the next screen. The next screen is used to identify the option you want to use as a default value, if any. In Figure 9-8, we have indicated that we don't want to have a default value in the option group. If the user doesn't select one of the options available, the corresponding field in the table will be left empty. You have two options to select from on this screen.

○ *No, I don't want to select a default*. Choose this option if you want to have the option of not entering a value in the option group field.

○ *Yes, the default is*. Choose this option if you want one of the values you entered on the previous screen to be used as a default. If you choose this option, you must select the value you want to use as a default from the list shown in the combo box on this line.

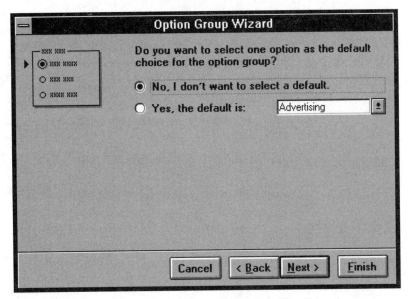

Figure 9-8: Option Group Wizard's default option dialog box.

6. Click the button representing the default to apply to the option group.

7. Click the Next > button to move to the next screen. When the user selects one of the options in the group, a value is stored that identifies the option chosen. You need to associate a unique numeric value with each option. In Figure 9-9, you see the default values for each option we entered on the first screen. There are two columns for each option: the first shows the descriptive text and the second the value associated with the option. The Wizard assigns the first option the value 1, the second 2 and so on.

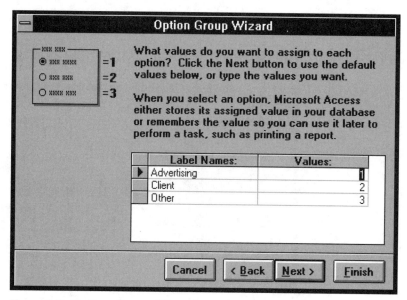

Figure 9-9: Option Group Wizard's option values dialog box.

It's important to understand how these values are used. The value associated with the label is what is stored when one of the options from this group is selected. If you want to use the value at a later time, such as in a report, you'll have to remember what each value means. If you print the field this option group updates, you'll see the number, not the label text. If you want to see the label text, you'll have to remember what each value represents when you create the report.

In the option group we are creating, if the user selects Advertising, the value 1 is what is actually stored. Where it is stored is determined on the next screen.

8. Enter a value to be stored for each label in the group.

9. Click the Next > button to move to the next screen. So far, you've identified the options to choose, which—if any—is the default option, and the value associated with each option. Next, you must determine what to do with the value. You have two options to choose from.

○ *Remember the value for later use.* When you choose this option, the associated value for a chosen option is not written to a field in the table. It is stored in memory and is available to any procedure you might choose to write.

○ *Store that value in this field.* When you choose this option, the associated value is written to the field you select from the field list to the right of this option.

Because we want to use this value later, and we won't be writing any procedures in this chapter, we've chosen the second option and selected the ReferredBy field from the field list. Figure 9-10 shows what the screen looks like after we've made these choices.

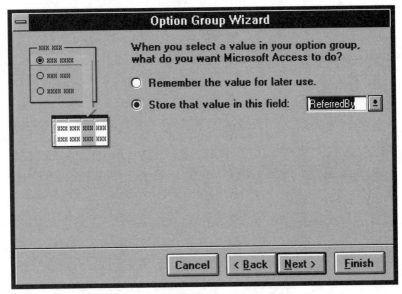

Figure 9-10: Option Group Wizard's control source dialog box.

10. Click the button describing where you want the associated value stored.

11. Click the Next > button to move to the next screen. All that's left to do is determine how you want the option group to appear on the form. There are two choices you need to make on this screen.

○ *What style do you want for your option group?* The selection you make here determines how the box around the buttons will appear. You have three choices:

Normal. The normal option creates a single-color line box.

Raised. The raised option creates a two-color box that causes the contents to appear to be above the surface of the form.

Sunken. The sunken option creates a two-color box that causes the contents to appear to be beneath the surface of the form.

○ *What type of buttons do you want?* The selection you make here determines the type of buttons created for the options in the group. You have three choices:

Option buttons. An option button appears as a circle with text next to it. When an option button is selected, a dot is shown inside the circle for the option. Unselected option buttons are identified by empty circles.

Check boxes. You should not place check boxes in option groups. Windows interface standards prohibit this. We will go into further detail about why interface standards exist and why following them will make your application easier to use in Chapter 14.

Toggle buttons. You've been using toggle buttons all along without even knowing it. The buttons on the toolbar and toolbox are toggle buttons. They can contain either text or graphic images. In many cases, using a toggle button containing an image describes the option much better than text. Remember the old saying, "A picture is worth a thousand words."

In Figure 9-11, we've chosen a sunken appearance for the group containing option buttons.

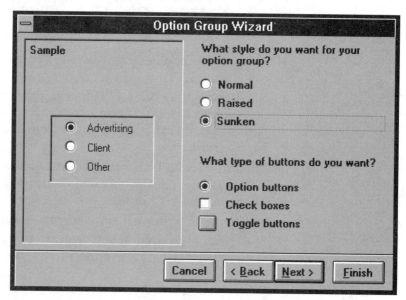

Figure 9-11: Option Group Wizard's style dialog box.

12. Click the button for the appearance style you want for the option group.

13. Click the button for the type of option button you want created in the option group.

14. Click the Next > button to move to the next screen. The last thing the Option Group Control Wizard needs to know is how to identify the option group. Just like other controls on your form, option groups can have identifying labels. On this screen, you are asked for the text to place in the associated label. The created label will be placed along the top line of the option group frame. To generate an option group without a label, delete the text from the label.

15. Enter the text to be placed in the generated label (see Figure 9-12).

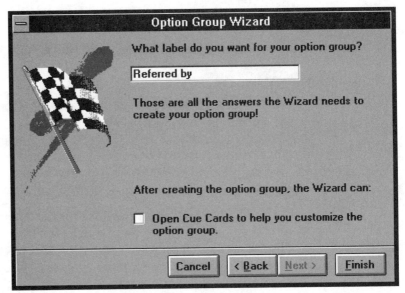

Figure 9-12: Option Group Wizard's identifying label text dialog box.

16. Click the Finish button to complete the Wizard and generate the option group on the form.

Figure 9-13 shows the Contacts form design after adding the option group. Notice that several fields have been moved in order to accomodate the option group (compare to the Contacts form generated in Chapter 8).

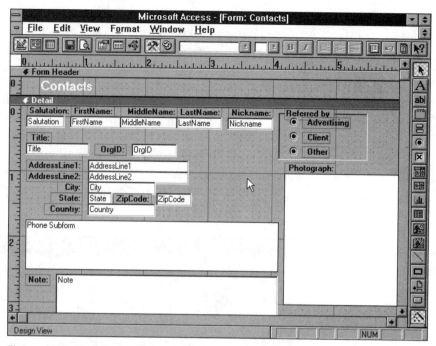

Figure 9-13: The Contacts form design after adding the option group for the Referred by field.

Combo Boxes

The next control we want to add is for the Salutation field. We'll use a combo box control for this field because there are several valid values from which we want to be able to choose. The values displayed in a combo box can be supplied either when you create the control or when the form is opened for use. If the values do not change, it is better to supply them when you create the control. We will supply the list of valid values when we create this control. The following procedure steps you through creating this control.

1. Click the Toolbox button on the Forms Design toolbar to open the toolbox.
2. Click the combo box tool in the toolbox.
3. Position the mouse pointer at the place on the form where you want to create the combo box and click. Specify in the first screen in the Combo Box Wizard where the list of values comes from. This indicates the type of list to be built. You have two options to choose from.

○ *I want the combo box to look up the values in a table or query.* Choose the first option if you want to create a list of values contained in a table or query in the database. This option is useful when the list of values changes depending upon the data contained in the database. For example, you would use this option to show a list of the organizations contained in the Organizations table.

○ *I will type in the values that I want.* Choose this option if there is a predetermined list of values the user should see. This option is useful when you can identify the list of values when you design the form. For example, you would use this option to show a fixed list of salutations.

In Figure 9-14, the second option has been selected. The list of values you see when you use the form will not change. We will enter the list of acceptable values in the Wizard.

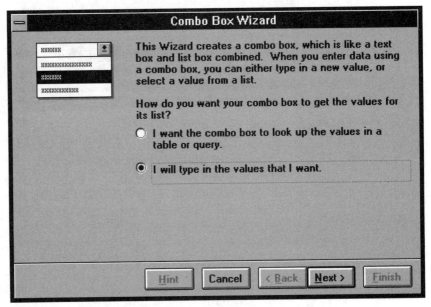

Figure 9-14: Combo Box Wizard row source type dialog box.

4. Choose the button to identify where the list of values comes from.

5. Click the Next > button to move to the next screen.

Next you must specify what values the list should contain. This is the actual source of the values displayed in the list. You can create multiple columns of values to use in the combo box. This is useful when you want to display one value but store a different value. For example, you could display a list of type descriptions and store identification codes.

The example shown in Figure 9-15 shows one column containing a list of the salutations we want entered into our database.

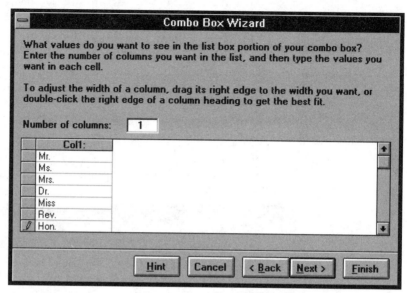

Figure 9-15: Combo Box Wizard row source dialog box.

6. Enter the number of columns to create in the list.

7. Type the values to display in the list.

8. Adjust the column widths to indicate how much of each column to display. If you don't want to see a column at all, you can shrink its width completely.

9. Click the Next > button to move to the next screen. Next, you must indicate what you want done with the value you select from the list. You have two options to choose from.

○ *Remember the value for later use.* Chose this option to store the selection in memory. This is useful when you want to use the value as part of a procedure associated with the form.

○ *Store that value in this field.* When you choose this option, the associated value is written to the field you select from the field list to the right of the option button.

We want to store the selected value in the Salutation field. Figure 9-16 shows what the screen looks like after we've made these choices.

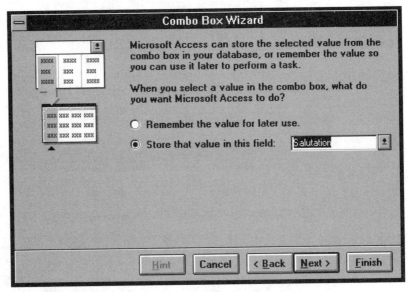

Figure 9-16: Combo Box Wizard's control source dialog box.

10. Click the button describing where you want the associated value stored.

11. Click the Next > button to move to the next screen. Just like you've seen before, the last screen of the Wizard is where you determine the label text associated with the control. Figure 9-17 indicates that the generated label should contain "Salutation:".

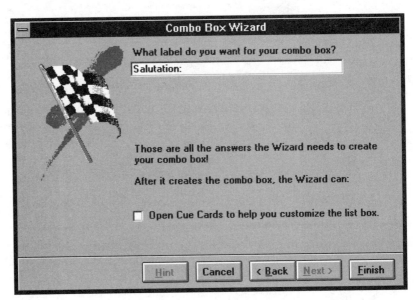

Figure 9-17: Combo Box Wizard's identifying label text dialog box.

12. Enter the text to be placed in the generated label.

13. Click the Finish button to complete the Wizard and generate the option group on the form.

Figure 9-18 shows the Contacts form design after adding the combo box. Notice that the original Salutation field has been deleted in order to make room for the new combo box (compare to Figure 9-13).

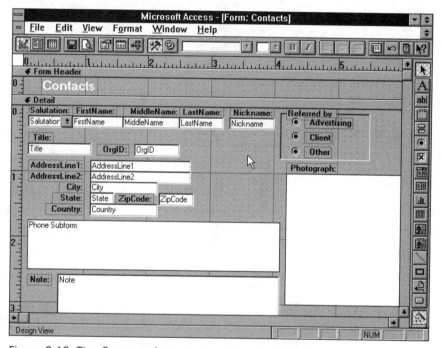

Figure 9-18: The Contacts form design after adding the combo box for Salutation field.

If you indicate that the list of values should be determined by the contents of a table or query, the Wizard uses a slightly different set of screens to retrieve the required information.

Let's create another combo box control to maintain the OrgID field. This control displays a list of organization names and stores the associated OrgID for the selected organization. The values to display in this combo box come from the records in the Organizations table.

The differences you'll see when creating this combo box and the previous involve identifying the source of the values in the list and what gets stored in the field when a selection is made.

You can begin to create this control the same way you created the last combo box.

1. Click the Toolbox button on the Forms Design toolbar to open the toolbox.

2. Click the combo box tool in the toolbox.

3. Position the mouse pointer at the place on the form where you want to create the combo box and click. The first screen in the Wizard specifies where the list of values comes from. This indicates the type of list to be built. You have two options to choose from.

4. To indicate that the values should come from the Organizations table, select the table/query option on the first screen instead of the text values option.

5. Click the Next > button to move to the next screen.

The next screen you see is where you identify the table or query containing the values to display in the list. To make it easier to locate the data to display the list shown can be limited to show just the table or queries in the database. The option group at the bottom of the screen contains buttons to limit the list to either tables, queries or both tables and queries.

6. Choose the option button to indicate what database object to display.

7. Highlight the name of the table or query containing the data you want displayed in the combo box.

8. Click the Next > button to move to the next screen. In Figure 9-19, we've identified the Organizations table as the source from the list values.

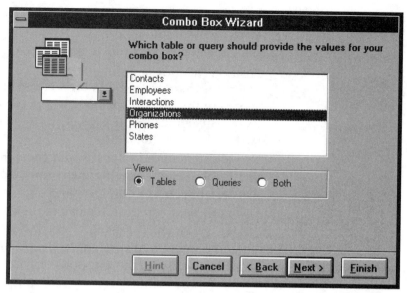

Figure 9-19: Combo Box Wizard's row source table/query identification dialog box.

The next screen contains two lists. The Available fields list on the left contains the fields contained in the table or query you selected on the previous screen. The Columns in my combo box list on the right shows the fields you've indicated you want to use in the generated combo box. There are several ways you can identify the fields to use in the combo box.

○ Double-click a field name to move to the opposite list.

○ Click a field name in the Available fields list box, and choose the > selector button to include a field.

○ Choose on the >> selector button to move all fields from the Available fields list box to the Columns in my combo box list box.

○ Click a field name in the Columns in my combo box list box, and choose the < selector button to not include a previously included field.

○ Choose the << selector button to remove all previously included fields.

9. Identify the fields to use in the combo box.

10. Click the Next > button to move to the next screen. In Figure 9-20, the OrgID, Name, AddressLine1, AddressLine2, City, State, ZipCode and Country fields will be used in the combo box.

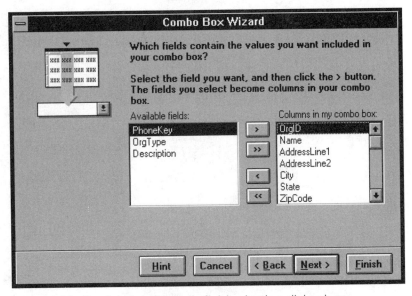

Figure 9-20: Combo Box Wizard's field selection dialog box.

11. Next, you need to determine how much of each of the identified fields should be displayed in the combo box and how wide the combo box should be. This screen shows a column for each field selected on the previous screen. You resize the columns to represent the width you want displayed in the combo box. In Figure 9-21, we've indicated that we don't want to see data from the first column (OrgID) in the combo box by dragging the right edge of the column to its left edge.

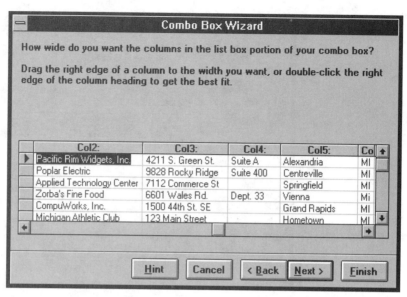

Figure 9-21: Combo Box Wizard's field display dialog box.

Adjust the column's width to indicate how much of each column to display. If you don't want to see a column at all, you can shrink its width completely.

12. Click the Next > button to move to the next screen. This screen shows the fields included in the combo box. Choose the field whose value you want to use when a selection is made from the combo box. For example, in Figure 9-22, the OrgID value will be stored when a selection is made from the combo box.

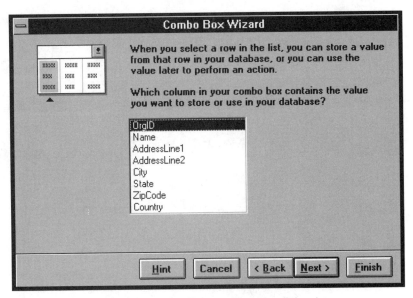

Figure 9-22: Combo Box Wizard's stored value dialog box.

13. Highlight the name of the field in the list whose value you want to store.

14. Click the Next > button to move to the next screen.

The last two screens are the same as the previous example of the Combo Box Control Wizard. You must identify what to do with the stored value and determine its identifying label.

The process of creating a list box is basically the same as a combo box and the Wizards follow the same basic steps.

Figure 9-18 shows the Contacts form design after adding the combo box. Notice that the original OrgID field has been deleted to make room for the new combo box (compare to Figure 9-18).

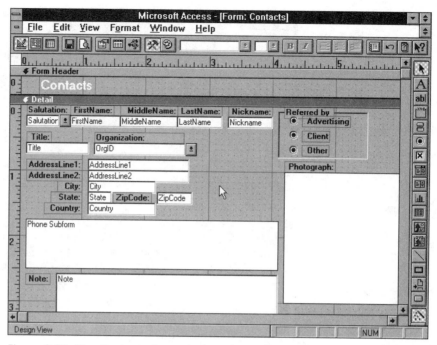

Figure 9-23: The Contacts form design after adding the combo box for the OrgID field.

For further practice adding combo box controls, you may want to add a combo box for the State field. First import the States table from the Ventana database. This table contains two fields: StateCode and StateName. Then replace the State field in the Contacts form with a combo box that looks up values from the States table and stores the correct two-letter code from the States table's StateCode field into the Contacts table's State field.

Command Buttons

You might also want to add some command buttons to help make your form easier to use. Command buttons execute associated procedures when clicked. You can do just about anything you want to the data, such as adding new records, deleting records, printing records and so on. Because we want to see the command buttons regardless of what part of the detail section is displayed in the window, we'll place the command buttons in the form header section. Remember, the form header and footer sections are always displayed at the top and bottom of the Form window. Let's take a look at the steps to create a command button to add a new contact record.

1. Click the Toolbox button on the Forms Design toolbar to open the toolbox.

2. Click the command button tool in the toolbox.

3. Position the mouse pointer at the place on the form where you want to create the command button and click. The first screen in the Command Button Wizard identifies the action you want the button to perform when clicked on the form. There are two lists of options on this screen.

   ○ *Categories*. The list on the left is called the Categories list. This is a list of the general type of action to perform. Highlighting an option in this list updates the task list on the right.

   ○ *When button is pressed*. The list on the right is called the When button is pressed list. This list shows the task to be performed when the button is clicked.

   In Figure 9-24, we've selected the Add New Record option from the Record Operations task list.

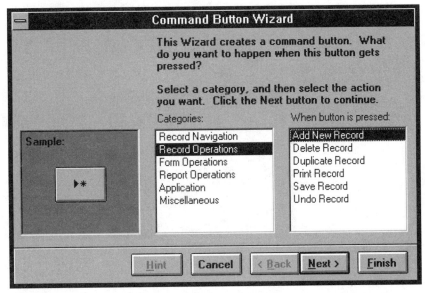

Figure 9-24: Command Button Wizard's action specification dialog box.

4. Click the category option to show the list of tasks available.

5. Click the task you want performed when the button is clicked on the form.

6. Click the Next > button to move to the next screen. The second screen in the Command Button Wizard is where you

decide what appears on the button face. You have two options to choose from.

○ *Text*. Choose this option if you want to see text on the button face. If you choose this option, the text entered in the area to the right will be shown as the button caption.

○ *Picture*. Choose this option if you want to see a picture on the button face. If you choose this option you have the option of selecting a picture from the list shown to the right of this option. Or, you can click the Browse... button to locate a file containing the picture to display.

At the bottom of the screen, there is a check box labeled Show All Pictures. If you check this box, the list shown to the right of the Picture option is updated to show the names of all the available pictures. In Figure 9-25, the Picture options is selected and the GoToNew will be used.

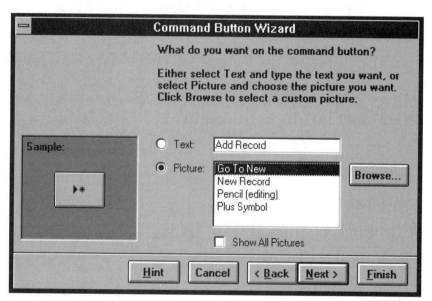

Figure 9-25: Command Button Wizard's button display dialog box.

7. Click the option button to indicate whether you want text or a picture on the button.

8. Enter the text to appear on the button face if you choose the text option. Or, if you choose the picture option, indicate the picture you want to see.

9. Click the Next > button to move to the next screen. The last screen of this Wizard is where the name for the generated command button is determined. You can allow the Wizard to

automatically generate a name or you can enter a name in the text box. In Figure 9-26, the name Go To New was entered and will identify the generated button.

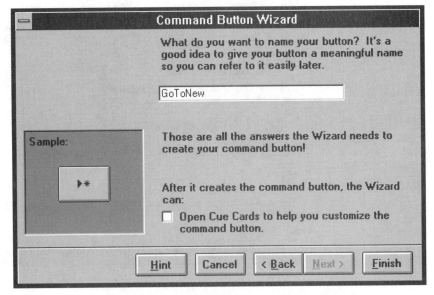

Figure 9-26: Command Button Wizard's button name dialog box.

10. Enter the name you want used to identify the generated command button.

11. Click the Finish button to complete the Wizard and generate the command button.

Take a few minutes to add command buttons to delete records, save changes to disk, undo changes to the current record and close the form.

Figure 9-27 shows the Contacts form design after adiing the control buttons.

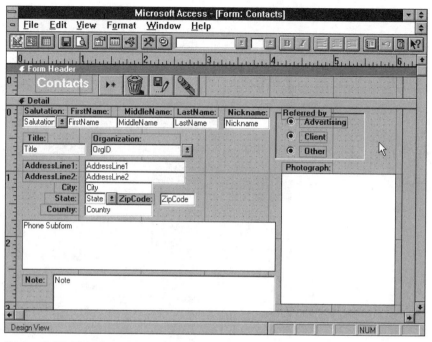

Figure 9-27: The Contacts form design after adding the New Record, Delete, Save and Undo command buttons.

For further practice workiing with forms, modify the Employees form that you created in Chapter 8 so that it resembles the form shown in Figure 9-28. To create the Phones subform, use the Copy commands on the Edit menu to copy the Phones subform from the Contacts form. Then use the Paste command on the Edit menu to paste the subform to the Employees form. Replace the State field with a combo box that looks up state codes from the States table, as you did earlier in this chapter in the Contacts form. Also add GoToNew, Delete, Save and Undo command buttons.

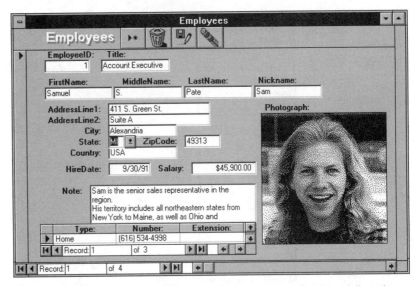

Figure 9-28: The Employees form after rearranging fields, adding the Phones subform, the State combo box, Contacts form design after adding the New Record, Delete, Save and Undo command buttons.

ADDING CONTROLS WITHOUT USING WIZARDS

The text box control is the most common control on most forms. It is also the easiest to create. It's so easy, you don't even need a Wizard to help. Check boxes and bound object frames are also easy to create without Control Wizards. There are two ways to create a control without using a Control Wizard.

With the Field List

If you want to create a control to update a field, you can use the following procedure:

1. Click the field list button on the toolbar to display a list of fields in the table or query associated with the form. The field list is also useful when you are unsure of the spelling of a field name in the record source for the form. Figure 9-29 shows the field list window; it shows the names of the fields in the Contacts table.

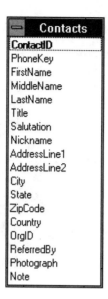

Figure 9-29: The field list window showing Contacts table fields.

2. Locate the field to place on the form in the list.

3. Drag and drop the field name from the list on the form where you want the control located. An appropriate type control is created at the location you drop the field name for the data type of the field selected. That's all there is to it; drag and drop the field name and you're done!

○ Text, Memo, Number, Currency, Date/Time and Counter fields are placed in a text box control.

○ OLE fields are placed in a bound object frame control.

○ Yes/No fields are placed in a check box control.

A label control is created next to the text box containing the name of the created text box control. This label control serves as a prompt for the text box area when using the form.

Take a few minutes to create controls for the rest of the fields in the Contacts table. Use Figure 9-2 as a guideline for where to place the controls or experiment with your own design.

With the Toolbox

So far we've discussed how to create controls that update fields in the table the form is based upon. But that's not the only thing you can do with a control. Controls can be used to perform calculations on data, and as temporary holding areas for values. You create these types of controls by choosing the Toolbox button for the type of control to create and clicking on the form where you want the control placed.

Once you place the control on the form, you need to indicate how to use the control. The Control Source property identifies the purpose of a control.

The other way to create a control without the help of the Control Wizards is to click a control button in the toolbox and place it on the form. If you do this when the Control Wizard button is not depressed, you'll have to modify the properties of the control to indicate how it is supposed to behave.

PROPERTIES

Properties are used to describe an object. When you describe a person, you usually mention their height, weight, age, sex, hair, eye color and so on. These things describe how the person appears. You might also mention activities the person takes part in, for example, tennis, golf, cycling, rock climbing, involvement in civic organizations and so on. These things describe how the person acts. You could further describe a person by telling something about their environment, for example, where they live or their family. If you know the person well enough, you might even be able to describe the person's behavior, how they'd respond under different circumstances.

Just like describing a person, when you create an object on a form, you describe the properties associated with the object. There are many properties associated with every object on a form. Even the form itself has properties you can set. We won't look at all of the properties associated with every type of object on a form. You don't need to understand them all to get a form up and running. So, we'll look at those properties you might need to modify as you design your form. Later in this book, when we discuss the Access Basic language, we'll look at several more properties for the object on your forms.

Properties define how an object looks on the form and how it responds to various events that occur when using a form. The property sheet displays a list of the properties for the currently selected object. Click the Properties button on the toolbar to activate the property sheet. Figure 9-30 shows the properties associated with the FirstName text box. Most of the properties we will look at in this chapter can be maintained with one of the tools accessible from the toolbar.

Figure 9-30: Property sheet in the FirstName text box.

You'll remember from our previous discussions, properties define how an object looks on the form and how it responds to the events that occur when using a form. There are form properties, section properties and control properties.

At first glance, you might be a little overwhelmed by all the properties available. Most properties are used for fine tuning an application. Many of the controls on your form use the property settings you defined when you created the fields in the table, for example, the Default Value, Validation Rule and Format properties.

The property sheet displays a list of the properties available for an object. There are a number of properties for each object. The combo box at the top of the property sheet can display all or just the properties for a selected category. The properties are grouped into four categories.

○ Data

○ Layout

○ Event

○ Other

Let's take a quick look at each of these categories and discuss a few properties from each category. Keep in mind, you don't need to memorize what every property does to create useable forms. As you gain more experience developing applications, you'll find yourself using more properties. Before you know it, you'll be an expert.

Click the Properties button on the Forms Design toolbar to open the property sheet. The property sheet shows the properties associated with the selected object. Each object type is selected in a slightly different manner.

○ *Form.* To see the properties associated with the form itself, click the white box in the upper-left corner of the Forms Design window.

○ *Section.* To see the properties associated with a particular section of the form, click the section divider bar in the Forms Design window.

○ *Control.* To see the properties associated with a control, click anywhere on the control.

Data

Data properties determine what an object displays and how it is displayed. These properties determine the table or query associated with a form, the data to display in a control, how data is displayed in controls and what you are allowed to do with the data on the form.

Let's take a look at a few data properties:

○ *Record Source.* The Record Source is a property associated with the form. The Record Source is the name of the table or query where the data is stored. This property is automatically set to the table or query you identify on the New Form dialog box when you start designing a new form.

○ *Control Source.* The Control Source property tells Access where to retrieve and store the data displayed in a control. If a control is used to update data in the Record Source, the Control Source property is set to the name of a field. The Control Source property can contain one of the following values:

FieldName   If the Control Source contains the name of a field, the value shown matches the value in the field. Any changes you make to the data on the form are written to the field. A control containing a field name in the Control Source property is called a *bound* control.

Nothing   If you leave the Control Source empty, data displayed in the control is not stored in the underlying table or query unless you write a procedure.

A control that has an empty Control Source is called an *unbound control*.

Calculation   If the Control Source contains a calculation, the control displays the results of the calculation. A control containing a calculation in the Control Source property is called a *calculated* control. The value displayed in a calculated control cannot be changed directly. You create a calculated control in much the same way as a formula in a spreadsheet: enter the calculation to perform preceded by an equal sign.

○ *Enabled*. The enabled property determines if the cursor can be placed in a control. If you set the enabled property to No, the control is still displayed, but you can't Tab or click into it. The default setting for the Enabled property is Yes. When a control is disabled (set to No), the control appears grayed on the form.

○ *Locked*. The locked property determines if the data in a control can be changed. If the locked property is set to Yes, the data is locked and cannot be changed. If it is set to No, the data is not locked and is changeable. The default setting for the Locked property is No. If a control is both disabled and locked, the control is not grayed (or the color set for disabled by Windows) on the form.

Layout

Layout properties determine how an object appears on the form. These properties determine an object's size and color, and how and under what circumstances it should be displayed.

Let's take a look at a few layout properties:

○ *Caption*. Both the form itself and label controls have Caption properties. As a form property, the Caption property determines the contents of the window's title bar. If the Caption property is empty, the window's title bar displays the name of the form as saved in the database. Otherwise, the window's title bar displays the caption. As a label control property, the Caption property contains the text to display in the label.

○ *Default View*. The Default View property is a form property that determines the manner a form is opened. There are three options for this property.

Single Form   Single Form view displays the contents of a single record at a time in the Form window.

Continuous Form   Continuous Form view displays as many records in the Form window as the design of the form allows. The detail section of the form is repeated within the window once for each record displayed.

Datasheet   Datasheet view displays a spreadsheet-like view of the data in the associated table or query. Each field on the form is displayed in a column and the records are displayed as rows.

○ *Scroll Bars.* The Scroll Bars form property determines which scroll bars to display in the Form window. There are two scroll bars available in each window. The Horizontal scroll bar enables right/left scrolling within the window. The Vertical scroll bar enables up/down scrolling.

○ *Navigation Buttons.* The Navigation Buttons form property determines if the Form window should include the VCR-like buttons used to move from record to record. These buttons are located in the bottom of the Form window in the left-hand corner. They also include the current record indicator number and the count of the number of records contained in the table or query.

○ *Grid X/Y.* The Grid X and Grid Y form properties are used when designing a form. These two properties divide the form into squares used to align controls. These numbers determine the number of divisions per inch. Grid X is the number of horizontal divisions and Grid Y is the number of vertical divisions.

○ *Visible.* The Visible property is a property of both form sections and controls on the form. If the visible property is set to No, the object, and any objects it contains in the case of a section, is not displayed.

Event

Event properties determine how an object responds to the events that occur while using a form. These properties specify tasks to perform when an event occurs. These tasks can be performed within a macro or an Access Basic procedure.

Let's take a look at a few event properties:

○ *Form Before Update.* The Before Update event of a form occurs just prior to any changes made to the data on the form being written to the underlying table or query. This event property can be used to trigger processing to determine if the data on the form has been completed properly before writing it to disk.

○ *Control: Before Update*. The Before Update event of a control occurs when you attempt to leave a control containing changed data. If no data has been changed in a control, the Before Update event does not occur. This event is triggered prior to the changes made to the control data written to the record update buffer. The record update buffer is where the changes to be written to disk are stored.

○ *Control: After Update*. The After Update event of a control occurs after the record update buffer is modified to reflect changes made to the data in the control.

○ *On Change*. The On Change event occurs when the value of an object changes. For example, typing a character into a text box control triggers the On Change event for the control.

○ *On Dbl Click*. The Dbl Click event occurs when an object is double-clicked. This event can be used to trigger a special process, such as a procedure to invoke another form.

Other

The properties listed under the Other topic describe general attributes about the object. These properties include the object name, where to locate help information regarding the object, custom menu associated with the form, how the window should function, how the Tab and Enter keys should function and a Tag area containing additional information for each object.

Let's take a look at a few of the properties in the Other category:

○ *Name*. The Name property is used to identify the form object. Every object on a form has a name. You'll use the name when you refer to an object in a procedure. The names of the objects on a form must be unique.

○ *Combo box: Auto Expand*. The Auto Expand property is available with combo box controls. If it is set to Yes, the closest matching item in the list is displayed in the combo box.

○ *Tab Stop*. The Tab Stop property determines if a control can be accessed by pressing the Tab key. If the Tab Stop property is set to No, the control can only be accessed by clicking it.

CREATING A FORM TEMPLATE

When you create a new form with the Design window, the default properties of the objects are determined by a form template. You can create your own template by

1. Creating a new form.
2. Setting the properties to your preferences.
3. Saving the form.
4. Setting the Form Template option in the Form & Report Design category of the options window to the name of the form created.

MOVING ON

In this chapter we looked at the components of the Form Design window. You learned about the sections that make up a form. You learned about the controls available on a form and how to use them. And how to make a form appear and behave to your needs by setting the properties of the objects that make up a form.

We'll look at how to create reports in the next two chapters. In Chapter 10, we'll learn to generate forms quickly using Wizards. In Chapter 11, we'll look at how easy it is to create great-looking reports without using Wizards.

10

CREATING ACCESS REPORTS QUICKLY

The subject of this chapter, as well as the chapter that follows it, is Access *reports*—printed output from your database. So far, this book has focused on designing, creating, querying and data entry. A database is of little value, however, if it doesn't present itself to its intended audience in a useful and informative way. Early in the design of your database you should be thinking about how your printed reports will look.

If you took the "whirlwind tour" in Chapter 1, you have already gotten a taste of what reports can do. In Chapter 2, "Designing Your Database," you learned that the "real-world" reports already produced by a business often help you determine what information needs to be collected in the database. Not surprisingly, real-world reports already produced by the intended users of your database often give you a good starting point for the reports you need to produce for your Access application. At least initially, you can base your report design on these existing reports.

In one sense, you already know how to create Access reports. Just print some or all of a datasheet. You can also print the contents of a form. More often than not, however, Access reports are designed separately from forms, specifically to be printed. Most reports are a cross between the tabular format of Datasheet view and the single-record-at-a-time format of Form view. While it is possible to use subforms to design a form that fits that description, Access' Report Wizards and the Report window's Design view are better suited for that purpose.

This chapter presents Access' Report Wizards. But first you'll learn how to print forms as reports, and how to create a quick report known as an *AutoReport*. Then you learn how to create several simple reports using the Report Wizards. After you finish this chapter, move on to Chapter 11, "Designing Custom Reports," to get the rest of the story on Access report design.

PRINTING DATASHEETS & FORMS

Sometimes the quickest and easiest report has not been originally designed as a report at all. In Access, it is simple to print the contents of a datasheet or the contents of a form. If you need to sort, arrange or summarize the data in some way, you should use a Report Wizard or design a report in Design view. But when you simply want to print out data from a table or query, you may want to just print a datasheet or form.

When you want to print any Access table or query from either the Database window or from the table's or query's datasheet, follow these steps:

1. Open the database that contains the table or query that you want to print. For example, if you want to print a list of contacts from the Contacts database, open CONTACTS.MDB.

2. Select the table name or query name in the Tables list in the Database window, or open the table or query in Datasheet view. For example, either select Contacts in the Tables list, or double-click Contacts to display the table in Datasheet view.

3. To preview a printout onscreen, before you send it to a printer, click the Print Preview button on the toolbar, or choose File, Print Preview from the menu bar.

4. Access displays a miniature version of the datasheet, as it will appear on the first page of the printout (see Figure 10-1). Move the mouse to the image and click to enlarge the image onscreen so that it is legible.

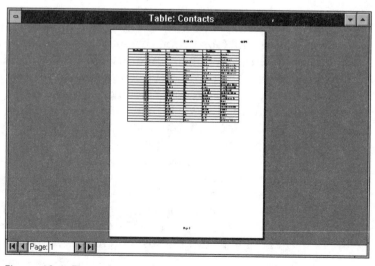

Figure 10-1: The print preview window showing the first page of the Contacts table printout.

If there is more than one page, use the navigation buttons at the bottom left of the window to flip through the pages. In the Contacts table examples, the print preview contains three pages.

5. If you are satisfied that you want to send the output to the printer, make sure your printer is turned on and click the Print button on the toolbar, or choose File, Print from the menu bar. Access displays the Print dialog box.

6. Check the settings in the Print dialog box and click the OK button. Access sends the datasheet to the printer (see Figure 10-2).

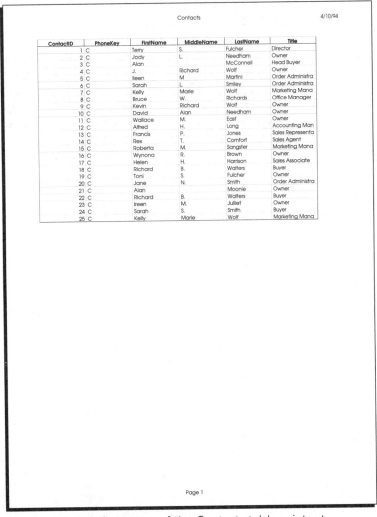

ContactID	PhoneKey	FirstName	MiddleName	LastName	Title
1	C	Terry	S.	Fulcher	Director
2	C	Jody	L.	Needham	Owner
3	C	Alan		McConnell	Head Buyer
4	C	J.	Richard	Wolf	Owner
5	C	Ileen	M	Martini	Order Administra
6	C	Sarah	L.	Smiley	Order Administra
7	C	Kelly	Marie	Wolf	Marketing Mana
8	C	Bruce	W.	Richards	Office Manager
9	C	Kevin	Richard	Wolf	Owner
10	C	David	Alan	Needham	Owner
11	C	Wallace	M.	East	Owner
12	C	Alfred	H.	Long	Accounting Man
13	C	Francis	P.	Jones	Sales Representa
14	C	Rex	T.	Comfort	Sales Agent
15	C	Roberta	M.	Sangster	Marketing Mana
16	C	Wynona	R.	Brown	Owner
17	C	Helen	H.	Harrison	Sales Associate
18	C	Richard	B.	Walters	Buyer
19	C	Toni	S.	Fulcher	Owner
20	C	Jane	N.	Smith	Order Administra
21	C	Alan		Moonie	Owner
22	C	Richard	B.	Walters	Buyer
23	C	Ireen	M.	Julliet	Owner
24	C	Sarah	S.	Smith	Buyer
25	C	Kelly	Marie	Wolf	Marketing Mana

Contacts — 4/10/94

Page 1

Figure 10-2: The first page of the Contacts table printout.

7. Choose View, Datasheet from the menu bar to return to the table's or query's datasheet.

8. Double-click the datasheet's Control-menu box to return to the Database window.

As you can see, when the table contains too many columns to fit on one page, Access breaks the table up horizontally onto multiple pages. Of course, when there are more records than will fit on one page, Access prints the excess records on subsequent pages. Access adds a header on each page that includes the table name as well as the date. Each page also is numbered at the bottom.

As you learned in Chapter 5, you can customize column widths and even hide columns in Datasheet view. It would be possible, therefore, to manipulate column widths and columns displayed until you can fit all the columns you want to see on one page. You could then print the table using the Print button. It is much easier, however, to create a query that displays the columns that you want to print and then just print the query's dynaset. For example, if all you want to see of the Contacts list is the ContactID and the contact's name, use the Contact List query that you created in Chapter 7. Figure 10-3 shows the report generated by printing the Contact List query.

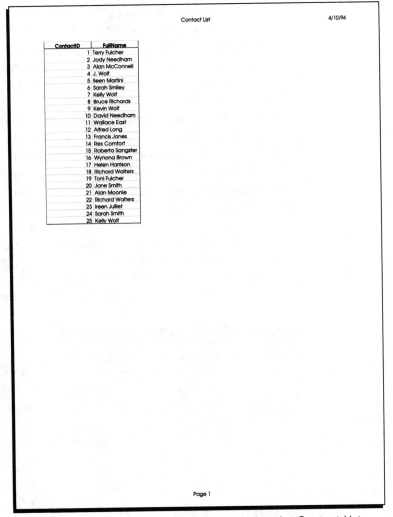

Figure 10-3: The report generated by printing the Contact List query.

It is also very easy to print the contents of an Access form. For example, you might want to make a hard copy of the data contained in the Employees form, which was created in Chapter 8. If you plan to print a form, however, and you want each form to print on a separate page—one employee per page in the Employees form example—you have to remember to add a page break control at the end of the form design (the page break control is covered later in this chapter).

To print a form, follow these steps:

1. Open the database that contains the table or query that you want to print. For example, if you want to print Alan

McConnell's record using the Contacts form from the Contacts database, open CONTACTS.MDB.

2. Click the Form button in the Database window to display the Forms list and select the form name from the list. For example, double-click Employees to display the Employees form in Form view.

3. Find the record you want to print and make a note of the record number.

4. To preview a printout onscreen, before you send it to a printer, click the Print Preview button on the toolbar.

5. Access displays a miniature version of the form as it will appear in the printout. Move the mouse to the image and click to enlarge the image onscreen so that it is legible.

6. Notice that the output will always start with the first record in the table. To print a specific record, you need to specify the correct page to print. Click the Print button on the toolbar. Access displays the Print dialog box.

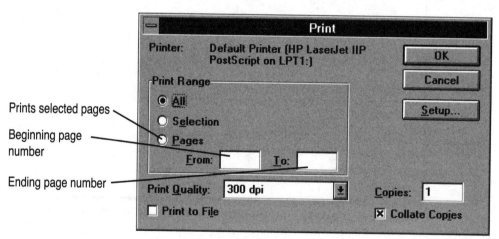

Figure 10-4: The Print dialog box.

7. Click the Pages option button in the Print dialog box to indicate that you want to print selected pages of the report. Type the starting page number in the From text box. Type the ending page number in the To text box. For example, to print Alan McConnell's record, which is the third record, type **3** in the From text box and type **3** in the To text box. (**Note:** If you didn't add a page break control to the end of the form design, you must do so before printing the form. Otherwise, multiple records will print on each page.)

8. Check the other settings in the Print dialog box and click the OK button. Access sends the form to the printer (see Figure 10-5) and returns to the Form window.

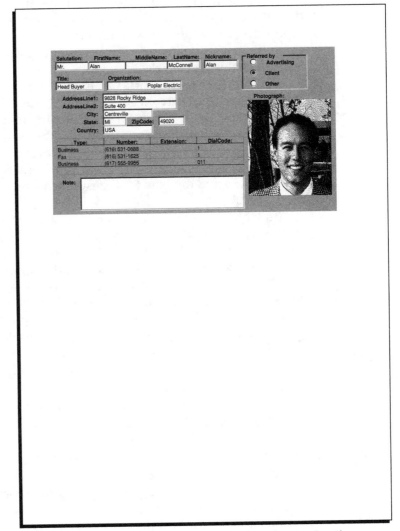

Figure 10-5: Alan McConnell's record printed out using the Employees form.

9. Double-click the Form window's Control-menu box to return to the Database window.

UNDERSTANDING ACCESS REPORTS

Although printing either a datasheet or a form is easy, neither method is very flexible. A printed datasheet shows all fields and all records from the table, not grouped in any meaningful way. Forms typically group information one record at a time. But Access' report designer enables you to generate reports that group and combine data from multiple records, and that compute statistics to assist in analyzing your data.

Like forms, Access reports can include lines, boxes and labels that surround your data. Access reports can also include all the controls available in Access forms, including text boxes, list boxes, combo boxes, check boxes, command buttons, option buttons, calculated controls and even graphics. Access also makes it possible to create reports that include data from several tables at one time. You can even add the new OCX custom controls, once they become available.

Similar to Form Wizards, covered in Chapter 8, Report Wizards enable you to quickly and easily create fairly sophisticated reports for your Access database. Each Wizard produces a complete report design, ready to print. You can also use the report design created by a Wizard as the basis for a custom report design. In the remainder of this chapter we will discuss how to create reports using Report Wizards. Then you should turn to Chapter 11 to learn how to modify Wizard-designed reports and how to design reports from scratch using the Report window's Design view.

Access Report Wizards can create six different styles of reports:

○ *Single-Column*. A single-column report is very similar to a single-column form. It displays data one record at a time. Fields are arranged vertically in a single column, with each field's name to its left.

○ *Group/Totals*. A group/totals report enables you to group records together by the value(s) in up to four fields in the underlying table or query. Each group of records is displayed in a tabular format. The Report Wizard can generate a report that calculates subtotals at the end of each group, and grand totals at the end of the report.

○ *Mailing Label*. A mailing label report prints mailing labels. Access enables you to design mailing label reports to fit any of more than 100 Avery label styles.

○ *Summary*. A summary report is a variation of a groups/totals report. It only includes the calculated totals—not the record data on which the totals are based.

○ *Tabular*. A tabular report displays records much as they appear in a datasheet—each field is a separate column and each record is a separate row.

○ *AutoReport*. An AutoReport is a very simple single-column report that you can generate either using a Report Wizard by clicking the AutoReport button on the toolbar.

The type of report you decide to create depends on the nature of your data and the message you want to convey. Your answers to the following questions can help you determine which style of report can best accommodate your data.

○ *Can you visualize the way the report will look?* Sketch the report on paper first. Or, if you are duplicating an existing report, work from that report. You can even include real data in the sketch so that you can get an idea of how the final product will look.

○ *Will your new report replace an existing report or form?* When practical, design your report to look as much like the current report or form as possible. The people who read the report will have an easier time understanding and accepting reports that resemble the reports to which they already are accustomed.

○ *Will data be arranged in rows and columns or in groups?* A telephone list of your contacts probably should be tabular in design, with each contact's name and phone number on a single row. But a mailing-label report to print labels to those same contacts should group data about each contact vertically in several rows.

○ *Will summary computations be necessary?* When your data includes numeric information, you often need to perform summary calculations. Subtotals, subaverages and so on require data to be appropriately grouped in the report.

○ *Is all the data in a single table or in multiple tables?* Using Access queries, you can combine data from multiple tables into a single dynaset. If your report needs to draw its data from multiple tables, you need to design an appropriate query on which the report will be based before you begin building the report.

CREATING AN AUTOREPORT

The easiest type of report to create in Access is the AutoReport. It's so easy, it almost creates itself. To create an AutoReport, follow these steps:

1. Open the database that contains the table or query that you want to print. For example, if you want to create an AutoReport to print records from the Contacts table in the Contacts database, open CONTACTS.MDB.

2. Select in the Database window the table (from the Tables list) or query (from the Queries list) on which the report will be based. For example, if you want to use an AutoReport to print contacts data, select Contacts in the Database window's Tables list.

3. Click the AutoReport button in the toolbar. Alternatively, you can explicitly go through the Report Wizards dialog box, discussed later in this chapter. The AutoReport button bypasses four steps and the end result is the same.

4. Access designs a simple single-column report and displays the report in Print Preview (see Figure 10-6). Each field in the table is in its own row and each record starts on a new page. Access displays the table or query name at the top of each page, along with the date that you are printing the report. Each page is also numbered at the bottom.

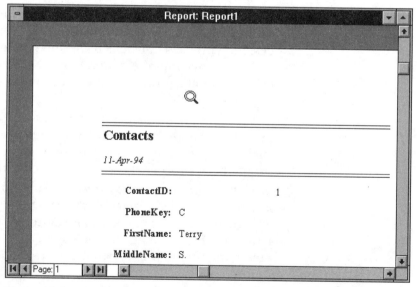

Figure 10-6: The AutoReport for the Contacts table in Print Preview.

5. Access initially displays the preview of the report in its zoomed-in mode. Only about 1/3 of the page is visible, but all text is legible. To see a miniature version of an entire page, either click the report with the magnifying-glass-shaped mouse pointer, or click the Zoom button in the toolbar.

6. The initial Print Preview screen for the AutoReport always shows the first record from the underlying table or query. If you want to preview the printout for other records, use the navigation buttons at the bottom of the window to scroll through the records.

7. If you are satisfied that you want to send the output to the printer, make sure your printer is turned on and click the Print button on the toolbar, or choose File, Print from the menu bar. Access displays the Print dialog box (see Figure 10-4).

8. Check the settings in the Print dialog box. If you don't want to print all records, you can print a range of records using the Pages option button. Choose the Pages option button and specify starting and stopping pages in the From and To text boxes, respectively.

9. Make sure that all other print settings are correct and click the OK button. Access sends the report to the printer (see Figure 10-7).

Contacts

11-Apr-94

ContactID: 1

PhoneKey: C

FirstName: Terry

MiddleName: S.

LastName: Fulcher

Title: Director

Salutation: Ms.

Nickname:

AddressLine1: 777 Kittyhawk Dr.

AddressLine2:

City: Gaithersburg

State: MD

ZipCode: 20877

Country: USA

OrgID: 13

ReferredBy:

Photograph:

Note:

1

Figure 10-7: The first page of the Contacts AutoReport printout.

10. If you want to immediately modify the design of the AutoReport in Design view, click the Close Window button on the toolbar. Refer to Chapter 11 for a discussion of Design view.

11. To close the report and save it for later use, double-click the Report window's Control-menu box. Access displays a message box that prompts you to save the report. Choose the Yes button in the message box. Access displays the Save As dialog box.

12. Type a name for the report in the Report Name dialog box. Access suggests the name Report1, but you can certainly

think of something more descriptive than that! For example, a good name for the Contacts report that you just created might be "Contacts AutoReport."

13. After you type the report name, choose the OK button. Access saves the report design and returns to the Database window.

CREATING A SINGLE-COLUMN REPORT

A single-column report, in the context of Access' Report Wizards, lists table or query fields vertically, one at a time. The AutoReport form, discussed in the preceding section, is a single-column report that includes all fields in the underlying table or query. If you want to create a single-column report that includes only some of the fields in the table or query, create a single-column report using a Report Wizard.

To create a single-column report,

1. Open the database that contains the table or query you want to print. For example, open the Contacts database.

2. Select in the Database window the table (from the Tables list) or query (from the Queries list) on which the report will be based. For example, if you want to create a single-column report that lists names and addresses from the Organizations table, select Organizations in the Tables list.

3. Click the New Report button on the toolbar or choose File, New, Report from the menu bar. Access displays the New Report dialog box with the name of the selected table or query already entered in the Select A Table/Query text box (see Figure 10-8).

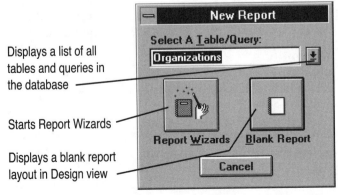

Displays a list of all tables and queries in the database

Starts Report Wizards

Displays a blank report layout in Design view

Figure 10-8: The New Report dialog box with the Organizations table name entered in the Select A Table/Query text box.

Alternatively, you can choose the Report button in the Database window to display the Reports list (see Figure 10-9) and then choose the New button. Access displays the New Report dialog box, but with the Select A Table/Query text box empty. Click the drop-down button at the right end of the text box to display a scrolling list of all the tables and queries in the database. Select a table or query from the list. **(Note:** From the Reports list you can also preview the printout of the selected report by choosing the Preview button, and you can open the selected report in Design view by choosing the Design button.)

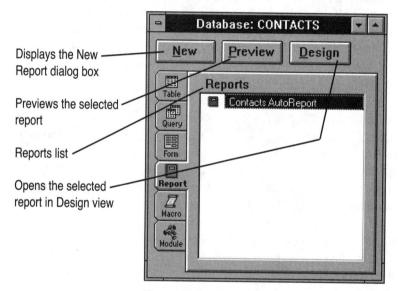

Displays the New Report dialog box

Previews the selected report

Reports list

Opens the selected report in Design view

Figure 10-9: The Reports list in the Database window.

4. Choose the Report Wizards button in the New Report dialog box. Access displays the Report Wizards dialog box (see Figure 10-10).

314

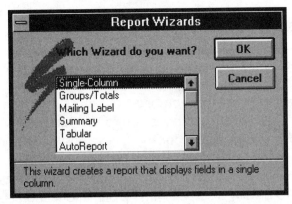

Figure 10-10: The Report Wizards dialog box, which lists available Report Wizards.

5. The Single-Column option is already selected, so choose the OK button to continue. Access displays the first Single-Column Report Wizard dialog box (see Figure 10-11).

Select fields for the report from this list

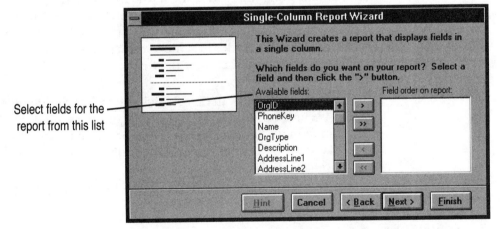

Figure 10-11: The first Single-Column Report Wizard dialog box, used to select fields for the report.

Navigating a Wizard

All Wizards share a common set of command buttons to control movement from one screen to the next. You tell the Wizard you are done with a screen by clicking the Next > button. Clicking the < Back button takes you back to the previous Report Wizard screen. Clicking Cancel returns you to the Database window. The Finish button is available once you have answered enough questions to allow the Wizard to generate the report. Most screens have a Hint button. Clicking this button causes the Wizard to display a screen with helpful information about questions posed by the current screen.

6. The Report Wizard asks, "Which fields do you want on your report?" and lists the table's or query's fields in the Available fields list box. For each field you want displayed in the report, either double-click the field name in the Available fields list, or select the field name and click the > button in the dialog box. Access moves the field name over to the "Field order on report" list box. The order in which you select the field names will determine the order the fields will appear in the report design.

   If you want to include all fields, click the >> button. If you want to use most of the fields in the table or query, click the >> button to move all fields to the "Field order on report" list box and then use the < button to move individual fields back to the Available fields list.

   In the Organizations example, move the following fields to the "Field order on report" list box:

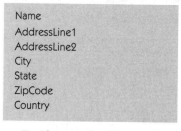

```
Name
AddressLine1
AddressLine2
City
State
ZipCode
Country
```

7. Choose the Next > button. Access displays the second Single-Column Report Wizard dialog box (see Figure 10-12).

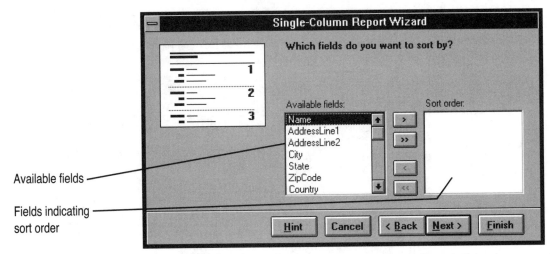

Available fields

Fields indicating
sort order

Figure 10-12: The second Single-Column Report Wizard dialog box, used to establish record sort order.

8. In this dialog box, the Wizard asks, "Which fields do you want to sort by?" The Available fields list box lists all fields from the table or query that you moved to the "Field order on report" list box in the first dialog box. If you want Access to print the records sorted by the values in one of the fields, either double-click the field name in the Available fields list box, or select the field name and choose the > button. Access moves the field name to the Sort order list box. To sort by more than one field, move additional field names to the Sort order list box. If you want records sorted by state, city and zip code, for example, you must choose the fields in that order.

   In the Organizations example, move the Name field name to the Sort order column to sort the report by values in the Name field.

9. Click the Next > button to display the third Single-Column Report Wizard dialog box (see Figure 10-13).

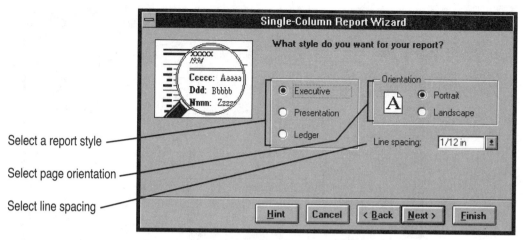

Select a report style ———

Select page orientation ——

Select line spacing ———

Figure 10-13: The third Single-Column Report Wizard dialog box, used to select a report style.

10. The Report Wizard asks, "What style do you want for your report?" Select Executive, Presentation or Ledger. The Wizard displays a small sample of the currently selected report style in the upper-left corner of the dialog box. If you want to see a different style, select the appropriate option button.

In the Organizations example, choose the Executive style (the default).

11. Also choose between the Portrait and Landscape option buttons to determine whether the report will be printed along the width of your paper (portrait–the default), or along the length of your paper.

In the Organizations example, choose the Portrait orientation (the default).

12. By default, the line spacing of the report is ¹⁄₁₂ inch. If you want to change the spacing, click the drop-down button at the right end of the Line spacing text box and select a different spacing.

In the Organizations example, choose ¹⁄₁₂ in as the line spacing (the default).

13. After determining how you want the report to look, click the Next > button to display the fourth Single-Column Report Wizard dialog box (see Figure 10-14).

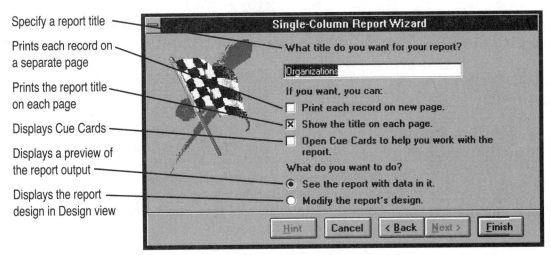

Specify a report title

Prints each record on a separate page

Prints the report title on each page

Displays Cue Cards

Displays a preview of the report output

Displays the report design in Design view

Figure 10-14: The fourth Single-Column Report Wizard dialog box, used to specify a report title, to determine whether each record prints on a separate page, as well as to determine what Access displays after the Wizard is finished designing the report.

14. By default, Access will print as many records as will fit on each page and will print the table or query name at the top of each page. In the dialog box shown in Figure 10-14, you have the option of changing the report title by typing a different title in the provided text box.

   To cause each record to start on a new page, mark the "Print each record on new page" check box.

   To suppress printing of the report title, unmark the "Show the title on each page" check box.

   In the Organizations example, accept the default options.

15. As is the case in Form Wizards, the Single-Column Report Wizard gives you the option of turning on Cue Cards. If you plan to display the report design in Design view, you may want to display Cue Cards by marking the appropriate check box in the fourth Single-Column Report Wizard dialog box.

16. Finally, the dialog box shown in Figure 10-14 asks which of the following you want to do next, after the Wizard finishes generating the report design:

   ○ *See the report with data in it.* Choose this option if you want to preview the report output, as a prelude to printing the report, without making any changes in the report design.

○ *Modify the report's design.* Choose this option if you want the Wizard to display the new report design in Design view, so you can customize the design.

In the Organizations example, we'll go directly to Print Preview, without displaying Design view.

17. Choose the Finish button. The Report Wizard first generates the report design, based on your answers to the Wizard's various questions. If you chose the "See the report with data in it" option button in the last Report Wizard dialog box, Access displays the report in Print Preview. Figure 10-15 shows the example single-column report for the Organizations table in Print Preview. You can use the scroll bars at the bottom and on the right side of the Report window to scroll the first page of the report.

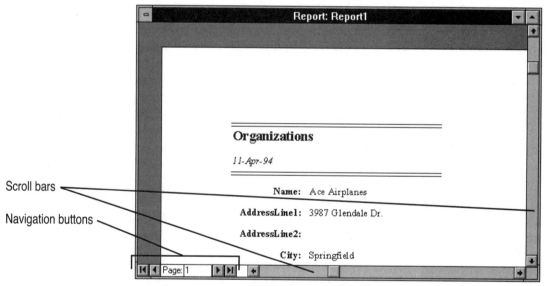

Figure 10-15: The single-column report for Organizations in Print Preview.

If, in the last Report Wizard dialog box, you chose the "Modify the report's design" option button, the Wizard displays the new report design in Design view (see Figure 10-16). Refer to Chapter 11 for a full discussion of how to modify the report design.

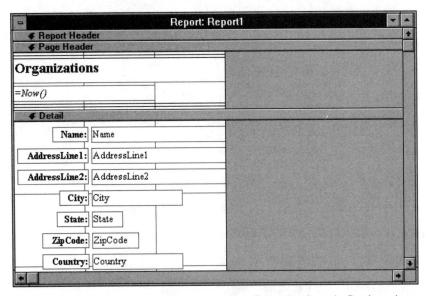

Figure 10-16: The single-column report for Organizations in Design view.

18. You can use the scroll bars at the bottom and on the right side of the Report window to scroll the first page of the report.

19. To print the report, either click the Print button in the toolbar or choose File, Print from the menu bar. Access displays the Print dialog box. Make sure all the print settings are correct, and choose the OK button to send the report to the printer.

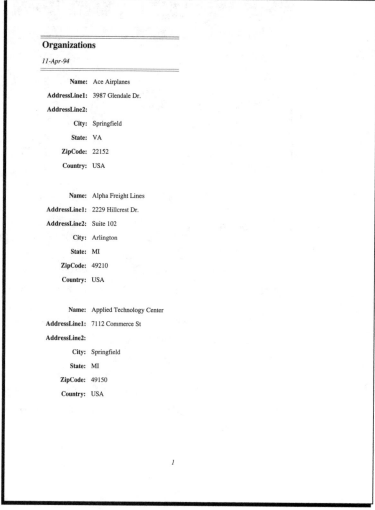

Organizations

11-Apr-94

Name:	Ace Airplanes
AddressLine1:	3987 Glendale Dr.
AddressLine2:	
City:	Springfield
State:	VA
ZipCode:	22152
Country:	USA

Name:	Alpha Freight Lines
AddressLine1:	2229 Hillcrest Dr.
AddressLine2:	Suite 102
City:	Arlington
State:	MI
ZipCode:	49210
Country:	USA

Name:	Applied Technology Center
AddressLine1:	7112 Commerce St
AddressLine2:	
City:	Springfield
State:	MI
ZipCode:	49150
Country:	USA

1

Figure 10-17: The first page of the single-column report for Organizations, generated by the Report Wizard.

20. To save the report design, either click the Save button in the toolbar (if it is displayed) or choose File, Save As from the menu bar. Access displays the Save As dialog box. Type a name for the report in the Report Name text box and choose the OK button.

   In the Organizations example, type **Organizations Single-Column Report** and choose the OK button.

21. To close the Report window, double-click the Control-menu bar in the upper-left corner of the window.

CREATING A TABULAR REPORT

Tabular reports, as created by a Report Wizard, are rather similar to the report that results from printing a datasheet. Each record in the underlying table or query generates a row in the report. Each field in the table or query generates a column in the report. When you use the Report Wizard, however, it is easier to control which fields are included in the report.

Tabular reports are most suitable when you want to see data in rows and columns. For example, if you want to compare employee salaries, a row-and-column orientation would be appropriate.

To generate a tabular report using a Report Wizard, follow these steps:

1. Follow steps 1 through 4 described in the "Creating a Single-Column Report" section of this chapter. Choose the Employees table.

2. From the list box in the Report Wizards dialog box (see Figure 10-10), double-click Tabular, or choose Tabular and choose the OK button. Access displays the first Tabular Report Wizard dialog box (this dialog box is very similar in appearance to the dialog box shown in Figure 10-11).

3. Move from the Available fields list box to the "Field order on report" list box the names of the fields you want included in the report. Each of the chosen fields will appear as a separate column in the report.

   In the Employees example, double-click each of the following field names in the Available fields list box:

   First Name
   Last Name
   Salary

4. Choose the Next > button to display the next dialog box.

5. Access displays the second Tabular Report Wizard dialog box, which is nearly identical to the second Single-Column Report Wizard dialog box, shown in Figure 10-12. In this dialog box, the Wizard asks, "Which fields do you want to sort by?" The Available fields list box lists all fields from the table or query that you moved to the "Field order on report" list box in the first dialog box. If you want Access to print the records sorted by the values in one of the fields, either double-click the field's name in the Available fields list box, or select the field name and choose the > button. Access moves the field name to the Sort order list box. To sort by more than one field, move additional field names to the Sort order list box.

In the Employees example, move the LastName field name to the Sort order column to sort the report by values in that field.

6. Choose the Next > button to display the next dialog box.

7. The third Tabular Report Wizard dialog box is also very similar to its counterpart in the Single-Column Wizard (see Figure 10-13). Use this dialog box to select report style (Executive, Presentation or Ledger), page orientation (Portrait or Landscape) and line spacing.

   In the Employees example, choose the Ledger style, Portrait orientation. Because of choosing Ledger style, line spacing is automatically set to 0.

8. Choose the Next > button to display the fourth Tabular Report Wizard dialog box (see Figure 10-18).

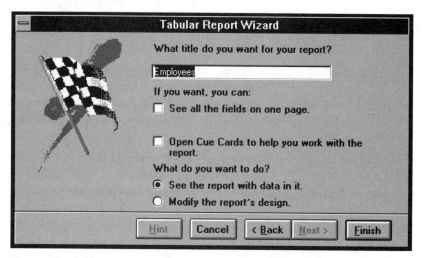

Figure 10-18: The fourth Tabular Report Wizard dialog box, used to specify a report title, to determine whether all fields appear on the same page, as well as to determine what Access displays after the Wizard is finished designing the report.

9. Access will, by default, print the table or query name at the top of each page. In the dialog box shown in Figure 10-18, you have the option of changing the report title by typing a different title in the provided text box.

   In the Employees example, type **Employees Salaries** as the report title.

10. By default, Access uses a standard column width to display all fields that you selected for use in the report, each field in its own column. If the table contains many fields, they may not

fit within the margins of a single page. Access uses landscape page orientation, by default, but there still may be too many fields to fit on one page width. If you want Access to reduce column width in an attempt to squeeze all fields on a single page width, mark the "See all the fields on page" check box in the fourth Tabular Report Wizard dialog box.

In the Employees example, accept the default option.

11. The fourth Tabular Report Wizard dialog box gives you the option of turning on Cue Cards. If you plan to display the report design in Design view, you may want to display Cue Cards by marking the appropriate check box in the fourth Single-Column Report Wizard dialog box.

12. Finally, the dialog box shown in Figure 10-18 asks which of the following you want to do next, after the Wizard finishes generating the report design:

○ *See the report with data in it.* Choose this option if you want to preview the report output, as a prelude to printing the report, without making any changes in the report design.

○ *Modify the report's design.* Choose this option if you want the Wizard to display the new report design in Design view, so you can customize the design.

In the Employees example, we'll go directly to Print Preview, without displaying Design view.

13. Choose the Finish button. The Report Wizard first generates the report design, based on your answers to the Wizard's various questions. If you chose the "See the report with data in it" option button in the last Report Wizard dialog box, Access displays the report in Print Preview.

Figure 10-19 shows the example tabular report for the Employees table in Print Preview. Notice that the Report Wizard generated a report that totals the number field Salary at the end of the report. The report doesn't correctly format the sum as currency, but we could easily correct that oversight in Design view.

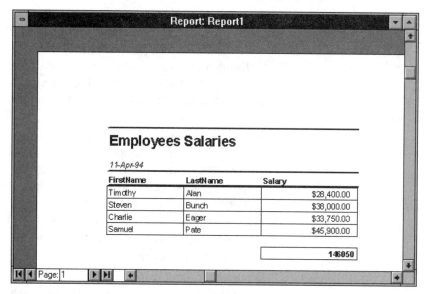

Figure 10-19: The tabular report for the Employees table in Print Preview.

If, in the last Report Wizard dialog box, you chose the "Modify the report's design" option button, the Wizard displays the new report design in Design view (see Figure 10-20). Refer to Chapter 11 for a full discussion of how to modify the report design.

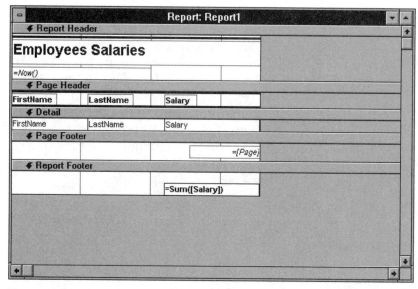

Figure 10-20: The tabular report for the Employees table in Design view.

14. To print the report, either click the Print button in the toolbar or choose File, Print from the menu bar. Access displays the Print dialog box. Make sure all the print settings are correct, and choose the OK button to send the report to the printer (see Figure 10-21).

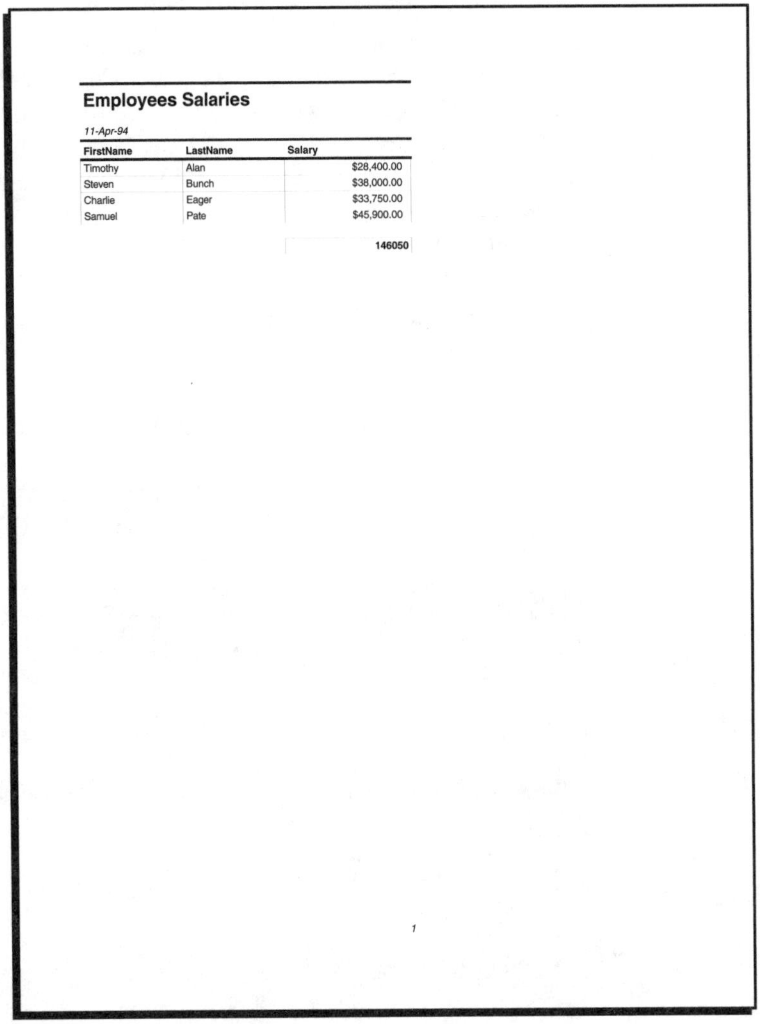

Employees Salaries

11-Apr-94

FirstName	LastName	Salary
Timothy	Alan	$28,400.00
Steven	Bunch	$38,000.00
Charlie	Eager	$33,750.00
Samuel	Pate	$45,900.00
		146050

1

Figure 10-21: The first page of the tabular report for the Employees table generated by the Tabular Report Wizard.

15. To save the report design, either click the Save button in the toolbar (if it is displayed) or choose File, Save As from the menu bar. Access displays the Save As dialog box. Type a name for the report in the Report Name text box and choose the OK button.

In the Employees example, type **Employees Salaries** and choose the OK button.

16. To close the Report window, double-click the Control-menu bar in the upper-left corner of the window.

CREATING MAILING LABELS

Virtually every business mails an ever-increasing volume of correspondence month after month. Many businesses have found that the most efficient way to address envelopes is using mailing labels. Access, therefore, includes a Report Wizard that can generate mailing labels that match over 100 varieties of Avery (brand) labels. In our Contacts database example, you may want to create a report to generate mailing labels from data in the Contacts table.

To create a mailing-label report using a Report Wizard,

1. Follow steps 1 through 4 described in the "Creating a Single-Column Report" section of this chapter. Choose the Contacts table.

2. From the list box in the Report Wizards dialog box (see Figure 10-10), double-click Mailing Label, or choose Mailing Label and choose the OK button. Access displays the first Mailing Label Wizard dialog box (see Figure 10-22).

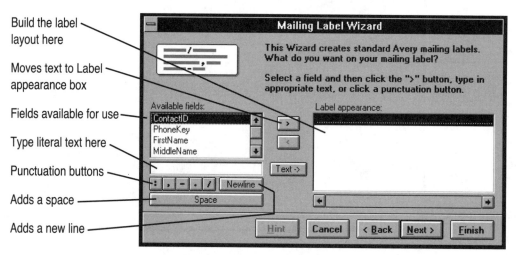

Figure 10-22: The first Mailing Label Wizard dialog box.

3. Similar to the procedure used in the other Report Wizards, you move the names of the fields you want to appear in the labels from the Available fields box, on the left side of the dialog box, to the Label appearance list box, on the right side

of the dialog box. To move a field name, either double- click the name, or select the name and click the > button.

Unlike the other Wizards, however, you have control over both the horizontal and vertical positioning of the fields. When you move a field to the Label appearance box, the Wizard adds fields from left to right. To cause a field to appear on the next line in the Label appearance box, you must first click the Newline button.

To cause a space to appear between fields, click the Space button in the dialog box before moving the second field name to the Label appearance box.

If you want punctuation to appear in the label—between the City and State fields, for example—click the appropriate punctuation button in the dialog box.

Sometimes you need to add certain text to all labels. For example, you may want to add "Or Current Resident" in a line below the name line when sending out an advertisement to home addresses. To add text to the label design, type the text in the text box on the left side of the dialog box and click the Text button. The Wizard moves the text to the Label appearance box.

In the Contacts mailing label example, create a mailing label design that resembles the following layout:

```
Salutation FirstName MiddleName LastName
AddressLine1
AddressLine2
City, State Country  ZipCode
```

The completed design should look similar to Figure 10-23.

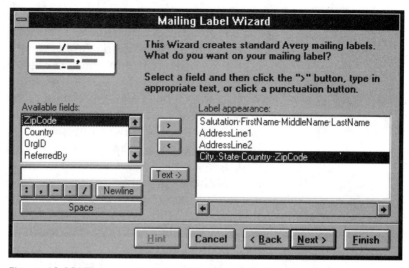

Figure 10-23: The completed mailing label design for Contacts.

4. Choose the Next > button to display the next dialog box.

5. Access displays the second Mailing Label Wizard dialog box, which is nearly identical to the second Single-Column Report Wizard dialog box, shown in Figure 10-12. In this dialog box, the Wizard asks, "Which fields do you want to sort by?" The Available fields list box lists all fields from the table or query. If you want Access to print the labels sorted by the values in one of the fields, either double-click the field name in the Available fields list box, or select the field name and choose the > button. Access moves the field name to the Sort order list box. To sort by more than one field, move additional field names to the Sort order list box.

   In the Contacts example, move the LastName field name to the Sort order column to sort the labels by values in that field.

6. Choose the Next > button to display the third Mailing Label Wizard dialog box.

7. The third Mailing Label Wizard dialog box contains a scrolling list box that lists built-in label sizes (see Figure 10-24). Each row in the list box corresponds to a particular Avery label style. The list box consists of three columns. The first column lists the Avery label number. The second column lists the dimensions of a single label. The last column lists the number of labels contained in each row of the label sheet. To scroll the list box, use the mouse and the scroll bar on the right side of the list box.

Label dimensions
Avery label number

Sheet-fed labels
Continuous labels

Number of labels
in a row

Lists labels with
English unit of
measure

Lists labels with Metric
unit or measure

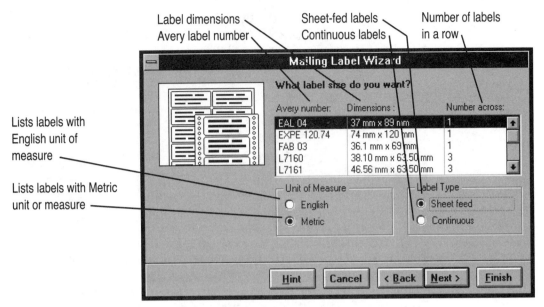

Figure 10-24: The third Mailing Label Wizard dialog box.

The label-size list box is actually three separate lists: a Metric sheet-feed list, an English sheet-feed list and an English continuous-feed list. When you first display the dialog box, the Wizard displays the Metric sheet-feed list. If you are using sheet-fed labels, but you don't find your labels listed, you may be using English measure labels (inches rather than centimeters).

To select the English sheet-feed list, choose the English option button and make sure the Sheet feed button is still selected.

If you want to print on continuous labels, choose the English option button and the Continuous option button. Then choose the correct label size from the list box.

In the Contacts example, display the English sheet-feed list and then choose Avery number 5160.

8. Choose the Next > button to display the fourth Mailing Label Wizard dialog box.

9. The fourth Mailing Label Wizard dialog box (see Figure 10-25) asks, "What font and color do you want?" Four drop-down list boxes enable you to select a different font (default is Arial), font size (default is 10), font weight (default is Bold) and text color (default is Black). (**Note:** These options are effective only if supported by your printer.) You can also cause the

labels to print in italic by selecting the Italic check box, or to be underlined by selecting the Underline check box.

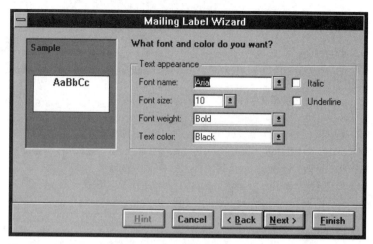

Figure 10-25: The fourth Mailing Label Wizard dialog box, used to specify font and color.

In the Contacts example, choose Times New Roman font, but leave all other options at their default settings.

10. After selecting font and color, choose the Next > button to display the fifth Mailing Label Wizard dialog box.

11. This final dialog box asks which of the following you want to do next, after the Wizard finishes generating the label design:

○ *See the mailing labels as they will look printed.* Choose this option if you want to preview the labels, as a prelude to printing them, without making any changes in the report design.

○ *Modify the mailing label design.* Choose this option if you want the Wizard to display the new label design in Design view, so you càn customize the design.

In the Contacts example, we'll go directly to Print Preview, without displaying Design view.

12. The final Mailing Label Wizard dialog box gives you the option of turning on Cue Cards. If you plan to display the label design in Design view, you may want to display Cue Cards by marking the appropriate check box in the Wizard dialog box.

13. Choose the Finish button. The Mailing Label Wizard first generates the label design. If you chose the "See the mailing

labels as they will look printed" option button in the last Mailing Label Wizard dialog box, Access displays the labels in Print Preview. Figure 10-26 shows the example mailing labels, from the Contacts table data, in Print Preview. You can use the scroll bars at the bottom and on the right side of the Report window to scroll the first page of the report.

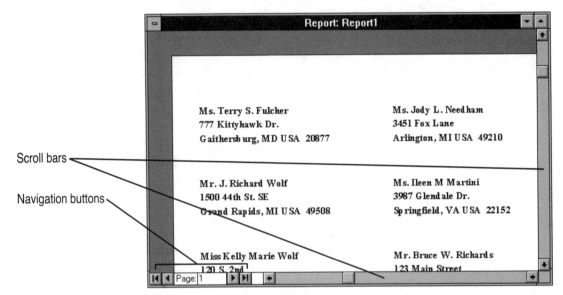

Figure 10-26: The mailing labels generated from the Contacts data in Print Preview.

If, in the last Mailing Labels Wizard dialog box, you chose the "Modify the mailing label design" option button, the Wizard displays the new report design in Design view (see Figure 10-27). Refer to Chapter 11 for a full discussion of how to modify the report design.

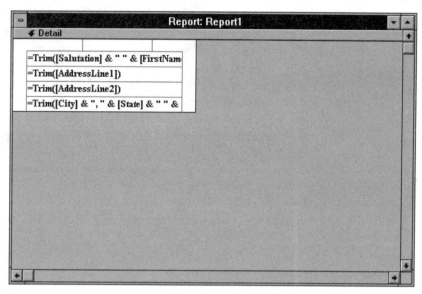

Figure 10-27: The mailing label report for Contacts in Design view.

14. To print the labels, either click the Print button in the toolbar or choose File, Print from the menu bar. Access displays the Print dialog box. Make sure all the print settings are correct, and choose the OK button to send the report to the printer (see Figure 10-28).

Ms. Terry S. Fulcher
777 Kittyhawk Dr.
Gaithersburg, MD USA 20877

Ms. Jody L. Needham
3451 Fox Lane
Arlington, MI USA 49210

Mr. Alan McConnell
9828 Rocky Ridge
Suite 400
Centreville, MI USA 49020

Mr. J. Richard Wolf
1500 44th St. SE
Grand Rapids, MI USA 49508

Ms. Ileen M Martini
3987 Glendale Dr.
Springfield, VA USA 22152

Mrs. Sarah L. Smiley
13 Baker St.
Suite 1700
Alexandria, VA USA 22213

Miss Kelly Marie Wolf
120 S. 2nd
Suite B
Springfield, VA USA 22152

Mr. Bruce W. Richards
123 Main Street
Hometown, MI USA 49000

Mr. Kevin Richard Wolf
770 Shaw Rd.
Suite 701
Alexandria, MI USA 49313

Mr. David Alan Needham
663 Yuppie Lane
Mail Stop #800
McLean, VA USA 22101

Mr. Wallace M. East
1211 Commerce St.
Springfield, VA USA 22150

Mr. Alfred H. Long
720 Port Royal
Building 33, Suite 4a
Fairfax, VA USA 22030

Ms. Francis P. Jones
2229 Hillcrest Dr.
Suite 102
Arlington, MI USA 49210

Mr. Rex T. Comfort
6601 Wales Rd.
Dept. 33
Vienna, MI USA 49180

Ms. Roberta M. Sangster
1411 Reservation Dr.
Springfield, VA USA 22152

Mrs. Wynona R. Brown
1711 Lakeview Dr.
Chapel Hill, NC USA 27514

Ms. Helen H. Harrison
7112 Commerce St
Springfield, MI USA 49150

Mr. Richard B. Walters
328A Front St.
Suite 100
Maui, HI USA 61010

Mrs. Toni S. Fulcher
9560 Shell Street
Sinajana, Guam 55523

Ms. Jane N. Smith
901 Wall Street
Tamuning, Guam 55522

Mr. Alan Moonie
9828 White Sands Dr.
Toto, Guam 55524

Mr. Richard B. Walters
328A Front St.
Suite 100
Maui, HI USA 61010

Miss Ireen M. Julliet
23 Jordan Lane
Suite 402
Hilo, HI USA 61012

Ms. Sarah S. Smith
1142 S. Orange Blvd
Sinajana, Guam 55523

Ms. Kelly Marie Wolf
33 Duke St.
Honolulu, HI USA 61016

Figure 10-28: The first page of the mailing labels from data in the Contacts table, generated by the Mailing Label Wizard.

15. To save the label design, either click the Save button in the toolbar (if it is displayed) or choose File, Save As from the menu bar. Access displays the Save As dialog box. Type a name for the labels in the Report Name text box and choose the OK button.

In the Contacts example, type **Contacts Mailing Labels** and choose the OK button.

16. To close the Report window, double-click the Control-menu bar in the upper-left corner of the window.

CREATING A GROUPS/TOTALS REPORT

The Report Wizards covered thus far enable you to print records in a particular order, sorted by the values in one or more fields. But sometimes you not only want to sort records, but you want to group them so that you can perform some type of numerical analysis of the grouped records. A group/totals report enables you to group records together by the value(s) in up to four fields in the underlying table or query. Each group of records is displayed in a tabular format. The Report Wizard can generate a report that calculates subtotals at the end of each group, and grand totals at the end of the report.

For example, you might want to group employee records by company department and then total the salaries per department. The Employees table that we have been working with only contains records for four account executives (salespersons). So that we can practice creating a group/totals report, use the File, Import command to import the All Employees table from the Ventana database into the Contacts database. This table includes the entire Sales department, as well as the Production department, the Accounting department and the Administration department.

To create a group/totals report using a Report Wizard,

1. Follow steps 1 through 4 described in the "Creating a Single-Column Report" section of this chapter. Base the report on the All Employees table.

2. From the list box in the Report Wizards dialog box (see Figure 10-10), double-click Group/Totals, or choose Group/Totals and choose the OK button. Access displays the first Group/Totals dialog box (this dialog box is very similar in appearance to the dialog box shown in Figure 10-11).

3. Move the names of the fields you want included in the report from the Available fields list box to the Field order on report list box. Each of the chosen fields will appear as a separate column in the report.

   In the All Employees example, double-click each of the following field names in the Available fields list box, in the following order:

   Department
   FirstName
   LastName
   Salary

4. Choose the Next > button to display the next dialog box.

5. Access displays the second Group/Totals Report Wizard dialog box, which asks, "Which fields do you want to group by?" To group records by one of the fields in the Available fields list box, move the field name to the Group records by list box. The Wizard will group records by up to four fields, if you need that many levels of grouping.

   In the All Employees example, to group the report by department, double-click the Department field name in the Available fields list box to move the field to the Group records by list box.

6. Choose the Next > button to display the third Group/Totals Report Wizard dialog box.

7. The third Group/Totals Report Wizard dialog box enables you to choose how you want to group records within each grouping that you specified in the preceding dialog box. Click the drop-down button at the right end of the Group list box (see Figure 10-29) and choose from among the available grouping options:

Click to display available grouping options

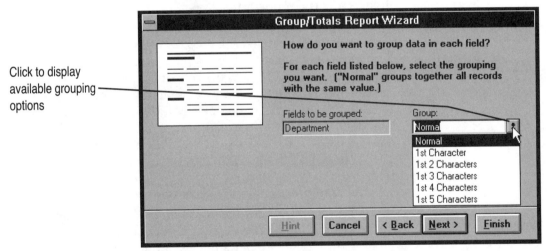

Figure 10-29: The third Group/Totals Wizard dialog box with the Group drop-down list displayed.

   In the All Employees example, there is no need to group records any more narrowly. Accept the default setting and click Next > to display the fourth Group/Totals Report Wizard dialog box.

8. The fourth Group/Totals Report Wizard dialog box asks "Which fields do you want to sort by?" Access automatically sorts the report by the grouping field(s). To sort records

within each grouping by the values in one of the other fields, select one of the remaining field names in the Available fields list box.

In the All Employees example, double-click LastName to sort employee records by last name within each department's grouping.

9. Click the Next > button to display the fifth Group/Totals Report Wizard dialog box.

10. Choose the report style, page orientation and line spacing from the fifth Group/Totals Report Wizard dialog box. In the All Employees example, choose the Presentation style and Portrait orientation. Leave line spacing at $\frac{1}{12}$ inch.

11. Click the Next > button once more to display the sixth and final Group/Totals Report Wizard dialog box.

12. Access will, by default, print the table or query name at the top of each page. You have the option of changing the report title by typing a different title in the provided text box.

In the All Employee example, type **All Employees Salaries** as the report title.

13. By default, the Wizard uses a standard column width to display all fields that you selected for use in the report, each field in its own column. If the table contains many fields, they may not fit within the margins of a single page. Access uses landscape page orientation, by default, but there still may be too many fields to fit on one page width. If you want Access to reduce column width in an attempt to squeeze all fields on a single page width, mark the "See all fields on the same page" check box in the sixth Tabular Report Wizard dialog box.

In the Employees example, accept the default option.

14. By default, the Wizard will calculate percentages of the total for each group. If you don't want percentages computed, unmark the "Calculate percentages of the total" check box. In the All Employees example, accept the default option.

15. The sixth Group/Totals Report Wizard dialog box gives you the option of turning on Cue Cards. If you plan to display the report design in Design view, you may want to display Cue Cards by marking the appropriate check box.

16. Finally, the dialog box asks which of the following you want to do next, after the Wizard finishes generating the report design:

○ *See the report with data in it.* Choose this option if you want to preview the report output, as a prelude to printing the report, without making any changes in the report design.

○ *Modify the report's design.* Choose this option if you want the Wizard to display the new report design in Design view, so you can customize the design.

In the All Employees example, we'll go directly to Print Preview, without displaying Design view.

17. The Report Wizard first generates the report design, based on your answers to the Wizard's various questions. If you chose the "See the report with data in it" option button in the last Report Wizard dialog box, Access displays the report in Print Preview.

If, in the last Report Wizard dialog box, you chose the "Modify the report's design" option button, the Wizard displays the new report design in Design view (see Figure 10-30).

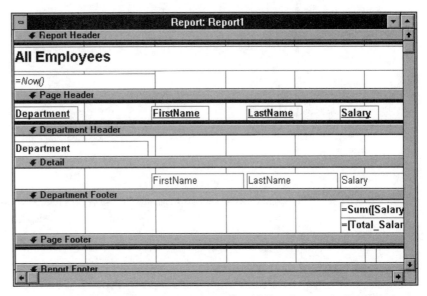

Figure 10-30: The group/totals report for All Employees in Design view.

18. To print the report, either click the Print button in the toolbar or choose File, Print from the menu bar. Access displays the Print dialog box. Make sure all the print settings are correct, and choose the OK button to send the report to the printer (see Figure 10-31).

All Employees

12-Apr-94

Department	FirstName	LastName	Salary
Accounting			
	David	Brown	$36,575.00
	Freda	French	$29,834.75
	Christopher	Harvey	$44,935.00
			111344.75
			12.76%
Administration			
	Bruce	Brown	$35,700.00
	Hercule	Plum	$44,887.50
	Sarah	Singer	$22,522.50
			103110
			11.81%
Production			
	Stanley	Harrell	$51,558.00
	Steven	Harrison	$44,616.00
	Angel	Smith	$46,280.00
			142454
			16.32%
Sales			
	Timothy	Alan	$28,400.00
	Sharon	Albertson	$22,744.80
	Tim	Bronson	$43,056.00
	Steven	Bunch	$38,000.00
	Susan	Carson	$22,000.00
	Charlie	Eager	$33,750.00
	Gertrude	English	$38,220.00
	George	Green	$51,312.56

1

Figure 10-31: The first page of the group/totals report for All Employees, generated by the Group/Totals Report Wizard.

19. To save the report design, either click the Save button in the toolbar (if it is displayed) or choose File, Save As from the menu bar. Access displays the Save As dialog box. Type a name for the report in the Report Name text box and choose the OK button.

    In the All Employees example, type **All Employees Salaries** and choose the OK button.

20. To close the Report window, double-click the Control-menu bar in the upper-left corner of the window.

CREATING A SUMMARY REPORT

The last type of report that can be created using a Report Wizard is the summary report. A summary report is essentially a group/totals report that displays only the totals. The steps for creating a summary report using the Summary Report Wizard are very similar to the steps for creating a group/totals report. Refer to the preceding section for a discussion of the Group/Totals Report Wizard. Figure 10-32 shows the summary report that is generated by grouping the All Employees table (discussed in the preceding section) by department and totaling salaries. If you generate this report, save it as All Employees Summary.

All Employees (Summary)

12-Apr-94

Department	EmployeeID	Salary
Accounting	49	111344.75
	19.37%	12.76%
Administration	31	103110
	12.25%	11.81%
Production	39	142454
	15.42%	16.32%
Sales	134	515809.36
	52.96%	59.10%
Grand Total:		
	253	872718.11

1

Figure 10-32: The summary report for All Employees, generated by the Summary Report Wizard.

MOVING ON

This chapter has introduced you to Access reports and Report Wizards. You have learned how to print tables, queries and forms. You have also learned how to create several different types of reports using Report Wizards.

Now that you are familiar with these easy ways to create reports, you are ready to take a look at how to design reports on your own using the Report window's Design view. Turn now to Chapter 11, "Designing Custom Access Reports," to learn more about creating reports from scratch.

11

DESIGNING CUSTOM ACCESS REPORTS

In Chapter 10 we discussed how to print tables and forms and how to create reports using Access's powerful Report Wizards. This chapter teaches you how to modify reports designed by a Report Wizard as well as how to design reports on your own from scratch in the Report window's Design view.

MODIFYING AN EXISTING REPORT

Often the most efficient way to design a report is to first let a Report Wizard do most of the work. You can then customize the report design to add the little bells and whistles that the Wizard overlooked. For example, you may recall from Chapter 10 that neither the Employees Salaries report (see Figure 11-1), which was designed by the Tabular Report Wizard, nor the All Employees Salaries report, which was designed by the Group/Totals dialog box, correctly formatted the sum that appears at the end of the report. The sum should be displayed as currency, but both reports display the sum as a number without a dollar sign or commas.

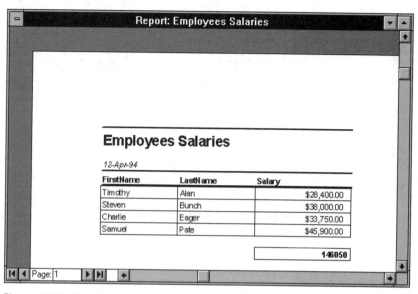

Figure 11-1: The Employees Salaries report incorrectly formats the sum at the end of the report.

In addition to changing the formatting of a field in a report design, you may want to add or remove other design elements, such as headers, footers, labels, lines, boxes, fonts and calculated fields.

To modify an existing report,

1. Open the database containing the report that you want to modify. For example, if you want to modify the Employees Salaries report, open CONTACTS.MDB.

2. Choose the Report button in the Database window to display the Reports list (see Figure 11-2).

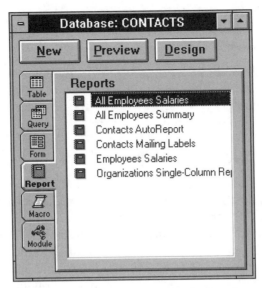

Figure 11-2: The Reports list in the Database window.

3. Select the name of the report you want to modify and choose the Design button in the Database window. Access displays the existing report design in the Report window, as shown in Figure 11-3. This view of the Report window is known as Design view.

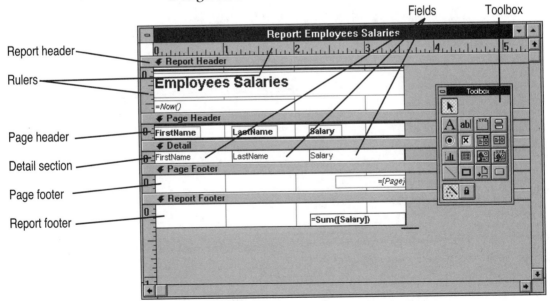

Figure 11-3: The Employees Salaries report in Design view.

4. Make the desired changes to the report's design. (We'll discuss changes you can make in the remainder of this chapter).

5. Click the Save button in the toolbar to save the changes.

6. Double-click the Control-menu box at the upper-left corner of the Report window to close the window and return to the Database window.

CREATING A NEW REPORT

Although you may often use Report Wizards to generate basic report designs, you may sometimes prefer to design a report yourself, from the ground up. For example, let's create the Follow-Up Report that you examined in Chapter 1. The Follow-Up Report displays pertinent information about the follow-up calls or meetings that an account representative should attend to on a particular date. Figure 11-4 shows a sample follow-up report for April 13, 1994.

Contact Follow-Ups for 4/13/94

Contact Name: Mr. Bruce Richards

Nick Name:

Description: Made an appointment for a sales call
on 4/13/94. Expressed an interest in
Deluxe and Super models.

Phone Numbers:

Type	Number	Extension
Business	(616) 555-8889	

Follow-Up Date: 4/13/94

Contact Name: Mr. Alan Moonie

Nick Name: Alan

Description: Send catalog. Call on 4/13/94.

Phone Numbers:

Type	Number	Extension
Home	(671) 555-0028	

Follow-Up Date: 4/13/94

Contact Name: Mr. Richard Walters

Nick Name: Rich

Description: Tentative phone order for 3 dozen
Super Widgets. Call on 4/13 to
confirm.

Phone Numbers:

Type	Number	Extension
Business	(808) 555-3884	
Fax	(808) 555-8285	

Follow-Up Date: 4/13/94

Contact Name: Ms. Kelly Wolf

Nick Name:

Description: Call requesting catalog. Call on 4/12.

Phone Numbers:

Type	Number	Extension
Business	(808) 555-2333	
Fax	(808) 555-2331	

Follow-Up Date: 4/13/94

Figure 11-4: The Follow-Up Report for April 13, 1994.

The Follow-Up Report that we're going to create will be based on a query that combines fields from the Contacts table with fields from the Interactions table. Before we can design the report, we must create the query on which it will be based.

1. Create a query named Follow Up that contains the following fields from the Contacts table and the Interactions table:

Contacts	Interactions
ContactID	EmployeeID
PhoneKey	FollowUpDate
FirstName	Description
LastName	
Salutation	
Nickname	

2. Add the following criteria to the criteria row for the FollowUpDate column in the QBE grid: **[To see a list of follow-ups, specify the date:]**

   Recall from the discussions in Chapter 7 that this entry in the criteria row will cause Access to display, at run time, a dialog box displaying the text that you typed within the brackets. The dialog box also will include a text box in which the user can enter a date. As a result, the query's dynaset will include records from the matching follow-up date only.

3. Sort the dynaset in ascending order by the values in the ContactID field.

4. Save the query with the name **Follow Up.**

5. Run the query. When Access displays the prompt, asking you to specify a date, type **4/13/94** and press Enter. Access displays follow-ups for April 13, 1994 (see Figure 11-5).

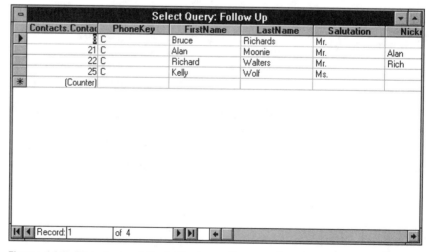

Figure 11-5: The dynaset that displays after running the Follow Up query and entering the date 4/13/94.

After you have decided on a table or query on which to base the report, you are ready to begin designing the report. To display a blank design, follow these steps:

1. Open the database containing the table or query on which you want to base the report. In our example, if you haven't already done so, open the CONTACTS.MDB database.

2. In the Database window, select the table or query on which you will base the report. In the Follow-Up Report example, display the Queries list and select the Follow Up query.

3. With the Database window displayed, click the New Report button in the toolbar. Alternatively, choose File, New, Report from the menu bar. Access displays the New Report dialog box (see Figure 11-6).

Figure 11-6: The New Report dialog box with the Follow Up query selected.

4. Choose the Blank Report button in the New Report dialog box. Access displays the Report window in Design view, containing an empty report design (see Figure 11-7).

Rulers

Page header

Toolbox

Detail section

Page footer

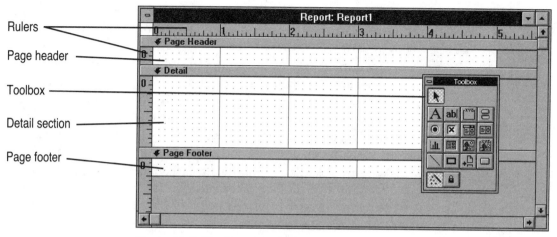

Figure 11-7: The Report window in Design view, containing a blank report design.

SAVING A REPORT DESIGN

Whether you are modifying an existing report design or creating a new one, you should save to disk any additions or changes to the design. To save the report design:

1. Click the Save button on the toolbar, or choose File, Save or File, Save As from the menu bar. Access displays the Save As dialog box.

2. Type the name you want to give the report in the Report Name text box and press Enter. In the example report, name the report **Follow-Up Report.**

TAKING A LOOK AT DESIGN VIEW

Think of the Report window, when in Design view, as a canvas on which you "paint" a report design. When you start with a blank report, you are starting with a blank canvas. The only things that print when you send the report to the printer are the items that you add to the canvas in Design view.

Report Sections

The body of the Report window, in Design view, is split into sections. The number of sections can vary. Figure 11-7, the blank report design in which we will design the Follow-Up Report, shows the Report window split into three sections. Figure 11-3, the Employees Salaries report design generated by the Tabular Report

Wizard (in Chapter 10), shows a Report window split into five sections. Figure 11-8 shows the All Employees Salaries report design, generated by the Groups/Totals Report Wizard (also in Chapter 10). The All Employees Salaries Report window is divided into seven sections. These sections determine where data will be printed in the final printed report:

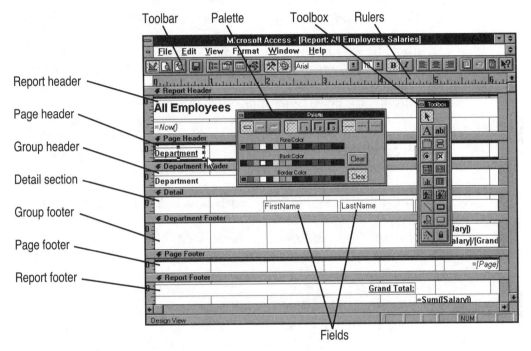

Figure 11-8: The All Employees Salaries report in Design view.

○ *Report Header*. The report header appears at the top of the Report window. It is bounded by the Report Header bar on the top and the Page Header bar on the bottom. Data placed in the report header appears at the beginning of the report, before the page header on the first page of the report. A report header typically contains the report title and often the date of the report. The report header in the All Employees Salaries report design, shown in Figure 11-8, includes the title All Employees as well as the current system date (generated by the =Now() expression).

To toggle a report header on or off, choose Format, Report Header/Footer from the menu bar.

○ *Page Header*. The page header section of the Report window is bounded by the Page Header bar on the top and the Detail bar on the bottom. Data placed in the page header section appears at the top of every page of the report. The page header typically contains labels of some kind. In the All Employees Salaries example, the page header includes column-header labels: Department, FirstName, LastName and Salary.

To toggle a page header on or off, choose Format, Page Header/Footer from the menu bar.

○ *Group Header.* When you use the sorting and grouping feature of Access reports, Access adds a group header section for each field by which you group records in the report. In the All Employees Salaries example, records are grouped by department. Access has added a group header for the Department field. All group header sections appear in the report design above the detail section and below the page header. Data placed in a group header appears in the report printout above the detail records. Most often, group headers include the name of the field on which the grouping is based. Sometimes the field itself is placed in the group header. In the All Employees Salaries report, the group header for the Department field contains the field name, Department.

○ *Detail.* The contents of the detail section appear once for every record in the underlying table or query. This section is bounded on the top by the Detail bar and on the bottom by the first footer.

○ *Group Footer.* For each group header, Access also adds a group footer. When you use the sorting and grouping feature of Access reports, Access adds a group header and group footer section for each field by which you group records in the report. In the All Employees Salaries example, Access has added a group footer for the Department field. All group footers appear after the detail section and above the page footer. Data placed in a group footer appears in the report printout below the detail records. Typically, group footers include summary calculations. In the All Employees Salaries example, the group footer for the Department field contains a calculated field that totals all salaries in the department as well as a calculated field that computes the percentage of all salaries that the department total represents.

○ *Page Footer.* Data placed in the page footer section appears at the bottom of every page in the report. The page footer area is bounded on the top by the Page Footer bar and on the bottom by the Report Footer bar. The page footer often includes a page number.

○ *Report Footer*. The report footer is found at the bottom of the report design. It is bounded on the top by the Report Footer bar and on the bottom by the end line of the report design. Data placed in the report footer appears once in the report: at the end of the last page, just before the page footer on the last page of the report.

Sometimes you need to adjust the vertical position of the bars that separate the various report sections, increasing or decreasing the size of the sections. To move a bar:

1. Place the mouse pointer on the top edge of the bar. The mouse pointer changes shape to a double-arrowhead, pointing up and down at the same time.

2. Click and drag the bar in the desired direction. It is often convenient to use the vertical ruler that appears on the left side of the Report window to judge how much space you need to add to a section.

   Figure 11-9 shows the blank Follow-Up Report design after moving the Page Footer bar downward in order to increase the size of the detail section.

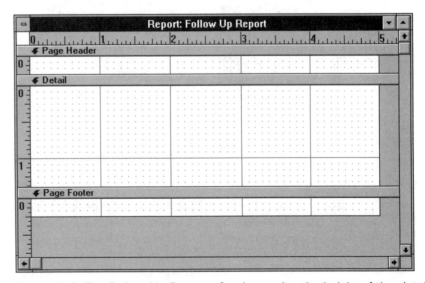

Figure 11-9: The Follow-Up Report after increasing the height of the detail section.

The Toolbox

Toolbox

Like the Form window (see Chapter 9), the Report window, in Design view, displays a toolbox (see Figure 11-10) for adding controls to the report. The toolbox can be toggled off and on. It is a sizable, movable window that "floats" on top of the Report window. If the toolbox is not already displayed, you can display it by clicking the Toolbox button or by choosing View, Toolbox from the menu bar.

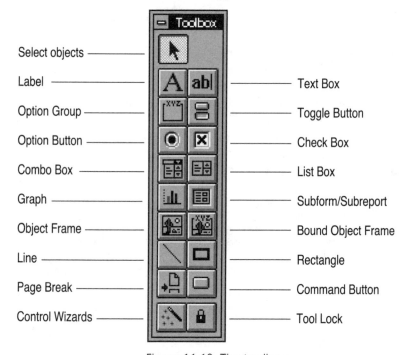

Select objects		
Label		Text Box
Option Group		Toggle Button
Option Button		Check Box
Combo Box		List Box
Graph		Subform/Subreport
Object Frame		Bound Object Frame
Line		Rectangle
Page Break		Command Button
Control Wizards		Tool Lock

Figure 11-10: The toolbox.

Each button in the toolbox represents a control that you can add to the report design, or a setting that affects how controls are created. Refer to Chapter 9, "Designing Custom Forms," for a description of each button.

Some of the controls—such as toggle buttons, check boxes and combo boxes—don't have much relevance in reports. But for consistency, all controls available in form design are also available in report design.

The Palette

As in the Form window's Design view, Access provides a Palette (see Figure 11-11) for your use in designing reports (see "The Palette" in Chapter 9 for a full description). The Palette is not displayed by default, but can be toggled on and off. Like the toolbox, the Palette "floats," and is sizable and movable. To display the Palette, either click the Palette button in the toolbar or choose View, Palette from the menu bar.

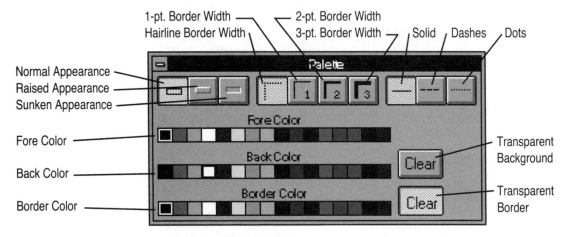

Figure 11-11: The Palette.

WORKING WITH FIELDS

Before data from your database will print in a report, you must add fields to the report design. Both the Employees Salaries report and the All Employees Salaries report include the FirstName, LastName and Salary fields in their respective detail sections (see Figures 11-3 and 11-8). Most often, you add fields to the detail section, but you can add fields to any section of the report design. *Where* you add the field, however, will determine where and how often the field's values will print in the report output.

Adding Fields

To add a field to a report design, follow these steps:

　　1. Open the report in Design view.

Field List

2. Either click the Field List button in the toolbar, or choose View, Field List from the menu bar. Access displays a field list window that lists the field names from the table or query on which the report is based. Figure 11-12 shows the field list for the Follow Up query on which the Follow-Up Report design is based.

Figure 11-12: The field list for the Follow Up query.

3. Click the name of a field that you want to add to the report and drag the field name to the appropriate section of the report window.

For example, in the Follow-Up Report, drag the Nickname, Description and FollowUpDate fields to the detail section of the Report window, as shown in Figure 11-13.

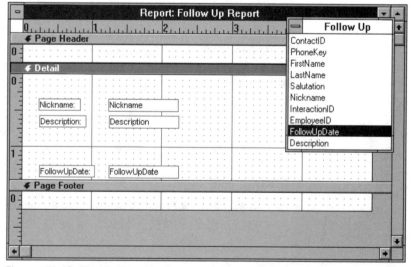

Figure 11-13: The Follow-Up Report design with Nickname, Description and FollowUpDate fields added.

Notice that each field appears to have been added twice to the report design. The control on the left side, however, is actually a label control that describes the contents of the control on the right. The control on the right is a *bound text box*—bound to the field that you selected in the field list. For convenience, this chapter refers to bound text controls in reports as *fields*.

When you print the report, the label prints in the report just as it appeared in the Report window. But the field (the bound text box) prints a value from the field to which it is bound—the contact's nickname, for example.

When you finish adding fields to the report design, double-click the field list's Control-menu box to close the field list.

Moving, Sizing & Deleting Fields

Both the label controls and the associated fields can be moved and sized in the Report window using the mouse.

Before you can move, size or delete a control you first must select the control with the mouse. Just click the control and Access displays small squares—known as *handles*—at the corners, top and bottom of the control's box. If you select the bound text box, Access also places a large handle at the upper-left corner of the bound control's label. For example, Figure 11-14 shows the Description field selected in the Follow-Up Report design.

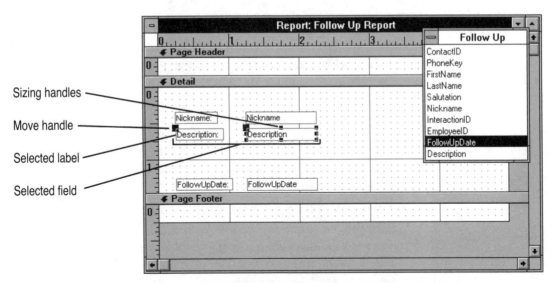

Figure 11-14: The selected Description field and its label.

If you want, you can select several controls at once by drawing a box around the controls. Simply click at the position that will be a corner of the box and drag to the diagonally opposite corner. For example, click in the upper-left corner, drag the mouse pointer to the lower-right corner and release the mouse button (see Figure 11-15). When you release the mouse, all controls in the box are selected.

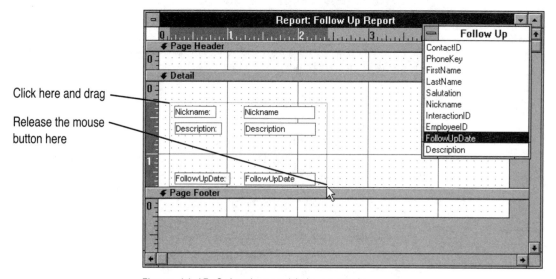

Click here and drag

Release the mouse button here

Figure 11-15: Selecting multiple controls.

After you have selected a control or controls, you are ready to move, size or delete the control. To move one or more selected controls, along with each control's attached label, if any, follow these steps:

1. Move the mouse pointer around over the selected control you want to move until the pointer becomes shaped like an open hand (*not* a hand with a pointing finger).

2. Click and drag the control(s) to a new position and release the mouse button.

To move a field *without* moving its attached label,

1. Select the control.

2. Move the mouse pointer to the *move handle*—the larger square at the upper-left corner of the control's box. The mouse pointer becomes shaped like a hand with a pointing index finger.

3. Click and drag the control to a new position and release the mouse button.

To move just a label, without moving the control to which it is attached,

1. Select the control.

2. Move the mouse pointer to the move handle at the upper-left corner of the label. The mouse pointer becomes a hand with a pointing index finger.

3. Click and drag the label to a new position and release the mouse button.

To resize a control,

1. Select a control.

2. Move the mouse pointer to one of the *sizing handles*–the small squares at the top, bottom or corner of the control.

3. Click and drag the sizing handle until the control is the desired size.

To edit the text in a label control,

1. Select the label control.

2. Move the mouse pointer over the selected label control. When the mouse pointer shape becomes an I beam, click inside the control's box. Access displays a blinking cursor inside the box.

3. Use the cursor-movement keys (the Home, End and arrow keys) to move the cursor around the box. Edit the text just as you would type text in any text box.

4. When you are finished editing the label, click in a blank area of the form.

To delete one or more controls,

1. Select the control(s).

2. Either press the Delete (or Del) key, or choose Edit, Delete from the menu bar. Access deletes the control(s) from the form.

In the Follow-Up Report example, use these techniques to move, size and edit controls to match the design shown in Figure 11-16.

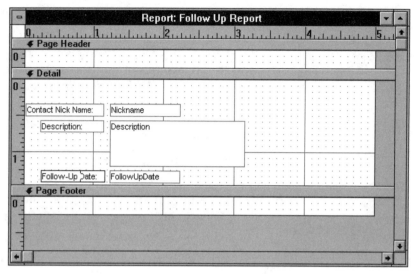

Figure 11-16: The Follow-Up Report design after resizing and editing controls.

SETTING PROPERTIES

In Chapter 9, "Designing Custom Forms," you learned how to display and modify the properties of controls. Properties in the Report window's Design view work in exactly the same way as properties in the Form window's Design view.

To display a control's property sheet, either double-click the control (before selecting it) or do the following:

1. Select the control.

2. Click the Properties button in the toolbar; choose View, Properties from the menu bar; or right-click the selected control and choose Properties from the pop-up menu.

For example, to display the property sheet for the Nick Name label, either double-click the label, or select the label and then click the Properties button in the toolbar. Access displays the label's property sheet, shown in Figure 11-17.

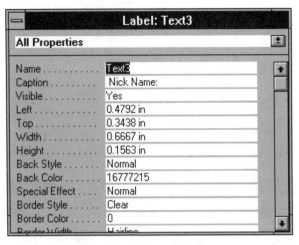

Figure 11-17: The Nick Name label's property sheet.

Changing a property value is straightforward. Each property is contained in either a simple text box or in a combo box. For example, let's change the Nick Name label's FontWeight property from Normal to Bold, and change the TextAlign property from General to Right:

1. Display the property sheet for the Nick Name label.

2. Click the Font Weight combo box in the property sheet and then click the drop-down button at the end of the combo box. Access displays the following choices:

   ○ Extra Light

   ○ Light

   ○ Normal

   ○ Medium

   ○ Semi-bold

   ○ Bold

   ○ Extra Bold

   ○ Heavy

3. Select the Bold option. Access changes the label to bold.

4. Select the Text Align combo box in the property sheet for the Nick Name label.

5. Click the drop-down button the end of the combo box to display the following list of options:

○ General

○ Left

○ Center

○ Right

6. Choose the Right option. This causes the selected label to be right justified within the field's box in the report design.

Repeat the property changes for the Description label and the Follow-Up Date label. The results should resemble Figure 11-18.

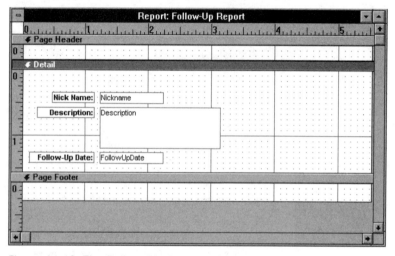

Figure 11-18: The Follow-Up Report after changing the FontWeight and TextAlign properties in the Nick Name label's property sheet.

ADDING CONTROLS TO REPORTS

As is the case with forms, each of the elements you add to a report design is known as a *control*. Access controls fall into three broad categories:

○ *Bound control.* A bound control, such as a field from the Contacts table or from the Follow Up query, is tied to a field in the table or query on which the report is based. As Access moves record by record through the table or query during report output, the value of a bound control changes.

○ *Calculated control.* A calculated control is based on an expression—a combination of fields, values, operators, control names, functions and constant values. If the expression is based on the value(s) in a field(s), the value displayed in the control will change as the report moves from record to record.

❍ *Unbound control.* An unbound control, such as the title at the
top of a report, is not tied to a field in the underlying table or
query, nor is it tied to an expression. Unbound controls, therefore, do not change as a report is processed.

Chapter 9 explains how to add controls to a form design. The
procedure for adding controls to a report design using the toolbox
(see Figure 11-10) is identical, except that many of the controls that
are used in forms are of little value in reports. Buttons and combo
boxes, for example, are not operational when you print the report.
We'll spend the rest of this chapter discussing some of the controls
that you *will* find useful in your reports.

The Pointer

The pointer is selected by default whenever you open the toolbox.
The pointer must be selected when you are attempting to select
and change the controls currently in the report design. Clicking
the pointer button causes the default mouse pointer to appear.

Adding a Label

You use the label control to place text into a report. Each field
placed in the report design automatically gets its own label. But you
can also use label controls to add text elsewhere in the report that
is not tied to a particular field. For example, let's use a label control
to add a report title to the Follow-Up Report's page header.

1. If the toolbox is not already displayed, click the Toolbox
   button in the toolbar.
2. Click the Label button in the toolbox. The mouse pointer
   takes the shape of a cross-hair next to the uppercase letter *A*.
3. Move the mouse pointer to the spot in the report where you
   want the upper-left corner of the control to be located. Click
   and drag the pointer until the box on the screen is the right
   size to hold the text that you want to include in the label.
   Release the mouse button.
4. A cursor blinks inside the control's box. Type the following
   text: **Contact Follow-Ups for**
5. Click outside the control's box. The control is defined.

To complete the page header, add the FollowUpDate field to the
right of the new label. Delete the label that is attached to the field. Use
the property sheet to change the FontWeight property to Bold and the
FontSize property to 14 for both the label and the FollowUpDate field.
Also change the TextAlign property of the FollowUpDate field to Left.
The results should resemble Figure 11-19.

The new label control   FollowUpDate field

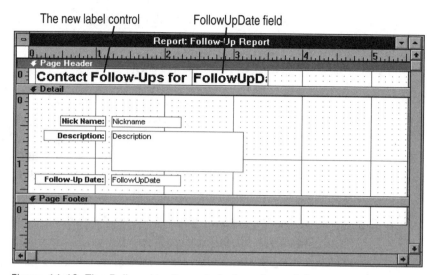

Figure 11-19: The Follow-Up Report design after adding a label control and a field to the page header.

Adding a Text Box

A text box control is the most common type of control in most reports. All fields that you place in the report using the field list are actually bound text box controls.

You can also add text box controls using the toolbox. When you want to add a calculated control to the report, you normally use a text box control.

In the Follow-Up Report we want to show the contact's name at the top of the detail section. Instead of showing Salutation, FirstName, MiddleName and LastName as separate fields, we want to combine these fields in one text box control in the report design. Such a control is often referred to as a *calculated control*. In addition to a combination of text fields, calculated controls can contain any valid Access expression. Most often such expressions are based on values in one or more fields in the underlying query or table.

To create a calculated control,

1. Display the toolbox.

2. Click the Text Box button in the toolbox. The mouse pointer takes on the shape of a cross-hair and the Text Box button.

3. Move the mouse pointer to the spot in the report where you want the upper-left corner of the control to be located. Click and drag the pointer until the box on the screen is the right size to hold the calculated output of the expression that you will enter into this control.

In the calculated contact name example, draw a box above the Nickname field that is long enough to accommodate the salutation and full name of a contact.

4. Click outside the control. You have added an unbound text box to the report.

5. Select the unbound text box and then click inside the text box. A cursor blinks in the text box.

6. Type an equal sign (=) followed by an Access expression (**Note:** If you prefer, you can display the property sheet for the text box and enter the expression in the ControlSource property. Using that method, you also have the option of using the Expression Builder.)

    In the Follow-Up Report example, type the following in the unbound text field:

    ="[Salutation] &" "& [FirstName] &" "& [LastName]"

7. Edit the label control that is attached the new calculated control. Change the label to **Contact Name:**. Select Bold as the FontWeight property. Position the label to be aligned with the other labels in the column.

8. When you have finished typing the expression, click outside the control. The result should resemble Figure 11-20.

The new calculated control

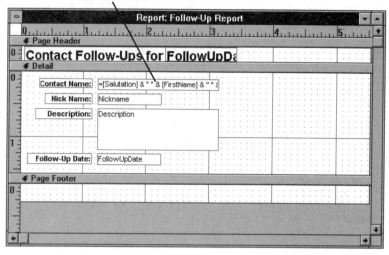

Figure 11-20: The Follow-Up Report after adding a calculated control.

Adding a Graph

You can use a graph control to display a graph on a report. Refer to Chapter 13 for a full discussion of adding graphs to forms and reports.

Adding a Subreport

A subreport control can display one report within another report. The most common use of a subreport control is to display multiple records from a related table. But it is possible to add an unbound subreport that displays data from an unrelated table.

In the Follow-Up Report example, we need to use a subreport to show the phone number records from the Phones table.

Before you can add a subreport to the main report, you have to create the subreport.

1. In the Follow-Up Report example, create a simple report, based on the Phones table, including only the Type, Number and Extension fields in the detail section.

2. Use the Format, Page Header/Footer command to toggle off the page header.

3. Use the Format, Report Header/Footer command to toggle on the report header.

4. Add the labels **Type, Number** and **Extension** in the report header, above the fields with the same names.

5. For each of the labels in the report header, set the FontWeight property to Bold and set the FontUnderline property to Yes.

6. Reduce the size of the report header and detail sections to the minimum necessary to contain the fields and labels.

7. Save the report as **Phone SubReport.**

The resulting report design for the Phone SubReport should resemble Figure 11-21.

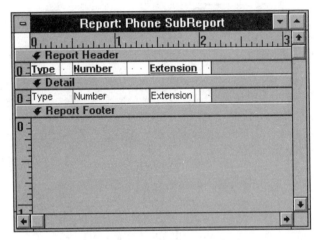

Figure 11-21: The Phone SubReport design.

After you have created the subreport, you can add it to the main report. To add the subreport:

1. With the main report design displayed, click the Database Window button on the toolbar, or press F11. Access displays the Database window, on top of the Report window.

2. If the Reports list is not already displayed, click the Report object button in the Database window.

3. Click and drag the name of the subreport to the detail section in the main report.

   In the Follow-Up Report example, drag the Phone SubReport to the detail section of the Follow-Up Report design (see Figure 11-22). Edit the label attached to the subreport. Change the label to **Phone Numbers:.** Apply the Bold FontWeight property.

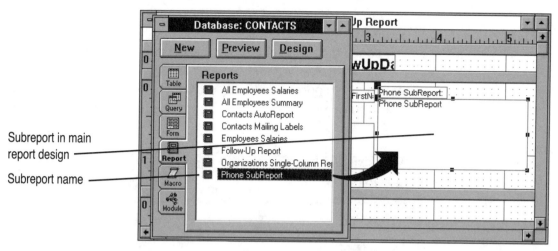

Subreport in main
report design

Subreport name

Figure 11-22: The Phone SubReport has been added to the Follow-Up
Report by dragging the report name from the Database window to the
Report window.

4. Select the subreport in the Report window and open the
property sheet. Add to the LinkChildFields property the
name(s) of the field(s) in the subreport (or underlying table/
query) that link the subreport to the main report. Add to the
LinkMasterFields property the name(s) of the field(s) in the
main report (or underlying table/query) that link the main
report to the subreport.

In the Follow-Up Report example, the ForeignKey and
PhoneKey fields in the Phones table link to the ContactID and
PhoneKey fields in the Contacts table (on which the Follow
Up query is based—the Follow-Up Report is based on the
Follow Up query). You can see the relationship graphically by
reviewing the Relationships window for the Contacts data-
base (choose Edit, Relationships on the menu bar to view the
Relationships window).

Apply the Normal BorderStyle property to the subreport to
cause a border line to be drawn around the phone numbers in
the report.

Apply the CanShrink property to the subform as well so
that the border line grows and shrinks to fit the number of
phone numbers available for each contact. Figure 11-23 shows
the completed property sheet.

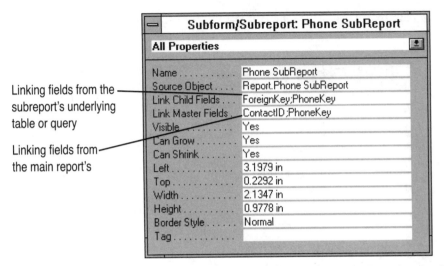

Linking fields from the subreport's underlying table or query

Linking fields from the main report's

Figure 11-23: The completed property sheet for the Phone SubReport.

Previewing a Report

It is often a good idea when your are modifying a report design to preview the report output once in a while. Access Version 2.0 has two preview modes: Print Preview and Sample Preview. Print Preview generates the report, just as it will be sent to the printer. Sample Preview, by contrast, displays only a limited number of records and ignores joins and criteria in underlying queries.

To preview a report in Print Preview, either click the Print Preview button in the toolbar, or choose File, Print Preview.

To preview a report in Sample Preview, either click the Sample Preview button in the toolbar, or choose File, Sample Preview.

To return to Design view from the preview, choose File, Print Preview or File, Sample Preview, as the case may be (only one preview option is available—the other option is dimmed).

Figure 11-24 shows a print preview of the Follow-Up Report for April 13, 1994.

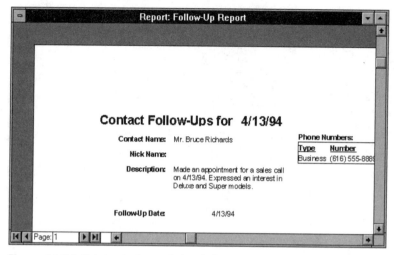

Figure 11-24: Print preview of the Follow-Up Report for April 13, 1994.

Adding an Unbound Object Frame

An unbound object frame control displays data from a source outside of Access tables. For example, you can use an unbound object frame to display your company logo in your report. First create an electronic version of the logo by scanning it or by using a paint or draw program. Then you can place the image into an unbound object frame.

Adding a Bound Object Frame

A bound object frame control displays data from an OLE data type field. The Photograph field in the Contacts table is displayed in a bound object frame control in the Contacts AutoReport, created by the AutoReport Wizard in Chapter 10. To add an OLE field to a report, from a table or query, display the field list and drag the OLE field name to the report design. Access adds a bound frame control to the report design.

Adding Lines

The line control is used to draw lines in your report. In many cases, placing a line between sections of the report helps make the report more readable.

In the Follow-Up Report, for example, a line between contacts would make it easier for a reader to quickly distinguish which information goes with which contact.

To add a line to a report design:

1. Click the Line button in the toolbox.

2. Move the mouse pointer to one end of the proposed line.

3. Click the mouse button and drag the mouse to the other end of the line. Release the mouse button. Access draws the line.

For example, place a line at the end of the detail section in the Follow-Up Report design (see Figure 11-25). The line prints each time the report moves to another contact, as shown in Figure 11-26.

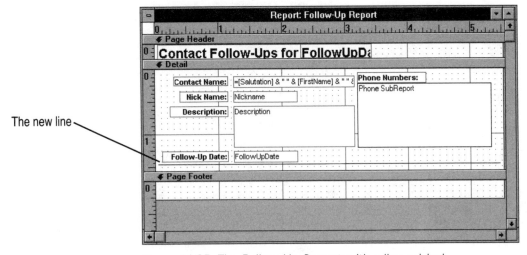

Figure 11-25: The Follow-Up Report with a line added.

Contact Follow-Ups for 4/13/94

Contact Name:	Mr. Bruce Richards
Nick Name:	
Description:	Made an appointment for a sales call on 4/13/94. Expressed an interest in Deluxe and Super models.

Phone Numbers:

Type	Number	Extension
Business	(616) 555-8889	

Follow-Up Date: 4/13/94

Contact Name:	Mr. Alan Moonie
Nick Name:	Alan
Description:	Send catalog. Call on 4/13/94.

Phone Numbers:

Type	Number	Extension
Home	(671) 555-0028	

Follow-Up Date: 4/13/94

Contact Name:	Mr. Richard Walters
Nick Name:	Rich
Description:	Tentative phone order for 3 dozen Super Widgets. Call on 4/13 to confirm.

Phone Numbers:

Type	Number	Extension
Business	(808) 555-3884	
Fax	(808) 555-8285	

Follow-Up Date: 4/13/94

Contact Name:	Ms. Kelly Wolf
Nick Name:	
Description:	Call requesting catalog. Call on 4/12.

Phone Numbers:

Type	Number	Extension
Business	(808) 555-2333	
Fax	(808) 555-2331	

Follow-Up Date: 4/13/94

Figure 11-26: The completed Follow-Up Report, with line added, for April 13, 1994.

Adding Rectangles

The rectangle control appears as a box in a report. You can place other controls within a rectangle control. Placing controls in a rectangle control gives the user a strong visual clue that the values in the controls are somehow related. Reports containing a lot of information can, in many cases, appear less cluttered by grouping the controls in rectangles. When you look the report output, your eye moves from rectangle to rectangle rather than looking at each control.

Adding a Page Break

The page break control in a report causes Access to send a message to your printer to eject a page. By placing a page break control in different sections of a report design, you can determine how often and under what circumstances Access starts a new page.

Using the Tool Lock

By default, once you place a control on a form, the pointer button is automatically selected. If you want to add several of the same type of control to a form, you must re-choose the control button prior to creating each control. Clicking the Tool Lock button causes the selected toolbox button to stay selected. You must click another toolbox button to select another tool.

Using Events

Event properties in reports are very similar to form event properties (see "Event" in Chapter 9). In the report's property sheet you can specify a macro (see Chapter 15) or an Access Basic procedure (see Chapters 16 and 17) to run at the occurrence of any of the following events:

○ OnOpen: This event occurs when you open (run) the report, before the report prints.

○ OnClose: This event occurs when the report closes, before returning to the Database window.

○ OnActivate: This event occurs when the Report window becomes the active window.

○ OnDeactivate: This event occurs when the Report window is no longer the active window and before another window becomes the active window.

○ OnError: This event occurs if an error occurs during the running of the report.

In a report section's property sheet you can specify a macro or an Access Basic procedure to run at the occurrence of any of the following events:

○ OnFormat: This event occurs when Access is ready to print data in a section, but before the data is formatted.

○ OnPrint: This event occurs when Access is ready to print data in a section, after the data is formatted.

○ OnRetreat. This event occurs if Access "backs up" to a preceding section as a result of a formatting property setting. This event occurs after the OnFormat event but before the OnPrint event.

MOVING ON

You now should have a better feel for what you can do with Access reports. You know how to create reports using the Report Wizards, how to modify a report design and how to design custom reports from scratch. Access's reporting capabilities are so extensive, however, that you still have many features left to explore.

This book next takes you beyond the fundamental capabilities of Access and begins to show you how to really polish your Access applications. Turn to Chapter 12 to learn how to take advantage of the powerful Windows integration tool known as Object Linking and Embedding, or OLE.

12

EXPLORING & ADMIRING OLE 2.0

*O*LE! Put down your sombreros and turn on your computer. We are about to have some fun exploring Microsoft's Object Linking and Embedding technology—or OLE for short—as it relates to Access.

With Microsoft's OLE technology, you can link Access to the power of Microsoft Excel, Microsoft Word or any other OLE-compliant product whether or not it comes from Microsoft. It's as if Microsoft built a little piece of every major software package available into Access to provide infinite power and flexibility.

Access had OLE technology built into it as early as Access Version 1.0, but both Access and OLE have come a long way since then. This chapter introduces you to OLE technology and how to take advantage of it in Access.

OLE: WHAT IT IS, WHAT IT WAS, WHAT IT SHALL BE

As mentioned earlier, OLE stands for *Object Linking and Embedding*—a term that is right on target with what OLE is all about. OLE allows you to link or embed a document from another software package. For example, you can link a Paintbrush Picture into your database, so that it appears whenever you look at a certain record. Whenever you need to update that picture, you can launch Paintbrush from within Access to make changes, then save the new picture right back into your database.

In effect, OLE actually links another application, such as Paintbrush or Excel, *into* Access, as if Access and the linked application were one. Think of it. Even though Access does not have its own graphics painting tool, OLE makes it possible to use such a tool within Access as if it were a part of Access itself. And Paintbrush is only the beginning! Access has powerful analytical capabilities like Excel, even though it doesn't have its own spreadsheet tool; Access has award-winning word-processing capabilities like Microsoft Word, even though it has no built-in word-processor—all thanks to the magic of OLE.

Some Background on OLE

For years, the brainy folks at Microsoft have been trying to think of new ways to leverage the multitasking environment in Windows toward making applications work together. As early as Windows 1.x, you could copy text from one DOS application, then paste that text into another DOS application under Windows control. Not a big deal by today's standards, but it wowed them all back in '85. For the first time, you could actually work in one application and duplicate that work in any other application without duplicating the effort.

Microsoft upped the ante in Windows 2.x with the introduction of DDE, which stands for *Dynamic Data Exchange*. Windows applications weren't just keeping an eye on the clipboard looking for something to paste; they were actually *talking* to each other! With DDE, a user could write a macro in Excel that instructed Microsoft Word to print a document, or a Visual Basic program could drive all of the applications in Microsoft Office to make up a single solution.

OLE is a relatively new Windows technology that represents the next step in the evolution of interprocess communication in Windows. It is also the most revealing of what is coming our way in future operating systems, where documents such as spreadsheets and databases will be the focus of your attention, while the applications that support these documents work quietly and harmoniously in the background, making it all happen.

OLE has an evolution of its own, starting out rather humbly as OLE 1.0 and turning into a very sophisticated OLE 2.0 in the latest wave of Microsoft product upgrades.

OLE in Access 1.x

OLE technology has been available in Access ever since Access has been around. Back in the Access 1.x days, OLE was really handy, but nothing to scream about compared to what OLE is today.

With the advent of OLE, you could link or embed a document, such as an Excel spreadsheet, into an OLE Object field in an Access table. You could take advantage of all the power of the spreadsheet program you use by editing the OLE Object field from an Access form. When you edit the OLE Object by double-clicking on it, the application that "owns" the document—the document's *host application*—appears onscreen so that you can edit the document.

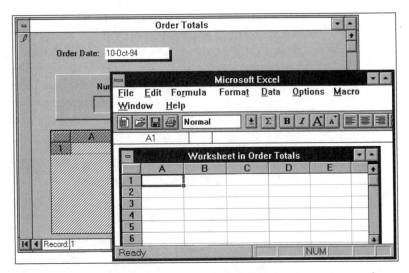

Figure 12-1: Double-clicking on an OLE 1.0 object in an Access form brings up the document's host application. In this case, the host application is Excel 4.0.

Once you completed the changes you wanted to make, you would close the OLE application and the document on the Access form would reappear with the new changes.

OLE opened up Access to many new possibilities never before seen in a database product. In addition to giving Access live graphics and charting capabilities thanks to add-on OLE "applets," an end-user could now coordinate database data with spreadsheet data, word-processed documents or any other OLE-compliant tool. Of course, Microsoft didn't stop improving on this new technology with Access 1.x. As you are about to discover, some radical and exciting changes have been made to OLE, and Access 2.0 is equal to the task of taking on this new and improved technology.

EXCITING NEW FEATURES OF OLE 2.0

Things are really getting exciting now that OLE is maturing into a nifty and powerful technology. The new version of OLE includes many enhancements that truly integrate and leverage other Windows applications and utilities. These new features are summed up in the next few sections.

In-Place Editing of External Documents

When you edit an OLE 1.0 document in an Access form, the document appears in its host application until you complete your

377

changes and close the host application; then the updated version of the document appears in the form (see Figure 12-1).

An OLE 2.0 document, on the other hand, can be edited *right on the Access form*! Rather than bringing up the document's host application, the document is "live" right where it is. In most cases, toolbars from the host application appear while you are editing the document, as if the toolbars were a part of Access.

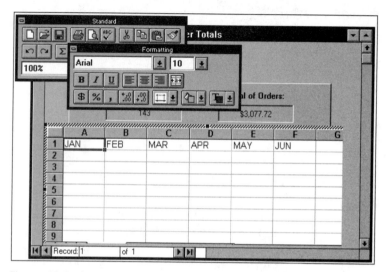

Figure 12-2: OLE 2.0 allows you to edit a document without leaving the Access form. In this case, an Excel 5.0 document is being edited; note the Excel toolbars, which appear within Access when the document is active.

Moving to any other control in the form automatically closes any of the OLE object's toolbars or other editing tools.

The Ability to Drag and Drop Parts of a Document From One Application to Another

Another really neat feature of OLE 2.0 is the ability to drag and drop data from one application to another. At first, it may not sound that impressive, probably because you are used to dragging and dropping all kinds of things within Access; but the key phrase here is "drag and drop *from one application to another*." For example, this means you could literally drag a selection of cells from a spreadsheet object on an Access form into a spreadsheet in Excel.

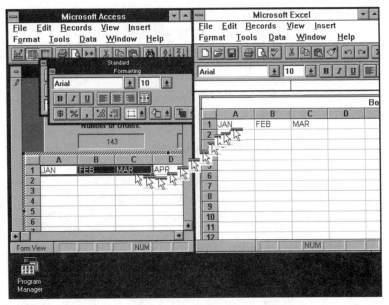

Figure 12-3: Dragging a selection of cells from an OLE object on an Access form into a new worksheet in Excel 5.

And it's as easy as it sounds. You simply select the data you want from one application, such as selecting a range of cells in Excel or highlighting a block of text in Word for Windows, then you drag it to the target application and drop it in the place where it should be placed.

Of course, since this is an OLE 2.0-specific feature, both the source OLE object and the target application must support OLE 2.0.

The Ability to Nest OLE Objects Within OLE Objects

OLE 2.0 allows you to link or embed documents within documents to form a complete subsystem. For example, an Access form can contain an embedded Word for Windows document, which may in turn contain an embedded Excel spreadsheet. In such a case, you could double-click on the Word for Windows document to edit it, then double-click on the spreadsheet within the WinWord document to edit it as well. All this happens within the Access form, effectively giving you three powerful tools in one.

The Ability to Create & Use Custom Controls for Access Forms

For a few years now, Microsoft's Visual Basic programming tool has allowed developers to create *custom controls*. Basically, rather than being tied down to all of the controls in the form toolbox, Visual Basic allows you to create your own special controls, called *VBX*

379

controls. A lot of Access 1.x developers were begging Microsoft to implement this capability into Access, since the Access and Visual Basic programming environments and form tools were so similar. As it turns out, the Access folks delivered on this request, and then some.

Microsoft has developed a new kind of custom control approach based on OLE 2.0 technology, and Access is the first beneficiary of these new custom controls. *OCX controls*, as they are called, will replace the Visual Basic VBX technology and will almost certainly catch on as an industry standard, just as VBX technology has done.

Now that you're all excited about OCX controls, I should let you know that we won't be discussing custom controls in this book because of the complexities involved. However, you can impress all your friends by telling them that your database product is the first to use OLE 2.0 custom controls!

The Future of OLE

As mentioned earlier, OLE 2.0 is just another step in the evolution of a document-based operating environment as envisioned by Microsoft. In such an environment, you won't worry about starting up Excel or WinWord or Access or whatever. You will work with any kind of document or object you need, and the host application will manage it in the background. These objects can exist separately, or can be part of one monolithic document.

At some point, we will probably see OLE technology enhanced to work simultaneously with different users on a network. Imagine the power of OLE in a multi-user environment, being able to link in documents from different workstations. If you're a computer nerd like me, the mere thought of it is giving you goose bumps right now!

Of course, we currently have our hands full with OLE 2.0. Although the future holds many exciting prospects, there's a lot to be excited about right now.

OLE TERMINOLOGY

Now that you have a general idea of what OLE is all about, we will begin discussing practical applications of OLE 2.0. Before we get into the nuts and bolts of taking advantage of this technology in Access, we have to learn some new buzzwords.

OLE Servers & Container Applications

When OLE is in action, there are always two applications involved: the host application that provides the document, and the application that is using it. For example, when an Excel spreadsheet is being edited in an Access form, there are two applications at work: Access and Excel.

In OLE terms, the application that *provides* the document is called the *OLE Server*; the application that *uses* the document is called the *Container Application*. In the spreadsheet example in the previous paragraph, Access would be the Container Application and Excel would be the OLE Server.

The Access form contains a linked spreadsheet; therefore it is called the *Container Application.*

This linked spreadsheet is provided to Access by Excel; therefore Excel is called the *OLE Server.*

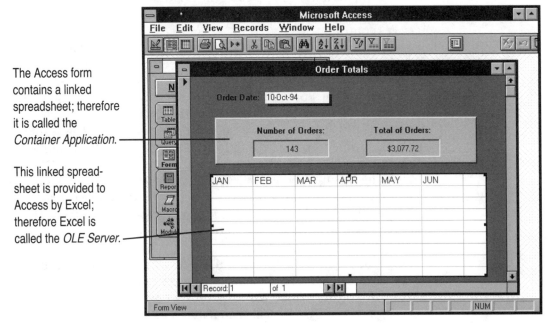

Figure 12-4: Definition of Container Application and OLE Server.

Linked vs. Embedded Objects

OLE documents are stored in an OLE Object field. There are two ways you can store an OLE document into an Access table: either by *embedding* the document, or *linking* the document.

Embedding the document into your table means that the entire document is stored in an OLE Object field. For example, rather than storing an Excel spreadsheet in an XLS file on the hard drive, it would be stored in an OLE Object field in an Access table. In addition to storing the document, the OLE Object would also contain information on the document's host application. When you double-click on the OLE Object field in a form, the host application becomes the OLE Server for the object stored in Access.

When an object is embedded in an Access table, it can only be updated from Access, since no other application has the capability to read the OLE Object data from the Access database.

Linking the document into your table means that only information on the document's location and its host application is stored in the OLE Object field. In this case, the document exists in a file by itself, and the OLE Server loads the object from its location under Access's control.

Since a linked object is accessible by its host application outside of Access, any changes made to it will be reflected when it appears in Access.

The method of storage you use depends upon how you intend to use these documents in your database. Do you want to link this document so that it is available outside of Access, or do you want to embed this object so that it is only accessible from within your database? In either case, the appearance and behavior of the OLE object is identical when it is being edited inside Access. Obviously, an embedded object takes up more space in your database, and subsequently, your database uses more hard-disk space. Of course, disk-space would also be used up by the document's native file if the object were linked.

One other issue to keep in mind is performance. When accessing a recordset—whether table or query—containing a embedded object field, performance will take a hit when compared to using links since Access has to deal with a much larger database.

BRINGING AN OLE OBJECT INTO AN ACCESS TABLE

Once you have created one or more OLE Object fields in a table, Access allows you to create a new OLE document or add an existing document to that table either from a datasheet or from a form. One difference between using a table or form is that you can't see the OLE document when you add it to a table; instead, you only see a text description of the object, such as: Microsoft Excel 5.0 Worksheet for an Excel spreadsheet.

OLE Object Field

Figure 12-5: In Datasheet view, OLE documents appear as a description.

There are potentially three routes you can take to bring in a project. The steps you use to accomplish this depend on which of the following you want to do:

○ Embed a New OLE document to the table.

○ Embed an Existing OLE document to the table.

○ Link an Existing OLE document to the table.

Creating & Embedding a New OLE Object

You can create and embed a new document to an OLE Object field by following these steps:

1. Give the OLE Object field focus by clicking on it once.

2. From the Edit menu at the top of the screen, choose Insert Object.

Access displays a dialog box that includes a list of application objects that support OLE.

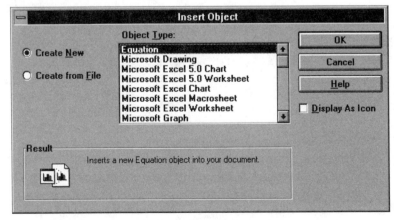

Figure 12-6: The Insert Object dialog box.

3. Make sure that the Create New radio button is selected.

You can choose to have the OLE document displayed as its host application's icon, rather than as the document itself, by clicking the Display As Icon check box so that an **X** appears in it. You will still be able to edit the document as you normally would, but you would click on a picture of the document's icon, rather than an image of the document itself. (You can only use this feature if the OLE document's host application supports OLE 2.0.)

4. From the Object Type list, choose the type of document you want to bring in and click the OK button.

At this point, one of the following occurs:

○ If the OLE Server supports OLE 2.0 and you are using a form rather than a datasheet, a new document will appear in the OLE Object field on the form.

○ If the OLE Server does not support OLE 2.0, or if you are editing from a datasheet rather than a form, the host application will start and appear in front of Access with a new document in it.

In either case, you can now edit the new document as needed. When you are finished with the document, close the host application if it is open, or move off of the OLE Object field if you are editing the document in place. The edited document will appear in the OLE Object field on a form, or a description of the document will appear in the OLE Object field in a datasheet.

Embedding or Linking an Existing Document Into a Table

You can embed or link an existing document to an OLE Object field by following these steps:

1. Give the OLE Object field focus by clicking on it once.

2. From the Edit menu at the top of the screen, choose Insert Object. Access displays the Insert Object dialog box.

3. Click the Create From File radio button. Access displays an entry area for a file name along with a Link check box.

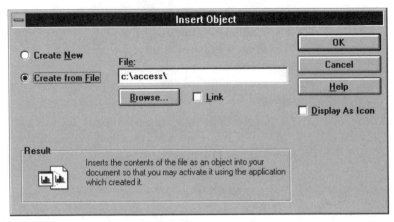

Figure 12-7: The Insert Object dialog box with the Create from File option selected.

4. Type in the name of the document file that you want to bring into the table. You can optionally click the Browse... button to locate the file with a File Open dialog box, rather than typing the name in.

   If you want to embed the document into the table, make sure the Link check box does *not* have an X in it; otherwise, click the Link check box so that an X appears in it.

   As mentioned in the prior example, you can choose to have the OLE document displayed as its host application's icon, rather than as the document itself, by clicking the Display As Icon check box so that an X appears in it. You will still be able to edit the document as you normally would, but you would click on a picture of the document's icon rather than an image of the document itself. (**Note:** You can only use this feature if the OLE document's host application supports OLE 2.0.)

5. Click the OK button to close the Insert Object dialog box.

At this point, one of the following occurs:

   ○ If the OLE Server supports OLE 2.0, and you are using a form rather than a datasheet, the document will appear in the OLE Object field on the form.

   ○ If the OLE Server does not support OLE 2.0, or if you are editing from a datasheet rather than a form, the host application will start and appear in front of Access with the document in it.

In either case, you can now edit the document as needed. When you are finished with the document, close the host application if it is open, or move off of the OLE Object field if you are editing the document in place. When you are finished editing, the edited document will appear in the OLE Object field on a form, or a description of the document will appear in the OLE Object field in a datasheet.

Linked OLE Documents

As mentioned earlier, a linked OLE document reflects changes made to it by its host application. In other words, if you link an Excel spreadsheet into an Access form, and you later modify the spreadsheet *in Excel*, the changes you made will appear in the linked document on your Access form.

There are two ways that the update can occur: by automatic updating or by manual updating. If you choose to have a linked document update automatically, the document will be updated anytime it is changed by its host application. If you choose to have a linked document update manually, it only changes when you explicitly tell it to update.

After you have completed adding a document into an OLE Object field as discussed in the previous section, you can specify whether you want it to be updated automatically or manually by choosing the Links menu item from the Edit menu. This displays the Links dialog box where you can do a number of different things to a linked OLE document.

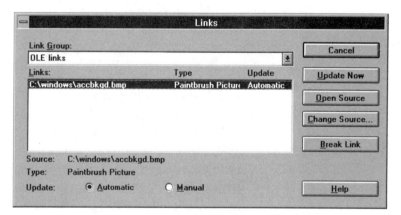

Figure 12-8: The Links dialog box allows you to do a number of things to a linked OLE document.

The Links dialog box displays all of the linked documents in the current record, along with a number of other controls and settings that apply to the OLE document highlighted in the Links list. Among the settings, you can specify Automatic or Manual updating by choosing the appropriate radio button at the bottom of the dialog box.

If you specify manual updating for an OLE document, you then can go into this dialog box and click the Update Now button every time you want to update the document's data. As long as you don't use the Update now option, the OLE document remains the same even if the document is modified in the meantime.

You can use the Open Source button to open the linked document in its host application for editing, and the Change Source button to link the document to a different host application. You can also disassociate the document from any host application altogether by using the Break Link button to turn it into an image (see "Converting an OLE Object to a Picture" below for more information on the ramifications of doing this).

EDITING EXISTING OLE OBJECTS INSIDE ACCESS

Once an OLE document has been linked or embedded into an OLE Object field, you can edit the object by simply double-clicking on it. This works the same way whether you are editing the object from a datasheet or from a form.

As with adding a new OLE document, editing an existing document goes like this:

○ If the OLE Server supports OLE 2.0, and you are using a form rather than a datasheet, the document will appear in the OLE Object field on the form, and you can edit it in place.

○ If the OLE Server does not support OLE 2.0, or if you are editing from a datasheet rather than a form, the host application will start and appear in front of Access with the document in it. You can then edit the document as needed and close the host application when you are finished. Before the host application closes, you will be prompted as to whether or not you want to save the changes you just made back to the OLE document in the table.

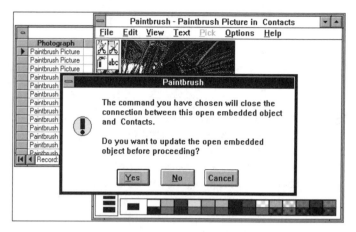

Figure 12-9: The OLE document's host application prompts you to save changes back to the Access table.

CONVERTING AN OLE OBJECT TO A PICTURE

As mentioned in the previous section, an OLE document can be edited from a datasheet or form simply by double-clicking it. In many cases, the data you add to an OLE Object field may be permanent; for example, you may be adding a picture of a contact in the Contacts table, and you may not want someone to come in and mess up the picture by allowing it to be edited in Paintbrush.

One way to do this would be to open the Contacts form in Design view and change the Photograph field's Enabled property to No, and its Locked property to Yes. Although this would prevent a user from double-clicking the picture to edit it, it would not prevent someone from going into the Contacts datasheet and editing the picture from there. In addition, the Photograph field would not only contain the data for the picture; it would also contain additional data for calling the host application. Storing this extra information is a waste of space since you never intend to edit the picture in Paintbrush.

Access addresses this issue in a very simple way: it allows you to save the OLE document *as an image* rather than as a "live" document, whether or not it is a picture. Even if the OLE document is a spreadsheet or word-processor document, you can save its image so that it will always appear the same and it would be impossible to edit.

This can be done by following these simple steps:

1. Give the OLE Object field focus by clicking on it once.

2. From the Edit menu at the top of the screen, choose the last menu item in the pop-up.

   The menu item will be different, depending on what type of OLE document is stored in that field. For example, if the OLE document is a Paintbrush Picture, the menu item will be called Paintbrush Object. If the OLE document is an Excel spreadsheet, the menu item will be called Worksheet Object and so on.

   Once you select the menu item, another pop-up menu appears.

3. From the second pop-up menu, choose Change to Picture.

At this point, Access warns you that what you are about to do can't be undone—once you change the current document to a picture, you will never be able to change it again, unless you re-embed or re-link the object. Choose Yes to continue, or No if you change your mind.

MOVING ON

This chapter has introduced you to OLE, what it is and how you can use it. If you don't already have one of the OLE server programs mentioned in this chapter, you may be thinking you are out of luck. But you're wrong. Microsoft Graph is one of the "applets" that supports OLE 2.0. Turn now to Chapter 13 to see how easy it is to add a graph to an Access form using the Graph Wizard and Microsoft Graph.

13 PRESENTING YOUR DATA GRAPHICALLY

In simple terms, the purpose of collecting data is to use it to make decisions. Suppose Congress must decide how much money to budget for training technical specialties in the Armed Forces. It is possible to provide a list of the names and technical specialties of every member of the Marines, Army, Navy and Air Force and give it to the Armed Services Committee. It is also possible to give a summary report that shows how many are in each specialty by branch of service. It is also possible to provide graphs of those same numbers, including percentages. If you were the committee member, which would you like to see? Most of us would like to see the graphical presentation first. Then, if we needed to see the details, we would turn to summary and/or detailed reports.

In this chapter, we'll create a graph using data from the Contacts database from the companion disk. Our graph will show the relationship between organizations and the states where they are located. The source for our graph will be the Organizations table. We will modify the graph to display both the graph and data simultaneously.

CREATING THE ORGANIZATIONS BY STATES GRAPH

Suppose management is interested in seeing where our advertising has helped us build a customer base. The Organizations table contains the data describing the organizations we work with, including the state where they are located. By counting the number of organizations in each state, we'll be able to see where our customers come from.

Let's walk through the steps you need to complete to create a graph showing this information.

1. Open the database containing the data you want to graph.

2. Choose the Form button in the Database window to view a list of the forms, if any, that have already been defined in the database.

3. Next, choose the New button in the Database window to start creating a new form. Access displays the New Form dialog box, as shown in Figure 13-1.

4. Select the table containing the data you want to graph from the combo box list. In Figure 13-1, we've selected the Organizations table.

5. Click the Form Wizard button to move to the next screen.

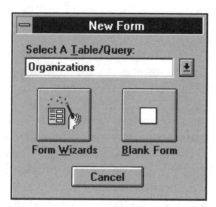

Figure 13-1: New Form dialog box.

6. Choose "Graph" from the list in the Form Query Wizards dialog box. Either highlight "Graph" and click the OK button, or double-click "Graph" in the list. Access displays the Graph Wizard dialog boxes. Figure 13-2 shows the Form Wizards dialog box with the "Graph" option selected.

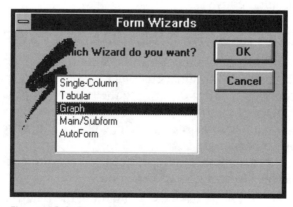

Figure 13-2: Form Wizards dialog box.

The Graph Wizard asks for information necessary to generate a graph. The Wizard generates a graph using the answers you provide. You already identified the location of the data to graph when you selected the table or query in the New Form dialog box.

The next thing the Wizard needs to know is which fields you want to use on the graph.

7. The first screen in the Query Wizard contains two lists. The Available fields list, on the left, contains all the fields in the table or query you specified in the New Form dialog box. The Fields for graph list, on the right, shows the fields containing the data you want to graph.

   Use the field selection buttons to build the list of fields to be checked for duplicate values. To move a field from the list on the left to the list on the right, highlight the desired field and click the > button. To select all fields, click the >> button. If you want to remove a field from the list on the right, highlight the field and click the < button. To remove all fields, click the << button. You may double-click the mouse pointer on a field in either list to move it to the other list.

   In Figure 13-3, we've selected the State and OrgID fields.

. . . .

Navigating a Wizard

All Wizards share a common set of command buttons to control movement from one window to the next. You tell the Wizard you are done with a window by clicking the Next > button. Clicking the < Back button takes you back to the Query Wizard type selection screen. Clicking Cancel returns you to the Database window. The Finish button is available once you have answered enough questions to allow the Wizard to generate the query. Some windows have a Hint button; pressing this button causes the Wizard to display a screen with helpful information about how to answer the questions posed by the current screen.

. . . .

8. Click the Next > button to move to the next screen.

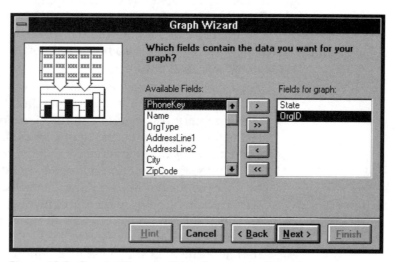

Figure 13-3: Graph Wizard's fields for graph dialog box.

9. Next, you must specify how you want the data summarized in the graph. There are three options you may choose from in this dialog box.

   ○ *Add (Sum) the numbers*. This option totals the values contained in the field you specify.

   ○ *Average the numbers*. This option calculates the average of the values contained in the field you specify.

   ○ *Count the number of records in each category*. This option counts the number of records found containing the same value.

10. Select the option representing the operation you want performed on the data.

    In Figure 13-4, we've selected the "Count the number of records in each category" option. We want to see the total number of organizations in each state in the generated graph.

11. Click the Next > button to move to the next screen.

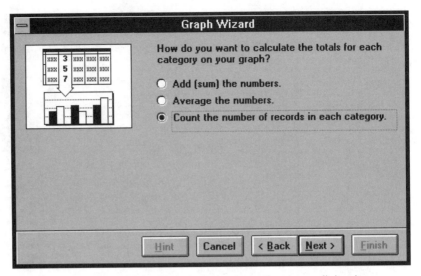

Figure 13-4: Graph Wizard's summary operation type dialog box.

The next thing the Wizard needs to know is the type of graph you want generated. The graph type dialog box displays three rows of buttons on the right-hand side of the screen, representing the types of graphs the Wizards can generate. You can see how the different types of graphs will appear by clicking on them. The Wizards process the data and display a sample graph. In Figure 13-5, we've chosen a two-dimensional bar chart.

12. Click on the button representing the type of graph you want to generate.

In the lower-right-hand corner of the dialog box is an option group labeled "Data Series in," used to determine how to present the data in the graph. The option you chose determines the number of column titles shown on the graph. In Figure 13-5, we've selected the Columns option; we want to see a label for each state.

○ *Rows*. The rows option generates a single label for all the categories displayed.

○ *Columns*. The Columns option generates a label for each category displayed.

13. Choose the option you want used by clicking the appropriate option button.

14. Click the Next > button to move to the next screen.

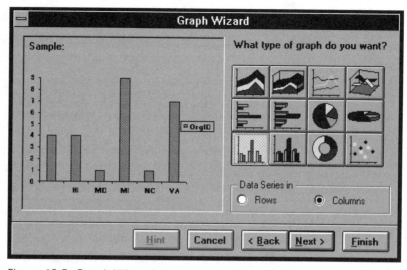

Figure 13-5: Graph Wizard's graph type dialog box.

The next screen is where you enter the title and legend information you want displayed on the graph, if any. The title you enter will be shown at the top of the graph. If you choose to include a legend, it will be shown along the right-hand side of the graph. The legend text displays the name of the field being used to calculate the data displayed. In the example in Figure 13-6, we've specified a title of "Organizations by State" and chosen not to display a legend by selecting the "No" option.

15. Enter the title you want displayed on the graph.

16. Indicate your legend preference by choosing either the "Yes" or "No" option button under the question "Do you want the chart to display a legend?"

17. Click the Next > button to move to the next screen.

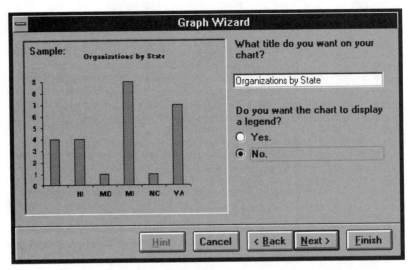

Figure 13-6: Graph Wizard's title/legend specification dialog box.

18. Select one of the following two options to determine how to proceed:

○ *Open the form with the graph displayed on it.* Selecting this option tells the Wizard to generate the graph and a form to display it, and immediately open the form to display the generated graph, once the Finish button is pressed. This is the default option.

○ *Modify the design of the form or the graph.* This option generates the graph and form and then opens the form in the Design window, allowing you to modify the design before saving.

We've chosen the default option in Figure 13-7.

19. Click the Finish button to generate the graph and form.

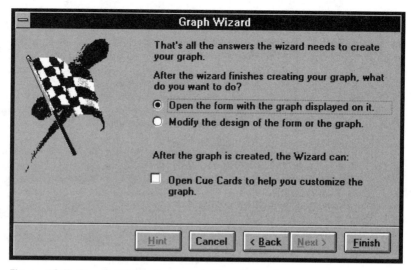

Figure 13-7: Graph Wizard's completion dialog box.

Figure 13-8 shows the generated graph and form.

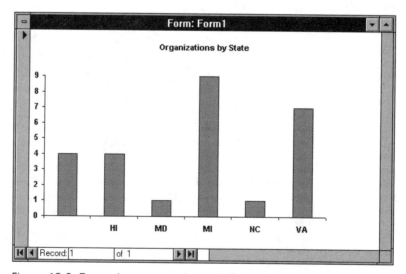

Figure 13-8: Example generated graph/form display.

Once you've reviewed the design, you must save the graph and form design. To save the form, choose the Save Form As option from the File menu. In Figure 13-9, we've entered **Organizations by State Graph** as the form name.

20. Enter the Form Name.

21. Click the OK button to save the form.

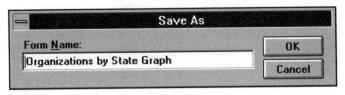

Figure 13-9: Save As dialog box.

Congratulations! You've created a useful and informative graph for management about the number of organizations by state.

MODIFYING THE ORGANIZATIONS BY STATES GRAPH

Although the new graph is quite nice, management has requested a few changes:

○ Remove the word "FORM:" from the Title.

○ Remove the Record Selector, Navigation buttons and scroll bars from the form.

○ Disable the Data Sheet icon on the toolbar.

○ Delete the unlabeled first bar of the graph.

Let's walk through the steps necessary to satisfy management's request.

1. Open the database containing the form you want to modify.

2. Choose the Form button in the Database window to view a list of the forms already defined in the database.

3. Click the Organizations by State Graph entry in the list.

4. Click the Design button to display the form in Design view (see Figure 13-10).

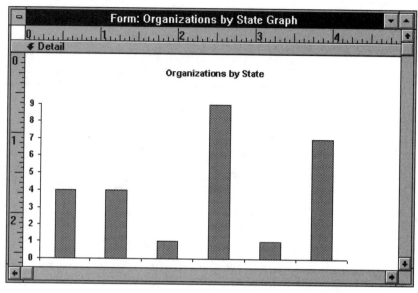

Figure 13-10: The Organizations by State Graph form in Design view.

There is only one object on this form: an object frame containing the graph we just designed. To accomplish the requests management made, the form's properties must be changed.

5. Click on White Square in the upper-left corner of the window to select the form.

6. Open the Properties window by clicking the Properties button on the toolbar.

(**Note**: For the rest of this chapter, set the properties category to All Properties.) Figure 13-11 shows the property sheet displaying the properties for the form.

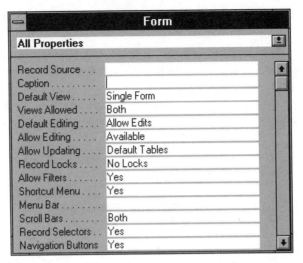

Figure 13-11: Unmodified form properties.

The first thing we'll do is change the title to eliminate the word "FORM" from the window title. The Caption property determines the title displayed on the Form window. If it is left blank, the window title displays the word "FORM" followed by the name you gave the form when you saved it. If the Caption property is not blank, the text it contains becomes the Form window title.

7. Change the Caption property to Organizations by State.

The ViewsAllowed property allows you to determine which view options can be selected from the toolbar to view the form. By default, the ViewsAllowed property allows both datasheet and form views. You can choose to limit the view to either Form or Datasheet by selecting the appropriate option.

8. Change the Views Allowed property to form to remove Datasheet availability.

The ScrollBars property chooses the scroll bars to display in the Form window. By default, both horizontal and vertical scroll bars are shown in the window. Since we don't have anything on this form to scroll, we can turn off the scroll bars altogether.

9. Change the ScrollBars property to Neither to remove Scroll Bars.

The RecordSelectors property turns on and off the record selector bar displayed along the left edge of the Form window. The record selector bar is the vertical bar where the record status indicators are displayed.

10. Change the RecordSelectors property to No to remove the Record Selectors.

Navigation buttons are used to move from record to record when looking at data in a table. Since this form is based upon a query that only returns one record, we don't need to confuse ourselves by displaying navigation buttons.

11. Change the NavigationButtons property to No to remove the Navigation Buttons.

Figure 13-12 shows the Form properties window after the modifications have been made.

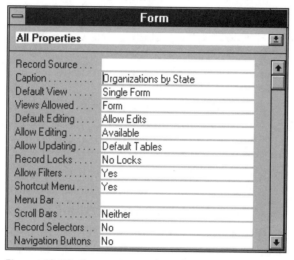

Figure 13-12: Form properties after modifications.

12. Next, we need to delete the unlabeled bar in the graph. By examining the Organizations table, we discover that there is no entry in the State field for organizations from Guam. The unlabeled bar in the graph represents these organizations because the graph labels were taken from the State field. We need to modify the query, and thus eliminate this bar.

While still displaying the form's property sheet, click the graph to display the graph object's property sheet. Select the RowSource property and then click the Builder button at the right end of the RowSource text box (the button that contains an ellipsis ...). Access displays the Query Builder window (see Figure 13-13).

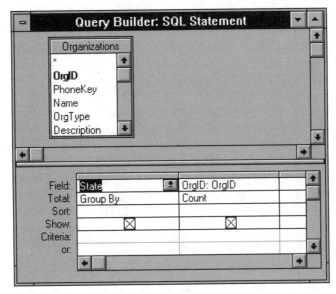

Figure 13-13: The Query Builder window.

13. Add the criteria **Not "Guam"** in Criteria row for the State field in the QBE grid. This criteria will prevent the query from retrieving data on Guam organizations, and therefore will eliminate the unlabeled bar in the graph.

14. Double-click the Query Builder window's Control-menu box to close the window and return to the Form window. When Access displays a message box asking whether you want to save the property, choose the Yes button. Access saves the change and returns to the Form window.

15. Since you aren't displaying scroll bars, record selectors and navigation controls, you'll need to resize the Form window. The easiest way to get the size right is to make the changes while in Form view. Figure 13-12 shows how the screen should look after you complete the modifications.

16. Click on the Form icon on the toolbar to show graph changes.

17. Resize the graph window by clicking and dragging the edge of the window with a double-headed arrow mouse cursor.

18. Save the modifications to the form.

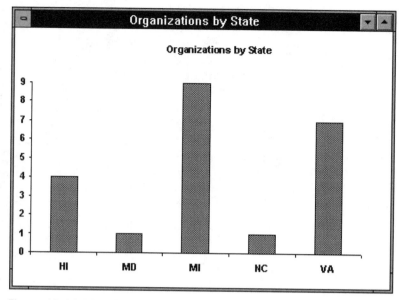

Figure 13-14: Modified Organizations by State form.

Congratulations! You have modified the graph to meet management's requests. The boss knows who to come and see next time she needs a graph done in a hurry!

CREATING A CONTINUOUSLY UPDATING GRAPH

The graph you just created uses a query to summarize the data presented. The query is executed when the form is opened. You might wonder what happens if another user changes the data in the Organizations table while you are looking at the graph. Will the changes be reflected in the graph? As it stands now, no. But where there's a will, there's a way. Let's take a look at how we can change the Organizations by State Graph to automatically reflect changes made to the Organizations table.

What we need to do is to find a way of telling the form to periodically look at the Organizations data to see if there have been any changes. We can do this by using one of the events on the form called the OnTimer Event. The OnTimer event occurs at a time interval you specify in the TimerInterval property. This all sounds more difficult than it is. What we are going to do is to write a procedure to execute every 30 seconds while using the Organizations by State form. This procedure updates the graph with the current information in the Organizations table every 30 seconds.

Let's see how easy this really is.

1. Open the Contacts database containing the form you want to modify.

2. Choose the Form button in the Database window to view a list of the forms already defined in the database.

3. Click the Organizations by State Graph entry in the list.

4. Click the Design button. Access displays the graph in Design view.

5. Open the Propery sheet by clicking the Properties icon on the toolbar.

As we discussed before, this form only contains one object: an object frame used to display the graph. In order to refresh its contents, we'll have to know its name, so we can tell Access what to refresh.

6. Click on the graph in the Form window.

Scroll to the top of the properties window, and you'll see the Name property. This is the name given to the object when we generated it. Let's change it to something a little more meaningful. Figure 13-15 shows the Object Frame properties window with the name we've given the object, "Graph1".

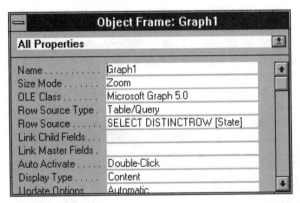

Figure 13-15: Object Frame properties window with Name property set to Graph1.

7. Click on the White Square in the upper-left corner of the window to select the form.

Figure 13-16 shows the Form window displaying the properties for the form we are interested in using: the OnTimer event property and the TimerInterval property. As you can see by default, the TimerInterval property is set to 0, and the OnTimer event property is empty.

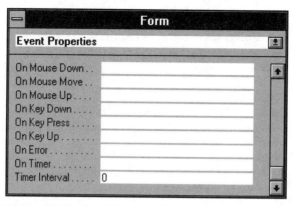

Figure 13-16: Organizations by State default form On Timer and Timer Interval properties.

The Timer Interval property determines the amount of time between execution of the On Timer events. The TimerInterval property can contain a value between 0 and 65,535: this number represents the number of milliseconds between timer events. A millisecond is 1/1000 of a second.

8. Enter **30000** (thirty thousand) in the TimerInterval property. This causes a 30-second pause between timer events.

The OnTimer event property executes a procedure whenever the time specified by the TimerInterval property elapses. In our example, every 30,000 milliseconds (30 seconds). All we have to do is to tell the On Timer event property what to do. But how? By writing an event procedure. Figure 13-17 shows the Form properties window with the Timer Interval property set to 30000.

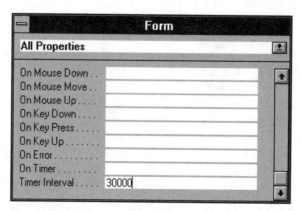

Figure 13-17: Form properties window with Timer Interval property set to 30000 (30 seconds).

Don't quit now. You'll be amazed at how easy this is going to be!

The first thing you need to do is figure out what you want to do in the On Timer event procedure. I'll give you a hint...refresh the graph. How do you do that? By using what is called a *method*. Without getting into a lot of unnecessary detail at this point, think of a method as a way of doing something to an object, like refreshing its contents. OK, but what object do we want to refresh, you ask? The object containing the graph, of course. You know the name of the object: Graph1. All you have to do is learn how to refresh its contents.

Creating an Event procedure is easy. Just follow along and you'll see.

9. Click on the On Timer property. Figure 13-18 shows the two buttons that appear once the cursor is in the property area.

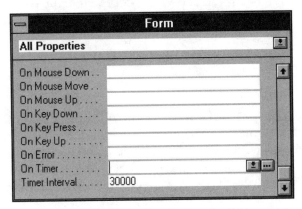

Figure 13-18: On Timer property selection.

10. Click on the Builder button (button displaying an ellipsis "..."). The Builder button invokes the Code Builder dialog box. You can use this dialog box to create Expressions, Macros or Code (Access Basic procedures).

In Figure 13-19, we've highlighted the Code Builder option. Here, we'll write a simple Access Basic procedure that refreshes the data used by the graph.

11. Choose the Code Builder and then click the OK button.

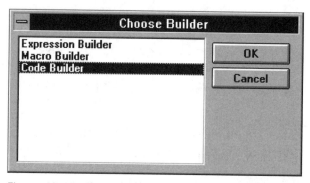

Figure 13-19: Choose Builder dialog box with Code Builder option highlighted.

Figure 13-20 shows the completed On Timer event procedure. All you need to enter is the code that invokes the Graph1 object's requery method.

12. On the second line of the procedure, enter the following Access Basic code.

```
Graph1.Requery
```

Graph1 is the name of the object frame containing the graph and Requery is the requery method. Please notice the period "." between the object name and its method. We'll discuss the syntax of Access Basic in the last few chapters of this book. This code runs whenever this event procedure is triggered (every 30 seconds).

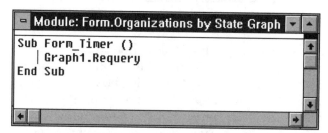

Figure 13-20: On Timer event procedure.

13. Close the Code Builder.

14. Save the modifications to the form.

Congratulations! You have just created a graph that is automatically updated to reflect the most current data on file.

MOVING ON

In this chapter we looked at how to create graphs on forms. You can also place a graph on a report in essentially the same way. You also learned about a few of the properties on a form and how to modify them to make your graph form more attractive. Finally, you learned how to write a simple procedure that updates the graph to display current data.

In the next chapter, we'll take a look at some of the ways you can make your application attractive and easy to use by following a few simple interface guidelines.

14

DESIGNING A "FRIENDLY" USER INTERFACE

The key to successful interface design is consistency. The term *interface* describes the parts of an application used to view data. That would describe forms and reports. You use forms when you want to provide an interactive interface, and reports when you want to provide a one-way interface. You don't have to be an artist to design an attractive interface.

The goal of this chapter is to introduce you to the basics of interface design using Access. We'll focus on how to make your applications easier to use, by applying the guidelines developed for the Windows platform. We will also briefly discuss some guidelines for report design.

THE IMPORTANCE OF INTERFACE DESIGN

There are many books available to help you learn the guidelines for producing attractive interfaces that have been developed through years of experience and study. IBM has developed a set of interface guidelines called "Common User Access" (CUA), published in *IBM Common User Access: Advanced Interface Design Guide*. Apple Computers publishes their guidelines in a book called *Human Interface Guidelines: The Apple Desktop Interface*. Microsoft's guidelines are published in *The Windows Interface: An Application Design Guide*. Other computer platforms also have published guidelines available.

The goal of these guidelines is to promote both visual and functional consistency. Consistency provides a familiar environment, and we are all more comfortable in familiar surroundings. Users learn best by experimenting with new systems, and you can encourage experimentation by providing a comfortable environment to explore.

About now you're probably asking yourself, "Why should I concern myself with all this stuff?" The answer is simple: to make your applications easier to use and to save you time while developing them.

Let me give you an example of what I'm talking about. Most of us drive a car, it doesn't matter if it's really a truck; they work the same way, right? Right! That's the point: you know when you get into a different car or truck that you'll be able to drive. The experience you have driving other vehicles applies almost universally. Sure, you'll have to adjust the seat and mirrors, and it might even take you a minute or two to find the lights. You already know the important stuff: how to use the steering wheel, accelerator and brakes. I bet you don't even have to look at your feet to position them on the pedals. Why? Because of a consistent interface.

Figure 14-1 shows the form generated by the Single-Column Form Wizard. You can use this to maintain the data in the Contacts table, but I think you'll agree that the design could use a little work.

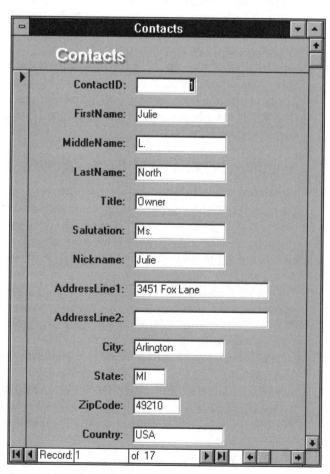

Figure 14-1: Contacts form generated with Single-Column Form Wizard.

There are a number of things you can do to make the form easier to use. They could be a simple as rearranging the controls so that they fit into a single form window. You can improve the design even further by changing the type of control used to maintain some of the fields. As we discussed in Chapter 9, each control type has unique features that improve the usability of your application. For example, the Salutation text box can be replaced with a combo box.

Figure 14-2 shows what the Contacts form, developed in Chapter 9, looks like after applying some of the guidelines we'll discuss in this chapter.

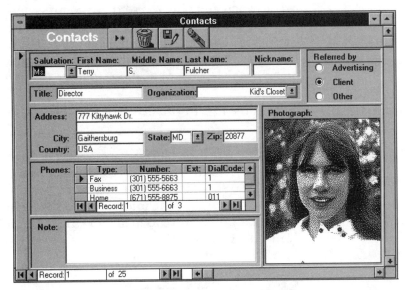

Figure 14-2: Contacts form after design modifications.

The saying "keep it simple" is something everyone designing an interface should keep in mind. One of the most common mistakes made is trying too many things. I'm not advocating dull, lifeless applications. Though a dull application is probably more usable than one that looks like a Picasso painting, sorry Pablo.

Keep in mind that the material in this chapter is intended as a guideline. Try the ideas out in your applications and see what works for you. Everyone has his or her own style, and you don't have to make your application look exactly like another to use these guidelines. The important thing is to understand your choices and the impact they have on your application.

Let's look at some guidelines for designing forms.

FORM DESIGN GUIDELINES

The time you spend designing your application should be spent where it will have the greatest impact on your users. The people using your application will spend a majority of their time using the forms you design. So it makes sense to start discussing interface guidelines with forms. Many of the guidelines we'll look at while discussing forms apply to reports as well. There are some guidelines unique to forms. For example, you typically won't use combo or list boxes on reports.

We'll start out by looking at a few guidelines for using some of the controls available in the tool box. Many new users are confused about when and how to use these controls. Once you understand how the controls work, you'll be able to make an intelligent decision about which one to use. Remember, these aren't hard-and-fast rules that you must always follow. They are guidelines you can use to help you design applications that are easier to use.

Selecting the Right Control for the Job

Text Boxes

Test boxes are the most common type of data control on most forms. You should use a text box when you want the user to maintain the value by typing information. For example, you'd probably use a text box control to maintain fields containing peoples names. Figure 14-3 shows the text box control used to maintain the FirstName field on the Contacts form.

Figure 14-3: Contact FirstName text box control.

Text boxes don't always have to be one line tall. When maintaining long text or memo fields you can choose to display more than one line of information. If you do decide to use multi-line text boxes, you should set the Scroll Bars property to Vertical. When the control has focus, a vertical scroll bar appears along the right edge. The user can use this scroll bar when the data exceeds the size of the control.

When you use a multi-line text box, you must adjust the height of the control to hold the number of lines you want to display at a given time. Here are a couple things to consider:

○ How much data will the field normally contain? If the control is going to be used to maintain a text field, you know the maximum amount of data the control needs to display—it can't hold more than the Field Size property setting. On the other hand, if you're maintaining a memo field, the amount of data will vary. Make a "best guess" at how much data you'll keep in the field.

○ Decide how much room you have to display the control. There is a limited amount of space available onscreen to display your form. When the amount of data a field normally contains is large, you usually can't show it all at one time. You need to decide how much you want to display at a given time. The amount of space you give the control should be large enough to display a meaningful amount of data. For example, if the text box is used for short notes about an individual, the control should be large enough to display at least one full note of a typical size. This might be as small as a single paragraph or as large as a whole page.

Figure 14-4 shows the text box control used to maintain the Note field on the Contacts form. The text box is 60 characters wide and 4 lines tall.

Figure 14-4: Contacts form Note text box control.

Combo Boxes

Combo boxes are like text boxes with attached lists of values from which the user can choose or, if the application allows, enter a value not shown in the list. Using a combo box is a great way of preventing users from entering incorrect data into a field. You provide users a list of valid values, and let them select the value that meets their need. The values in the list can come from records in a table or query, or you can enter the values you want displayed in the list in the Row Source property when you create the control.

Combo boxes are a good choice when the list of values to display is relatively small—less than 200 or so. If the number of choices available gets too big, the combo box can appear sluggish when opened.

The List Rows property determines the number of values to show in a list at one time. The guideline is to show at least 3 and not more than 15 values at a time. You want to show enough values to allow the user to select a value without excessive scrolling. On the other hand, if you show too many values at one time the user will have difficulty finding the correct value to select.

Figure 14-5 shows the combo box control used to maintain the Salutation field. The values shown in the list were determined when we created the control. The Row Source Type property is set to Value List, meaning that the values to display in the combo box were specified when the control was created. The Row Source property contains the values to display in the combo box. Each value is separated by a comma. In this case the list of salutations the users may select from are: Mr., Ms., Mrs., Miss, Dr., Rev. and Hon. If you want the user to enter values other than those displayed, you must set the LimitToList property to No. This tells Access to accept whatever the user enters as a valid value.

Figure 14-5: Salutation combo box.

List Boxes

At first, many users are confused about the similarities between list boxes and combo boxes. Both controls display a list of values for selection. And, both controls store the selected value in the associated field. But there is a reason why both control types are available.

List boxes serve a unique function on your forms despite the apparent similarities they have with combo boxes. You should use a list box when the following two criteria are met:

1. The values available for selection can vary.

2. The only values that can be stored in the associated field are the values shown in the list.

Like combo boxes, the list of values can come from a table, or you can build the list when you create the control.

If you want to allow the user to enter a value not shown in the list use a combo box.

The user chooses a value from the list by clicking the desired option in the list. The value chosen replaces the current contents of the associated field. The current value is indicated by a highlighted value in the list. If there are more options available than will fit in the defined list box area, a scroll bar is displayed on the right edge of the control. The user can scroll the list by pressing the Up and Down arrow keys or by using the mouse on the scroll bar.

Figure 14-6 shows an example of a list box. In this example, the user is presented with a list of values from which to select an Organization Type. The current value contained in the field associated with the list box is highlighted.

Organization:	Kid's Closet					
Kid's Closet	777 Kittyhawk Dr.		Gaithersburg	MC	20877	USA
WRB Consulting	1711 Lakeview Dr.		Chapel Hill	NC	27514	USA
Outback Boutique	1211 Commerce St.		Springfield	VA	22150	USA
Friendly Farms	13 Baker St.	Suite 1700	Alexandria	VA	22213	USA
Metro Athletic, Inc.	720 Port Royal	Building 33, :	Fairfax	VA	22030	USA
Tyson Plumbing	770 Shaw Rd.	Suite 701	Alexandria	MI	49313	USA
Surf's Up Discount	328A Front St.	Suite 100	Maui	HI	61010	USA
Prince Wallace Pearls, Inc.	1142 S. Orange Blvd		Sinajana		55523	Guam

Figure 14-6: Organization Type list box.

Option Groups

You should consider using an option group when you have a field that can only contain a small number of possible values. For example, in the Contacts application we want to track how our customers heard of our company. The Contacts table contains a field called ReferredBy. We've decided we only need to determine if a customer came to us through our Advertising, from another Client or some Other means. Figure 14-7 shows an option group to track these referral types. There is an option button representing each of the three types of referrals we want to track: Advertising, Client and Other.

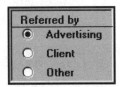

Figure 14-7: ReferredBy option group using option buttons.

Figure 14-8 shows the same option group using toggle buttons instead of option buttons. Toggle buttons can display either text or a picture to describe the option they represent. As the saying goes, "A picture is worth a thousand words." Using toggle buttons with pictures can, in many cases, more clearly describe the option than using a few words. A word of caution: be careful when choosing pictures for your buttons. Though you might understand the thought the picture represents, it is a good idea to ask the opinion of several other people. I've often been surprised to hear how some people interpret pictures I thought were perfectly clear.

Figure 14-8: ReferredBy option group using toggle buttons.

To use an option group, the user selects the appropriate option by clicking the option or toggle button representing that option. When a button is selected, any previous selection is replaced with the new selection. This works like the buttons on an old car radio: only one button can be pushed at a time.

Option groups are a good choice when there are a few (five or less) options and the options never change.

Check Boxes

Check boxes are a great way to maintain fields that can only contain one of two possible values, such as Yes/No data fields. The check box will appear checked if the field contains a Yes value or it will appear unchecked if the field contains No. The user changes the value stored in the field by clicking on the check box to switch between checked and unchecked or vice versa.

Most people with experience using other Microsoft Windows products know how check boxes work. Users know that they can check one or more boxes to indicate the status of each option. Figure 14-9 shows the Permissions dialog box; notice the check boxes used to indicate the permissions assigned to the group. You may check any one or more of these check boxes to assign the associated permission to the group.

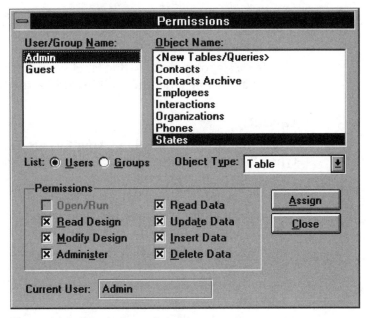

Figure 14-9: Permissions dialog box.

Labels

By default, a label is created with all of the controls used to maintain data, with the exception of toggle buttons. When labels are used this way, they identify the contents of the associated control. Here are a few things to keep in mind when using labels:

○ Use mixed case for the text in the label. The first letter should be capitalized for each word except for words such as *a, and, the, to,* etc.

○ Use all uppercase to send important messages, such as required fields. For example, using a label containing the text "FIRSTNAME" next to a label containing the text "Middle Name" attracts attention to the First Name field.

○ When you disable a control the label is dimmed along with the control.

○ Use a bold font to make the label easier to read, especially when the label is disabled.

○ Don't use any label at all for controls that are self descriptive. For example, the second line of the street address probably doesn't need a label if it is placed directly below the first line.

○ Create labels to help guide users to use the form properly or to identify areas of the form containing related data.

○ Be as concise as possible. Whenever you can, use one or two words to convey the message. Users should be able to read the entire label at a glance.

○ It is easier to read a two-line label spread across half the form than a one-line label the entire width of the form.

Layout

Where you place the object on your form is just as important as the type of control you use. Here are a few guidelines that will help you design understandable forms:

○ Group related controls together on the form. For example, the fields containing address information can be grouped together. Grouping saves valuable space on your form and improves the flow when maintaining data.

○ Use rectangles and lines to separate groups of related controls. This helps the user associate the controls with the topics they describe.

○ Use space between controls to indicate relationships.

  Little or no space between controls (the width of one character or less) indicates that the controls depend on each other to describe a particular piece of information. For example, first name, middle name and last name controls together describe a person's name.

  A moderate amount of space between controls (the width of two or three characters) indicates that the data contained in the controls describes related pieces of information. For example, the group of controls containing name information is related to the group of controls containing address information.

○ Use alignment to help indicate related controls. Staggering groups of related controls gives a visual clue that they are included in a group.

○ Align controls both horizontally and vertically to give the form an orderly appearance.

○ Balance the placement of controls on the form. Evenly distribute the controls over the form.

○ Large rectangle controls can be used to either frame or separate information on the form.

  Figure 14-10 shows a form before making layout changes. Each control is on a separate line. The relationship between controls is unclear because the spacing between controls doesn't give any indication of the relationships.

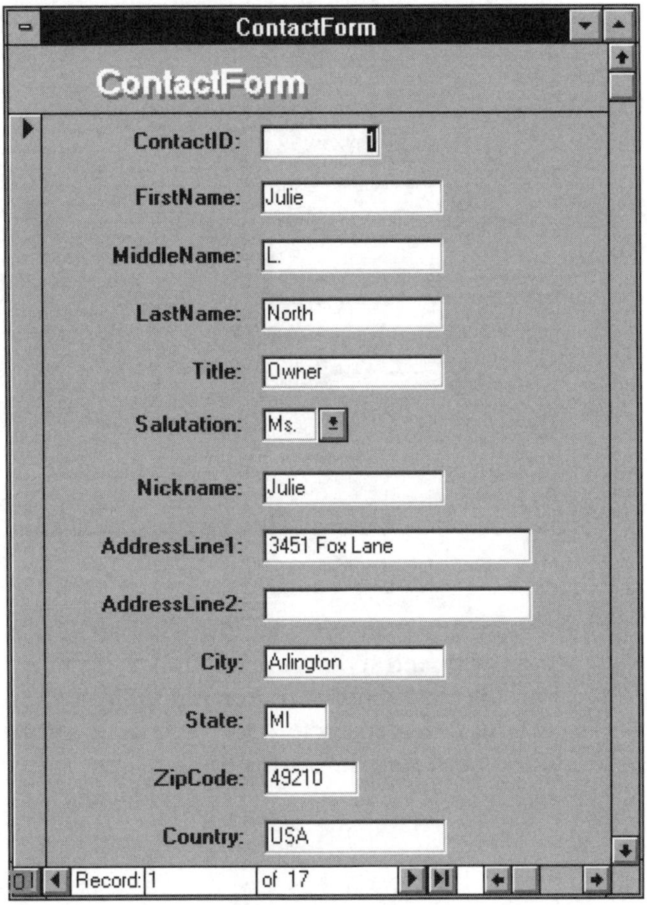

Figure 14-10: Contacts form before layout changes.

Figure 14-11 shows the form after making changes based upon the guidelines presented in this chapter.

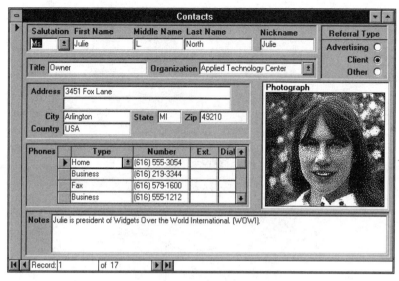

Figure 14-11: Contacts form after layout changes.

Figure 14-12 shows what the Contacts form would look like using the boxed style. This style takes up more room because each control is placed inside a rectangle. The style you choose is a matter of personal preference. The same guidelines apply to any style you use for your form.

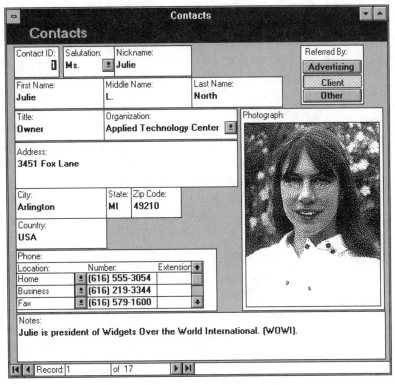

Figure 14-12: Contacts form using boxed style after layout changes.

Using Color Effectively

The colors you use on your form should give visual clues about the data. Clues can be intuitive, like changing the color of a number displayed in a text box from black to red when negative. You can use clues to help identify certain types of data. For example, you can make required fields a certain color and optional fields another. You can help organize the data on your form by using different colors for controls containing related information.

Be careful not to use too many colors on your form. As far as the number of colors you use on a form goes, less is more. Using fewer colors on a form will give those colors you use more impact. Every color you add to a form reduces the effectiveness of the other colors. You also run the risk of ending up with a form that looks more like modern art than a form for maintaining data. As a general guideline keep the number of colors on a form to four or less. If you need to use more colors, consider using shades of gray instead. You can use twice as many shades of gray as colors without overpowering the user.

You should not rely on color alone to send clues to your users. It's a good idea to give a second clue, such as using different fonts or using the Status Bar Text property, to reinforce the clues. For example, you might place "[Required]" in the text displayed for those fields that the user must fill in on the form.

Color blindness is very common, especially among men. Studies have shown that 8 percent of males and 0.5 percent of females have some color vision deficiency. In most cases, certain colors are seen as shades of gray. The most common forms of color blindness are red/green and yellow/blue deficiencies, where the two colors appear as gray. Keep this in mind when choosing colors for your form. That's not to say that you shouldn't use red, green, yellow or blue on your forms. Just keep in mind that the red/green or yellow/blue pairs could be indistinguishable from gray.

Some colors are more visible than others. Blue is the least visible color in the spectrum. It is a good choice for objects you don't want to draw attention to, such as a line or rectangle. Red seems to jump off the screen, unless the user has a deficiency in this area. I know what you're thinking: fire trucks aren't red anymore because they found that yellow is more visible. You're right, but I don't think I want that color hanging around my forms.

We associate some colors with certain conditions, such as green with proceed, yellow with caution and red with stop. Take advantage of this by using these colors in an appropriate manner. For example, use green when you'd like to draw the user's attention, yellow when it is important for the user to notice an object and red when it is critical for a user to notice an object.

One way to really improve the use of color on your forms is to let users choose their own colors. There are several ways of doing this. We won't discuss the details of how you might implement this type of feature in your applications in this book. Keep it in mind if you decide you want to market a commercial application though.

Fonts

There are hundreds of fonts you can choose from for your application. Some fonts are designed to display information onscreen while others are designed to be printed. There are some fonts designed to be both screen and printer fonts.

All of the fonts available fall into two basic categories: serif and sans serif. The fonts most commonly used on forms are sans serif fonts. As a general rule, sans serif fonts are a good choice when you need to use a small font size or when you want a "cleaner" looking interface. Use a serif font when you want a "fancier" interface. The section headings in this book are set in sans serif fonts. The text in this book is set in a serif font.

Here are a few guidelines to keep in mind regarding fonts, and text in general:

❍ Mixed-case letters are easier to read than all capitals.

❍ Using all capital letters is a good way to draw ATTENTION!

❍ Bold type adds emphasis to text.

❍ Attention-getting clues, such as boldface or capitalization, are only effective if you use them sparingly. If you put too many of them on a form you run the risk of reducing their effectiveness.

Figure 14-13 shows the Contacts form after making a few font changes. Compare this figure to Figure 14-11. The fields with uppercase labels seem to stand out. The first name, last name and referral type controls contain the data that is required on the form.

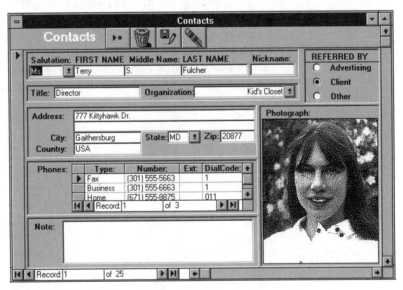

Figure 14-13: Contacts form with font changes.

REPORT GUIDELINES

Many of the guidelines we've looked at for forms design apply to report design as well. There are a few differences you should be aware of:

❍ Because of the static nature of reports, you have more flexibility as far as font selection is concerned. It is a good idea to limit the number of typefaces, and vary the size for emphasis. You can also add emphasis by using the Bold, Italic or Underline properties.

425

○ Consider using shaded rectangles to help create groups of related information. Most printers can support several shades of gray. Take advantage of this to create some informative reports.

○ Avoid putting too much information on a single report line. A line with more than 8 to 10 data items on standard 8½ by 11 paper looks crowded. Try separating the data into multiple lines to avoid making the report look congested.

○ Use "white space" to indicate groups of related data.

○ Make sure columns of data align across report sections. If you are printing total information in a footer section, make sure to align the total with the column used in the calculation.

○ Use controls normally thought of as form controls, such as option groups, check boxes and toggle buttons, to help the user relate the data on the report to the forms used for maintenance.

○ Use graphs to present comparisons of data. As I said before, a picture is worth a thousand words. In most cases, people can understand data comparisons presented graphically much easier than by looking at numbers alone. The graph shown in Figure 14-14 demonstrates this point. It shows the states our customers reside in. It is easy to see the differences in numbers of customers between the states shown.

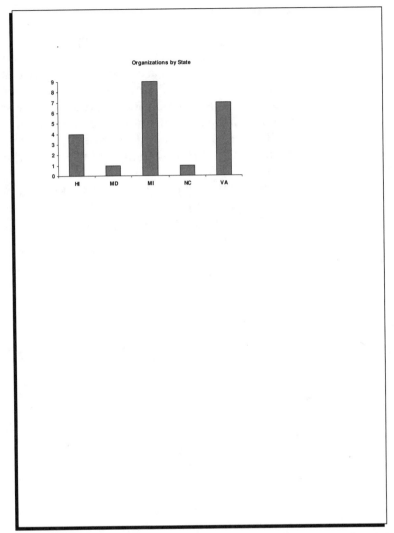

Figure 14-14: Sample graph showing number of customers by state printed as a report.

MOVING ON

In this chapter we discussed the importance of following a few simple guidelines to help make your applications easier to use. Many of the guidelines are so intuitive that we take them for granted, like placing related controls together on a form. Others are less obvious, like considering color blindness when choosing the colors for our application. The most important things to remember are to keep your application's interface as simple as possible and to be consistent in how you use the tools at your disposal.

In the next chapter we will look at how you can add power to your application by using macros. Macros provide an easy way of performing simple tasks to help make your application easier to use.

15

Switching on the Power with Access Macros

Assuming that you've been reading this book straight through, you thus far have experienced the challenge of designing a relationally correct database schema, the thrill of looking at data in a new light via Access queries, the joy of creating forms with all kinds of buttons and other gadgets, and, of course, the visual stimulation of your first printed report. After all of that, you may feel like you have conquered a great mountain, and you may have difficulty trying to think of new ways to satisfy your hunger for adventure. If this is you, then you're in for a real treat!

Using Access macros is a great way to really liven up all those tables, queries, forms and reports you've been working so hard on, and to give your Access objects extra functionality. For example, the Contacts form in the VENTANA.MDB sample application contains a button labeled Today's Follow Ups. When you click this button, a filter is applied to the data on the form so that you only see those records that have a follow-up appointment for today's date. This magic is done with Access macros. Basically, you can use Access macros to write small programs, or to tie all of your Access objects together into a full-on application.

This chapter will begin by explaining just what an Access macro is, and will take you all the way to writing complete macro programs. On the way, we'll talk about the different elements that make up an Access macro, including actions, conditions, group names and more.

"FILL-IN-THE-BLANK" PROGRAMMING

If you are not an experienced programmer, or if the thought of learning a new language seems intimidating, don't fear; Access macros make programming easy, and even a little fun. Unlike working with traditional programming languages, using Access macros does not involve writing programming code or coming up with obscure formulas and algorithms. Instead, you simply choose from a list of *actions* you'd like a macro to accomplish. (A macro *action* is a predefined command that tells Access to do something, such as opening a form or filtering a set of records.) Once you choose a particular action–OpenForm, for example–you can fill in the detailed information required by that command, such as which form you want to open. You can also fill in other areas of a macro, such as a condition that determines whether or not an action or a set of actions should be executed.

The clever marketing folks at Microsoft call this "fill-in-the-blank" programming–an accurate summary of what Access macros are all about. There is no language to learn and no rigid syntactical structure to follow; you simply choose actions from a list and fill in the blanks with the appropriate information. (In some cases, you won't even have to do *that* much.)

Does this all sound too easy? To give you an idea of how easy it really is, let's go ahead and try a couple of simple macros now, before we get into heavy-duty macro toil. These examples, along with most of the examples in this chapter, will take place in the CONTACTS.MDB sample application. Open the CONTACTS.MDB database if you haven't already done so.

Both of the macros we are about to create will open the Contacts form when executed; the only difference will be in *how* we create them.

Follow these steps to create the first macro:

1. From the Database window, choose the Macro tab (see Figure 15-1).

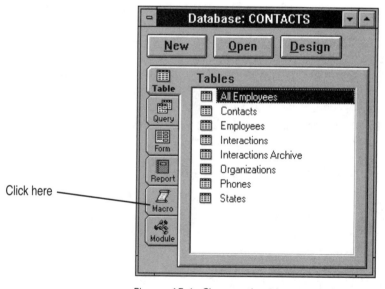

Click here

Figure 15-1: Choose the Macro tab in the Database window.

430

2. Click the New button in the Database window. A new Macro window appears labeled Macro: Macro1.

3. Display the list of available macro actions by clicking the button in the Action column of the macro sheet. You can scroll down the list to see more actions (see Figure 15-2).

Click here to show a list of macro actions

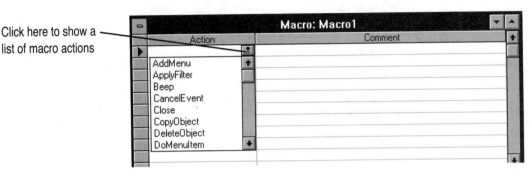

Figure 15-2: The list of macro actions appears right in the Macro window.

4. Scroll through the action list and choose OpenForm. Several arguments appear at the bottom of the window, including Form Name.

5. Type **Contacts** at the Form Name prompt, or click on the right side of the white entry area and choose the Contacts form from the list that appears.

6. Choose the File menu item from the menu bar, and select Save from the pull-down menu. Access displays a prompt allowing you to name the macro.

7. Name the macro **Open Contacts Form** and close the Macro window by choosing the File menu from the menu bar and choosing Close from the pull-down menu.

Voila! You have just created your first macro! You can try out the macro by highlighting it in the Database window and choosing the Run button.

Believe it or not, there is an even easier way to create an identical macro, using a really nifty drag-and-drop feature. (You may have discovered by now that Access is replete with nifty drag-and-drop features.) Follow these steps to try this out:

1. As with the previous example, make sure that the Macro tab in the Database window is selected, and choose the New button.

2. Size and position the Macro window so that it appears next to the Database window and is not obscuring the Database window (see Figure 15-3).

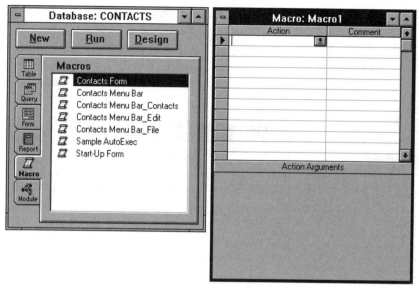

Figure 15-3: Size and position the Database window and Macro window as shown here.

3. Click the Form tab in the Database window, so that the list of forms is displayed.

4. Here's the fun part: drag the Contacts form from the Database window and drop it into the first line of the Action column in the Macro window.

5. Notice that Access automatically adds an OpenForm action and fills in the Form Name entry at the bottom of the window. At this point, you can save and close the macro as you did in the previous example.

This macro will also open the Contacts form using the OpenForm action. After saving the macro, you can run it by choosing the Run menu item from the Macro menu.

Now that you have had a little experience creating macros, let's move on to the heavy-duty stuff. There's a lot more you can do with macros than simply executing a set of actions. We'll begin by examining the various components of the Macro window. You may want to open a new Macro window right now to better follow the discussion.

MACRO ACTIONS & ARGUMENTS

As you have already seen, a macro sheet includes an Action column and a Comment column. In each of the previous examples, we created a macro with only one action, but a macro of course can contain many actions.

Action ———

Action Column ———

Comment Column ———

Action Arguments ———

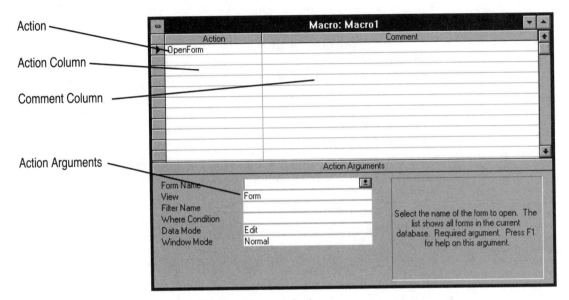

Figure 15-4: The Macro window.

You can add an action to a macro in one of four ways:

○ Display the list of actions by clicking on the right side of the Action column; then choose an action from the list.

○ Type the name of the action.

○ Type the first few letters of the action name until the action appears.

○ If you want to add an OpenTable, OpenQuery, OpenForm, OpenReport, RunMacro or OpenModule action, you can drag the object you want to open from the Database window to a new line in the Action column. As we discovered earlier, adding a macro action this way automatically fills in all of the action arguments you need to open the object.

Each action has a set of arguments that appears at the bottom of the Macro window (see Figure 15-5). These arguments differ from one action to another, since each action has a different purpose and requires different information. For example, adding an OpenForm action to the macro causes these arguments to appear at the bottom of the Macro window:

433

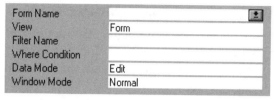

Figure 15-5: Arguments for the OpenForm action.

Since the purpose of the OpenForm action is to open an Access form, it is important to know what the form name is. The other arguments can be equally important, depending on the context in which the OpenForm action is being used.

But the TransferDatabase action, for instance, has a different set of arguments. The TransferDatabase action imports, exports or attaches data to or from Access, and it doesn't need a form name or a window mode as does the OpenForm action. Instead, these arguments are displayed when you select the TransferDatabase action:

Transfer Type	Import
Database Type	Microsoft Access
Database Name	
Object Type	Table
Source	
Destination	
Structure Only	No

Figure 15-6: Arguments for the TransferDatabase action.

Access makes it as easy as possible to fill in these arguments. In many cases, the arguments are already filled in for you with Access's default. Many arguments (such as the Form Name argument for the OpenForm action) have a drop-down pick-list that appears when you click on the right end of the argument entry area. Many arguments also have an Expression Builder available to them. The Expression Builder appears when you click on the button with the three dots in it (this button only appears when applicable). The Expression Builder is pretty handy, but—in my opinion—if you're proficient enough with Access to understand how to use the Expression Builder, you're probably better off manually typing the expression into the argument entry area.

Expressions in Action Arguments

The term *expression* may sound like another one of those intimidating buzzwords, but it's really a fairly simple concept. Basically, an expression is a formula that represents a value. For example, 2+2 is an expression that represents the number 4. If you wanted to represent the number 4 in a macro action argument, you could literally type the number 4, or you could type the expression =2+2. Since an expression can be anything that evaluates to some value when you feed it to Access, you might have an expression like =Time( ), since Time( ) is an Access Basic function that evaluates to the current time of day. (See Chapter 16 for more information on Access Basic functions.)

If the concept of Access expressions is new to you, then the following example will demonstrate what expressions are all about. Note the arguments and their settings for the MsgBox action shown in Figure 15-7:

Message	This is a message
Beep	Yes
Type	None
Title	

Figure 15-7: Arguments for the MsgBox action with settings filled in.

Since the purpose of the MsgBox action is to display a box with a message, one of the arguments we are prompted for is a Message. Executing this action with the argument values we specified here would produce the following message box:

Figure 15-8: The action arguments in Figure 15-7 produce this message box.

Since we wanted the message "This is a message" to appear, we literally typed **This is a message** into the Message argument for this action. Sometimes, however, we may need the MsgBox to display a value that we represent as an expression.

When you work with macros, there are many cases where you might need to use an expression as an argument because the value of the argument is not known at the time that you design the macro. Suppose you want to create a MsgBox that displays today's date. What would you specify for the Message argument in such a case? You can't just type in today's date—the message box might display the proper date today, but it wouldn't automatically change for tomorrow.

The solution to this problem would be to type in some kind of expression that evaluates to today's date, rather than typing in a literal date. The expression we need in this case is the Access Basic Date( ) function, which evaluates to today's date when it is used in an expression. To tell Access that you are specifying an expression for an argument, you must precede the expression with an equal (=) sign. Figure 15-9 shows the =Date( ) function in the Message argument, along with the message box that would result. (You'll have to pretend that today's date is May 4, 1994.)

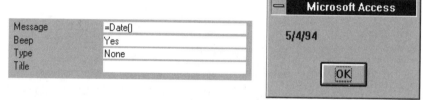

Figure 15-9: The Date() function in the MsgBox action's Message argument displays the current date in the resulting message box.

The equal sign (=) is necessary when you are specifying an expression. If you omit the equal sign, Access interprets the entry you made as a literal string of characters to display, as shown in Figure 15-10:

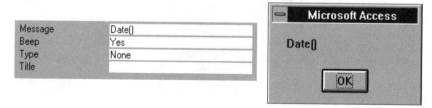

Figure 15-10: Omitting the equal sign produces an unwanted result.

As mentioned earlier, an expression can be an Access Basic function, such as the Date( ) function, or one that you define (as discussed in Chapter 16). It can be an arithmetic or other kind of Access expression. It can also be a reference to a control on a form, such as a text box, representing the value of that control. (We'll discuss how to write an expression that references a control in the next section.) For example, you might want to use the TransferDatabase action to export an Access table specified by the user. Rather than type in the name of the Access table to be exported, you would specify a reference to a textbox control on a form you created, where a user will type the actual name of a table.

Referencing Controls in Arguments

Arguments that you use with certain actions may require a reference to a control on a form or report. For example, suppose you want to create a macro that, when executed, changes the caption of a button called FollowUpFilter on a form called Contacts to Show All Records. To do this, we need to set the value of the button's Caption property to the expression "Show All Records" using a SetValue action. (The SetValue action expects an expression as opposed to a literal value, such as "Show All Records" rather than Show All Records. If you do not enclose the caption value in quotes, Access will interpret the caption as a name of a form or control. This would result in an error, since Show All Records is not a valid name for a form or control, as you will learn in the next few paragraphs.)

The SetValue action has two arguments: Item and Expression (see Figure 15-11). The Item argument wants to know *what* you are setting, and the Expression argument wants to know what *value* to give to the Item.

Figure 15-11: Arguments for the SetValue action.

The *what* in this case is the FollowUpFilter button's Caption property; but how do we refer to the FollowUpFilter button on the Item line? I am about to give a detailed answer to this question in the next couple of pages. I urge you to pay close attention to this (as if you haven't been glued to your seat already), since what you are about to learn is an important fundamental when working with macros, Access Basic programming, and even forms, reports and queries.

Whenever you want to refer to an object on a form, you must follow this convention:

Forms!<form name>!<control name>.<property>

For example, the reference to the FollowUpFilter button and its Caption property would be:

Forms!Contacts!FollowUpFilter.Caption

This may seem a bit confusing and off-the-wall at first, but it makes a lot of sense once you understand the idea behind this naming convention. Let's consider each element of the complete reference to the FollowUpFilter button shown above.

○ The *Forms* element specifies that the button is located on an active form. Access keeps track of all the active forms in something called the forms collection, which we'll learn more about later. If we were referring to an object on a report, we would substitute the *Forms* element with the word *Reports*, meaning that the object is on an active report rather than a form. If we wanted to refer to a property of the Contacts form rather than to a property of a control *on* the Contacts form, we would omit the control name from the reference. For example, we would refer to the Contacts form's Caption property as follows:

Forms!Contacts.Caption

○ The *Contacts* element identifies the specific form that the control is located on. If the form name consisted of more than one word, such as Contacts Form, the name would need to be enclosed in square brackets:

Forms![Contacts Form]!FollowUpFilter.Caption

○ The *FollowUpFilter* element identifies the actual control. As with the form reference, the control name must be enclosed in square brackets if it contains spaces.

○ Finally, the property we are interested in, *Caption*, appears at the end of the of the reference.

None of the reference elements are case sensitive, but you may want to use proper capitalization for neatness and ease of reading.

You might have noticed that the first few elements of the reference are separated with exclamation points, and the last argument is preceded by a period. There is a good reason for this. An exclamation point precedes the name of an object that is created by the user. For example, notice that an exclamation point appears in front of *Contacts* and *FollowUpFilter*. Forms and buttons are objects that you create. On the other hand, the Caption property is something you didn't create—it is a predefined property that some genius developer type at Microsoft threw together so that you could display any caption you want on a button. That's why *Caption* is preceded by a period.

Because Microsoft decided to go this route with the exclamation points and periods, you can create objects with the same names as properties without conflict. For example, you could create a button called Caption, even though Caption is a predefined property, and refer to the Caption button like so:

Forms!Form1!Caption

If you preceded *Caption* with a period rather than an exclamation point, you would actually be referring to the Caption property of Form1:

Forms!Form1.Caption

Of course, I would never recommend using the name of a predefined property as an object name, but this feature allows Access to be forgiving if you accidently use an existing property name as an object name. It also avoids compatibility problems in case future versions of Access happen to use a name for a property that you are now using for an object.

Now, with all of this in mind, let's get back to the problem at hand. We have a SetValue action sitting in a Macro window on the screen, and it's waiting for us to enter something into the Item and Expression arguments. Remember that we want to set the value of the FollowUpFilter button's Caption property to "Show All Records." Remember also that the button exists on a form called Contacts. With our newfound wisdom on object references in Access, this should be a snap! Figure 15-12 shows the arguments we want.

| Item | Forms!Contacts!FollowUpFilter.Ca [...] |
| Expression | "Show All Records" |

Figure 15-12: The arguments for setting the FollowUpFilter button's Caption property to "Show All Records."

This naming convention works with all controls except subforms and subreports. If the FollowUpFilter button were situated on a subform called Contacts Subform, we would have to reference its Caption property this way:

Forms!Contacts![Contacts SubForm].Form!FollowUpFilter.Caption

Whoa! What the *heck* is that?! Let's break this reference apart as we did for the previous example, and you'll see that it actually makes sense.

○ As with the previous example, the *Forms* element specifes that the button is located on an active form, and the *Contacts* element identifies the form we are referring to.

○ *Contacts SubForm* is the name of the subform control. It is important to distinguish between the name of the subform control and the name of the subform itself. For example, the form you created that eventually became Contacts Subform may appear in the Database window under some other name, such as Subform for Contacts. In that case, Subform for Contacts would be the name of the form itself, but its *control name* on the Contacts form is *Contacts Subform*. A lot of people understandably get hung up on this concept, and they are bitten once or twice before they figure out the distinction. However, thanks to me, you are now one step ahead of all of them.

○ *Form* is a property of the Contacts Subform control. It means that you want access to the information on the form that is contained in Contacts Subform, as opposed to some other property of Contacts Subform such as its height or width. Notice that Form is preceded by a period rather than an exclamation point, since it is a predefined property of the Contacts Subform control. For a report/subreport reference, you would *not* use the word *Report* instead of *Form*. Form is a property that is valid for both subform and subreport controls, since subform and subreport controls are essentially the same thing. To draw an analogy, a label control has a property called Caption, and the name of this property doesn't change just because you might use it on a report instead of a form.

○ As with the previous example, *FollowUpFilter* refers to the control we want and *Caption* refers to the property of the control we want.

Understanding expressions in Access not only helps you in writing useful macros, but it also comes in handy for writing Access Basic programs and complex queries. Speaking of useful macros, we will now proceed to put what you have learned so far into practical use.

INCORPORATING MACROS INTO AN APPLICATION

With a little practice and a little experience with the different macro actions, you already know enough to be dangerous. Now that you know how to create macros, you need to know how to incorporate them into your forms and reports.

Running a Macro From a Button on a Form

The purpose of a button is to perform some action. Thus, running a macro from a button is perhaps the most common way to incorporate a macro into your application. It is also the easiest way to run a macro from a form. And once you understand how to run a macro from a form, it will be easy for you to understand how to run a macro in one of the zillions of other places that a macro can be executed from.

Just to get warmed up, I'd like to start off by showing you an interesting trick you can do to add a button that executes a macro to a form. Follow these steps for a bit of fun:

1. Create a macro with one MsgBox action in it. Specify **Hello world** for the Message argument.

2. Save the macro, naming it **Push Me**. The Push Me macro appears in the Database window when the Macro tab is selected.

3. Create a new blank form by clicking the Form tab on the Database window, then clicking the New button in the Database window. When you are prompted to choose either Form Wizards or Blank Form, choose Blank Form.

4. Size and position the form so that it appears next to the Database window and is not obscuring the Database window.

5. Click the Macro tab in the Database window, so that a list of macros appears.

6. Drag the Push Me macro from the Database window to the detail section of the new form, as shown in Figure 15-13. A button appears with a Push Me caption.

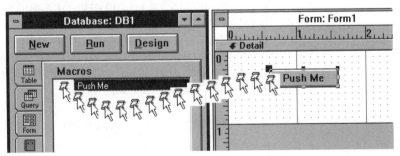

Figure 15-13: Drag the Push Me macro onto the form.

Now switch the form into Form view and click the new Push Me button. Notice that it runs the Push Me macro.

This is an easy way to add any macro to a form. Access automatically did what we would normally do in several steps. Now let's manually create an identical macro by following the steps below. (Anyone caught cheating by using drag-and-drop has to stay after class and bang erasers.)

1. Switch the form back to Design view.

2. First make sure the Control Wizard button on the toolbar is not pushed in, then add a new command button to the form from the toolbox. Do not erase the original button—we'll try both of them out later.

3. Change the caption of the new button to **Push Me**.

4. If it isn't already on the screen, bring up the button's property sheet. Make sure the new Push Me button is highlighted, so that its properties appear in the property sheet.

5. If it isn't already selected, choose Event Properties from the combo box list at the top of the property sheet. This displays a list of all the button events you can run a macro from.

6. Click once anywhere in the row labeled OnClick, so that the cursor appears in the entry area. Notice that a drop-down list button appears to the right.

7. Click the drop-down list button. This displays a list of macros in your database.

8. Choose the Push Me macro.

9. Save the form as **Hello world.**

By specifying the Push Me macro in the OnClick event property, you are instructing the form to execute the Push Me macro when the button is clicked.

Now switch the form into Form view and click each button. Notice that the button you created manually behaves identically to the button that you dragged and dropped onto the form. If you were to look at the button that you dragged and dropped, you would notice that Access specified Push Me for the OnClick event of that button, just as we did.

Running a Macro From Other Form Event Properties

Up to this point, we've gone as far as hooking up a macro to a button on a form. But a macro can be executed from any other event property as well. I mentioned earlier that a button is one of the most common places to run a macro from, since the purpose of a button is to do something when it is clicked. Another common use for macros on a form is data validation. For example, you could write a macro for a State field that pops up a list of state abbreviations that a user can choose from, rather than requiring the user to type the state abbreviation. This kind of macro would be executed when the user tabs into the State field, as opposed to taking a more obvious action, such as clicking a button.

Still another common use for macros is to execute something when a form is opened. For example, in the VENTANA.MDB sample application, the number of Follow Up contacts for today is displayed when you open the Contacts form. You don't have to click a button for this to happen; it just happens when the form is opened. This is possible because Access provides an event property called OnLoad, which allows us to run a macro or an Access Basic program when the form is opened.

To learn about other event properties on a form, see Chapter 9.

Using Macros With Reports

Like forms, reports and report controls have various event properties from which you can execute a macro. It may not seem obvious why you would ever need to use a macro with a report, since reports don't interact with users like forms do, but you should know this stuff in case it ever comes up (as it has for me on several occasions).

OnFormat and OnPrint are two very important report event properties that can execute a macro (and they are the only ones you need to know about for now):

○ The OnFormat event takes place before a report section is formatted in memory, or in other words, when Access is figuring out where to place items on a page so that the report prints the way you designed it. You would run a macro from the OnFormat event property when you want something to happen *before* Access commits to formatting a page. For example, you may need to use a macro to recalculate the value of a text box on the report each time the text box is printed, based on the value of the current record. If you choose to run the macro any time after the OnFormat event occurs, the text box will not be changed, because Access has already committed to printing the text box as is, even though the formatted page hasn't gone to the printer yet.

○ The OnPrint event takes place after the section has been formatted, but before Access sends it to the printer. You would run a macro from the OnPrint event when you need to take some kind of action after Access finishes formatting the page. You might use the OnPrint event to run a macro that keeps a running total for weekly sales figures being printed on your report. You wouldn't use the OnFormat event in this case, because the number you need to add to the running total isn't available until after the section is formatted.

Refer to Chapter 11 for more detailed information on reports and report events.

SOME USEFUL MACRO ACTIONS

By dropping down the list of macros in the Action column of a macro sheet, you can scroll through all the actions available to you. The purpose of some actions is obvious from their names, and the help message appearing at the lower right-hand side of the Macro window ought to be enough to clue you in for most actions. (The description of an action appears when you select that action from the list.)

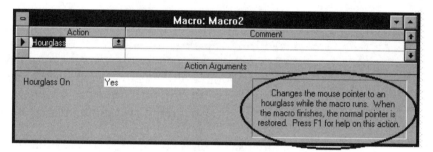

Figure 15-14: Help message in a Macro window.

In this book, we won't discuss every single macro action, since many of the actions are self-explanatory, and we don't want to get distracted from the real issues you need to know about. However, there are a few actions that are very important, although you wouldn't know it just by looking at their names. In this section, you will be subjected to some serious application of what you have learned so far, and you'll get some practical experience working with macros.

The ApplyFilter Action

The ApplyFilter action *filters* records on an open form—that is, it restricts the records that can be viewed with a form based on a certain condition (such as City = "Los Angeles"). ApplyFilter can filter out records based on a query you created, or you can type in the filter criteria.

To practice using ApplyFilter, we'll create a small form that displays data from the Contacts table in the CONTACTS.MDB sample database. This form will have a combo box from which you can choose either a letter from the alphabet or an item called **All**. Choosing a letter will filter the records on the form so that you only see those people whose last names begin with the letter you clicked. Choosing All will remove the filter, and you'll see all records in the table.

Follow these steps to create the form and the macros to go with it—I'll explain what you're doing as we go along. (In this section I am assuming that you've already read Chapters 8 and 9 and are familiar with designing forms.)

1. With the Contacts table highlighted in the Database window, create a new blank form by clicking the New Form button on the Database toolbar. When you are prompted to choose either Form Wizards or Blank Form, choose Blank Form.

2. Turn off the Wizards option if it is toggled in the tool box.

3. Add a combo box to the form. Name the combo box **Alphabet List**.

4. Modify the RowSourceType property of the combo box to Value List. Modify the RowSource property to read All;A;B;C;D;E;F;G;H;I;J;K;L;M;N;O;P;Q;R;S;T;U;V;W;X;Y;Z.

5. Modify the AfterUpdate event property for the combo box so that it executes a macro called Alphabet Filter. We will create this macro a few steps from now.

6. Change the Caption of the combo box's label control to **Alphabet.**

7. Click the Field List button to display the field list for Contacts. Add FirstName and LastName text boxes to the form by dragging the field names onto the form from the field list (see Figure 15-15).

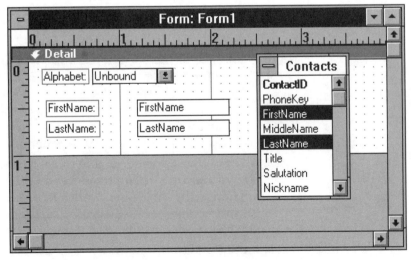

Figure 15-15: Drag the field names onto the form.

8. Close and save the form, naming it **Alphabet Form**.

9. Bring up a new Macro window by clicking the Macro tab followed by the New button in the Database window.

10. Add an ApplyFilter action to the macro. This action will only be executed when All is not selected from the combo box on the form. We'll add the condition that checks for All as we go along.

11. Modify the arguments for the ApplyFilter action as indicated below:

Argument	Value
Filter Name	
Where Condition	Left(LastName,1)=Forms![Alphabet Form]![Alphabet List]

○ The Left(LastName,1) function in the Where Condition is an Access Basic function that tells us what the first character on the left of LastName is. For example, if the value of LastName is Madoni, Left(LastName,1) returns M. Don't be intimidated by the fact that we're using an Access Basic function here. You don't need to know Access Basic to use macros, but there are a handful of functions that come in handy. You'll learn about them in the upcoming sections of this chapter and in the Access Basic chapters later on.

○ You might have noticed that the reference to LastName in the function didn't have Forms![Alphabet Form]! in front of it. The reason for this is that LastName in this context doesn't mean the value of LastName *on the form* as it appears for the current records. We want to filter based on *all* of the LastName values *in the set of records that the form is using.* Think of it like this: Forms![Alphabet Form]!LastName means "the value of the LastName text box on the form as we see it right now," and LastName by itself means "the LastName field in general."

12. Add a ShowAllRecords action to the next line of macro. The ShowAllRecords action removes any filter that has been applied to the record set. Notice that there are no arguments for this action, because Access doesn't need to know anything else about it.

13. If the Condition column is not displayed, click the Conditions button on the toolbar, or choose View, Conditions from the menu bar. In the Condition column for the ShowAllRecords action, add the following:

Forms![Alphabet Form]![Alphabet List] = "All"

Suppose we didn't add this condition, and the user selected the letter *A* from the combo box. The ApplyFilter would filter the records, but then the ShowAllRecords action would be executed, since there is no condition specified in the Condition column. Adding the condition above ensures that ShowAllRecords occurs only when **All** is selected from the combo box.

14. Close and save the macro, naming it **Alphabet Filter**.

Now we're ready to try this out. Open Alphabet Form and select different letters from the list, or select the All option.

The CancelEvent Action

The CancelEvent action is really handy for macros that do something "destructive," such as deleting a record from a table, deleting an object such as a query or form, or in some other way destroying something. You can use CancelEvent as part of a macro that handles the deletion of a record or object. Although Access already does this for you, you may want to customize the process to make it more user-friendly and more consistent with the way your application works. This is very important, since deleting something is usually serious business—you want to make sure that your user knows what he or she is doing.

Suppose someone using the Contacts form wants to delete the current record. When a record on a form is deleted, Access displays a generic warning message that looks like this:

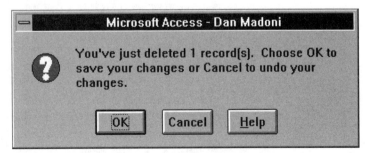

Figure 15-16: Generic Access delete warning message.

As I mentioned earlier, deleting data is serious business, and this message may be *too* generic for your taste. In addition, you may want to do other things "behind the scenes" when a user deletes a record (such as copying the record to some sort of backup table before the deletion actually takes place).

Access forms have an event property called *OnDelete*, which you can use to run a macro when a user chooses to delete the current record. From this macro, you can display your own warning message, and you can use the CancelEvent action to prevent the record from being deleted if the user responds to the warning accordingly. The event taking place in this case is OnDelete, so the CancelEvent action is *canceling* the OnDelete *event*, preventing the record from being deleted. Of course, you can use CancelEvent to cancel *any* pending event that calls a macro—I don't want you to get the impression that CancelEvent only exists for the purpose of preventing a record from being deleted.

To demonstrate the CancelEvent action, we will create a form that displays information from the Contacts table in the CONTACTS.MDB database. From this form's On Delete event, we will call a macro that displays our own user-friendly warning that allows the user to change his or her mind.

Before we begin with the example, choose Options from the View menu at the top of the screen. In the Options dialog box, change the Confirm Record Changes setting to No. This will give us complete control over what happens when a record is deleted. (After you have completed this section, and the Requery action section that follows, you may want to change the Record Changes setting back to Yes just to be extra safe.)

Follow these steps to test drive the CancelEvent action:

1. Open the Contacts form (developed in Chapters 8, 9 and 14) in Design view.

2. Modify the OnDelete event property for the form so that it executes a macro called Delete Contacts Record. We will create this macro a few steps from now.

3. Close and save the form.

4. Bring up a new Macro window by clicking the Macro tab followed by the New button in the Database window.

5. Add a CancelEvent action to the first line of the macro. As mentioned earlier, this action cancels the OnDelete event from which it was called. We will add a condition in the next step that ensures that the CancelEvent action only occurs if the user decides not to go ahead with the deletion.

6. Open up the Condition column in the Macro window and add the following condition to the first line (*The whole condition must appear on one line even though it is broken up here to fit on the page.*)

MsgBox("Are you sure you want to delete the record for" &
Forms!Form1!FirstName & " " & Forms!Form1!LastName & "? If you
choose 'Yes', this record will be permanently removed.",36) = 7

You're probably wondering what the heck this is. This is
another Access Basic function that you will use fairly often as
part of your macro conditions. The MsgBox( ) function does
the same thing that the MsgBox macro action does, except
that it allows you to display Yes and No buttons as part of the
message. This MsgBox( ) function will display a warning
message that includes the name of the person whose record
will be deleted. The concept of adding values to the message,
such as FirstName and LastName, is called *concatenation*.
Concatenation is discussed further in the Access Basic
chapters.

The numbers 36 and 7 in this function have special
meanings. The number 36 means that we want to display a
question mark icon and Yes/No buttons in the message. The
number 7 means that the user chose the No button in
response to this MsgBox. If the user chooses the Yes button,
then the result of the MsgBox( ) function will not be 7; the
condition will evaluate to False, and the CancelEvent action
on this line will not be executed. It probably seems pretty
obscure to you that the numbers 36 and 7 actually mean
something. Don't fret—these numbers are listed in Access's
online help, so you don't have to memorize them.

7. Close and save the macro, naming it **Delete Contacts
Record**.

Now go ahead and try out this example. Open Contacts,
click the record selector on the left of the form, and click the
form's Delete button (the one with the trash can—created in
Chapter 9) or choose Delete from the Edit on the menu bar.
Try it once by responding Yes to the custom message, and
again by responding No. Notice that the No response stops
the On Delete event and returns control to the form
immediately.

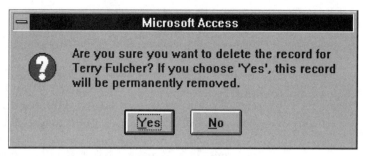

Figure 15-17: Custom delete warning message.

Don't delete any of the work you just did. In the next section, we will build on the form and macro you just created.

The Requery Action

As you learned in Chapters 8 and 9, some of the controls that you can put on a form can get their information from a table. For example, you can create a combo box or list box full of LastName values from the Contacts table, or you might have a subform that lists records from the Phones table, etc.

When a record is deleted from a table that a combo box or list box is using as a source of data, the deleted item is not removed from the list box. Instead, Access displays the record with the word #Deleted appearing in every column for that item.

J. Richard	Wolf
David	Needham
#Deleted	#Deleted
Alan	McConnell
Ileen	Martini
Timothy	Alan

Figure 15-18: #Deleted appears in place of a deleted record.

The Requery action forces a control to requery its data source for the data it needs to display. Once a Requery action is performed for the list box we've been talking about, the #Deleted record would disappear and everything would be just dandy.

If you're programming only with macros, it isn't very often that your application would delete a record from a table that is the data source of a control on an open form. However, it isn't so uncommon when you are using Access Basic, which gives you much greater and more efficient control over the data that underlies all of your forms and controls. I mention this because the value of learning Requery will become more apparent when we talk about Access Basic later on, though it is helpful to learn about it now.

For our Requery example, we'll build on the example we created in the previous section. In that example, we modified the Contacts form so that it executes a macro named Delete Contacts Record when the OnDelete event occurs. In our next example, we will create an new form with a combo box that gets its data from the Contacts List query that was created in Chapter 7 (you can import the query from the Ventana database if you haven't completed Chapter 7). We will create a macro that will requery the combo box in the new form so that no #Deleted records appear.

1. Create a new form for the Interactions table using the Single-Column Form Wizard. Include all fields from the Interactions table. Save the form with the name **Interactions.** If you created a form by that name in Chapter 8, either rename the other form or just replace it with the new form. Display the new Interactions form in Design view.

2. Delete the ContactID field and its label from the form and add a combo box control in its place (first toggle off the Control Wizard button so that the Combo Box Wizard is not invoked).

3. Modify the combo box properties as indicated in the following table:

Property	Value
Name	ContactID
ControlSource	ContactID
RowSourceType	Table/Query
RowSource	Contact List
ColumnCount	2
ColumnWidths	0 in;1 in

With these property settings, the combo box will display the FullName column from the Contact List query (created in Chapter 7), which draws its data from the "Contacts table". The ContactID field from the query doesn't appear, because its column width is set to zero inches. (See Chapter 9 for more on combo boxes.) But if the user selects a name from the combo box, the correct ContactID is stored in the ContactID field in the Interactions table.

Also edit the property sheet for the combo box's label, changing the label control's Name property to **Contact** and its Caption property to **Contact:** (see Figure 15-19).

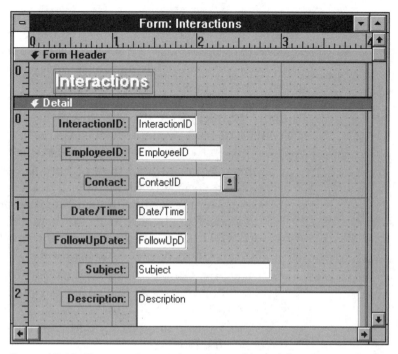

Figure 15-19: The new Interactions form after adding the combo box.

4. Modify the OnActivate property of the form so that it executes a macro named Requery Combo Box. We will create this macro next. This macro will run each time the Interactions form becomes the active window.

5. Save and close the Interactions form.

6. Create a new macro named Requery Combo Box. We will use this macro to cause the Interactions form to update the ContactID combo box.

7. Add the Requery action to the macro. A single argument labeled Control Name appears.

8. Specify ContactID for the Control Name argument. Notice that we simply indicate ContactID rather than Forms!Interactions!ContactID. Requery only works on the active form, and it only accepts the name of a control by itself, rather than the complete reference. Microsoft decided to implement Requery this way because—well, just because.

9. Save and close the macro.

Okay, let's try it out. Open both Contacts and Interactions. Drop down the ContactID combo box in the Interactions form (next to the Contact: label). This list box contains a list of all the individuals in the Contacts table. Now switch to the Contacts table and delete a record. You are prompted to confirm the deletion, as in the preceding example. Switch again to the Interactions form and display the ContactID combo box list again. The record you deleted in the Contacts form is gone, just as you wanted, and no #Deleted record is listed.

For practice, modify the Interactions form again and replace the EmployeeID text box and label with another combo box. Set the combo box's properties as follows:

Property	Value
Name	EmployeeID
ControlSource	EmployeeID
RowSourceType	Table/Query
RowSource	Employee List
ColumnCount	2
ColumnWidths	0 in;1 in

Modify the Requery Combo Box macro to add another Requery action. Specify EmployeeID as the action's argument. Now, each time you activate the Interactions form, the Requery Combo Box macro looks up the current values for both the ContactID and EmployeeID combo boxes. Whether the user has added or deleted records from Contacts or Employees, the combo boxes will always be up to date.

THE COMMENT AREA

You may have noticed that macro sheets have a column labeled *Comment,* where you can type comments about each line of your macro. Access doesn't require you to put anything in the Comment column in order for your macro to run, but it's a good idea to use comments liberally. Not only do comments help you keep track of why you designed your macro the way you did, but they also help others who may have to maintain your work after you get promoted for having revolutionized your company with Access macros.

CONDITIONS

Programming, whether by macro or with a programming language, typically involves checking for a certain condition, then doing one of two different things depending on that condition. For example, suppose you designed an order form that shows the total cost of the items ordered. Let's say that you're a national operation, and people in Los Angeles, Dallas and Charlotte will be using your order form. Since this form displays the total amount owed by the customer for the items purchased, it has to be able to factor in a tax rate, which differs from city to city.

Here's where macro conditions come into play. You can create a macro that checks which city the order is taken in and applies the appropriate tax rate using a SetValue macro action.

The example in Figure 15-20 calculates the Total Cost by multiplying the Sub Total by the tax rate for Los Angeles. (The tax rate shown here might be inaccurate, since I'm not sure what it is off hand—I only remember that the amount of tax you pay for a gallon of milk in Los Angeles is roughly equivalent to the price of a new Buick.)

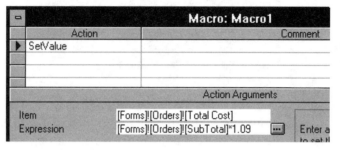

Figure 15-20: This SetValue action calculates the tax for the Total Cost field on our Orders form.

Now, we will add SetValue actions for Dallas and Charlotte. (Make sure the tax rate you're using in each Expression argument is correct.) Although there is now one SetValue action for each city, only *one* action will be executed, because we will specify a condition for each line that checks the value of a text box called City on the Orders form.

To add a condition to an action, open up the Condition column by clicking the Conditions toolbar button at the top of the screen. A new column labeled Condition appears in the Macro window.

In the Condition column, we can identify what condition to check for in order to execute the action on that line. If the condition is True, the action on that line is executed; otherwise, it is ignored.

Macro: Macro1		
Condition		Action
▶ [Forms]![Orders]![City]="Los Angeles"		SetValue
[Forms]![Orders]![City]="Dallas"		SetValue
[Forms]![Orders]![City]="Charlotte"		SetValue
		Action Arguments
Item	[Forms]![Orders]![Total Cost]	
Expression	[Forms]![Orders]![SubTotal]*1.09	

Figure 15-21: The conditional expressions determine which SetValue action will be executed.

Using a conditional expression, we were able to calculate a Total Cost depending on which city the transaction took place in. In this example, we were only concerned with executing one SetValue action if the condition evaluated to True; but what if we wanted to execute a *group* of actions if a given condition is True? Fortunately, the bright people at Microsoft realized that some of you out there may need to do this.

To describe how this is done, let's expand the example we are working with. Suppose that, in addition to showing the total cost with tax on the Orders form, we also wanted to print a special catalog for that area to give to the customer. In this case, two actions will be executed for each condition: one to set the Total Cost, and another to print an Access report.

You can execute multiple actions by placing three consecutive periods (...) in the condition column for each line that should be executed as long as the condition is True (see Figure 15-22). Access will execute each line following the True condition, until it encounters a line with a different condition. If a Condition column has nothing in it, Access executes the action on that line no matter what. In the example below, only one pair of SetValue/OpenReport actions will be executed, depending on the value of the City text box; however, the MsgBox action will execute in every case, since there are no conditions or periods.

Macro: Macro1	
Condition	**Action**
▶ [Forms]![Orders]![City]="Los Angeles"	SetValue
...	OpenReport
[Forms]![Orders]![City]="Dallas"	SetValue
...	OpenReport
[Forms]![Orders]![City]="Charlotte"	SetValue
...	OpenReport
	MsgBox

Action Arguments	
Item	[Forms]![Orders]![Total Cost]
Expression	[Forms]![Orders]![SubTotal]*1.09

Figure 15-22: If a condition evaluates to True, Access continues executing actions that contain three consecutive periods in the Condition column.

MACRO GROUPS

Microsoft Access allows you to organize a group of macro actions and refer to that group by giving it a name. And you can have several groups of macro actions within a single macro window. Thus, rather than calling a group of actions by referring to the name you saved the Macro window with, you call a group *within* the macro window by referring to its group name.

This is helpful for maintaining your application by minimizing clutter in the Database window. For example, you might want to keep all macros associated with the Contacts form in one Macro window called Contacts Form (which is how we did it in the VENTANA.MDB sample application).

This is accomplished by appropriately labeling groups of actions using the Macro Name column of a macro sheet. (These names are also used for creating menus, but we'll talk about that later on.) To open the Macro Name column, choose the Macro Names toolbar button at the top of the screen.

Using Labels in the Macro Name Column

To understand how to use the Macro Name column to group macros, first consider the macro in Figure 15-23. If you were to run this macro as is, the five actions would be executed one at a time from top to bottom.

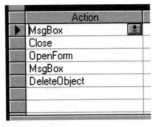

Figure 15-23: If you were to run this macro as is, all of the actions would be executed.

Now look at the example in Figure 15-24. Here we added labels in the Macro Name column to group the actions into two separate macros, *even though they exist in the same Macro window*. If you wanted to execute the Next Form macro, Access would execute the actions beginning with the Next Form line, until a line with another label is encountered. If you wanted to execute the Delete Temp Query macro, Access would execute the actions beginning with the Delete Temp Query line, until there are no more actions to process.

Macro Name	Action
Next Form	MsgBox
	Close
	OpenForm
Delete Temp Query	MsgBox
	DeleteObject

Figure 15-24: Macro names group macro actions together.

Referencing Macro Groups From an Event Property

Hooking up a macro to a form or control event property is pretty straightforward, as we have seen. You simply type the name of the macro or choose it from a drop-down list in the property sheet of a form or report. Hooking up a macro group is basically the same thing—the only difference is in the naming of the macro.

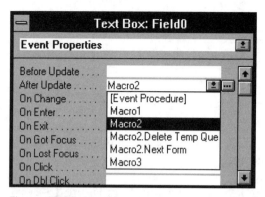

Figure 15-25: Hooking up a macro group is just like hooking up a regular Macro window with no groups in it.

A Macro window is identified by its name in the Database window, whether or not it has any macro groups in it, so a macro called Macro2 would appear in a Properties window as Macro2. However, if we wanted to refer to a group that exists *within* Macro2, we would use this convention: <macro name>.<group label>. For example, the Next Form macro group in the example above would appear as Macro2.Next Form in a property sheet. Access makes this even easier by including macro groups in the property sheet's drop-down list.

USING MACROS TO CREATE BAR MENUS

Whenever you want to create custom menus for a form, it is easiest to use the Menu Builder. To start the Menu Builder, either click the Build button at the end of the form's MenuBar property, or choose File, Add-Ins, Menu Builder from the menu bar. Then just select options from the screens.

In fact, menus are actually macros in Access. The Menu Builder simply creates a macro and automatically attaches it to a form via the form's Menu Bar property.

Considering how easy it is to use the Menu Builder, there really isn't any value in creating a menu from scratch using the macro actions you are about to learn. Nonetheless, we strive for excellence here, and knowing this stuff will come in handy someday. (Of course, that's what my high school math teacher said about Advanced Algebra!)

To build a menu using macros, you need to do the following three things:

1. Create one macro for each pull-down menu.

2. Create a macro that "ties" all of these pull-down menus together into one bar menu.

3. Hook the bar menu macro up to a form via that form's Menu Bar property.

The following three sections describe these steps in detail.

Creating a Macro for Each Pull-Down Menu

Earlier, we learned that you can group macros together in a single Macro window using the Macro Name column. In a bar menu macro, you use the Macro Name column to identify the name of each menu item in the pull-down menu.

For example, suppose your pull-down menu will contain two items: Display Contacts Table and Close This Form. You would type these names into the Macro Name column, each on its own line, as shown in Figure 15-26:

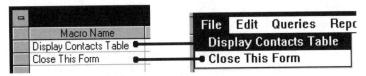

Figure 15-26: The entries in the Macro Name column identify the menu items.

You assign an action, or a group of actions, to each menu item by filling in the Action column for each item.

Macro Name	Action
Display Contacts Table	Hourglass
	OpenForm
Close This Form	Close

Figure 15-27: Each menu item executes a set of actions.

In the illustration above, the Display Contacts Table menu item will execute two actions, and then stop once it encounters the next macro name. This is consistent with the way named macro groups work, as we learned earlier.

You optionally can put an ampersand (&) in front of a letter in a menu item name that you want to create a hot key for. When the menu appears, the letter that you preceded with an ampersand is underlined, and you can access that menu item by pressing that letter on the keyboard. For example, if you specified **&Close This Form** in the Macro Name column, the menu item would appear as CloseThisForm when the pull-down menu is selected. You could then press **C** to select that menu item.

Another way to customize your menu is to include separator bars. A separator bar is a line that runs across a pull-down menu, separating one group of commands from another (see Figure 15-28).

Figure 15-28: A Menu separator bar.

To create a separator bar, place a dash (-) in the Macro Name column instead of a menu item name. Since separator bars cannot be highlighted in a menu, any action you place in the Action column is ignored.

When you save one of these pull-down menu macros, it is a good idea to give the macro the same name as the bar menu item it will be associated with. For example, if the pull-down menu is to be associated with a File menu item in the bar menu, you should name the macro *File* or *File Menu*. This will make it easier for you when you build the macro that ties all of these menus together.

Tying All the Pull-Down Menus Together

Once you have defined the pull-down menu macros, you are ready to create the final bar-menu macro, which ties all of the pull-down menus together. To accomplish this, you create a new macro and use AddMenu actions for each menu item in the menu bar. For example, suppose you have created three pull-down menu macros: File Menu, Edit Menu and Reports Menu. The final macro you create would contain three AddMenu actions, one for each pull-down menu macro.

When you add an AddMenu action, three action arguments appear at the bottom of the screen:

○ *Menu Name.* This is the name of the menu item on the bar menu at the top of the screen. As with pull-down menu items, you can place an ampersand in front of the character you want to make a hot key for. In this case, the menu item is selected when the user presses Alt plus the underlined character.

○ *Menu Macro Name.* This is the name of the macro containing the pull-down menu that should appear when you select the bar-menu item identified by the Menu Name argument above.

○ *Status Bar Text.* When this bar-menu item is selected, you can display a message in the status bar to indicate the purpose of this menu item to the user.

It is a good idea to give this macro a name that includes the form that it is to be associated with. For example, if you created this menu for a form called Contacts, you might consider naming this macro Contacts Menu.

To make this menu appear with a form, you simply specify the name of the bar-menu macro for the Bar Menu property of the desired form.

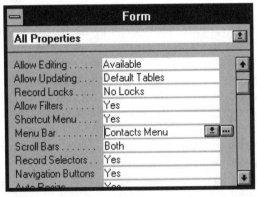

Figure 15-29: Hooking up the menu to a form.

Duplicating Existing Menus

When you add a custom menu to a form, it completely replaces the menu that normally appears when you open a form. This is kind of a bummer, because forms normally include some very useful pull-down menus. For example, a form with no custom menu has an Edit menu item on the menu bar that drops down a menu chock full of great editing options, including Undo, Copy, Paste, Find and other goodies.

If you wanted to include the existing Edit menu in your custom menu, you'd have to duplicate it using DoMenuItem actions in a pull-down menu macro. The DoMenuItem action does just what its name implies—it acts as if you selected a standard Access menu item. This is easy to do, but it can be tedious because there are so many menu items to duplicate. You can make things easier for yourself by using the Menu Builder from the form. The Menu Builder can automatically duplicate an entire menu upon your request.

THE AUTOEXEC MACRO

When you open a database, Access looks for a macro called AutoExec. If a macro with this name exists, Access executes it automatically. From a programming standpoint, this allows you to have control over the database as soon as it is opened. For example, the Sample AutoExec macro in the VENTANA.MDB application opens the Start-Up form and hides the Database window. Then a user of the VENTANA.MDB application needs only to open the database to start the application.

The AutoExec macro is no different from any other macro as far as what you can put in it. It executes actions like any other macro. You can even run the macro any time after the database has been opened.

As with the VENTANA.MDB example, the AutoExec macro is usually used to open up the main menu form of an application. This makes it easier for the user, since he or she does not have to fish through a list of forms in the database looking for the one that starts the application. The AutoExec macro also provides a measure of security to your application. If you design the rest of your application so that the user cannot get to any design screens, then you have complete control over your application from the moment the database is opened to the moment it is closed.

Once you create an AutoExec macro, you may find it frustrating to open your database if you don't intend to start your application. We all know the trauma of having to sit there for a whole five seconds, waiting for the AutoExec macro to execute, and of having to close any unwanted forms that it opens. Because Microsoft cares so much, they have provided a way for you to bypass the AutoExec macro: hold down the Shift key while you open the database, and keep it down until the Database window appears.

THE AUTOKEYS MACRO

Access allows you to define hot keys for your application, in a macro called AutoKeys. Like the pull-down menu macros, the AutoKeys macro relies on the Macro Name column to identify something; in this case, it identifies key combinations. The AutoKeys macro is no different from any other macro as far as what you can put in it—it executes actions like any other macro.

Creating the AutoKeys macro is similar to creating a pull-down menu macro. In the Macro Name column, you place names that represent key combinations. After you save the macro, pressing a defined key combination executes the macro group associated with it in the AutoKeys macro.

The key combination labels are the same ones you use for the SendKeys macro action; you can find a list of them in Access's online help by searching on SendKeys codes.

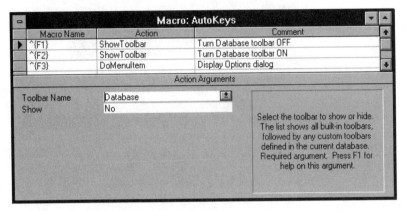

Figure 15-30: A sample AutoKeys macro.

DEBUGGING MACROS

Imagine you've just spent hours writing the perfect macro. It's 16 pages long and it's a technical marvel. You feel the excitement as you hook up the macro to a button on a form that you have poured your heart and soul into. You open the form in browse mode. You're so excited to see this baby come alive for the first time that it seems to take an eternity for you to drag your mouse to that magic button that runs your masterpiece. You click it. It goes! It is running smoothly and you're about to pat yourself on the back, when all of a sudden, out of nowhere, some strange form appears that has nothing to do with this macro.

"It can't be!" you say to yourself. "I didn't do *anything* to this macro to make it open that form." Worse yet, there are a zillion OpenForm actions in this macro. How are you going to find the offending line when it all runs so quickly?

To help you solve these kinds of problems, Access includes a feature called *Single Step mode*, which allows you to suspend execution of your application and single-step through a macro. You can run your application up to the point just before the problem macro is executed, then execute each macro action one at a time until you find the offending line. When your macro is running in Single Step mode, the dialog box shown in Figure 15-31 appears for each action in the macro.

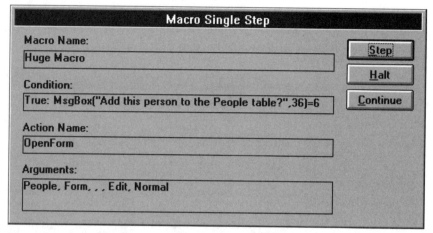

Figure 15-31: The Macro Single Step dialog box contains lots of handy information.

As you can see, this dialog box offers plenty of the information you need to narrow down a problem like the one I described. Once the dialog box appears, you can either Step to the next action in the macro, Halt execution of the macro, or let the macro Continue without stopping.

Getting a macro to run in Single Step mode is a piece of cake. You simply open any Macro window and choose the Single Step mode button from the toolbar at the top of the screen. Once you've done that, any macro that executes will do so in Single Step mode. To turn Single Step mode off, bring up a Macro window and click the Single Step toolbar button again.

MOVING ON

Hold on to your seat! If you think that macros have opened up a new world for you, wait'll you experience the ultimate driving machine: Access Basic! The next couple of chapters will introduce you to the real programming power of Microsoft Access.

16

Access Basic:
The Basics

Welcome to the world of hard-core Access programming. Chapter 15 discussed creating macros to write simple programs in Access, and there is enough depth in Access macros to meet most of your programming and automation needs. However, the real programming power in Access lies in Access Basic. Access Basic picks up where macros leave off, and it takes you as far as you'll ever need to go.

This chapter introduces you to Access Basic—the programming language in Microsoft Access. It's important to note that there will be more to learn about developing applications in Access even after you have read the Access Basic chapters. Access has so much development capability you could write an entire book on the subject. Because of this, we won't be dabbling with really complex topics like Access libraries or Custom Wizards; but by the time you've completed these chapters, you'll be empowered with plenty of knowledge of the deepest layer of Access, enabling you to develop powerful database applications.

KNOWING WHEN TO USE ACCESS BASIC

A common reaction from new Access users goes something like this: "Why are there two programming languages in Access—Macros and Access Basic?" You may be asking yourself this question right now. You may also be wondering how on earth you're supposed to know which one to use for your application.

Actually, these two programming languages complement each other. Access macros provide an easy transition from Access user to Access programmer. As an Access programmer, you are granted the simplicity of macros for most of your programming needs, and the power of Access Basic for more challenging solutions. With this in mind, you're probably best off by following this rule of thumb: *Always consider using macros first*. The decision to use Access Basic should be made only in the following cases:

○ Macros are too limited to accomplish the given task.

○ Macros would be too inefficient for the given task.

Moving to Access Basic doesn't necessarily mean that you solve a programming task exclusively with Access Basic and abandon macros altogether. There is some overlap within the capability of macros and Access Basic, and there are easy ways for a macro to make a transition into an Access Basic procedure and vice versa. As an example of this, take a look at the Dial Form macro in the VENTANA.MDB application. This macro handles the functional requirements for the Dial Form dialog box, and, in doing so, uses a RunCode action to incorporate an Access Basic procedure. On the other side of the coin, Access Basic can execute macros to take advantage of the simplicity of macro programming for simpler tasks.

Limitations of Macros

There are enough macro actions to accomplish the most common database programming tasks. The VENTANA.MDB sample application, for example, accomplishes the vast majority of its programming tasks using macros.

Even with the robustness of macros, however, the VENTANA.MDB application relies on a handful of Access Basic procedures to complete its functional requirements. For example, the VENTANA.MDB sample application includes an Access Basic procedure that counts the number of follow-up contacts for today. Although a macro can run a query that counts the number of follow-up contacts, it can't do anything reasonably meaningful with the resulting information, such as displaying a custom message indicating how many follow-up contacts there are.

The VENTANA.MDB application includes another Access Basic procedure that dials your modem. This type of procedure requires interaction with the Windows operating system directly, and macros simply don't have that kind of capability.

Program Efficiency

There are some things that a macro can do, but not very efficiently. One really good example is complex branching. The NWIND.MDB sample application that comes with Access includes a Suppliers form that allows you to filter supplier names by letter. There are buttons on the form labeled A-Z, and another labeled All. When you click one of these buttons, the macro in Figure 16-1 is executed.

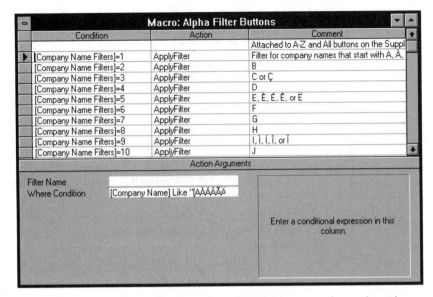

Figure 16-1: You might consider an Access Basic procedure when there are many conditions.

As you can see, the Alpha Filter Buttons macro has many conditions, making the macro harder to read and more difficult to maintain. Access Basic handles this sort of thing much more efficiently. Consider the following Access Basic function procedure, which can accomplish the same thing with a little modification to the Suppliers form:

```
Function FilterSupplyForm
    DoCmd ApplyFilter , "[Company Name] Like '" & [CÇ] & "*'"
End Function
```

This is not to question the wisdom of the people at Microsoft who put this sample application together. Among other things, the intention of the NWIND.MDB sample application is to demonstrate all that you can do with Access without ever having to write a single line of programming code.

Of course, it would be impossible for me to anticipate every possible scenario you may encounter that would call for making the move to Access Basic; this is something you'll be able to do with a little bit of experience.

EVENT-DRIVEN PROGRAMMING (THIS IS NOT YOUR FATHER'S BASIC)

The BASIC language has been around a long time—in fact, the first Microsoft product ever was a BASIC interpreter. BASIC has come a long way since then, as is evidenced by Access Basic as well as Microsoft's successful Visual Basic package.

If you haven't had any experience with Windows languages like Visual Basic, then you may initially feel a little uncomfortable with Access Basic. Access Basic is an *event-driven* language, which means that you write a bunch of programming code, and all of that code just sits there until something tells it to go. Traditionally, you think of a computer program as starting at the top, then executing each command one at a time until the end of the program is reached.

For example, the following English-like instructions illustrate how to change a light bulb:

```
START
   OBTAIN LIGHT BULB
   EXECUTE PROCEDURE REMOVE_OLD_LIGHT_BULB
   EXECUTE PROCEDURE INSTALL_NEW_LIGHT_BULB
END

PROCEDURE REMOVE_OLD_LIGHT_BULB
   DO WHILE NOT REMOVED
      GRASP LIGHT BULB
      TURN LIGHT BULB COUNTER-CLOCKWISE
   LOOP
   DISCARD LIGHT BULB
END OF PROCEDURE

PROCEDURE INSTALL_NEW_LIGHT_BULB
   HOLD LIGHT BULB IN SOCKET
   DO WHILE NOT INSTALLED
      GRASP LIGHT BULB
      TURN LIGHT BULB CLOCKWISE
   LOOP
END OF PROCEDURE
```

It is easy to understand this set of instructions because they are *procedural*. The processes for removing and installing a light bulb are defined for us in procedures, and we know when to execute those procedures, because the instructions at the top indicate the order in which they should be executed.

Now imagine trying to install a light bulb for the first time, given these instructions:

```
PROCEDURE REMOVE_OLD_LIGHT_BULB
    DO WHILE NOT REMOVED
        GRASP LIGHT BULB
        TURN LIGHT BULB COUNTER-CLOCKWISE
    LOOP
    DISCARD LIGHT BULB
END OF PROCEDURE


PROCEDURE INSTALL_NEW_LIGHT_BULB
    HOLD LIGHT BULB IN SOCKET
    DO WHILE NOT INSTALLED
        GRASP LIGHT BULB
        TURN LIGHT BULB CLOCKWISE
    LOOP
END OF PROCEDURE
```

The processes for removing and installing a light bulb are still defined for us in procedures, but we don't have a set of instructions telling us what to do with those procedures. Should they be executed in the order that they appear? Should we do something before installing a light bulb, or after removing the old light bulb? The answer to these questions is that either of these procedures could be executed at any time. We were instructed how to remove an old light bulb and install a new one; now we have to wait for someone to come along and tell us to do one of these two things. We could be told to install a light bulb before removing an old one, or to remove an old light bulb many times in a row—it doesn't matter. Our job is just to sit there and wait for someone to tell us to do something we know how to do.

This is what event-driven programming is like. You basically define a bunch of routines, and they all just sit there until an event, such as clicking a button or opening a form, triggers one of them.

If you are new to event-driven programming, or if you are new to programming in general, then this model might feel a bit uncomfortable at first. When I first started writing event-driven programs, I felt as if it would be impossible to keep an application under control. I didn't like the idea of all these procedures and functions floating around with no way to anticipate the order in which they would be executed. Experience soon showed me that my fears were unfounded; in fact, I've gotten to the point where I try to avoid writing procedural programs because they make me feel so limited.

WHERE ACCESS BASIC PROGRAMS "LIVE"

Access Basic programs are broken down into *procedures*. A procedure is a set of instructions that represents a single task, a lot like the procedures in the light bulb example. We'll get into more detail about different kinds of procedures later on.

Access Basic procedures can exist in two different places:

○ In an Access module.

○ In a form module, otherwise referred to as storing procedures "behind" a form.

You store Access Basic procedures in one of these two places, depending on how the procedures are scoped. The term *scoped* refers to the availability of something in Access Basic.

For example, the VENTANA.MDB application includes an Access Basic procedure that counts the number of follow-up contacts for today. Since this procedure is potentially usable in many different places in the application, including forms, reports and other procedures, we want Access to keep the procedure loaded in memory at all times. If we only allowed the procedure to be available to the Contacts form, we would have to duplicate it in another form if it needed the same functionality. A procedure that is available in memory at all times is said to be scoped *globally*. Procedures that need to be globally available are stored in Access modules.

On the other hand, some procedures may exist for only one purpose, and we only want Access to load that procedure into memory when it is needed by the one form that uses it, then unload the procedure when the form goes away. A procedure that is available in memory only when the object that uses it is loaded is said to be scoped *locally*. Procedures that are needed only by a particular form are stored along with that form in a form module, or—in Access lingo—such procedures are stored "behind" the form.

ACCESS MODULES & MODULE FUNDAMENTALS

So far in this book, you've clicked all of the tab-shaped buttons in the Database window, except for the one labeled "Module." Well, here's your chance, so savor the moment; go ahead and click the Module button in the VENTANA.MDB database. Access displays the Modules list in the Database window (see Figure 16-2).

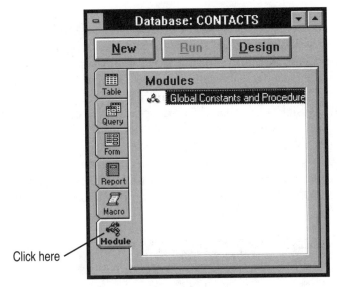

Click here

Figure 16-2: Choose the Module button in the Database window.

Getting Around in a Module Window

In this sample database, we only have one module called Global
Constants and Procedures. This module contains global procedures
that the VENTANA.MDB application uses. To open the module,
click the Design button in the Database window. Access displays
the Module window, as shown in Figure 16-3.

```
Module: Global Constants and Procedures
' MsgBox parameters
Global Const MB_OK = 0                      ' OK button only
Global Const MB_OKCANCEL = 1                ' OK and Cancel buttons
Global Const MB_ABORTRETRYIGNORE = 2        ' Abort, Retry, and Ignore
Global Const MB_YESNOCANCEL = 3             ' Yes, No, and Cancel butto
Global Const MB_YESNO = 4                   ' Yes and No buttons
Global Const MB_RETRYCANCEL = 5             ' Retry and Cancel buttons

Global Const MB_ICONSTOP = 16               ' Critical message
Global Const MB_ICONQUESTION = 32           ' Warning query
Global Const MB_ICONEXCLAMATION = 48        ' Warning message
Global Const MB_ICONINFORMATION = 64        ' Information message

Global Const MB_APPLMODAL = 0               ' Application Modal Message
Global Const MB_DEFBUTTON1 = 0              ' First button is default
Global Const MB_DEFBUTTON2 = 256            ' Second button is default
Global Const MB_DEFBUTTON3 = 512            ' Third button is default
Global Const MB_SYSTEMMODAL = 4096          'System Modal

' MsgBox return values
```

Figure 16-3: The Global Constants and Procedures module in
VENTANA.MDB.

471

If this is the first time you have opened a module window with code in it, I can hear you say "Ughh! What's all *that* stuff?" What you're looking at is called the *Declarations* section of a module, something every module has. The Declarations section of a module contains definitions of variables and constants that are to be scoped locally to that module; however, in this case, all these constants are globally available because they are specifically defined as Global Constants. We'll talk more about constants and variables later on.

This module contains two procedures, but you can't get to those procedures by scrolling down past the Declarations section in the Module window. Instead, Access provides a pick list of procedures for this module at the top of the screen in the toolbar (see Figure 16-4).

Click here to display a list of procedures in the current module

Figure 16-4: Access provides an easy way to get to the procedure you want to edit.

When you click one of the names in the list, Access displays the selected procedure. The check marks next to each procedure name in the list indicate that the procedure has something in it other than just a name. This may sound useless right now, but it will make more sense when we look at form modules.

Adding Procedures

Now let's create a small procedure to put some of this stuff to practice, and to learn some new things. This procedure is intentionally simple so that we can discuss some fundamental concepts. We'll get into more complex concepts as we go along.

To create a new procedure, follow these steps:

1. Choose the New Procedure menu item from the Edit menu. Access displays the New Procedure dialog box (see Figure 16-5).

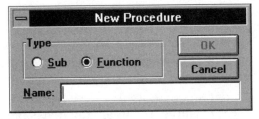

Figure 16-5: The New Procedure dialog box.

2. Click the Sub option button in the New Procedure dialog box. Sub and Function are two different kinds of procedures. The differences between them will be discussed later.

3. Type **HelloWorld** into the Name prompt in the New Procedure dialog box and click the OK button.

Access creates the new procedure, and you are ready to start pounding out some code.

The top of a procedure includes the procedure name followed by parentheses (the parentheses are used for defining parameters for this procedure, but that's another thing we'll be discussing later). The bottom of the procedure is always End Sub or End Function, depending on what type of procedure this is. All of the programming code you write goes between the Sub line at the top and the End Sub line at the bottom; you cannot write programming code above the Sub line or below the End Sub line.

From the current cursor position in the Module window, type three spaces, then type:

```
msgbox "Hello World"
```

The three spaces aren't necessary, but proper use of indentation makes a procedure more readable.

After you have typed the line, press the Down arrow key to move off the line. Notice that Access changes msgbox to MsgBox when you move off the line. Access not only formats lines of code you type; it also checks the line for proper *syntax*. If you type a command that is improperly used according to the rules of the Access Basic language, Access beeps and displays a message indicating that there is a problem with the line you just typed. This is a very nifty feature in Access—catching mistakes as you make them is a real time-saver for a couple of reasons:

○ Since Access catches syntax errors as you make them, you don't have to wait to run your program to find out that you made a zillion mistakes coding your procedures.

○ Since Access verifies each line as you type it, Access does not have to check the entire program for mistakes before you run it.

For example, in Microsoft FoxPro, you have to wait for a program to *compile* each line of code before it can be executed. Access compiles as you go, so you can execute programs instantaneously after having written them. (This is not to criticize FoxPro; I love the product.)

Some program errors are impossible for Access to catch one line at a time. For example, the following line is perfectly valid by itself:

```
Do Until Contacts.EOF
```

As you will learn later, every Do While statement has to have a matching Loop statement somewhere below it. Access has no way of knowing whether or not you intend to add the Loop statement to your procedure until you try to run it. The same goes for references to bogus procedure names or variable names, among other things. Since you can't rely on the automatic syntax-checking capability to find these kinds of errors, you might want to use the Compile Loaded Modules option every now and then to keep your program in check.

To use the Compile Loaded Modules option, click the Compile Loaded Modules button on the toolbar, or choose the Run-Compile Loaded Modules menu item.

"Compiling" means that Access translates all of the English-like Basic code into symbols Access can understand. The Compile Load Modules option compiles all of the Access modules in your database, checking for errors as it goes along. As mentioned earlier, the Compile Load Modules process is practically instantaneous, because most of the work is done as you type code into the module.

We are now ready to try this procedure out. You can run a procedure one of four ways:

○ Call the procedure from a form or report event.

○ Call the procedure from another procedure.

○ Call the procedure from a macro.

○ Call the procedure from the Immediate Window.

For now, we'll call the procedure from the Immediate Window.

The Immediate Window

The Immediate Window is a very helpful programming tool you can use to test and debug procedures. You can also use the Immediate Window to check the value of a field, control or property setting on a form or report. To access the Immediate Window (see Figure 16-6), choose the Immediate Window button in the toolbar, or choose the View-Immediate Window from the menu.

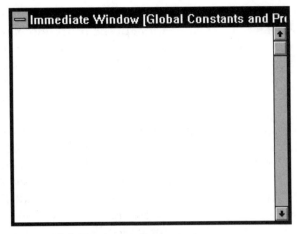

Figure 16-6: The Immediate window.

The Immediate Window always remains in the foreground as long as a module is opened and has focus. It disappears when the module is closed or loses focus.

To run the HelloWorld procedure, type **Call HelloWorld** in the Immediate Window and press the Enter key. The HelloWorld message box appears, and you feel really great having written your first Access Basic procedure.

We'll learn more about using the Immediate Window for debugging programs later on; for now, we'll do some more programming.

Calling an Access Module Procedure From a Form

Just like macros, we can "hook up" procedures to form events. The only catch is that the procedure must be a *function* procedure rather than a *sub* procedure, which poses a problem in the case of the HelloWorld procedure, since it is a sub procedure. Let's go ahead and change the HelloWorld procedure to a function procedure so that we can call it from a form:

1. If it isn't already onscreen, open up the Global Constants and Procedures module.

2. From the combo box procedure list in the toolbar, select the HelloWorld procedure.

   The HelloWorld procedure appears in the module window.

3. Backspace over the word **Sub** at the top of the procedure and replace it with the word **Function**.

4. Move off the line by pressing the Down arrow key.

When you move off the line, Access automatically replaces the End Sub line at the bottom of the procedure with an End Function line. If you'd had an Exit Sub command in the procedure, Access would have changed it to an Exit Function command.

Now that HelloWorld is a function procedure, we are ready to hook it up to a form. Hooking up a procedure to a form or to a control on a form is very similar to hooking up a macro. You find the event you want to use to invoke the macro, then you specify the name of the function procedure. The procedure name must be preceded by an equals sign (=) and must be followed by a pair of parentheses, as in =HelloWorld( ). If you designed your procedure to receive parameters, then you would include the parameters you want to pass within the parentheses (we'll talk more about using parameters to pass information later).

To demonstrate the process of hooking up a procedure, let's create a simple brain-dead form with a button on it. We'll hook up the HelloWorld procedure to the button so that the procedure is executed when the button is clicked:

1. Create a new form by clicking the Form button in the Database window and then clicking the New button. When you are prompted to choose the Form Wizards or Blank Form, choose Blank Form.

2. Add a new Command button to the form from the toolbox.

3. Change the caption of the new Command button to Push Me.

4. If it isn't already onscreen, bring up the Properties window. Make sure the Push Me button is highlighted, so that its properties appear in the Properties window.

5. If it isn't already selected, choose Event Properties from the combo box list at the top of the Properties window.
   This displays a list of all the Command button events you can run a procedure or macro from.

6. Find the row labeled On Click and click once anywhere in that row so that the cursor appears in the entry area.

7. Type **=HelloWorld( )** in the entry area (see Figure 16-7).

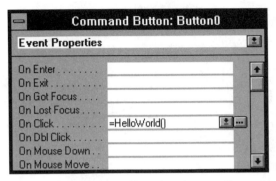

Figure 16-7: Calling a Function from a Control Event.

Now save the form as Form1 and switch into Form view mode and click the Push Me button. Voila! You might say that you've just written your first application. Sure, it's dull and useless, but we learned a few things along the way and had some fun at the same time. In the next section, we'll advance to something a bit more complicated and far more useful.

FORM MODULES, OR "CODE BEHIND FORMS"

Access 2.0 allows you to store procedures along with forms, rather than storing them in an Access module. Procedures that are stored with forms are called *event procedures*, and the concept of storing procedures with forms is generally referred to as *code behind forms*. Storing procedures this way offers a couple of nifty advantages:

○ You don't have to fish through your Access modules to find the name of the appropriate procedure.

Remember in the previous section we hooked up a procedure to a button by typing in the procedure's name. This was easy enough with one procedure, but it gets more difficult to remember the names, purposes and parameters of all your procedures when they start to multiply. Rather than creating the procedure in one place, then going over to another to hook it up, Access allows you to write an event procedure for a form or control event right from the Properties window.

○ It is easy to view a procedure associated with a particular event.

If you want to know what a button's On Click property does, you simply select the property in the Properties window and click the procedure button to display its event procedure. If the procedure existed in an Access module, all we would see is a reference such as =HelloWorld( ), and we'd have to hop over to an Access module to look at it.

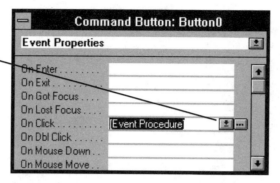

If there is a procedure associated with this event, you can click here to see it

Figure 16-8: Viewing a button's On Click procedure is a snap!

○ Storing procedures with forms makes more efficient use of memory.

Procedures stored in Access modules are always loaded into memory as long as your database is open. Procedures stored in a form module are loaded into memory when the form is loaded, then removed from memory when the form is closed.

Creating Event Procedures

With macros and Access modules, you first created the macro or procedure; then you hooked up the macro or procedure to a form. The approach to creating event procedures is the other way around: you first create the control or form; then you jump into a module window and write code.

To demonstrate this, we are going to add a Command button to the Contacts form that displays the number of follow-ups for today. The procedure for this button will call an exisiting procedure called CountFollowUps, which exists in the Global Constants and Procedures module. Follow these steps now:

1. Open the Contacts form in Design view by highlighting the Contacts form in the Database window and clicking the Design button.

2. Add a button from the toolbox to the form. Place the button in the upper left-hand side of the form in the blue area of the form header. Label the button Count Follow-Ups, as shown in Figure 16-9.

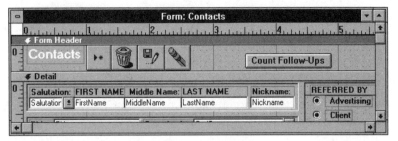

Figure 16-9: The Count Follow-Ups button.

3. If it isn't already onscreen, bring up the Properties window. Make sure the Count Follow-Ups button is highlighted so that its properties appear in the Properties window.

4. If it isn't already selected, choose Event Properties from the combo box list at the top of the Properties window.

5. Find the row labeled On Click and click once anywhere in that row so that the cursor appears in the entry area.

   The drop-down button and the build button appear to the right (the build button is the one with the three periods in it).

6. Click the build button.

   Access displays a list of builders.

7. Choose Code Builder from the list of builders.

   Access displays a Module window with an empty sub procedure. Notice that you don't have to create a new procedure like we did with the HelloWorld procedure. All the event procedures in a form are automatically created when you create the form and the controls in it. All you have to do is fill in the procedures you want with Access Basic code.

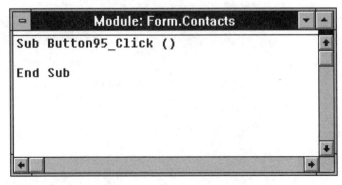

Figure 16-10: Access automatically creates event procedures; all you have to do is fill them in.

8. Type the following commands into the event procedure between the Sub and End Sub lines. Remember that indentation is not necessary, but it is a good habit to get yourself into:

```
Dim todaysfollowups As Integer
todaysfollowups = CountFollowUps()
If todaysfollowups = 0 Then
    MsgBox "There are no follow ups for today"
Else
    MsgBox "There are " & Str(todaysfollowups) & "follow ups"
End If
```

9. Close the Module window and switch the form to browse mode to try out your work.

Now that you have had a taste of event procedures, let's talk about the Module window for this form. If you haven't done so already, switch the form back to Design view and open the event procedure we just created.

Just like the Access module procedure we created earlier, a Module window for an event procedure also has a procedure pick list in the toolbar; however, some of the characteristics of the pick list that seemed useless with an Access module procedure turn out to be very handy for an event procedure. Let's examine the procedure pick list again. With the event procedure open, drop down the procedure list by clicking the drop-down button (see Figure 16-11).

Click here to display a list of event procedures for this control.

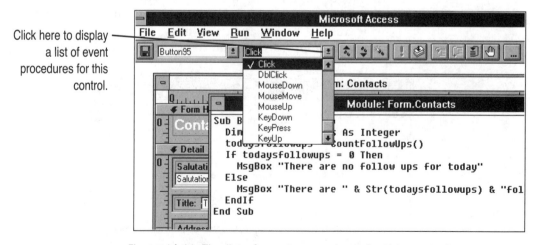

Figure 16-11: The list of event procedures for this control.

Notice that a list of events appears, and there is a check mark next to the Click event. By choosing one of these events, you can go directly to the event procedure for that event without first going to the Properties window and choosing the Code Builder as we did for the On Click event procedure (see Figure 16-12). If an event procedure has code in it, as our Click procedure has, a check mark appears next to that event in the list.

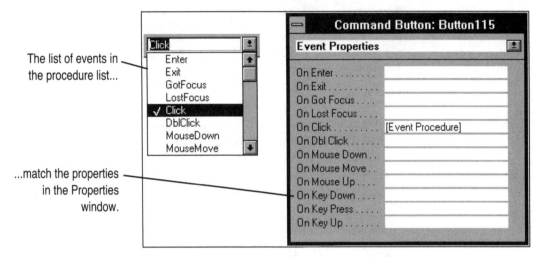

Figure 16-12: There is a procedure for every event.

By now, you're probably dying to know what the combo box to the left of the procedure list is for (see Figure 16-13). This is yet another list that is really helpful for managing the code on your form without having to jump to a zillion different places. This is the object list, and it serves a similar purpose as the event procedures list. In the same sense that the procedures list allows you to jump to different event procedures for the control you are currently working on, the object list allows you to jump around to other controls on the form.

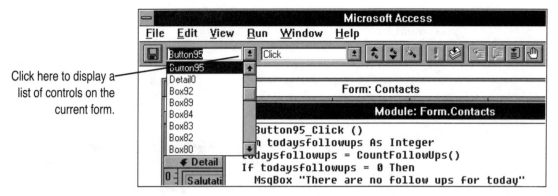

Click here to display a list of controls on the current form.

Figure 16-13: The object list allows you to view event procedures for other controls on the form.

For example, if you were currently working on the Click event procedure for the Count Follow-Ups button, and you wanted to write a procedure for the After Update event of the ContactID text box, you would select ContactID from the object list on the left, then select the AfterUpdate event procedure from the procedures list on the right.

The ability to jump to any event procedure and to any control on the form makes the Form Module window a powerful programming control center. You might say that it is your "one-stop shopping center for programming" at the form level (having worked in marketing at Microsoft, I couldn't resist the temptation to throw in a corny tag line).

Form-Level Procedures

In addition to creating event procedures for controls on a form, we can also create general usage procedures that load and unload with the form. For example, suppose we wanted to alert the user that the current record requires a follow-up contact. We would want the user to be alerted of such a condition when he or she moves to the current record, or when an attempt is made to delete the record. In order to accomplish this, we would have to create the following IsFollowUp function procedure that tells us if the follow-up date for the current record matches today's date, then use that function procedure in the Contacts form's On Current event procedure and in the Contacts form's On Delete event procedure.

```
Function IsFollowUp ()
  Dim ws As WorkSpace, db As Database, rs As Recordset

  Set ws = DBEngine.WorkSpaces(0)
  Set db = ws.Databases(0)
  Set rs = db.OpenRecordset("SELECT FollowUpDate FROM
Interactions WHERE ContactID = " & Forms!Contacts!ContactID & "
ORDER BY FollowUpDate DESC;")

  IsFollowUp = False
  If rs.RecordCount > 0 Then
    If rs!FollowUpDate = Date Then IsFollowUp = True
  End If
End Function
```

This particular function procedure needs to be available to two different procedures on the form, but we won't need it anywhere else in the application. Ideally, we would like this procedure to be loaded into memory only when the form is loaded. Access allows us to include this procedure in the form module, and to call the procedure from other event procedures on the form. To add this procedure to the module and to hook it up to the form's On Current and On Delete events, follow these steps:

1. If you haven't done so already, open the Contacts form in Design view and bring the event module to the front. As a shortcut to bring the form's event module to the front of the screen, click the Code toolbar button at the top of the screen.

2. Choose the New Procedure menu item from the Edit menu.
    Access displays the New Procedure dialog box, just like the one we saw when we were working with Access module procedures.

3. Click the Function radio button in the New Procedure dialog box.

4. Type **IsFollowUp** into the Name prompt in the New Procedure dialog box and click the OK button.
    The IsFollowUp function procedure appears in the form Module window.

5. Type the procedure code into the IsFollowUp function procedure as shown in the preceding example. Of course, the Function and End Function lines are already inserted for you, so you should not duplicate these lines.
    Notice that the word "general" appears in the object list when you add this procedure. The "general" selection from the object list refers to all the functions you add to the form

483

module that are not event procedures. With "general" selected in the object list, you can choose a form-level procedure from the event procedures list.

6. From the object list, choose Form.

7. From the event procedures list, choose Current. Add the following code to the Form_Current sub procedure that appears in the Module window:

```
If IsFollowUp() Then
    MsgBox "You have a scheduled follow-up call today for this
person.", MB_OK + MB_INFORMATION
    End If
```

8. From the event procedures list, choose Delete. Add the following code to the Form_Current sub procedure that appears in the Module window:

```
If IsFollowUp() Then
    MsgBox "Warning: you have a scheduled follow-up call today
for this person.", MB_OK + MB_EXCLAMATION
    End If
```

You can now switch to Design view and try this out. Upon moving to a new record or attempting to delete a record, the IsFollowUp function procedure is called, and a message is displayed if there is a scheduled follow-up contact for today. You may have to add an interaction with a follow-up for today's date in order to get this to work.

Now that you have learned how to get around in the module editing tools, in addition to some very important fundamental concepts, we are ready to start talking turkey. Beginning with the next section, we will shift our focus from general conceptual stuff to learning the Access Basic language itself.

SUB PROCEDURES & FUNCTION PROCEDURES

In our light bulb example, we defined two procedures: one that instructed us to remove an old light bulb, and another that instructed us to install the new bulb. In Access Basic, we define procedures that instruct Access on how to accomplish a particular task, just as the light bulb procedures instructed us on how to remove and replace a light bulb.

So far, we have already worked with a few procedures. We started out by creating an ultra-simple HelloWorld procedure, whose only purpose in life was to display a message that reads "Hello World". Most recently, we created an IsFollowUp procedure that tells us whether or not there are any follow-up contacts scheduled for today's date.

In Access Basic, there are two kinds of procedures: *sub* procedures and *funtion* procedures. The difference between a sub procedure and a function procedure is that a function procedure returns some kind of value and a sub procedure does not. The HelloWorld sub procedure and the IsFollowUp function procedure illustrate this difference. We originally designed the HelloWorld procedure as a sub procedure because it performs some action, but does not return any information. We designed the FollowUp procedure as a function procedure because it returns a True or False value, depending on whether or not it found a follow-up contact scheduled for today's date.

Procedure Syntax

The syntax for a sub procedure is shown below:

```
Sub procedurename ([parameters])
    statements
End Sub
```

The syntax for a function procedure is shown below:

```
Function procedurename ([parameters]) [As type]
    statements
End Function
```

As you can see, the syntax for the two different kinds of procedures is very similar. The *procedurename* reference is the name you want to give the procedure. Access allows 40 characters for a procedure name, and you should take advantage of this flexibility, so that the names you use are descriptive. You can use any name you want as long as you follow these naming rules:

❍ The name cannot exceed 40 characters.

❍ The name must begin with a letter.

❍ The name can't contain any punctuation or spaces; it can only contain letters, numbers and underscore characters (_). However, you can mix case the letters for better readability.

❍ The name can't be the same as an existing Access Basic command or function. These are also referred to as Reserved words.

You can optionally pass parameters to a procedure, as you can see from the *parameters* reference. This allows you to provide some information to the procedure when you call it. As an example, let's take a look at the DialPhoneNumber procedure in the Global Constants and Procedures module in the VENTANA.MDB sample database (see Figure 16-14).

```
 ─                  Module: Global Constants and Procedures          ▼  ▲
Function DialPhoneNumber (phonenumber As String, comport As String) ↑
   ' Go through all of the characters of the phonenum parameter
   ' to strip out any characters other than numbers.  The
   ' resulting phone number will be stored in the variable
   ' called "dialnumber$"

  dialnumber$ = ""
  For i = 1 To Len(phonenumber)
    If Mid(phonenumber, i, 1) >= "0" And Mid(phonenumber, i, 1) <
        dialnumber$ = dialnumber$ & Mid(phonenumber, i, 1)
    End If                                                           ↓
 ◄ ▮                                                              ► 
```

Parameters for the DialPhoneNumber procedure

Figure 16-14: The DialPhoneNumber procedure needs to know what phone number to dial and what COM port your modem is hooked up to.

As its name implies, the purpose of this procedure is to dial a phone number through your modem (if you have one). Of course, in order to dial the number, the procedure needs to know what the phone number is and which COM port to direct it to. When the function is executed, it can be provided with this necessary information because of the phone number and comport parameters defined on the top line of the procedure.

You can optionally identify the *data type* for each parameter value by using the As clause. In short, this allows us to identify whether that particular parameter is numeric, text or some other Access Basic data type (we'll get into a more heavy-duty discussion about data types later). As you can see in Figure 16-14, the DialPhoneNumber procedure expects both the phone number and comport parameters to be String (text) values.

Function procedures can optionally include an *As type* clause at the end of the top line. Similarly to the As clause that can be used with each parameter, this allows you to specifically define what *data type* will be returned by the function. The CountFollowUps function procedure shown in Figure 16-15 calculates the number of scheduled follow-up contacts that matches today's date, then returns that number as an Integer data type.

```
Module: Global Constants and Procedures                    ▼ ▲
Function CountFollowUps () As Integer                          ↑
  ' Count the number of FollowUps for today
  Dim ws As WorkSpace, db As Database, rs As Recordset
  Set ws = DBEngine.WorkSpaces(0)
  Set db = ws.Databases(0)
  Set rs = db.OpenRecordset("SELECT Count(FollowUpDate) AS CountOf

  If rs.RecordCount = 0 Then
    CountFollowUps = 0
  Else
    CountFollowUps = rs!CountOfFollowUpDate                     ↓
◀                                                              ▶
```

This function returns an Integer data type.

Figure 16-15: The CountFollowUps function from VENTANA.MDB.

Of course, you fill the procedure with the appropriate Access Basic code to accomplish the desired task.

Calling Procedures

Once you define your procedures, you need to know how they can be executed. Calling a sub procedure is very straightforward, while calling a function procedure can be done a number of ways, depending on the context in which it is used.

Sub Procedures

To call a sub procedure from another procedure, you can either use the Call statement or you can just specify the name of the sub procedure by itself. For example, you can use either one of the following two statements to call the HelloWorld sub procedure we created earlier:

○ Call HelloWorld

○ HelloWorld

If the sub procedure to be called includes parameters, you simply follow the procedure name with the values you want to send to the procedure, separated by commas. If the HelloWorld procedure expected a string parameter and a numeric parameter, the call to HelloWorld might look like this:

HelloWorld "This is a string value", 10

You can only call a sub procedure from another sub procedure or function procedure.

Function Procedures

A function procedure can be called anywhere that a value can be stated. For example, you can display the number 10 in a text box on the Contacts form by executing the following statement:

    Forms!Contacts!FollowUps = 10

However, rather than stating the value of 10 for the FollowUps text box, you can reference the name of a function procedure that calculates how many follow-ups there really are:

    Forms!Contacts!FollowUps = CountFollowUps()

By referencing the name of a function procedure, you are telling Access to execute that function procedure and store its results to the FollowUps text box.

As a rule of syntax, a function procedure is always followed by a set of parentheses, as shown by the CountFollowUps( ) function above. If the function procedure to be called includes parameters, you follow the procedure name with the values you want to send, separated by commas and *enclosed in parentheses*. If the CountFollowUps procedure expected a date parameter representing today's date and a numeric parameter, the call to CountFollowUps might look like this:

    Forms!Contacts!FollowUps = CountFollowUps(Date, 2)

Practically speaking, a function procedure can be used almost anywhere in Access: on forms, reports, in macros, and even in queries.

WORKING WITH PROGRAM VARIABLES & CONSTANTS

Like any other programming language, Access Basic allows you to store values into *variables*. You need variables in your program because you often work with values you don't know ahead of time. For example, the Form_Load event procedure for the Contacts form uses a variable called "numoffollowups" (as in "number of follow ups") (see Figure 16-16). The numoffollowups variable stores the number of follow-up contacts scheduled for today as returned by the CountFollowUps function procedure.

```
-                          Module: Form.Contacts                    ▼ ▲
Sub Form_Load ()                                                       ↑
   Dim numoffollowups As Integer

   numoffollowups = CountFollowUps()

   If numoffollowups = 0 Then
     MsgBox "There are no Follow Up contacts for today", MB_OK +
   Else
     MsgBox "There " & IIf(numoffollowups = 1, "is ", "are ") &
   End If
End Sub
                                                                      ↓
←  ▌                                                                → ▶
```

Figure 16-16: The numoffollowups variable stores the result of the
CountFollowUps function procedure.

Later on in the procedure, the MsgBox statement displays the
value of the numoffollowups variable.

The name you give to a variable is limited to the same naming
constraints as procedure names:

○ The name cannot exceed 40 characters.

○ The name must begin with a letter.

○ The name can't contain any punctuation or spaces; it can only
   contain letters, numbers and underscore characters (_). However, you can mix case the letters for better readability.

○ The name can't be the same as an existing Access Basic command or function.

Data Types for Variables

Variables in Access Basic can have different data types. You learned
about data types earlier in this book when you created your first
table. Remember that fields in a table can be Text, Number, Date/
Time or one of a few other data types. The same idea applies to
Access Basic variables, except the data types are a tad different.
The table that follows lists the different Access Basic data types and
what you can store in each type of variable.

Data Type	What you can store in a variable with this data type
String	The String data type is like the Text or Memo field data type. You can use it to store letters, numbers or any other character. Unless you plan to do any kind of arithmetic or date calculation with a value, or unless you plan to store a value from an Access table that could potentially be Null, I would recommend you always make your variables a String data type for greatest efficiency.

Integer	An Integer variable is for storing numbers that don't have decimal places. If the number could potentially exceed 32,767 or be less than -32,767, you should define the variable as a Long Integer instead. If not, you should define the variable as an Integer data type so you use memory most efficiently.
Long Integer	A Long Integer variable is for storing numbers that don't have decimal places, and that could potentially exceed 32,767 or be less than -32,767. However, if the number could potentially exceed 2,147,483,648 or be less than -2,147,483,648, you'll have to resort to using a Double Precision data type, which can store huge floating-point numbers.
Single Precision	A Single Precision variable is for storing a floating-point number that can fit in 4 bytes of memory, regardless of where the decimal place is.
Double Precision	A Double Precision variable is for storing a floating-point number that can fit in 8 bytes of memory, regardless of where the decimal place is.
Currency	The Currency data type is designed specifically for storing and performing calculations with monetary data. Currency data is always fixed to four decimal places for greatest possible accuracy with monetary calculations.
Variant	A Variant variable automatically figures out what data type to use when storing a value. When you define a variable as a Variant, you don't have to figure out which one of the above data types you should use. The drawback to using Variant is that it is the most inefficient, since it needs to first figure out how to type itself and it typically takes up more memory to accommodate data of an unknown size.

You must define a variable as a Variant data type if you plan to store data from an Access table because of the potential of having a Null value in a table. Variant is the only data type that can store a Null value.

You should also use the Variant data type for storing date and time values. Technically, date and time values are Double Precision data, but using a Variant allows more flexibility for treating the date flexibly. For example, a date stored in a Variant can either be used as a number that Access interprets as a date, or as something more familiar such as 10/20/94.

Creating Variables

There are two ways you can create variables in Access Basic: *Explicit* variable declaration and *Implicit* variable declaration. Don't worry; the concept isn't as intimidating as the buzzwords.

Explicit Variable Declaration

"Explicitly" creating a variable means you use the Access Basic Dim command to define the variable before you ever use it. The word "Dim" stands for "Dimension," which means that you want Access to allocate some space in the computer's memory to store a value. The syntax for the Dim command goes like this:

Dim <variable name> [As <data type>]

The <variable name> reference is the name you want to give to the variable you are creating. The optional <data type> reference is one of the following, depending on which data type you want this variable to be: String, Integer, Long (for Long Integer), Single (for Single Precision), Double (for Double Precision), Currency or Variant. Hence, if you wanted to create a variable called numoffollowups as an Integer, you would use the following command in your program:

Dim numoffollowups As Integer

You can optionally omit the As clause. If you leave out the As clause, Access defines the variable as a Variant data type.

At the moment the variable is created using Dim, the variable is automatically given a default value. The value given depends on the data type of the variable being created, as shown in the following table:

If the data type is...	...the default value will be...
String	A *zero-length string*, which means the variable contains no characters.
Integer	Zero.
Long	Zero.
Single	Zero.
Double	Zero.
Currency	Zero.
Variant	Variant variables are given a special value called *Empty*. Empty is not the same as Null or Zero-Length String; it is a unique state that means the variable contains nothing at all. When a variable is given a value later on in the program, Access determines what data type the variable should be, then stores the value into the variable.

At some point after the variable is created, you can give the variable a value by using the following convention:

<variable name> = <value>

For example, if you wanted to give the numoffollowups variable the value of 10, you would add the following statement to your program:

```
numoffollowups = 10
```

Or, if you wanted the numoffollowups variable to contain the value returned by the CountFollowUps function procedure, you would add this statement to your program:

```
numoffollowups = CountFollowUps()
```

Implicit Variable Declaration

"Implicitly" creating a variable means you define the variable and give it a value all at the same time, without using a Dim statement. In the previous section, we discussed the example of creating a variable called numoffollowups using the Dim statement, then giving the variable a value later on. We could do the same thing without the Dim statement using one line of code as shown below:

```
numoffollowups% = CountFollowUps()
```

This line of code creates an Integer variable called numoffollowups and stores the result of the CountFollowUps function procedure to that variable. The data type of the variable depends on the *type-declaration suffix* you give to the variable name. In this case, the type-declaration suffix is %, which means Integer. The list of type-declaration suffixes you can use for implicit variable declaration appears in the following table.

To implicitly declare this data type...	...use this type-declaration suffix...
String	$
Integer	%
Long	&
Single	!
Double	#
Currency	@
Variant	<none>

If you implicitly create a variable using a type-declaration suffix, you must always refer to the variable *with* the suffix. For example, if you create a string variable called name$, you must always refer to that variable as name$.

At first, it may sound like implicit declaration is the way to go, because it saves having to write extra lines of code to define variables, but there are a few advantages to defining variables using explicit declaration:

○ Using the Dim statement makes a program more readable and thus easier to maintain. Since there could potentially be several variables in a procedure, debugging a procedure could be hampered by not being able to identify immediately the origin and type of the variable.

○ As you will find out in an upcoming section, you must use the Dim statement in a module's Declarations section in order for a variable to be scoped globally or scoped to all the other procedures in the module. In order to declare a variable in the Declarations section, you must use the Dim statement. If you implicitly define variables in your procedures and use Dim statements in the Declarations section of the module, your program may feel and work inconsistently. This is something that will become more meaningful as you gain more experience with Access Basic programming.

Option Explicit

Even the best of programmers are always making typographical mistakes, and these kinds of mistakes can lead to hours of debugging a problem that can be fixed with one keystroke. Access prevents some typographical mistakes by checking syntax after you type each line of code, but there are some typographical mistakes you could make that Access doesn't catch because such mistakes are syntactically correct even though they may produce the wrong results.

For example, consider the sub procedure below, (the ... in the procedure indicates that there is some programming code, but we don't care what the programming code is for right now):

```
Sub DisplayNumberOfContacts ()
    Dim NumberOfContacts As Integer

    ...
    NumberOfContacts = NumberOfContacts + 1
    MsgBox Str(NumberOfContact)
End Sub
```

This procedure executes some programming code, adds 1 to NumberOfContacts, then displays the value of NumberOfContacts. However, if you look carefully, this procedure will never properly do what it was designed to do. After having gone through all the trouble of calculating the NumberOfContacts variable, the MsgBox line that displays the variable has the variable name misspelled, (the "s" is missing). Instead of displaying the value of the NumberOfContacts variable, Access assumes that you want to display the value of a new variable called NumberOfContact, which has no value.

Once you try to test this procedure and you see that it is producing incorrect results, you may overlook the subtle spelling error and spend hours banging your head against the wall trying to figure out what went wrong. (At Microsoft, I encountered many cases where Access users insisted they had found a bug, until I took a look at their code with fresh eyes and found the typo.) Because of this potential problem, you might consider using the Option Explicit statement. Option Explicit forces you to define all of the variables in a module using the Dim statement. If there are any variables that are not defined explicitly, Access points out the variable and refuses to run your program until you first define that variable or correct its spelling if you mistyped it.

To use the Option Explicit statement, you type Option Explicit on a line by itself in the Declarations section of each module in which you want Option Explicit to be enforced (see Figure 16-17). From then on, Access does the rest—just define your variables before you use them and nobody gets hurt.

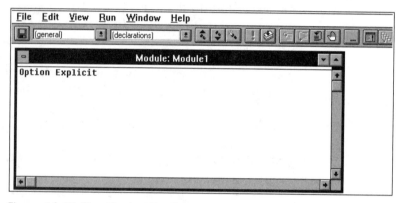

Figure 16-17: The Option Explicit statement in the Declarations section of a module.

Array Variables

An *array variable* allows you to store several values of like kind using one variable name and to refer to a particular value by an index number. For example, you might want to store a list of five Contact phone numbers to a variable called ContactPhoneNumbers. In Access Basic, you can use the Dim statement to create a variable array called ContactPhoneNumbers, then store the five phone numbers into each *element* of the array:

```
Dim ContactPhoneNumbers(1 To 5) As String

ContactPhoneNumbers(1) = "(909) 555-7273"
ContactPhoneNumbers(2) = "(714) 555-9826"
ContactPhoneNumbers(3) = "(206) 555-0937"
ContactPhoneNumbers(4) = "(909) 555-9045"
ContactPhoneNumbers(5) = "(909) 555-5667"
```

The (1 To 5) part of the Dim statement means that the ContactPhoneNumbers variable can contain five values, numbered from one to five. The statements that follow the Dim statement store different phone numbers to each of the five elements of the array. As you can see, the name of the variable is the same even though it is storing five different values; the only thing that distinguishes each one is the *index number* in the parentheses. The following lines of code do the same thing, except that the five elements are numbered from three to seven:

```
Dim ContactPhoneNumbers(3 To 7) As String

ContactPhoneNumbers(3) = "(909) 555-7273"
ContactPhoneNumbers(4) = "(714) 555-9826"
ContactPhoneNumbers(5) = "(206) 555-0937"
ContactPhoneNumbers(6) = "(909) 555-9045"
ContactPhoneNumbers(7) = "(909) 555-5667"
```

Creating an array with the Dim statement is almost exactly the same as using the Dim statement to create any other kind of variable. The only difference is that you follow the variable name with a set of parentheses containing the number of elements the array should have. You can indicate the number of elements in an array two different ways, as shown in these two examples

1. Dim ContactPhoneNumbers(1 To 5)

2. Dim ContactPhoneNumbers(4)

In both examples, an array variable called ContactPhoneNumber is created with five elements, even though it may appear at first that example #2 only has four elements. The reason why there are five elements in example #2 is because the number of elements you specify is zero-based, meaning you start counting at zero instead of one. Thus, in example #2, the elements are numbered 0 to 4 as illustrated below:

```
Dim ContactPhoneNumbers(4) As String

ContactPhoneNumbers(0) = "(909) 555-7273"
ContactPhoneNumbers(1) = "(714) 555-9826"
ContactPhoneNumbers(2) = "(206) 555-0937"
ContactPhoneNumbers(3) = "(909) 555-9045"
ContactPhoneNumbers(4) = "(909) 555-5667"
```

If you don't like the idea that arrays are zero-based, and you want the Dim statement above to really mean *four* elements when it says 4 in the parentheses, you can change the base to 1 by using the Option Base statement. The Option Base statement appears in the Declarations section of the module in which you want to change the default base of an array. To use the statement, you simply follow the keywords Option Base with the number that is to be the new base. The following example changes the base to 1:

```
Option Base 1
```

The index number you use to reference a particular value in the array can be a variable, which makes arrays particularly useful. For example, suppose you wanted to write the phone numbers from the ContactPhoneNumbers array above to the Immediate window. The Access Basic code you would need in order to do this *could* be written like this:

```
Print ContactPhoneNumbers(0)
Print ContactPhoneNumbers(1)
Print ContactPhoneNumbers(2)
Print ContactPhoneNumbers(3)
Print ContactPhoneNumbers(4)
```

However, since this is an array, we can potentially save lots of lines of code and make this program more efficient by coding it this way:

```
For i = 0 To 4
    Print ContactPhoneNumbers(i)
Next
```

The For...Next loop above counts from 0 to 4, changing the value of *i* each time so that each array element is printed. In this specific example, we only saved two lines of programming code compared to the previous example; but imagine how many lines of programming code you would save if the array consisted of a hundred or a thousand elements!

Multi-Dimensional Arrays

The ContactPhoneNumbers(1 To 5) array example above consists of five elements, or five "rows" of data as illustrated by the table below:

ContactPhoneNumbers Index	
1	(909) 555-7273
2	(714) 555-9826
3	(206) 555-0937
4	(909) 555-9045
5	(909) 555-5667

This array consists of only one *dimension*, or column of data, as you can tell by the fact that there is only one column of phone numbers in this array. However, what if you wanted to store phone *and* fax numbers for each row?

Access Basic allows you to create arrays that can store a matrix of information in several rows and columns. Arrays with more than one column of data are called *multi-dimensional arrays*. You create a multi-dimensional array in much the same way you create a one-dimensional array. The only difference is that you include another number in the definition that specifies the number of columns you want in the array. For example, the following Dim statement creates a multi-dimensional array with five rows and two columns, so that we can store both phone and fax numbers:

```
Dim ContactPhoneNumbers(1 To 5,1 To 2) As String
```

Given this definition, you could fill the array with data as shown here:

```
ContactPhoneNumbers(1,1) = "(909) 555-7273"
ContactPhoneNumbers(1,2) = "(909) 555-7274"

ContactPhoneNumbers(2,1) = "(714) 555-9826"
ContactPhoneNumbers(2,2) = "(714) 555-9827"

ContactPhoneNumbers(3,1) = "(206) 555-0937"
ContactPhoneNumbers(3,2) = "(206) 555-0938"

ContactPhoneNumbers(4,1) = "(909) 555-9045"
ContactPhoneNumbers(4,2) = "(909) 555-9046"

ContactPhoneNumbers(5,1) = "(909) 555-5667"
ContactPhoneNumbers(5,2) = "(909) 555-5668"
```

You can illustrate this data as being stored in memory like this:

ContactPhoneNumbers Index	1	2
1	(909) 555-7273	(909) 555-7274
2	(714) 555-9826	(714) 555-9827
3	(206) 555-0937	(206) 555-0938
4	(909) 555-9045	(909) 555-9046
5	(909) 555-5667	(909) 555-5668

To add columns to this array, you could increase the second number from 2 to whatever number of columns you need, as shown in the following two examples:

```
Dim ContactPhoneNumbers(1 To 5, 1 To 27) As String
Dim ContactPhoneNumbers(5, 27) As String
```

You can carry out the array to yet another dimension, as shown in the Dim statement below:

```
Dim ContactPhoneNumbers(5, 27, 20)
```

At this point, you've gone beyond the "rows and columns" metaphor into some really complicated array handling. Access Basic allows up to 60 dimensions in an array, although you will rarely, if ever, need more than two dimensions.

Dynamic Arrays

In every ContactPhoneNumbers array example we have been using thus far, we have defined the number of elements in the array by specifying the number of numbers within the parentheses. However, there are many times when you don't know how many rows an array might have. For example, you might create an array that is used to temporarily store all of the phone numbers in the Phone table, even though you can't predict ahead of time how many records will exist in the Phone table.

To solve this problem, Access Basic provides *dynamic arrays*, which allow you to define an array without a number of elements, then redefine the array later on when you know how many elements you need. To define a dynamic array, you use the Dim statement in the same way as you used it to create any other array, leaving nothing in the parentheses:

```
Dim ContactPhoneNumbers()
```

Later on in the program, when the number of elements is determined, you use the ReDim statement to give the array some elements. In the example below, the Phone table is opened, then the ContactPhoneNumbers array is ReDim'ed so that it has the same number of rows as there are records in the Phone table:

```
Set rs = db.OpenRecordset("Phone")
rs.MoveLast
ReDim ContactPhoneNumbers(rs.RecordCount)
```

You can ReDim as many times as you need within a procedure. By default, everytime you ReDim an array that has data in it, the data is erased. If you need to ReDim an array, and you want to make sure that changing its size doesn't erase any data in the array, you can use the Preserve keyword in the ReDim statement:

```
ReDim Preserve ContactPhoneNumbers(rs.RecordCount)
```

Variable Scoping

As with procedures, variables can be scoped globally or locally. When you create a variable in a procedure using a Dim statement, that variable is only available to that procedure. If you tried to reference that variable from another procedure, Access would generate an error indicating that it doesn't recognize that variable. With this is in mind, if you created a variable called numofcontacts in one procedure, and a variable in another procedure with the same name, you could change the values of one numofcontacts variable without affecting the other variable in the other procedure.

If you wanted to make a variable available to all procedures in a module, you would define the variable in the Declarations section of that module using the Dim statement. In this case, you could change the value of a variable called numofcontacts in one procedure, allowing any other procedure in the module to recognize that change.

If you wanted to make a variable available to all procedures in all modules everywhere in Access, you would need to define the variable in the Declarations section of an Access module using the Global statement. The Global statement is used the same way as the Dim statement, as shown in the following examples:

```
Global numofcontacts As Integer
Global numofcontacts%
Global numofcontacts(5, 27)
```

Constants

A *constant* is like a variable in that you assign a value to a name, but a constant is defined only once in your program, and its value can never change. Constants can be used to make a program more readable by substituting obscure numbers with more understandable names, and they can also make it easier for you to maintain programs that rely on changing information, such as tax rates.

To define a constant, you use the Constant keyword in the following convention:

```
Constant <constant name> = <value>
```

For example, to define a constant tax rate called TAX_RATE with a value of .085, you would add the following command to your program:

```
Constant TAX_RATE = .085
```

Once the constant is defined, any reference to the word TAX_RATE in the scope of the constant's definition "translates" to the value .085. In this case, the constant happens to be numeric; however, a constant can be any Access Basic data type.

The scoping of a constant works the same way as scoping a variable. If you define it in a procedure, it is local to that procedure. If you define it in the Declarations section of a module, it is global to all the procedures in that module. If you define the constant in the Declarations section of an Access module using the Global Constant statement, it is available everywhere in Access.

Using Constants to Improve Readability

The Access Basic MsgBox function allows you to display a message along with some kind of message icon and a combination of OK, Yes, No and Cancel buttons (see Figure 16-18). You can also determine which button the user pressed in response to the message.

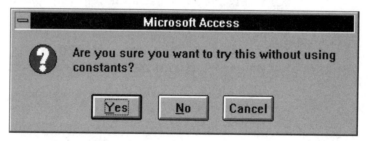

Figure 16-18: A sample MsgBox.

To create the sample message box in Figure 16-18, you could issue the following command in a program:

```
answer = MsgBox("Are you sure you want to try this without using
constants?",32 + 3)
```

The numbers 32 and 3 in the MsgBox statement above mean that you want to display a question mark icon (32) and that you want to display the Yes/No/Cancel button combination (3). The MsgBox function returns either a 6, 7 or 2, depending on which button the user chose. You can find all of these numbers in the manual when you need them, but you will probably never memorize them and they certainly don't make your program very readable.

By defining and using constants, you can more easily remember the various attributes of a MsgBox function, and you can make your program more readable:

```
answer = MsgBox("Are you sure you want to try this without using
constants?",MB_ICONQUESTION + MB_YESNOCANCEL)
```

The Global Constants and Procedures module in the VENTANA.MDB database defines a slew of constants for making the code more readable throughout (see Figure 16-19).

```
Module: Global Constants and Procedures

' MsgBox parameters
Global Const MB_OK = 0                      ' OK button only
Global Const MB_OKCANCEL = 1                ' OK and Cancel buttons
Global Const MB_ABORTRETRYIGNORE = 2        ' Abort, Retry, and Ignore b
Global Const MB_YESNOCANCEL = 3             ' Yes, No, and Cancel button
Global Const MB_YESNO = 4                   ' Yes and No buttons
Global Const MB_RETRYCANCEL = 5             ' Retry and Cancel buttons

Global Const MB_ICONSTOP = 16               ' Critical message
Global Const MB_ICONQUESTION = 32           ' Warning query
Global Const MB_ICONEXCLAMATION = 48        ' Warning message
Global Const MB_ICONINFORMATION = 64        ' Information message

Global Const MB_APPLMODAL = 0               ' Application Modal Message
Global Const MB_DEFBUTTON1 = 0              ' First button is default
```

Figure 16-19: Constants used in the Global Constants and Procedures module in VENTANA.MDB.

There is a file included in the Access program directory called CONSTANTS.TXT. This file includes constants used with various Access commands and functions.

Of course, MsgBox is only one example of something that uses obscure numbers. Your own program may use a constant to make different calculations, such as a tax rate. It would be easier to understand a formula with the word TAX_RATE in it as opposed to the tax rate number itself.

Using Constants to Better Maintain a Program

Speaking of tax rates, suppose you wrote a program that involved a tax rate of .085 in calculations scattered throughout the procedures in your program. Three months later, the tax rate goes up to .087, and the program is now producing incorrect results because it is using an obsolete number in all of its calculations.

Maintaining this type of program is greatly simplified by defining the tax rate as a Global Constant in the Declarations section of an Access module:

```
Global Constant TAX_RATE = .087
```

Rather than using the number .087 in all of the calculations in your program, you would use the word TAX_RATE, as shown in the example below:

```
queryset!TotalCost = queryset!SubTotal * TAX_RATE
```

With this in place, changing all of the calculations in your program to reflect a new tax rate can be done simply by changing the value of the TAX_RATE constant.

Intrinsic Constants

To make your life easier, Access provides a number of pre-defined constants called *intrinsic constants*. Intrinsic constants are stored in SYSTEM.MDA—an Access database loaded into memory that is full of information and utilities that Access needs. Since these constants are loaded into memory along with the SYSTEM.MDA database, they are always available to an Access program even though you can't get to them.

Specific examples of intrinsic constants will be discussed as we go along.

ARITHMETICAL, LOGICAL & STRING OPERATORS

Sure, you have some data stored in variables, but what can you do with it? You may need to add, subtract, multiply or divide numeric variables. You may need to design your program to make decisions based on whether or not some condition is true or false. You may have firstname and lastname variables you want to "glue together" into one fullname variable.

Access Basic supports common mathematical and logical operators the same way you learned them in elementary school and use them in your day-to-day work. Operators are symbols or words that you use to perform calculations, such as the symbols + (plus) and - (minus), or the words "And" and "Or". Access Basic also allows you to "add" text characters together—a concept we'll delve into later.

Mathematical Operators

Access Basic uses the following symbols and words to perform calculations with numbers stored in variables:

Operator	Description
+	Plus sign. Use this symbol to add numbers together.
-	Minus sign. Use this symbol to subtract one number from another.
*	Multiplication sign. Use this symbol to multiply numbers.
/	Division sign. Use this symbol to divide one number by another.
\	Integer Division. Use this symbol to divide one number by another, giving a result with no decimal places.
^	Use this symbol to raise a number to a specified power. For example, 3 ^ 2 means that you want to raise 3 to the power of 2, or 3^2, which is 9.
Mod	Use this number to find the modulus of two values. A modulus is the remainder of two numbers divided together. For example, 5 divided by 3 is 1 with a remainder of 2. 5 Mod 3 is 2.

Usage of most of these symbols is pretty straightforward. For example:

```
Forms!Orders!Tax = (Forms!Orders![Sub Total] + additems@) *
TAX_RATE
```

In a mathematical calculation that contains more than one type of operator, such as the example above, Access resolves the expression in the following order:

1. Expressions enclosed in parentheses
2. Multiplication
3. Division
4. Addition
5. Subtraction

Note that in the expression above, parentheses are placed around the items being added together, so that Access multiplies the result of that addition times TAX_RATE. If the parentheses weren't there, Access would first multiply additems@ times TAX_RATE, then add the result to Forms!Orders![Sub Total]. This, of course, would have an undesired effect on the whole calculation.

The Mod operator may seem obscure, but it comes in handy when you want to check for every *n*th number in a loop. For example, if you wanted to loop 21 times and display a message every third time, you would use Mod this way:

```
For i = 1 To 21
  If i Mod 3 = 0 Then
    MsgBox "This is a message"
  End If
Next
```

Logical Expressions & Operators

Don't worry—you haven't landed on the planet Vulcan as the title of this section may imply. In Access programming, you frequently need to test for the outcome of a condition and tell your program what to do as a result. For example, your program might look through a list of customer accounts and execute one set of actions if a customer owes you money, or another set of actions if the customer has paid in full.

In this section, you will learn how to create the logical expressions that test for different conditions.

Boolean Expressions

Logical operators allow you to derive a *boolean value* from multiple conditional statements. A boolean value simply means True or False. For example, consider the following English-like conditions:

[HAS 1 CAT]

...and...

[HAS 1 DOG]

Now consider the following statement:

DAN [HAS 1 CAT] AND [HAS 1 DOG]

For this statement to be True, Dan would have to have BOTH a Cat and a Dog. If Dan had only one of the two or neither of the two, the statement would evaluate as False. If you replaced the AND operator in this example with an OR operator, Dan could have either a Cat *or* a Dog to make this statement True; but if he had neither, the statement would be False. Now let's look at an example of Access Basic code that illustrates how this is used in programming:

```
num_of_cats = 1
num_of_dogs = 0

If num_of_cats = 1 And num_of_dogs = 1 Then
    MsgBox "He has both"
End If

If num_of_cats = 1 Or num_of_dogs = 1 Then
    MsgBox "He has at least one of them"
End If
```

As you can see from the Access Basic example, you use the words "and" and "Or" as logical operators to determine how to derive a boolean value. You can also use the logical operator *Not* to "invert" the value of a logical expression:

```
If num_of_cats = 1 And Not num_of_dogs = 1 Then
    MsgBox "He has a cat, but no dog"
End If
```

Order of Precedence

Like the mathematical operators in the previous section, logical operators have an order of precedence that Access Basic follows when resolving a logical expression. The order of precedence goes like this:

1. Expressions in parentheses
2. NOT
3. AND
4. OR

Equality Operators

In the dog and cat example, we define the has_dog and has_cat variables as having a True or False value at the beginning of the routine. In the real world, the programming code you write will more often test for a condition with an *equality operator*, such as the = (equals) sign, as shown here:

```
If CountFollowUps() = 0 Then
    MsgBox "There are no follow-up contacts for today."
End If
```

In this case, if the result of the CountFollowUps( ) function procedure is zero, the MsgBox is to be displayed. You can also use the > (greater than) equality operator to make the If statement true if the result of the CountFollowUps() function is greater than zero:

```
If CountFollowUps() > 0 Then
    MsgBox "You have follow-up contacts scheduled for today."
End If
```

The following table contains the equality operators and their meanings.

Operator	Purpose
=	Expression on the left *equals* the expression on the right.
<>	Expression on the left *does not equal* expression on the right.
<	Expression on the left *is less than* expression on the right.
<=	Expression on the left *is less than or equals* expression on the right.
>	Expression on the left *is greater than* expression on the right.
>=	Expression on the left *is greater than or equals* expression on the right.

- -

I used to have a hard time remembering which operator was for "greater than" and which was for "less than." The way I remember now is that the "less than" operator (<) kind of looks like an "L" that is leaning forward. Of course, "L" stands for "less than."

- -

The Concatenation Operator for Strings

You will frequently come across situations where you have two or more string variables or expressions, and you want to "glue" them together into one variable. For example, suppose you defined two string variables as shown below:

```
firstname$ = "Theodore"
lastname$ = "Roosevelt"
```

Access Basic supports the & operator, which you use to add the names together into one name. After executing the line below, the value of fullname$ would be Theodore Roosevelt:

```
fullname$ = firstname$ & " " & lastname$
```

The concept of adding, or "gluing" characters together is called *concatenation*.

PROGRAM CONTROL STRUCTURES

Program control structures control decisions and loops in your program.

The structures If...Then and Select Case allow you to *branch* control to a set of commands based on the outcome of a certain condition, or based on the value of some variable or expression. "Branching control" means that Access jumps to different areas in your program as it needs to, as illustrated in the example below:

If this logical expression is True...

...then your program branches to this set of commands.

```
If num_of_cats > 0 And num_of_dogs = 0 Then
    MsgBox "He has a cat, but no dog"
    dog_insurance = False
ElseIf num_of_cats = 0 And Not num_of_dogs > 0 Then
    MsgBox "He has a dog, but no cat"
    cat_insurance = False
ElseIf num_of_cats > 0 And Not num_of_dogs > 0 Then
    MsgBox "He has a cat and a dog"
    cat_insurance = True
    dog_insurance = True
End If
```

The Do...While and For...Next structures allow you to create a program *loop*. A loop is a set of commands that is repeated a certain number of times. The number of times a loop occurs depends on what kind of loop structure you use.

This line determines how many loops to execute.

```
For i = 1 To numberofowners
    If cats(i) > 0 Or dogs(i) > 0 Then
        animals = animals + 1
    End If
Next
```

This is the set of commands that will be repeated.

If...Then

The purpose of the If...Then statement in Access Basic is to test for a particular logical expression, then execute a block of programming code if the result of that expression is True.

The syntax of Access Basic's If statement is shown below:

```
If <condition> Then
    <statement block>
[ElseIf <condition> Then
    <statement block>...]
[Else
    <statement block>]
End If
```

In its simplest form, you would have an If statement at the top, a statement block in the middle, then the word "End If" at the bottom. As you can see, you can check for more If conditions using the ElseIf statements.

```
If num_of_cats > 0 And num_of_dogs = 0 Then
    MsgBox "He has a cat, but no dog"
    cat_insurance = True
    dog_insurance = False
ElseIf num_of_cats = 0 And Not num_of_dogs > 0 Then
    MsgBox "He has a dog, but no cat"
    cat_insurance = False
    dog_insurance = True
ElseIf num_of_cats > 0 And Not num_of_dogs > 0 Then
    MsgBox "He has a cat and a dog"
    cat_insurance = True
    dog_insurance = True
End If
```

In this case, the statement block under the first logical expression evaluating to True would be executed; then the program continues from the line of code that follows End If.

507

If you are only testing one logical expression, you can shorten the If...Then statement to one line, as shown below:

```
If num_of_cats > 0 And num_of_dogs = 0 Then MsgBox "He has a
cat, but no dog"
```

Notice that there is no End If when you format your If...Then statement on one line.

Select Case

The Select Case structure makes it really easy to branch to a set of commands based on the value of some variable or expression. In other words, you can write different blocks of code and allow Access to choose which block to execute, depending on the value of a variable. The complete syntax for Select Case is shown below:

```
Select Case <test expression>
  [Case <expression list 1>
    <statement block>...]
  [Case Else
    <statement block>]
End Select
```

The example below checks the value of a variable called payment_type. If the value of payment_type is "Credit Card", Access executes the block of code under the Case "Credit Card" line. The same is true for "Check", "Draft", and "Cash".

```
Select Case payment_type
  Case "Credit Card"
    pay_code = 1
    cc_number = InputBox("Please enter Credit Card number.")
  Case "Check", "Draft"
    pay_code = 2
    ck_number = InputBox("Please enter Check number.")
  Case "Cash"
    pay_code = 3
End Select
```

Notice that you can specify more than one value to compare against. In the example above, the same block of code would be executed if the value of payment_type were either "Check" or "Draft".

The sample above would be functionally equivalent to the following If...Then statement:

```
If payment_type = "Credit Card" Then
    pay_code = 1
    cc_number = InputBox("Please enter Credit Card number.")
ElseIf payment_type = "Check" Or payment_type = "Draft" Then
    pay_code = 2
    ck_number = InputBox("Please enter Check number.")
ElseIf payment_type = "Cash" Then
    pay_code = 3
End If
```

Notice that using the If...Then statement in this case requires you to repeat a logical expression for each If and ElseIf line. Select Case handles this much more cleanly, and you should always use the Select Case structure when you are testing for the value of a single variable or expression, and use If...Then when you need to check for different unrelated conditions.

Do...Loop

The Do...Loop structure is a flexible way to repeat a block of commands based on a given logical expression. There are two ways you can use Do...Loop:

```
Do While/Until <condition>
    <statement block>
    [Exit Do]
    [<statement block>]
Loop
```

...and...

```
Do
    <statement block>
    [Exit Do]
    [<statement block>]
Loop While/Until Condition
```

In each case, the statement block is repeated *as long as the condition is true* (While) or *until the condition becomes true* (Until) or until an Exit Do command is encountered. The difference between the two Do...Loop structures above is that the first checks the condition at the top of the loop, meaning it will not execute the statement block unless the condition is true to begin with. In the second Do...Loop structure, the condition is tested at the bottom of the loop, guaranteeing at least one iteration of the statement block.

For...Next

The For...Next structure is a straightforward way to repeat a block of commands a specified number of times. The difference between For...Next and Do...Loop is that For...Next is specifically designed to loop a number of times while Do...Loop is designed to continue looping until or while a condition is met. The syntax for For...Next is shown below:

```
For <countervar> = <start value> To <end value> [Step <increment
value>]
   <statement block>
   [Exit For]
   [<statement block>]
Next
```

The counter variable (countervar) must be a numeric variable; you don't have to define the variable before you use it in a For...Next loop. At the beginning of loop execution, the counter variable is initialized to the start value. When the Next line is encountered, the counter variable is incremented by one, or, if you include the Step clause at the end of the For line, the counter variable is incremented by the number in the Step clause. The statement block is repeated until the end value is reached or an Exit For command is encountered.

EXECUTING MACRO ACTIONS FROM ACCESS BASIC

As we learned in Chapter 15, you can use the RunCode macro action to complement macros with Access Basic code. Using the Access Basic DoCmd statement, you can complement an Access Basic program by running macro actions. This capability gives you access to the same simple functionality that macros provide.

To use the DoCmd statement, you follow the word "DoCmd" with the macro action you want to execute, followed by the parameters for that action. When you use DoCmd, macro action parameters are expressed by a number that indicates the position of that selection in a macro window. For example, suppose you wanted to issue a DoCmd statement that executes the DoMenuItem macro action. In a macro window, the DoMenuItem action has 4 parameters that allow you to choose the menu item you want to execute. When you drop down the list for the Menu Bar parameter, the first choice on the list is Form, the second choice is Database and so on. As far as DoCmd is concerned, all choices are numbered starting with zero, so the Form choice represents choice #0, the Database represents choice #1 and so on.

For this example, we want DoMenuItem to execute the Permissions menu item from the Security menu on the Database menu bar. You must indicate to DoMenuItem that you want the Database choice in the first macro window list, which is choice #1. The next parameter shows a list of menu items from the database menu bar, and from that parameter we would choose Security, which is choice #3. The Permissions menu item in the next parameter is choice #0, and we do not need to specify anything for the last parameter.

When you put all of this together, you end up with a DoCmd statement like the one shown in figure 16-20:

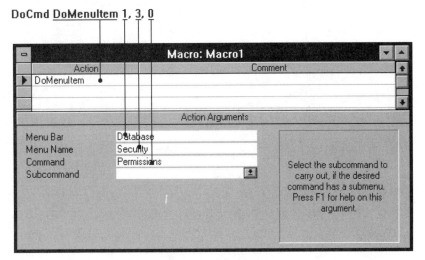

Figure 16-20: The DoCmd statement runs a macro action.

You cannot use DoCmd to perform a macro action for which there is already an Access Basic command. For example, there is a MsgBox Access Basic command and a MsgBox macro action. You must use the Access Basic MsgBox statement instead of the MsgBox macro action, since they are functionally identical. There are also other macro actions off limits to DoCmd, because they are macro-only functions. Below is a list of all of the macro actions that cannot be used with DoCmd:

○ AddMenu–because it is a macro-only function

○ MsgBox–because there is a MsgBox statement in Access Basic

○ RunApp–because there is a Shell function in Access Basic

○ RunCode–because there is a Call statement in Access Basic

○ SendKeys–because there is a SendKeys statement in Access Basic

○ SetValue–because you can set values in Access Basic using Let, Set or with an expression such as x = 1

○ StopMacro–because it is a macro-only function

MOVING ON

In this chapter, we covered some of the bottom-line fundamentals in Access Basic programming. In the next chapter, we will graduate to some more advanced topics, such as data access and manipulation, working with forms, debugging your programs and much more.

17

GETTING PAST BASIC

This chapter gets into some of the more interesting and useful things you can do with Access Basic. We will start out by discussing some important string functions—you're going to use a lot of string manipulation commands if you're going to be an Access Basic programmer, so we'll make sure you're covered.

After getting past some of the more challenging concepts, learning how to access and manipulate data using Access Basic should be a downhill coast. Being a database product, Access really focuses on data-intensive functionality and provides a wealth of capabilities.

Finally, just before you receive your official Access Basic hat and tassel, we'll discuss maintaining and debugging your programs. I'll even help you get off to a flying start before it's all over. When you have completed this final chapter on Access Basic, you won't quite have reached guru status, but you'll be well on your way.

STRING FUNCTIONS

The topic of string functions may not sound terribly exciting, but there are a few that you should know about because you'll need to use them very frequently. String functions solve a variety of problems, including:

○ Converting string data to numeric data so that you can do arithmetic with numbers that may be stored as string values.

○ Extracting part of a string, such as the leftmost *n* characters, the rightmost *n* characters, or anything in between.

○ Trimming spaces off string values.

You will realize the important role these functions play as we go over them and show some examples.

Converting & Formatting String Variables

As you have already learned, there are different types of Access variables to store different types of values. You use numeric types such as Integer or Single Precision to do math, and you can use a string type variable to store data such as names and addresses. You can add two numeric variables together, or you can concatenate two string values together, but you can't always add a numeric variable to a string variable containing numbers, nor can you always concatenate a string variable with a numeric variable to "glue" a string of numbers together. Access is unusually forgiving when it comes to mixing data types in the same expression, but there are certain situations involving mixed data types that Access has no way of knowing how to interpret.

You might wonder when this kind of situation would even come up, but these things occur more often that you might think. One common example is when a program accepts a number from a user and subsequently performs some mathematical operation with that number. If the user inadvertently includes some leading spaces or a non-numeric character anywhere in the input number, Access will return a Type mismatch error and halt your program as soon as it attempts to do math with the user's number.

You can test this problem by typing in the sub procedure below and running it from the Immediate Window by typing **TestProblem**:

```
Sub TestProblem
  x = InputBox("Enter any number.  Put spaces in it to cause an
error.")
  x = x + 1
  MsgBox x
End Sub
```

If you type a number by itself into the InputBox and click the OK button, the procedure successfully adds 1 to the number you entered, then displays the result. However, if you include a space or some other non-numeric character anywhere in the number you type, Access will display a Type mismatch error and bomb out of your program.

Figure 17-1: Typing a space as part of the number causes Access to generate an error.

The Type mismatch error occurs because Access interprets any value containing a non-numeric character as a string data type. When the procedure wanted to add the number 1 to the character string, Access could not convert the number you typed because the non-numeric character in it made its value ambiguous. Should the number 1234x5 be interpreted as 12345? 1234.5? 1234? In this example, we used an InputBox to illustrate the point, but the value could just as well have come from a text box on a form, or from a field in a table, or from somewhere else.

To make sure that this problem will never rear its ugly head, you can use the Access Basic Val function to convert a string value to a numeric value. The Val function accepts a single string value, collects all the numbers it can find from left to right until it encounters a non-numeric character other than a space, and returns a numeric value of all the numbers it finds. For example, Val("1234 5") would return the number 12345; Val("1234x5") would return the number 1234.

With this in mind, we can now modify the TestProblem procedure so that it never chokes on erroneous user entry again:

```
Sub TestProblem
    x = InputBox("Enter any number.  Put spaces in it to cause an
error.")
    x = Val(x) + 1
    MsgBox x
End Sub
```

The Access Basic Str function does the opposite: it accepts a numeric value and converts it to a string value so that you can concatenate it without risking a Type mismatch error. The following modified version of the TestProblem procedure concatenates

the resulting value of x into a string data type that can be displayed
with the MsgBox statement:

```
Sub TestProblem
    x = InputBox("Enter any number.  Put spaces in it to cause an
error.")
    x = Val(x) + 1
    MsgBox "The resulting value is " & Str(x)
End Sub
```

Although the Val and Str functions cover 90 percent of your
conversion needs, they are only two of many data type conversion
functions in Access Basic. The conversion functions shown below
can be used to convert any value to any data type. These functions
accept any kind of value and, as long as it can be converted to the
desired data type, return the value as that data type.

Conversion Function	Resulting Data Type
CCur	Currency
CDbl	Double Precision
CInt	Integer
CLng	Long Integer
CSng	Single Precision
CStr	String
CVar	Variant

Another way to convert variables from one type to another is to
format them. Actually, you can kill two birds with one stone when
you format a variable because you are applying a *template* to the
variable as you change its type. (A template is a format style that
you can add to data to make it more meaningful; for example, you
can enhance a number like 9095551212 with a phone number
template including parentheses and a dash to make it look like this:
(909) 555-1212.)

For example, suppose we stored today's date to a variable called
todaysdate using the Access Basic Date function, then displayed
that date with a MsgBox:

```
todaysdate = Date()
MsgBox todaysdate
```

If today's date were November 18, 1994, the result of executing
the MsgBox statement above would appear as 11/18/94. What if we
wanted the date to appear spelled out, as in November 18, 1994?
To do so, we would have to convert the todaysdate variable to a
string (right now, it's a Double Precision type, because dates are
stored in variables as Double Precision numbers). One way we

could convert the variable to a string would be to use the CStr function, as shown below:

```
todaysdate = CStr(todaysdate)
```

However, you've only done half the job. The value of todaysdate is still 11/18/94, only now it's a *string* of "11/18/94" rather than a Double Precision number representing the date 11/18/94. To convert the date to a string and spell it out at the same time, we can use the Access Basic Format function.

The Format function accepts a variable that you want to format, and a string of characters representing the way you want to format the result. To format todaysdate so that it is spelled out, we could use the format function below:

```
todaysdate = Format(todaysdate, "mmmm dd, yyyy")
```

After this line of code executes, the value of todaysdate would be a string value of November 18, 1994. The "mmmm dd, yyyy" argument is what tells the Format function to spell the date out. The format characters aren't anything you have to figure out; I originally learned how this particular set of characters formats the date by looking in the manual, and it's since found its way into my memory along with some other format characters, from using them so much.

As you might have figured, the Format function does a lot more than spell out dates. There is a slew of special characters you can use to indicate how to format values of different types. To get a list of all of these characters and descriptions of how they are used, search Access's online help facility for Format$.

Trimming Spaces off String Values

When dealing with data provided by users via a form or some other type of input, you cannot always be assured that character values will not end up with leading or trailing spaces. For example, suppose you had the following lines of code in your program:

```
Dim homecity As String
homecity = InputBox("Enter the name of the city you live in")
MsgBox "You live in " & homecity & " and it is very beautiful this time
of year"
```

If a user typed in the name of a city with some leading and trailing spaces, the resulting message displayed might look like this:

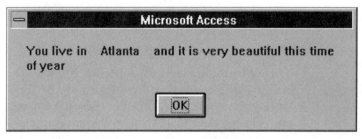

Figure 17-2: The result of leading and trailing spaces.

Notice the spaces before and after the word *Atlanta*. These spaces appear because the user typed a space before and after *Atlanta*, and the spaces were passed on to the string displayed in the MsgBox. Of course, this is just a cosmetic problem, but passing unwanted spaces among different operations in your program could cause unwanted results.

Access Basic provides three functions to solve the problem of leading and trailing spaces: LTrim, RTrim and Trim. Each function accepts one argument representing the string value you want to trim spaces from, and returns the trimmed result. LTrim trims leading spaces from the left side of the string, RTrim removes trailing spaces from the right side, and Trim removes leading *and* trailing spaces.

Try adding a Trim function to the code example:

```
Dim homecity As String
homecity = (InputBox("Enter the name of the city you live in"))
MsgBox "You live in " & Trim(homecity) & " and it is very beautiful
this time of year"
```

Now the sentence in the MsgBox is not broken up by extra spaces from the user's input:

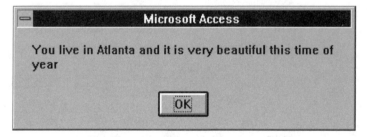

Figure 17-3: The Trim function removes leading and trailing spaces.

Manipulating & Parsing String Variables

In the VENTANA.MDB Global Constants and Procedures module, there is a sub procedure called DialPhoneNumber, which accepts a phone number as an argument and sends that phone number to your modem (if you have one). In order to work, the procedure has to send the phone number without all of the extra characters you and I use to make phone numbers easy to read. For example, if the procedure receives a phone number such as (909) 555-1212, the number would have to be converted to 9095551212 before it could be sent to the modem.

One of the first things the DialPhoneNumber procedure does is to strip out all these non-numeric characters. This allows flexibility in the way the phone number is passed to the procedure. To accomplish this, the procedure starts out with an empty string variable called dialnumber$, then goes through each character in the phone number argument and concatenates to dialnumber$ each character that falls between 0 and 9.

```
Module: Global Constants and Procedures
Function DialPhoneNumber (phonenumber As String, comport As String)
    ' Go through all of the characters of the phonenum parameter
    ' to strip out any characters other than numbers.  The
    ' resulting phone number will be stored in the variable
    ' called "dialnumber$"

    dialnumber$ = ""
    For i = 1 To Len(phonenumber)
        If Mid(phonenumber, i, 1) >= "0" And Mid(phonenumber, i, 1) <= "9" Then
            dialnumber$ = dialnumber$ & Mid(phonenumber, i, 1)
        End If
    Next
```

Figure 17-4: The For...Next loop goes through each character in the phone number and copies all the numbers to dialnumber$.

The For...Next loop provides a counter so that we can move from one character to the next in the phone number parameter. The Len function on the For line of the For...Next loop indicates how many characters there are in the phone number parameter. The key to making this work, however, is the Mid function. The syntax for Mid is shown below:

    Mid(<string expression>, <position>, <length>)

The Mid function accepts a string expression, a position within the string expression at which to begin reading, and a length value indicating how many characters to read. Mid reads the characters according to the values you specify and returns the resulting value.

In the case of the DialPhoneNumber routine we have been discussing, the Mid function extracts one character from the

519

phone number argument beginning at the current position in the For...Next loop. In the first iteration of the loop, the Mid function returns the first character from the phone number; in the second iteration, the Mid function returns the second character, and so on. Each time, the result of the Mid function has to be between the values of 0 and 9 in order for the If...Then statement to be true, in which case the number is concatenated on to the end of the dialnumber$ variable.

To complement Mid, Access Basic also includes the Left and Right functions. These functions return a specified number of characters from the left or right side of a string value. The syntax for Left and Right is identical:

Left(<string expression>, <length>)

Right(<string expression>, <length>)

In both cases, you provide a string expression and the number of characters you want to get from either the left or right of that expression.

The Left and Right functions are commonly used for *parsing out* a word from a text string that has more than one word in it, such as a full name. *Parsing out* means that your program pulls words out of a variable containing more than one word. Suppose you wanted to write some code to parse out a first name from a variable called fullname, so that you could store the first name into a variable called firstname.

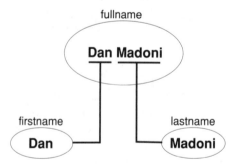

Figure 17-5: *Parsing out* means looking through a character string for different words. Here the first name and last name are parsed out of a variable called fullname, then stored into their own variables.

Using the Left function, you can get the firstname from the text box by specifying the number of characters to the left of the space that separates the firstname and the lastname. For example, in the name Dan Madoni, the space is the fourth character. Thus, if the name were stored in a variable called fullname, Left(fullname, 4) would return the first name Dan (along with the space). Of course, you don't always know where the space is, because the number of characters in a first name can be different every time. To solve this problem, we can use the Access Basic InStr function to tell us where the space is (the function name InStr stands for In String).

The InStr function accepts the variable that you want to find the string in and the string that you want to find. If the string exists in the variable, InStr returns a number representing the starting location of the string. If the string does not exist in the variable, InStr returns zero. In the following example, we can extract the name Dan from the string by using InStr to find the space that separates the first name from the last name:

```
fullname = "Dan Madoni"
findspace = InStr(fullname, " ")
firstname = Left(fullname, findspace)
```

Or we can embed the InStr function in the Left function to reduce the number of lines of code:

```
fullname = "Dan Madoni"
firstname = Left(fullname, InStr(fullname, " "))
```

Since the Left function will return the first name with a trailing space, we might want to throw in an RTrim function to make sure we get the first name without any trailing spaces:

```
fullname = "Dan Madoni"
firstname = RTrim(Left(fullname, InStr(fullname, " ")))
```

Now suppose we wanted to get the last name out of the fullname variable. One way we could do this would be to use the Right function to return the rightmost number of characters from the space, the same way we did with the first name. The problem with this is that we can't use InStr the same way we did with the first name; remember in the example that InStr returns 4 because the space is in the fourth position, but Right(fullname, 4) would return doni rather than Madoni.

What we need instead is a way to tell Access that we want to start at position 4, and return all of the characters up to the end of the string. We can do this with the Mid function we learned about earlier. Remember that the Mid function allows us to specify a starting position and a number of characters we want to get beginning from that position. If you leave out the number indicating how many characters to get, Mid returns everything from the starting position all the way to the end of the string. The following lines of code would correctly store Madoni into the lastname variable:

```
fullname = "Dan Madoni"
findspace = InStr(fullname, " ")
lastname = Mid(fullname, findspace)
```

Or we can write the code this way:

```
fullname = "Dan Madoni"
lastname = Mid(fullname, InStr(fullname, " "))
```

METHODS

In Access, objects such as forms can do different things. For example, a form can give itself focus, repaint itself, or do one of a number of other things. A program can tell a form to do something by executing one of the form's *methods*. To put it simply, a method is nothing more than a command that relates to a specific object. If you wanted the Contacts form to give itself focus, you could use its SetFocus method like this:

```
Forms!Contacts.SetFocus
```

Some methods, such as a form's GoToPage method, require arguments. In such cases, you follow the method with the appropriate arguments just like you would when you call a sub procedure with arguments:

```
Forms!Contacts.GoToPage 2, 100, 100
```

Although forms, reports and their controls have only a handful of methods, other objects you work with in Access Basic have all kinds of methods. Data objects, which you will learn about later, are practically useless unless you take advantage of the methods that go along with them.

INTRODUCTION TO COLLECTIONS

From the title of this section, you may be under the impression that we are about to discuss unpaid debts. Don't worry—the subject of collections in this case is related to Access. The concept of collections in Access is fundamental to understanding how to use Access Basic to work with objects such as forms and tables.

Many of the objects that you work with in Access are collections of other objects. For example, an Access database can be loosely interpreted as a collection of forms, reports, tables and so on. From the standpoint of Access Basic programming, the concept of collections has greater significance and a more complex meaning.

The Forms Collection

In Chapter 15, we touched briefly on the idea of a forms collection. Remember that a forms collection is the set of forms that are currently open, and that we refer to the forms collection every time we access a value from a form, such as *Forms*!Form1!Field1. In Access Basic, the forms collection becomes a lot more interesting (and it turns out to be a good example of how collections work). In addition to referring to a form by its name, as in Forms!*Form1*, you can also refer to it by an index number. Index numbers for forms begin with 0. For example, the first open form in the forms collection can be referred to as Forms(0), the second open form in the forms collection can be referred to as Forms(1), and so on. With this in mind, we could hide all of the forms currently open by looping through the forms collection and setting each open form's Visible property to False:

```
For i = 0 To Forms.Count - 1
    Forms(i).Visible = False
Next
```

In this loop, the counter variable i starts at 0 and executes the line below it each time as it counts to Forms.Count - 1. The Count property of the forms collection returns the number of forms that are currently open. Since the index number for referring to forms in the forms collection is zero-based, we have to start at 0 and end at Forms.Count - 1.

Each form has a couple of collections of its own: the controls collection and the sections collection. The controls collection includes all of the controls on an open form. Like the forms collection, you can refer to each control with an index number, beginning with 0. You can see from the code example below that the way you can work with a controls collection is consistent with the way you can work with a forms collection. Each form has a Count property that returns the number of controls on the form, and you can loop through each control and do something with it. Note also that the controls collection belongs to the forms collection, so you have to specify which form in the forms collection has the controls you want to work with:

```
For i = 0 To Forms!Contacts.Count - 1
    Forms!Contacts(i).Visible = False
Next
```

To make this even more interesting, we can loop through all of the forms in the forms collection, then loop through all the controls within that form to hide all of the controls on the screen. This example isn't very practical in real life, but it illustrates the relationship between these collections:

523

```
For i = 1 To Forms.Count
   For j = 1 To Forms(i).Count
      Forms(i)(j).Visible = False
   Next
Next
```

The sections collection of a form refers to all of the sections in a form, such as the form header, page header, detail section and so on. Unlike controls and forms, sections are predefined, so you always know what section is being referred to by a particular index number. For example, the first control in the controls collection could be a button, a text box or whatever, depending on how the form was designed. In the sections collection, however, Section(0) is always the detail section, Section(1) is always the form header, and so on. The table below lists all of the sections and the index numbers you can use to access them.

Index Number	Section
0	Detail Section
1	Form Header
2	Form Footer
3	Page Header
4	Page Footer

As mentioned earlier, the forms collection is a good example of Access collections in general, and of the way that you work with collections in Access Basic.

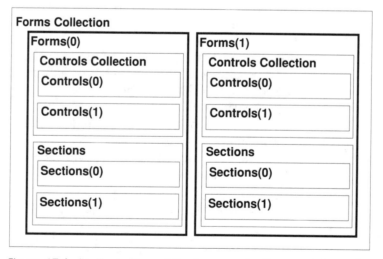

Figure 17-6: An illustration of the forms collection, and the collections that belong to it.

The Reports Collection

The reports collection is almost identical to the forms collection, since reports also contain controls and sections. The only differences between the forms and reports collections are:

○ When referring to a member of the reports collection, you use the word Reports rather than Forms.

○ Since reports can have group sections, the sections collection for reports also includes index numbers for group sections, as listed in the table below:

Index Number	Section
0	Detail Section
1	Report Header
2	Report Footer
3	Page Header
4	Page Footer
5	Group 1 Header
6	Group 1 Footer
7	Group 2 Header
8	Group 2 Footer

If a report has more than two groups, you number each group in pairs, beginning with 9 and 10.

Other Collections

Now that you have an idea of what collections are all about, we can start talking about data access. The next section will introduce you to some new collections that involve data handling. These collections are not as tangible as the forms and reports collections because you can't see them the way you can see a form and its controls and sections. The important thing here is that you understand the collection concept.

OBJECT DATA TYPES & VARIABLES

In Chapter 16, we discussed the different data types you can use in Access Basic. These data types are specifically designed to store different kinds of data for different purposes.

In the same sense that you can store an integer value in an Integer data type variable, or a monetary value in a Currency data type variable, you can also use an *object variable* to store references to forms, reports and other objects.

In the case of forms and reports, this allows you to write procedures that can be used with any form or report. For example, consider the following function procedure:

```
Function WarnAndCloseForm ()
   Const MB_YES = 6

   If MsgBox("Are you sure you want to close this form?") = MB_YES
Then
       DoCmd Close A_FORM, "Contacts"
       WarnAndCloseForm = True
   Else
       Forms!Contacts.SetFocus
       WarnAndCloseForm = False
   End If
End Function
```

Because this function makes direct references to the Contacts form, it can only be used with the Contacts form; however, you may want to use this function with other forms, too. Because Access allows you to refer to a form with an object variable, you can modify the function as shown below, and call it from a procedure with a reference such as isclosed% = WarnAndCloseForm(Forms!Contacts):

```
Function WarnAndCloseForm (formtoclose As Form)
   Const MB_YES = 6

   If MsgBox("Are you sure you want to close this form?") = MB_YES
Then
       DoCmd Close A_FORM, formtoclose.FormName
       WarnAndCloseForm = True
   Else
       formtoclose.SetFocus
       WarnAndCloseForm = False
   End If
End Function
```

Unlike other Access Basic data types, you can't simply assign a form object to an object variable by issuing a command like formvar = Forms!Contacts; you must use the Set statement whenever you work with object variables:

```
Set formvar = Forms!Contacts
```

The function procedure below is another modified version of WarnAndCloseForm. In this case, a form variable is set to the current active form using the Screen.ActiveForm object reference. Thus this function always works with the current active form, rather than using an explicit reference to a form:

```
Function WarnAndCloseForm ()
    Const MB_YES = 6
    Dim formtoclose As Form

    Set formtoclose = Screen.ActiveForm
    If MsgBox("Are you sure you want to close this form?") = MB_YES
Then
        DoCmd Close A_FORM, formtoclose.FormName
        WarnAndCloseForm = True
    Else
        formtoclose.SetFocus
        WarnAndCloseForm = False
    End If
End Function
```

As you will learn in the next section, there are lots of object data types in Access other than forms and reports. Using object data types becomes even more interesting when you are working with data objects; you can't "see" them like you can see forms and reports, yet you still need some way to refer to them.

WORKING WITH DATA

Being that Microsoft Access is a database product, Access Basic provides a wealth of functionality for working with data in Access tables. There are a number of different ways you can work with data, and you'll now get a chance to learn all kinds of fun new buzzwords like dynaset and snapshot.

As you will learn in this section, an understanding of collections is very helpful when you are working with data, as are many of the other fundamentals you have learned thus far.

Recordsets

In Access Basic, as well as Access in general, you work with data by retrieving a set of records and performing some action. For example, a form retrieves the set of records defined in its RecordSource property and displays those records according to your form design. A report retrieves a set of records, formats them according to your design, then sends an image of those records to the printer.

In Access Basic, you can retrieve a set of records and perform a number of operations on the recordset, including

○ Going through the records one at a time to change something.

○ Finding a record based on search criteria.

○ Adding new records to the set.

○ Deleting records.

And there are more operations that you can perform as well. The set of records that your program is working with at any one time is called a *recordset* (this is one of those rare occasions where a buzzword in Access actually means what it says).

Before you do anything with data from a table, you have to retrieve the data you want to work with into a *recordset object*, (which we will learn how to do a little further on). Like other data access objects you will learn about in this section, a recordset object is kind of like a form in that you can refer to it by a name and change its properties. But unlike a form, it isn't something you can see on the screen. The techno-folks at Microsoft sometimes refer to recordset objects as "virtual tables," because they are objects that you can work with even though you can't see them.

There are three different kinds of recordset objects: *dynaset*, *snapshot* and *table*. You will learn a little later how you can choose the type of recordset to work with.

Dynasets

A dynaset is the most flexible kind of recordset you can use. Using a dynaset, you can obtain data from a table, or several tables, in a particular order and with a particular filter if needed. When you use a dynaset, you don't have to worry about taking advantage of indexes you may have created for the source tables. A dynaset automatically determines the best use of indexes when you need to locate a record within a recordset.

A dynaset also gives you an updatable view of data, meaning that you can modify records in the dynaset even though they come from different data sources. Conversely, data retrieved into a dynaset is "live." In other words, if the data in the source tables changes, then the data in the dynaset changes accordingly.

For working with data, you should consider using a dynaset in your program by default. Dynasets are easiest to work with because they don't require you to figure out the best way to use indexes. If your program needs to obtain a recordset from an Access query, from multiple tables or from attached tables, and if the data obtained needs the ability to be updated, you must use a dynaset.

Snapshots

A snapshot is similar to a dynaset, but with a couple of differences. First, a snapshot is a static view of the data retrieved. Unlike a dynaset, data in a snapshot does not change even if the data in the underlying tables changes. And changes you make to a snapshot's data will not be reflected in the underlying table.

If your program needs to read through a set of data, but does not need to make changes to it, you should consider using a snapshot. Since snapshots do not need to constantly "look" at the underlying tables to make sure nothing has been updated, they offer better performance than dynasets and tables.

Table Recordsets

Using a table recordset is the most direct way to work with a table and its indexes. Unlike a dynaset or snapshot, a table recordset is not a view of data, but a direct link to data in an Access table.

When you use a table recordset, you cannot access data from more than one table in a single view. You also must manage indexes manually when you perform record searches.

If you play your cards right with table recordsets, you will gain the best possible performance from data-intensive operations in your program, which is one factor to consider when you decide which type of recordset to use for a given task. Some programmers may use the table recordset simply because they prefer to have complete control over data rather than allowing Access to work like a "black box," as it does when it retrieves data into dynasets and snapshots.

Opening Recordsets

Now that you know something about the different types of recordsets, we can discuss how you actually use them in practice.

Earlier, we learned about collections in Access, specifically with reference to forms and reports. When you work with data, you have to access a number of collections, which are layered, before you get to the collection of tables from which you retrieve data.

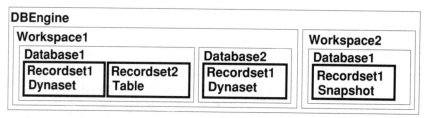

Figure 17-7: To open a recordset, you first have to get access to different layers of collections.

At first, this may seem like a lot of unnecessary steps just to get a set of data to work with, but a little bit of practice will demonstrate to you the value of the flexibility this model offers.

The DBEngine Object

Figure 17-7 illustrates the data access objects in Access, along with their collections. (There are actually other kinds of collections in some of these objects, but we are not concerned about them for now.)

At the top of the hierarchy of collections is the DBEngine object. The DBEngine object represents *Jet*, the mechanism that Access uses to manage data.

. . . .

The Jet Engine

Jet is not a part of Access itself; it is a component that Access interfaces with to manage data stored in Access tables or external data sources. If this sounds confusing, it might help you to think of Jet as a separate product from Microsoft that is bundled with Access in order to give it its data management capability. Jet is also bundled with other Microsoft products, such as Visual Basic and Microsoft Excel.

. . . .

Workspace Objects

Within the DBEngine object exists a collection called workspaces, which contains *workspace objects*. Workspace objects represent different "sessions" of database activity. By working with data in different workspaces, your program can meet the specific needs of users with different passwords and different levels of security. We won't be getting into the intricacies of the workspace object as it relates to workgroup programming, but we need to know how to access the workspace object in order to get access to the databases collection.

Database Objects

The databases collection contains *database objects*. A database object allows access to data and data definitions in an Access database, including tables, queries and relationships. One of the collections contained in a database object is the recordset collection, which contains recordset objects.

Creating & Using Variables for Database Access Objects

In order to gain access to these different layers of collections, you have to create some object variables with some new data types. We will use these object variables to refer to the different objects in Figure 17-7, so that we can work our way down to creating a recordset object:

```
Dim ws As Workspace
Dim db As Database
Dim rs As Recordset
```

Now that the object variables are available to the program, the program can begin working its way through the different layers of objects to get to the data it needs. The first step in this process is to ask the DBEngine object to provide a workspace from its workspaces collection (sort of like setting a form object variable to an open form in the forms collection). Like forms and reports, open workspace objects in the workspaces collection are enumerated beginning with 0, and there is always at least one workspace in the workspaces collection. Thus the program can get access to that workspace by setting the ws object variable to the first workspace in the workspaces collection:

```
Set ws = DBEngine.Workspaces(0)
```

With access to a workspace object via the ws object variable, the program can get access to the database containing the data it needs by asking the workspace object for a database in its databases collection. Like the workspaces collection, the databases collection is enumerated beginning with 0. The first database object in the databases collection always refers to the current open database. As long as the data needed by the program exists in the current database, the program can get access to the database object it needs by setting the db object variable to the first database in the databases collection of the ws workspace object:

```
Set db = ws.Databases(0)
```

Now that we have gone through the trouble of defining a workspace object and a database object, let me fill you in on a shortcut. Since the databases collection belongs to the workspace object, and since the workspaces collection belongs to the DBEngine object, we can shorten all the work we have done thus far down to two lines of code:

```
Dim db As Database
Set db = DBEngine.Workspaces(0).Databases(0)
```

As long as you are working with the current database, you can always use this shortcut. However, you can't use it if you are creating a new workspace, or creating or opening a database other than the current database.

The OpenRecordset Method

At this point, the db object variable refers to the database in which the desired data exists. To actually get to the data, the program needs to ask the database object for a set of data using the OpenRecordset method. The resulting recordset will be available via the rs recordset object:

```
Set rs = db.OpenRecordset("Contacts")
```

In this example, the db database object retrieves all of the data from the Contacts table in the current database and creates a dynaset recordset object. The reason that the OpenRecordset created a dynaset rather than a table or snapshot is because no type was specified. You can specify what type of recordset you want to create using one of the following intrinsic constants as a second argument in the OpenRecordset method:

○ DB_OPEN_DYNASET

○ DB_OPEN_SNAPSHOT

○ DB_OPEN_TABLE

> Set rs = db.OpenRecordset("Contacts", DB_OPEN_DYNASET)

The OpenRecordset method is very flexible as far as retrieving views of data is concerned. In addition to retrieving a set of data from a table as in the example above, you can also specify the name of a query to retrieve a set of records based on that query definition:

> Set rs = db.OpenRecordset("Contact List")

Yet another more flexible way to retrieve a view of data is to specify an SQL statement rather than the name of a table or query:

> Set rs = db.OpenRecordset("SELECT Contacts.*, Organizations.*
> FROM Organizations INNER JOIN Contacts ON Organizations.OrgID
> = Contacts.OrgID ORDER BY Contacts.OrgID;")

Structured Query Language

SQL, which stands for Structured Query Language, is a common query language used with many software packages—even on mainframe computers. Access uses SQL to talk to the Jet engine. Jet does not understand Access Basic, but you can use the OpenRecordset method to pass an SQL statement to Jet and retrieve a set of records as a result.

If you do not know SQL, your best bet is to design a query that represents the view of data your program needs, then specify the name of that query as the first argument for OpenRecordset.

Using an SQL statement with OpenRecordset is the easiest way to get a sorted and/or filtered view of data, in my opinion. You can specify a sort order using an ORDER BY clause, and a filter using a WHERE clause. If you specify the name of a table rather than an SQL statement in the OpenRecordset method, and you want to sort and filter data, you would have to create another recordset, as you will learn in the next section.

Recordset Object Properties & Methods

Now that you know what a recordset object is, let's talk about the kinds of things you can do with it. As you might expect, you can perform all kinds of data manipulation tasks with a recordset object, such as sorting and filtering data, navigating through a set of records, and changing or adding records.

Sorting & Filtering a Recordset

As mentioned earlier, the easiest way to sort and filter data in a recordset is to create the recordset with an SQL statement, which sorts and filter the recordset as it creates it. However, if you don't know SQL, or if you prefer the simplicity of defining a recordset with a table or query reference, you can use the Sort and Filter recordset properties.

To change the sort order of data in a recordset object, you set the recordset's Sort property to the field that you want to order the data as follows:

```
rs.Sort = "LastName"
```

If you want to sort the recordset by more than one field, specify the additional fields separated with commas. In this example, the Sort property setting indicates that the recordset is to be sorted first by the LastName field, then by the FirstName field, then by the MiddleName field:

```
rs.Sort = "LastName, FirstName, MiddleName"
```

By default, each field specified in the Sort property is sorted in ascending order. If you want to sort any of the fields in descending order, follow the field name with DESC, as shown here:

```
rs.Sort = "LastName DESC"
```

Changing the Sort property of a recordset object does not change the contents of the recordset in any way. You must create a second recordset variable to hold the recordset that results from changing the sort order. You then copy the sorted set to the new recordset using the OpenRecordset method. The following example covers the whole sort from the beginning. Note how OpenRecordset is used once to retrieve data from the Contacts table, then used again, without any parameters, by the rs recordset object to copy the sorted data to the rs_sorted recordset object.

```
Dim db As Database
Dim rs As Recordset
Dim rs_sorted As Recordset

Set db = DBEngine.Workspaces(0).Databases(0)
Set rs = db.OpenRecordset("Contacts", DB_OPEN_DYNASET)
rs.Sort = "LastName, FirstName"
Set rs_sorted = rs.OpenRecordset()
```

After this code is executed, the rs_sorted recordset contains the contents of the Contacts table, sorted by LastName and FirstName.

The Filter property of a recordset works very much the same way. You set the Filter property of a recordset object to a filter criteria, then you use OpenRecordset to copy the sorted data to a new recordset object. After the code in the following example is executed, the rs_filtered recordset object contains only Contacts table records for people who live in Michigan:

```
Dim db As Database
Dim rs As Recordset
Dim rs_filtered As Recordset

Set db = DBEngine.Workspaces(0).Databases(0)
Set rs = db.OpenRecordset("Contacts", DB_OPEN_DYNASET)
rs.Filter = "State = 'MI'"
Set rs_filtered = rs.OpenRecordset()
```

The filter criteria specified for the Filter property is a string expression, so it can be stored in a variable:

```
michiganfilter = "State = 'MI'"
rs.Filter = michiganfilter
```

Note that the MI in the filter expression is surrounded by single quotes. Since a string expression needs to be surrounded by double quotes, Access allows you to use single quotes to denote string expressions *inside* string expressions. For example, what we *really* want for our filter criteria is the following:

```
State = "MI"
```

However, we can't just enclose the filter criteria in quotes, since the criteria already has quotes in it. The following statement would generate a syntax error in your program:

```
michiganfilter = "State = "MI""
```

If the filter involves a numeric field, then we don't have to worry about using quotes within the expression:

```
orgfilter = "OrgID = 10"
```

535

The filter criteria you use is simply an SQL WHERE clause in quotes that Access sends to Jet. If you don't know SQL, you can think of the filter criteria as an Access Basic logical expression, even though that wouldn't be a completely accurate analogy. In either case, however, you can use AND and OR operators to round out a more complex filter expression. The following filter criteria would produce a recordset containing only those contacts whose last names start with the letter *M*:

```
rs.Filter = "LastName >= 'M' AND LastName < 'N'"
```

Of course, you can create a recordset by modifying *both* the Sort and Filter properties of a recordset object:

```
Dim db As Database
Dim rs As Recordset
Dim rs_newset As Recordset

Set db = DBEngine.Workspaces(0).Databases(0)
Set rs = db.OpenRecordset("Contacts", DB_OPEN_DYNASET)

rs.Sort = "LastName, FirstName"
rs.Filter = "State = 'MI'"
Set rs_newset = rs.OpenRecordset()
```

Not to beat a dead horse, but the code sample above can be significantly shortened by defining a sorted and filtered recordset in the first place using an SQL statement:

```
Dim db As Database
Dim rs As Recordset

Set db = DBEngine.Workspaces(0).Databases(0)
Set rs = db.OpenRecordset("SELECT * FROM Contacts WHERE State
= 'MI' ORDER BY LastName, FirstName;", DB_OPEN_DYNASET)
```

Moving Through a Recordset

When your program retrieves a recordset, it is only able to work with the records one at a time. For example, your program can move to the first record in the Contacts table and store the value of the LastName field to a variable, then move to the next record and store *its* LastName field value to another variable. The record that your program is working with at any given time is called the *current* record. When a recordset object is created, the first record in that recordset becomes the current record.

There are a number of ways in Access Basic to position a recordset object to a different current record. Among those ways are the recordset object Move methods, which allow you to move back and forth through a recordset, or move directly to the bottom or top record. The Move methods are listed here:

○ *MoveNext* moves to the next record in the recordset and makes it the current record.

○ *MovePrevious* moves to the previous record in the recordset and makes it the current record.

○ *MoveFirst* moves to the first record in the recordset and makes it the current record.

○ *MoveLast* moves to the last record in the recordset and makes it the current record.

○ *Move* moves by a specified number of records. The record that it lands on becomes the current record.

In the following example, we create a recordset object containing data from the Contacts table. The program uses the recordset object's MoveNext method to store the first 10 LastName field values into an array called lastnames:

```
Dim currdb As Database
Dim contacts As Recordset
Dim lastnames (1 To 10) As String
Dim i as Integer

Set currdb = DBEngine.Workspaces(0).Databases(0)
Set contacts = currdb.OpenRecordset("Contacts",
DB_OPEN_DYNASET)

contacts.MoveFirst
For i = 1 To 10
   lastnames(i) = contacts!Lastname
   contacts.MoveNext
Next
```

Now what if we wanted to create a program that stored *all* of the LastName values into an array? This would pose a problem for a couple of reasons:

○ We can't anticipate how many records there will be in the Contacts table, so we can't just create an array with a finite number of elements, such as 10.

○ We can't just MoveNext a finite number of times. If we create a For...Next loop that loops 10 times, and there are more than 10 records, we will miss out on LastName values beyond the tenth record. If there are fewer than 10 records, Access will generate an error when the MoveNext method attempts to advance beyond the last record in the recordset.

We can solve these problems by using the *RecordCount* and *EOF* properties of the recordset object.

As its name implies, the RecordCount property tells your program how many records there are in a recordset object. Using the RecordCount property, you can create an array variable big enough to hold all of the LastName field values because you know how many records there will be.

The only catch to the RecordCount property is that it does not return an accurate count of records until your program has forced the recordset object to move to the last record in the set. This is because, in the interest of speed, Access normally doesn't fill up an entire recordset object right away. If it did, your program would have to wait for Access to retrieve all of the records you requested before it could continue to the next line of code. As your program moves through the recordset, Access retrieves records as it needs them.

The EOF property tells your program when there are no more records to read in a recordset object (EOF stands for End Of File). As long as there is a current record to read, the EOF property has a logical value of False. Once a MoveNext method moves the current record pointer past the last record in the recordset, the value of EOF is a logical True. By using the EOF property, your program can open a recordset object and loop through all of the records using MoveNext, as long as the EOF property remains False (or *until* it becomes True).

The sub procedure example below puts into practice what we've just discussed. After creating a recordset object full of records from all of the Contacts living in Michigan, the procedure, using the RecordCount property, creates an array to hold all of the LastName values in the recordset. The procedure then loops through all of the records in the recordset and stores the LastName value of each record into an array element. As this is happening, each LastName value from the array prints to the Immediate Window, so you'll be able to see the program in action if you run the procedure from the Immediate Window:

```
Sub LoadLastNameArray ()
  Dim currdb As Database
  Dim contactinfo As Recordset

  Set currdb = DBEngine.Workspaces(0).Databases(0)
  Set contactinfo = currdb.OpenRecordset("SELECT LastName
FROM Contacts WHERE State = 'MI';", DB_OPEN_DYNASET)

  contactinfo.MoveLast
  Dim lastnames (1 To contactinfo.RecordCount)
  Dim indexcounter As Integer

  indexcounter = 0
  contactinfo.MoveFirst
  Do Until contactinfo.EOF
    indexcounter = indexcounter + 1
    lastnames(indexcounter) = contactinfo!LastName
    Debug.Print lastnames(indexcounter)

    contactinfo.MoveNext
  Loop

  contactinfo.Close
End Sub
```

Note that we use the Close method at the end of the procedure to close the contactinfo recordset object. Although it isn't necessary, it is good programming practice to close a recordset object when it is no longer needed.

In the same sense that the EOF property tells your program that the record pointer has moved beyond the last record, the *BOF* property can tell your program that the pointer has moved above the first record in a recordset object (BOF stands for Beginning Of File). If it were necessary to move through a recordset backward, from the bottom to the top, you could use MovePrevious instead of MoveNext and check to see if there are no more records using the BOF property. The example below is taken from the LoadLastNameToArray procedure example above, except the loop begins at the bottom and continues reading records until it reaches the top of the recordset:

```
indexcounter = 0
contactinfo.MoveLast
Do Until contactinfo.BOF
    indexcounter = indexcounter + 1
    lastnames(indexcounter) = contactinfo!LastName
    Debug.Print lastnames(indexcounter)

    contactinfo.MovePrevious
Loop
```

Finding Data in a Recordset

One very common thing your program will need to do with recordsets is to locate specific records. For example, your program may need to look up a name and change the address that goes with it, or you might simply need a program that looks up a record based on some key value in order to display that record's information.

Access Basic offers two ways to find data: using one of the Find methods (for a dynaset or snapshot recordset) or using the Seek method (for a table recordset).

To find a record in a dynaset or snapshot recordset, you use one of four Find methods:

○ *FindFirst*, to locate the first record meeting the specified criteria.

○ *FindLast*, to locate the last record meeting the specified criteria.

○ *FindNext*, to locate the first record meeting the specified criteria, beginning with the current record and searching forward.

○ *FindPrevious*, to locate the first record meeting the specified criteria, beginning with the current record and searching backward.

All of the Find methods work with search criteria in the same way that the Filter property works with filter criteria. For example, if your program needed to locate the first record in the recordset with MI in the State field, you might use the following statement:

```
contactinfo.FindFirst "State = 'MI'"
```

Or, if your program needed to find the *next* record where the State was MI, you might use this statement:

```
contactinfo.FindNext "State = 'MI'"
```

When a Find method is executed, Access figures out the quickest way to find data based on the indexes you have defined in the source tables.

Of course, there will be times when the record your program is looking for does not exist. For example, there might *not* be a record in the contactinfo dynaset that has a State field value of MI. To determine the success of a Find method, you can use a recordset's NoMatch property. When a Find method is issued, the Access sets the recordset's NoMatch property to True if the record was not found, or False if the record was successfully located.

The following sub procedure displays an input box that you type a last name into. The procedure searches a recordset with data from the Contacts table for the given last name. If it finds the name, then the City field value for that name is displayed; otherwise, a message appears indicating that no matching record was found:

```
Sub ShowCity ()
    Dim currdb As Database
    Dim contactinfo As Recordset
    Dim searchstr As String

    Set currdb = DBEngine.Workspaces(0).Databases(0)
    Set contactinfo = currdb.OpenRecordset("Contacts",
DB_OPEN_DYNASET)

    searchstr = InputBox("Enter a Last Name")
    contactinfo.FindFirst "LastName = '" & searchstr & "'"
    If contactinfo.NoMatch Then
        MsgBox "Name not found"
    Else
        MsgBox contactinfo!City
    End If

    contactinfo.Close
End Sub
```

The criteria used for the FindFirst line may seem a little confusing at first because of the unfamiliar use of single quotes and double quotes:

```
contactinfo.FindFirst "LastName = '" & searchstr & "'"
```

But it makes a lot of sense when you think about it a bit. If you ran this procedure and typed **Harrison** at the InputBox, you would want the criteria for FindFirst to be LastName = 'Harrison'. By breaking up the criteria argument above, you can see how the criteria ends up as LastName = 'Harrison', just the way we want it:

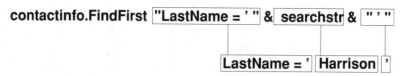

LastName = ' | **Harrison** | **'**

Figure 17-8: The FindFirst criteria example seems confusing at first, but it makes a lot of sense when you break it apart.

As mentioned earlier in this section, a table recordset object gives you more control over the way you can use indexes to find a record. Actually, you have no choice but to control the search process, since table recordset objects cannot use the Find methods. Instead, you use the Index property to set the index that the recordset will utilize in the search, then you use the Seek method to actually perform the search.

To set the Index property, simply specify the name of the existing index you want to use. For example, if you want to use the LastName index of the Contacts table to find a LastName value, you would set the Index property as shown below:

```
contactinfo.Index = "LastName"
```

The name of the index is almost always the same as the name of the field. The only exceptions are when you are setting the Index property to the name of a custom index or the name of the primary key of a table.

In the case of a custom index, you set the Index property to the name of the existing custom index you want to use:

```
contactinfo.Index = "CompoundNameIndex"
```

In the case of a primary key, you literally set the Index to the word PrimaryKey:

```
contactinfo.Index = "PrimaryKey"
```

Once you've set the Index property, you can use the Seek method. The Seek method only looks for data based on the Index you have set. For example, if you set the Index property to LastName, then you can't use Seek to look for a State field value.

The Seek method expects two parameters: a string value representing an equality operator and the value to look for. In the example below, a Seek is used to find the word Needham in the LastName index of the contactinfo recordset object:

```
contactinfo.Index = "LastName"
contactinfo.Seek "=", "Needham"
```

The equal sign (=) means that the Seek is to look for an exact match of the word Needham. If the program needed to find a LastName of Needham or anything following the name alphabetically, you could use a the greater than/equal to (>=) operator with the Seek method:

    contactinfo.Seek ">=", "Needham"

The operator you specify can be any one of the following:

=	to find data that matches the search value
<	to find data that has any value lower than the search value
<=	to find data that has any value less than or equal to the search value
>	to find data that has any value higher than the search value
>=	to find data that has any value greater than or equal to the search value

As with the Find methods, you can check the recordset's NoMatch property after the Seek has been executed to see if the Seek was successful.

The example below is another version of the ShowCity procedure in the previous section. In this case, however, a Seek is used with a table rather than a Find method with a dynaset:

```
Sub ShowCityWithTable ()
    Dim currdb As Database
    Dim contacts As Recordset
    Dim searchstr As String

    Set currdb = DBEngine.Workspaces(0).Databases(0)
    Set contacts = currdb.OpenRecordset("Contacts",
DB_OPEN_TABLE)

    searchstr = InputBox("Enter a Last Name")
    contacts.Index = "LastName"
    contacts.Seek "=", searchstr

    If contacts.NoMatch Then
        MsgBox "Name not found"
    Else
        MsgBox contacts!City
    End If

    contacts.Close
End Sub
```

Adding, Editing & Deleting Records

Access allows you to programmatically add, edit and delete dynaset or table recordset records using the AddNew, Edit and Delete methods.

The AddNew method adds a new record *in memory*, and allows your program to modify the values of the fields in the new record:

```
contactinfo.AddNew
contactinfo!FirstName = "Dan"
contactinfo!LastName = "Madoni"
contactinfo!Salutation = "Mr."
```

An Update method physically adds the new record to the recordset's underlying table:

```
contactinfo.Update
```

If your program used a Move, Find or Seek method to move to another record without first issuing an Update method, no new record would be added to the underlying table.

After a record is added, Access restores the record pointer to the record that was current before the AddNew method was executed. This is a very important point to remember; many new Access programmers forget this little tidbit and write their programs with the assumption that the new record becomes the current record. To make the new record current, your program must issue a Seek or Find method to locate the new record, based on a value that matches the index (Seek) or some other criteria (Find). For example, after adding the record below, a FindFirst method is used to position the record pointer on the new record:

```
contactinfo.AddNew
contactinfo!FirstName = "Dan"
contactinfo!LastName = "Madoni"
contactinfo.Update

contactinfo.FindFirst "LastName = 'Madoni' AND FirstName = 'Dan'"
```

The Edit method works just like the AddNew method, except you work with an existing record rather than creating a new one. To use the Edit method, follow these steps:

1. Locate the record you need to edit.

2. Issue an Edit method.

3. Change the values of the fields in the record.

4. Issue an Update method.

In the following example, we change the Title field value for the record we added above to Sales Associate, and we change the Salutation field to Mr.:

```
contactinfo.FindFirst "LastName = 'Madoni' AND FirstName = 'Dan'"

contactinfo.Edit
contactinfo!Title = "Sales Associate"
contactinfo!Salutation = "Mr."
contactinfo.Update
```

As with the AddNew method, leaving out the Update method and moving the record pointer will cause Access to ignore any changes the program has made.

Deleting a record is very simple to do with a recordset object— your program simply locates the record to delete and issues the Delete method:

```
contactinfo.FindFirst "LastName = 'Madoni' AND FirstName = 'Dan'"
contactinfo.Delete
```

Unlike the AddNew and Edit methods, you don't use an Update method to confirm the deletion. Access deletes the record as soon as the Delete method is executed—it does not prompt the user for confirmation. Because of this, it would be a good idea to add your own warnings in your programs to make sure that users will not inadvertently delete important data:

```
contactinfo.FindFirst "LastName = 'Madoni' AND FirstName = 'Dan'"

If MsgBox("Are you sure you want to delete this record?") = 6 Then
    contactinfo.Delete
End If
```

Once a record is deleted, your program must issue a Find, Seek or Move method to move off the spot where the deleted record was and make an existing record current.

Bookmarks

If you have ever worked with a database product like FoxPro or dBASE, you might have picked up a bad habit and become comfortable with the idea of record numbers. In these products, and in other popular database packages, a number uniquely identifies each record in a table. The first record in the table would be record #1, the second would be record #2, and so on.

The whole record-number thing is "politically incorrect" as far as true relational databases are concerned. The only way a record should be uniquely identified is by a unique key value—not some random number assigned to a record when it is created. (This is not to knock FoxPro or dBASE—my roots are in Xbase and I still enjoy using these products as part of my software development arsenal.) Access, as a better example of relational correctness, does not make use of record numbers.

From a programming standpoint, it may seem that record numbers are necessary to solve some of the most common programming tasks. In the following Xbase example, the program needs to move to a different record in the table, then move back to where it left off. To accomplish this, the program stores the record number of the current record before jumping to a different spot, then moves back to the first record as identified by its record number:

```
USE customers ORDER special_id
DO WHILE .NOT. EOF()
   IF special_id = 0
      current_rec = RECNO()
      GO TO BOTTOM
      new_id = special_id + 1
      GO TO current_rec
      REPLACE special_id WITH new_id
   ENDIF
   SKIP 1
ENDDO
```

If you were faced with a similar need in Access, you would not be able to rely on record numbers to make your program work.

To solve this problem, you can use the Bookmark property of an Access recordset object. The Bookmark property is an unintelligible string value that uniquely identifies each record in a recordset. The big difference between Bookmarks and record numbers is that Bookmarks are not a permanent part of an Access table—they are generated when a recordset is retrieved from that table. This is an important difference to understand: in an Xbase or Paradox table, record #5 will *always* be record #5, until it is deleted. In Access, a Bookmark can be one value in a particular record for one recordset, or another value for the exact same record in a different recordset.

To obtain a Bookmark for a record, you simply store the Bookmark property of the recordset into a string or Variant variable:

```
current_rec = contactinfo.Bookmark
```

Later, when your program needs to move back to the original record, you set the Bookmark property of the recordset to the original value:

```
contactinfo.Bookmark = current_rec
```

To put this into perspective, let's take a look at a few lines of code that do basically the same thing as the Xbase example a few paragraphs up:

```
Dim db As Database
Dim rs As Recordset
Dim current_rec As String
Dim new_id As Long

Set db = DBEngine.Workspaces(0).Databases(0)
Set rs = db.OpenRecordset("SELECT * FROM customers ORDER BY
special_id;")

Do Until rs.EOF
  If rs!special_id = 0 Then
    current_rec = rs.Bookmark
    rs.MoveLast
    new_id = rs!special_id + 1
    rs.Bookmark = current_rec
    rs.Edit
    rs!special_id = new_id
    rs.Update
  End If
  rs.MoveNext
Loop
```

By the way, don't be too impressed that the Xbase version was several lines shorter than the Access version; although Xbase has many advantages as a database language, Access Basic's object-based language delivers a more elegant, better thought-out, and arguably more powerful approach to data manipulation.

Transaction Processing

Database information processing frequently requires that all of the tasks making up an operation must be completed, or that none of the tasks should be completed at all. Think of grocery shopping as a real-life example of this concept: you put groceries on your shopping cart; then you pay for them at the checkstand. If you don't pay for the groceries, then you haven't completed your grocery shopping, because the clerk will not allow you to take the groceries home. If you don't put groceries in your shopping cart, then you haven't completed your grocery shopping, even if you give the nice clerk at the checkstand a hundred dollars. The point is, *both* of the shopping tasks have to take place before shopping is completed.

In Access, you may be writing a program that has this requirement. For example, your program may need to debit one expense account and credit another. If either the debit or the credit transaction is unsuccessful, neither should take place.

To facilitate this sort of programming, Access Basic provides *transaction processing* methods for workspace objects. Using the transaction processing methods, your program can begin a process that modifies data and adds records as needed. If at any time your program decides that the process cannot complete as a whole, all of the changes made up to that point can be undone, or *rolled back*.

The three transaction processing methods are listed below:

- ○ *BeginTrans* begins a transaction. If the process needs to be rolled back, BeginTrans defines the point that the process needs to be rolled back to.

- ○ *RollBack* rolls back any changes made since the BeginTrans method was issued.

- ○ *CommitTrans* closes a transaction. After a CommitTrans method is executed, any changes made to the data since the BeginTrans method are committed to the underlying tables. You cannot roll back a transaction after a CommitTrans method is executed.

In the following example, $1,200 is transferred from the expense account for department 295 and credited to department 307. If department 295 does not have enough funds to cover the expense, then the transaction will be rolled back with no action taken:

```
Dim translog As Workspace
Dim accounts As Recordset

Set translog = DBEngine.Workspaces(0)
Set accounts = translog.Databases(0).OpenRecordset("[Expense
Accounts]", DB_OPEN_DYNASET)

translog.BeginTrans

accounts.FindFirst "Department = '307'"
accounts.Edit
accounts!Amount = accounts!Amount + 1200
accounts.Update
```

```
accounts.FindFirst "Department = '295'"
If accounts!Amount - 1200 < 0 Then
    MsgBox "Department 295 does not have enough funds to
complete the transaction"

    translog.Rollback
Else
    accounts.Edit
    accounts!Amount = accounts!Amount - 1200
    accounts.Update

    translog.CommitTrans
End If
```

Manipulating Form Recordsets

Access Basic gives you complete control over the data a user sees on a form. You can move to a different record on the form, you can delete or edit a record from the form's underlying recordset, and more.

The key to all this wonderful power is the form's RecordsetClone property, which you can access from your program. The RecordsetClone property returns a copy of the recordset that the form is using as its source of data. Using this copy, you can treat the form's data in the same way you can treat any recordset object. To use the RecordsetClone property, you create a recordset object variable and simply Set it to the form's RecordsetClone property:

```
Dim formdata As Recordset
Set formdata = Forms!Contacts.RecordsetClone
```

Notice that you don't have to create a database object in order to get to the form's recordset.

When your program obtains a copy of the form's recordset in this manner, the current record is *not* the same current record that the user sees on the open form. However, you can easily match the record position of the recordset copy by setting its Bookmark to the form's Bookmark:

```
formdata.Bookmark = Forms!Contacts.Bookmark
```

You can also do the opposite: move the record pointer in the recordset copy, then position the form's recordset to match. This actually changes the data on the form so that the user sees the record:

```
formdata.FindFirst "LastName = 'Needham'"
If Not formdata.NoMatch Then
   Forms!Contacts.Bookmark = formdata.Bookmark
End If
```

You can easily see how all of this works by adding a button to the Contacts form in the VENTANA.MDB sample, and typing the following code into the button's On Click event procedure:

```
Dim contactrs As Recordset
Dim searchstr As String
Set contactrs = Me.RecordsetClone
searchstr = Trim(InputBox("Enter a last name to search for"))
If Len(searchstr) > 0 Then
   contactrs.FindFirst "LastName = '" & searchstr & "'"
   If contactrs.NoMatch Then
      MsgBox "The name was not found."
   Else
      Me.Bookmark = contactrs.Bookmark
   End If
End If
contactrs.Close
```

Take a Shortcut With Me

The Me reference in the code example above is a shortcut referring to the form in which this code resides. This is the line we used above:

```
Set contactrs = Me.RecordsetClone
```

We could have used this line instead:

```
Set contactrs = Forms!Contacts.RecordsetClone
```

However, since this procedure "belongs" to the Contacts form, using the Me reference is the better choice. It makes for shorter and cleaner code, and it is more efficient, since Access does not have to go searching through the forms collection to find the reference to the Contacts form.

ERROR HANDLING

There are three things in life that are completely unavoidable: death, taxes and program errors. Being the responsible programmer that you are, you will test the software you write to make sure it is free of bugs. However, it is very difficult to write large applications that are bug-free; there are so many different scenarios that could occur, and chances are something will slip by you and manifest itself as a program error. Even if you could test for every possible scenario, any bug fixes you make in one place could affect another area you have already tested without your realizing it. Some errors aren't even your fault—they may be occurring because someone is using your application incorrectly. Because errors are such a fact of life, you should always plan for handling them in your program.

Setting Error Traps in Your Program

One way to handle errors is by setting *error traps* in vulnerable spots. An error trap is like a trigger that goes off when an error occurs. The trap causes some code to be executed that keeps your application from dumping out as a result of the error. A good error trap will inform the user of the problem and allow the user to correct the mistake that caused the error, or it might allow your program to recover from the error on its own, without ever letting on that something went wrong.

Using the On Error Statement

To set up the error trap in a procedure, you use the On Error statement. The On Error statement can direct your program to branch to another part of the procedure where you keep your *error handling code*. An On Error statement placed at the top of a procedure will handle the errors that can occur in that procedure, and in the procedures that are *called* by that procedure.

In the example below, the On Error statement directs the procedure to branch to a label called OpenContactsErrorHandler (a *label* is used to define a specific point in a procedure). The error handling code uses the Err function to check for the possibility that there is no LastName field on the form passed to this procedure:

```
Sub FindLastName (searchstring As String, forminuse As Form)
  On Error GoTo OpenContactsErrorHandler

  Const CANT_BIND_NAME = 3070

  Dim rs As Recordset
  Set rs = forminuse.RecordsetClone

  rs.FindFirst "LastName = '" & searchstring & "'"
  If FindFirst.NoMatch Then
    MsgBox "'" & searchstring & "' not found"
  Else
    forminuse.Bookmark = rs.Bookmark
  End If

  Exit Sub

OpenContactsErrorHandler:
  Select Case Err
    Case CANT_BIND_NAME
      MsgBox "You cannot search for a Last Name with this form"
    Case Else
      MsgBox "An error has occurred while searching for a Last
Name using this form.  Try re-opening the form and performing the
search again."
  End Select

  Exit Sub

End Sub
```

Each error in Access Basic has a number associated with it. As you can see from the example, the Err function returns the error number and allows the Select Case statement to take some kind of action based on which error occurred. To find a list of error numbers and their associated errors, search Access's online help facility for "error messages: trappable errors."

Note in the example that an Exit Sub statement appears before and after the error handling code. If there were no Exit Sub before the error handler, Access would execute the error handler code every time the procedure was executed—the label doesn't *prevent* the code from being executed; it only *defines a starting point* that the procedure can branch to using the GoTo statement. After the error handling code, you must have an Exit Sub/Function, *Resume*

Next or *Resume* statement to indicate the end of the error handling code. Access returns an error if it encounters an End Sub or End Function statement at the end of error handling code.

The Resume Next statement tells Access to pick up where it left off when the error occurred. Using the Resume Next statement, you can create an error handler that acknowledges the fact that an error has occurred, but attempts to recover and continue execution. For example, the following procedure loops through a table called Expenses, calculating a Total Amount field for each record by adding the result of Sub Total * Tax Rate to the Sub Total. If a Null value is encountered in the Tax field, Access generates an error. The error is trapped, and the error handler recovers by copying the Sub Total to the Total Amount, since no tax rate was entered for that record:

```
Sub CalculateTax ()
  On Error GoTo CalculateTaxError

  Dim db As Database
  Dim rs As Recordset
  Dim tax As Currency

  Set db = DBEngine.Workspaces(0).Databases(0)
  Set rs = db.OpenRecordset("Expenses", DB_OPEN_DYNASET)

  Do Until rs.EOF
    tax = CCur(rs![Sub Total] * rs![Tax Rate])

    rs.Edit
    rs![Total Amount] = rs![Sub Total] + tax
    rs.Update

    rs.MoveNext
  Loop

  rs.Close

  Exit Sub

CalculateTaxError:
  tax = 0
  Resume Next

End Sub
```

The Resume statement by itself tells Access to continue from the same line that caused the error. You could use Resume in the example above to change the Tax Rate field itself, rather than just setting the tax variable to 0. This corrects both the program error and the source of the error:

```
CalculateTaxError:
    rs.Edit
    rs![Tax Rate] = 0
    rs.Update
    Resume
```

On Error Scoping

When you set an On Error trap in a procedure, its effect extends to any procedure called by the On Error procedure. For example, if ProcedureA sets an On Error trap and calls ProcedureB, any error that occurs in ProcedureB will be handled according to the error trap in ProcedureA. If ProcedureB had its own On Error trap, then the error trap in ProcedureB would be invoked in case of an error. In addition, if ProcedureB had its own On Error trap, any procedures called from ProcedureB would honor its error handling code.

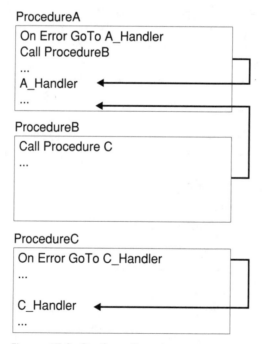

Figure 17-9: On Error Scoping.

Turning off the Error Trap

At some point in a procedure, you may want to disable an error trap. This is particularly useful in the case of a local error trap in a procedure that is already subject to an error trap in its calling procedure. For example, ProcedureA sets up an error trap and calls ProcedureB. ProcedureB sets up an error trap of its own, but only needs it for a few lines of code; otherwise, it can utilize the error trap already set up by ProcedureA.

To disable an error trap, use the On Error GoTo 0 statement. This statement disables the error trap *in the current procedure*. If there is another active error trap set up by a calling procedure, that error trap stays in effect until an On Error GoTo 0 statement is issued in the calling procedure.

Error Events

An *error event* is like an On Error statement that is automatically set up for you when you work with forms and reports. Rather than branching to a label in a procedure, an error event runs an event procedure whenever an error occurs in a form or report.

You can write error handling code in an event procedure similar to the way you write it with an On Error trap. You can get to the error event procedure by clicking the "..." button for the On Error event in a form or report property sheet, as shown in Figure 17-10.

Click here to open the On Error event procedure window.

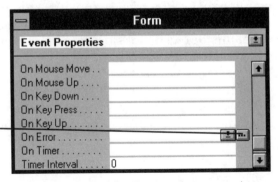

Figure 17-10: The On Error event procedure can be accessed from the property window.

Since form-level errors aren't always caused by Access Basic code, it wouldn't always make sense to include a Resume or Resume Next statement in an error event procedure. More often than not, you will probably use error event procedures to check for specific errors and report the error to the user, rather than trying to recover from an error.

MAINTENANCE & DEBUGGING

Some errors that occur in your program are easy to determine and fix. For example, if your program is trying open a table that doesn't exist (maybe you misspelled it), you'll find out right away when you run your program. When your program runs into one of these kinds of errors, Access displays an error message along with the offending line of code in a module window.

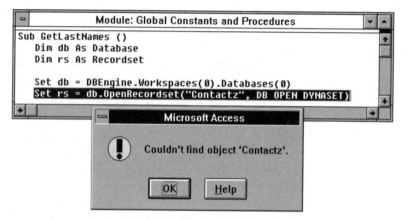

Figure 17-11: Access displays an error message and shows you where the problem occurred.

You can either correct the error in the module window and continue executing the program by choosing the Continue menu item from the Run menu, or stop the program by choosing the Reset menu item from the Run menu.

There are other kinds of errors that are not so easy to track down and that end up as bugs in your program. These are called *logical errors*. A logical error is one that doesn't stop your program from running, but it makes your program produce unintended results. For example, consider the following procedure:

```
Sub CalculateTax ()
    Dim db As Database
    Dim rs As Recordset
    Dim tax As Integer

    Set db = DBEngine.Workspaces(0).Databases(0)
    Set rs = db.OpenRecordset("Expenses", DB_OPEN_DYNASET)
```

```
    Do Until rs.EOF
        tax = rs![Sub Total] * rs![Tax Rate]

        rs.Edit
        rs![Total Amount] = rs![Sub Total] + tax
        rs.Update

        rs.MoveNext
    Loop

    rs.Close
End Sub
```

This procedure would seem to run without a hitch. However, if you were to check the resulting values in the Expenses table, you would find the wrong Total Amount values for some of the records. The reason for this is that the tax variable was accidentally defined as an Integer variable type, so the tax amount always ended up with no decimal places.

Using Access Basic Debugging Tools

You could bang your head against the wall trying to figure out why the CalculateTax procedure above did not work properly. Sure, the problem seems obvious after it has been revealed to you, but looking at the seemingly inconsistent results may have thrown you off and left you wondering if there was something wrong with Access. Other logical errors may be the result of many layers of procedures doing zillions of different things, making it very difficult to pinpoint the problem. Fortunately Access provides an ample set of debugging features that help you track down these kinds of problems.

To debug a program you need to follow these steps:

1. Set a *breakpoint* at a strategic location in your program.

2. Run your program and allow it to proceed until it encounters the breakpoint.

3. Step through the program one line at a time and check for results in the Immediate Window. Change the breakpoint if and when it is necessary to do so.

4. When the logical error has been located, correct the error and continue, or reset the program, fix the error, and restart the program.

Setting a Breakpoint

A breakpoint is a line of code at which you want Access to pause your program. Once you set a breakpoint, you can *step* through each line of code one at a time and check for results using the Immediate Window. To set a breakpoint, simply click once on the desired line in the module window, then choose the Toggle Breakpoint menu item from the Run menu. Doing so causes the line of code to appear in bold style characters.

The breakpoint line —

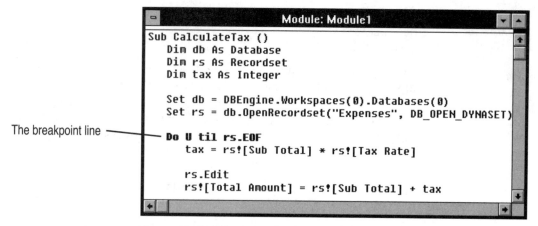

```
Module: Module1
Sub CalculateTax ()
   Dim db As Database
   Dim rs As Recordset
   Dim tax As Integer

   Set db = DBEngine.Workspaces(0).Databases(0)
   Set rs = db.OpenRecordset("Expenses", DB_OPEN_DYNASET)

   Do Until rs.EOF
      tax = rs![Sub Total] * rs![Tax Rate]

      rs.Edit
      rs![Total Amount] = rs![Sub Total] + tax
```

Figure 17-12: When this line of code is encountered, Access will pause execution and allow you to step through the program.

Stepping Through Code

Once you set the breakpoint, you can run the procedure either from the Immediate Window or in the way that you'd normally run the program. Once the breakpoint is encountered, Access brings the Module window to the front of the screen with the breakpoint line highlighted. At that point you can step through the code one line at a time, with the ability to check for values and other results in the Immediate Window during the whole process.

Single Step

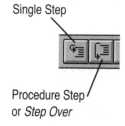

Procedure Step
or *Step Over*

Use the F8 key or the single-step toolbar button to execute each line of code. You can use Shift-F8 or the Procedure-step toolbar button to step through each line of code without stepping into any sub procedures that the procedure you are in refers to. This is really handy when you know the problem has nothing to do with any procedure other than the one you are in—it saves you from having to execute the other procedures one line at a time when it isn't necessary. Procedure-stepping is also known as *Stepping Over*.

If we were stepping through the CalculateTax program, we could check for the value of the tax variable in the Immediate Window each time it is calculated. Once we realize that the tax variable has no decimal places, we might deduce right then that the problem was the result of defining the tax variable as an Integer.

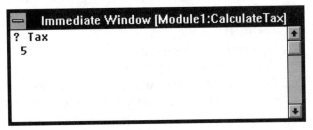

Figure 17-13: The tax variable mysteriously gives a value with no decimal places. Perhaps the problem is due to defining the tax variable with the wrong data type?

Once the problem is discovered, we could reset the program by choosing the Reset menu item from the Run menu, correct the problem, then try it again to make sure it works right next time.

The Set Next Statement

While you are stepping through code in a procedure, you may want to experiment with different orders of execution to help debug the problem. For example, you might want to see what would happen if the program skipped a few lines of code, or what would happen if the program went back and repeated a few lines. By selecting a line of code and using the Set Next Statement menu item from the Run menu, you can tell Access to proceed with the program beginning at that line.

Good Programming Practice

You can reduce the chance of making logical errors in your program and make the program run more efficiently by practicing good programming habits.

Commenting

You can radically enhance the maintainability of your programs by making good use of comments in your procedures. Comments help in a number of ways:

○ You can use comments to describe the intent of a piece of code. Programming code is not always self-explanatory, particularly if you are dealing with a complex programming task. Describing the intent of a piece of code makes it easier for you and others to follow the logic you originally laid out—and it is better to spend time figuring out why something doesn't work as intended rather than figuring out what the heck you meant to do in the first place.

○ You can use comments to describe how a piece of code works. There will probably be times when you literally spend hours figuring out how to make something work the way you want it to. These problems tend to involve complex algorithms that are hard to figure just by looking at them, even if you know what they are supposed to do. Adding comments that discuss how the code works, in addition to what it's supposed to do, can save you lots of time. After spending hours figuring something out once, you don't want to spend hours figuring out the same thing to fix a problem.

○ You can use comments to identify yourself. Perhaps you are working on a project with other programmers. Speaking from experience, it is very frustrating when you have to work with someone else's complicated code not knowing who that "someone else" is. Even if the code contains lots of helpful comments, it is nice to know that you can get insight to the design and intention of the code straight from the horse's mouth.

○ You can use comments to temporarily disable a line of code. One helpful debugging technique is to *comment out* one line of code at a time until an error no longer appears. By using the process of elimination in this way, you can narrow down the problem to one or two lines of code and take it from there.

To place a comment in your program, you begin a line with the comment character ('), then type the comment. You can also place a comment at the end of a line by placing a comment character at the end of the code and typing the comment after the comment character. The example below shows how comments make the procedure more maintainable:

```
Sub FindLastName (searchstring As String, forminuse As Form)
  ' Author  : Dan Madoni
  ' Date    : 11/18/94
  ' Purpose : Accepts a last name search value and a form
  '           and looks for the given value in the form's
  '           recordset. If the value is found, display it
  '           on the form. Otherwise, alert user that there
  '           is no such value in the record set.

  ' Set an error trap in case the form passed to this
  ' procedure is bogus, (i.e. it doesn't have a LastName
  ' field.
  On Error GoTo OpenContactsErrorHandler

  Const CANT_BIND_NAME = 3070

  ' Get the form's recordset
  Dim rs As Recordset
  Set rs = forminuse.RecordsetClone

  ' Look for the given last name
  rs.FindFirst "LastName = '" & searchstring & "'"
  If FindFirst.NoMatch Then       ' The record was not found
    MsgBox "'" & searchstring & "' not found"
  Else
    forminuse.Bookmark = rs.Bookmark ' Position the record
  End If

  Exit Sub

OpenContactsErrorHandler:
  Select Case Err
    Case CANT_BIND_NAME ' The form has no LastName field
      MsgBox "You cannot search for a Last Name with this form"
    Case Else         ' An unexpected error has occurred
      MsgBox "An error has occurred while searching for a Last
Name using this form.  Try re-opening the form and performing the
search again."
  End Select

  Exit Sub

End Sub
```

Modularity, Efficiency & Brevity

As much as possible, you should try to make your program *modular*. This means that you break your program down into procedures that accomplish one task each and that can work independently. A modular program makes it easier to locate potential problems because you always know where to look when something goes wrong. A modular program also makes it easier to make changes that affect a number of other procedures, since the same task is not repeated unnecessarily in other areas of your program.

In a nutshell, your code should accomplish its tasks in as few steps as is reasonably possible. It is easier to find your way around in shorter programs, and the possibility of writing erroneous code is reduced, at least as far as the law of averages is concerned. In addition, shorter programs are typically more efficient and run faster than larger programs.

HOW TO START WRITING A PROGRAM

Once you practice enough Access Basic to feel confident on your own, the first dilemma you'll probably run into is how to begin writing a program. This is a phenomenon that even experienced Access Basic programmers frequently deal with. It's like writing a term paper: you know what you want to say, and you've come up with clever ideas and thorough research, but writing that first paragraph is a big hurdle.

One of many advantages of developing an application in Access is that it forces you to do a little bit of designing before you begin creating forms, reports, macros and code. In the case of the VENTANA.MDB application, we began by designing the tables that would contain the information necessary for tracking contacts. Once you get the tables down, the rest kind of falls into place.

When I approach the development of any application, I tend to start with the component of the application that will receive the most use—even if I'm working from a prepared set of design specifications. Taking this approach, developing the VENTANA.MDB sample application went something like this:

1. After the tables were worked out (courtesy of Walt Bruce), I started developing the VENTANA.MDB application by creating the Contacts form, since that is where users would spend most of their time managing their contacts.

2. From there, I added some code and macros to increase the form's functionality.

3. With help and input (courtesy of Rich Wolf), I rounded out the application with forms to support the other data in the tables as they were defined.

4. Finally, I tied all of it together with a "front-end" form called Start-Up Form.

To start the application, I created an AutoExec macro that opens the Start-Up Form. (We actually called it Sample Autoexec in VENTANA.MDB so that you would be able to open up the database and play around in it without being immediately confronted with the application.)

Voila! A simple contact management application!

MOVING ON

Now the ball's in your court. With the information you have absorbed in these last three chapters, and in the book as a whole, you are on your way to becoming an expert Access developer. It's simple, but it takes practice and creativity. If you're lucky enough to really love it as I do, then it'll be no time before you master Access programming!

APPENDIX

A

THIRD-PARTY RESOURCES

As a busy working professional in your own field of business, you may find that you don't have time to master Access to the point that you could create and implement an entire system. Even if you knew how, you simply may not have the time. Or, your company may have just decided to standardize on Access, leaving you with a number of new Access users who need training.

The large user base created by Access has also created a demand for various services, such as training and application development. When these circumstances arise, Access professionals are here to help.

Perhaps you are one of those people in need at this very moment. After having read this book, perhaps you realize that Access is the tool of choice, but you need some extra help so you can concentrate on other things, or simply so you can learn more about this valuable product. This chapter informs you of your options when considering hiring outside help. We'll also discuss some considerations you should take into account when looking for a professional, and where you can find them.

DIFFERENT KINDS OF SERVICES

Of course, before you think about hiring outside help, you should know what kind of help there is. Services available for Access can be categorized as follows:

○ Application development
○ Consulting
○ Training
○ Technical support
○ All of the above

Application Development

One of the most common services available is application development. In other words, you hire someone to write an application in Access that you have designed to suit your needs. Access application developers are the easiest kinds of professionals to find. All you need to be an Access developer is a strong knowledge of Access programming, and there are lots of people with lots of Access knowledge out there.

When you work with a developer—as opposed to a consultant—you'll probably do most of the design work yourself, although the developer may have some ideas or suggestions based on his or her knowledge and experience of Access. Once the design is laid out and understood by both parties, the developer usually works out of his or her home or office; however, if your needs require, most developers are willing to work on-site.

Consulting

An Access consultant is someone who examines your business needs and provides a complete solution using Access. If necessary, a consultant will do all the legwork for you, including:

○ Helping you determine your own business needs.

○ Designing a complete software package in Access to meet those needs.

○ Developing the software.

○ Implementing the application and training your employees on how to use it.

○ Providing you with technical support and application maintenance as your needs change.

A consultant may also go as far as setting up a network complete with a network operating system and all the workstations you need.

Access consultants do a lot of on-site work because so much of what they do requires it (i.e., meeting with you and your employees to develop a design or install software and hardware). Depending on the size of the project, a consultant may decide to subcontract some of the work.

Training

Training services are available on a number of levels: from Access basics to hard-core Access programming. These services vary greatly in subject matter covered and length of classes offered.

Some training services come to your place of business and work completely on-site. Others may have their own training facility, complete with computers, overhead projectors and other expensive equipment you might otherwise need to facilitate the training. In addition, many training services also provide catering for meals, snacks and refreshments so that those participating in the training are comfortable and more receptive to the trainer and the subjects discussed. If you wish to hire a training service that does not offer catering service, I would recommend that you make your own arrangements. Having done training with and without a catering service, I can tell you first-hand that class members are more willing to participate on a full stomach.

Technical Support

If you have several employees who depend on Access for completing their daily tasks—and if you have the money—you might consider hiring a dedicated technical support professional rather than relying on long-distance calls and potential wait times to Microsoft's excellent product support staff.

A local Access specialist will usually be immediately available, and—having been exposed to your business—will have the advantage of understanding your business better than a Microsoft support engineer. Hiring your own technical support engineer saves you and your employees a lot of time in service issues as well. For example, a technical support engineer can be responsible for upgrades, registration and other services.

Technical support engineers are most effective when they are on-site; however, this may be the most expensive utilization of a support person. Another way to work with a technical support engineer is to have that person work in his or her own home or office "on call." In this case, the technician charges "per instance" rather than by the hour on-site. This saves you money and allows the technician to work on other projects or commitments.

WHEN TO HIRE A PROFESSIONAL

Now that you know *what* services are available, here are some things to think about before hiring some Access help.

Can You Do It Yourself?

On the surface, this may seem to be an obvious question. But you should really think it through—you might be surprised to find out that a seemingly insurmountable problem can be solved with a little practice using Access, or by a service available to you for free!

Take Advantage of the Simplicity of Access

From designing tables to querying for information to reporting to developing applications, Access *really is* simple to use.

Perhaps you need to create an application, but the idea of programming sounds intimidating. Don't be misled—try creating a couple of forms and writing a couple of macros. If at first you don't succeed, try a second, third and fourth time. You may fumble through your first few macros and programs; however, you might find yourself writing a complete working system before you realize it.

Is It Cheaper to Learn On Your Own?

Perhaps the problem you are faced with can be solved by "hitting the books." Spending a few days locked up with this book and the Access manuals may teach you everything you need to know. You may lose some work time or some sleep in the process, but hiring a professional may prove much more expensive. In addition, the experience you gain by learning Access can save you money in the future by allowing you to troubleshoot Access problems rather than hiring an expensive professional.

Microsoft Offers Free Assistance to Registered Access Users

Maybe the only thing between you and getting started on your own solution is a technical question or two. As long as you're a registered Access user, you can call and get *free* technical support.

The Microsoft support staff member at the other end of the phone is a professional, just like one that you could hire with your own money. I have worked personally with them and I can vouch for the quality of work they do. They're friendly, bright, helpful, tireless and—most important—*free*! To take advantage of this service, call (206) 635-7050. Call between 6:00 a.m. and 6:00 p.m. Pacific time, Monday through Friday.

In addition to person-to-person support, Microsoft also offers a 24-hour download service for most common questions. When you call, you can choose from a variety of topics covering common Access support issues and have them automatically downloaded to you via modem. Dial (206) 936-MSDL to use this service.

Can You Afford Professional Help?

Professional help can be very expensive. Once you begin pricing some of these services, you might realize you don't need them so badly. Later on in this appendix, we'll discuss the costs of professional services.

Do You Trust This Task to an Outsider?

No matter how experienced and bright a consultant is, it is often difficult for an outsider to really understand your business. Consultants and developers make a sincere effort to meet your needs with the solutions they create, but it is not uncommon that the final solution misses the mark in meeting the original needs due to a misunderstanding between the consultant and the client. Strangely, this happens even when the application is spec'ed to the finest detail—even though it all sounded good on paper, the consultant may have missed a minor detail that an insider with Access expertise would have caught, resulting in a completely different outcome.

It may be more cost-effective to allow one of your employees to become an Access guru so that the system you want benefits from both the experiences of someone who knows your business and the expertise of a good Access developer.

WHAT TO LOOK FOR IN A PROFESSIONAL

You're the one who is going to put the money into professional services. You're the one who is going to have to live with the work that is done. Selecting the person or firm for the job should be like hiring a full-time employee and like shopping around for a photocopier all at the same time. Don't be intimidated by someone who knows more than you about computers—if you don't understand what they are talking about, ask them to clarify. These are professionals who want *your* business.

With all of this in mind, here are a few specific things to look for when hiring a professional.

Different Kinds of Professionals

Although professional services come in all shapes and sizes, the businesses behind the services generally fall into two categories: independent contractors and consulting firms.

An independent contractor is usually a "one-man show" (or a "one-woman" show for that matter). You generally hear about independent contractors through word-of-mouth, contact on CompuServe, cheap flyers or chance meeting. Many independent contractors do consulting work "on the side"—that is, they have a regular computer job somewhere and they do consulting work to earn some extra cash. Others diversify enough to make a living of it.

Although the contractor/customer relationship is theoretically like any other relationship involving a business and an outside service, it may feel more like an employer/employee relationship.

This is because you are dealing one-to-one with the contractor as his or her "boss," and there is generally more legwork on your end when it comes to paying the contractor.

A consulting firm consists of a group of professionals all working for one business entity. Rather than hire a single person, you are hiring the firm to perform the services. This means you may deal with many different consultants depending on the scope of the project. However, this also means you don't have to deal with payroll hassles or work issues, and you can feel more confident knowing you are dealing with an established business.

Because a professional image is important to businesses who want to appeal to larger corporate clients, consulting firms tend to be more formal than independent contractors. This kind of formality also brings with it a higher price tag in most cases. In addition to the importance that price points have in making an impression on potential clients, consulting firms have to make up for the overhead of payroll, office space and other operating expenses that aren't as hard-hitting to an independent contractor working out of his or her home.

As you can see, both types of relationships have advantages and disadvantages. Although you should be educated on all of your options, the decision to go with one or the other shouldn't play too heavily in the overall decision of whom you end up hiring.

Qualifications

As with any other occupation, experience can speak volumes about the skill of the person or people you hire and how much their work is worth. If someone is good enough to have been in demand by reputable businesses and/or to have been quoted or published, then you can bet they are credible enough to be given the responsibility of defining and implementing lasting solutions to the most critical of your business operations.

As mentioned earlier, deciding whom you want to hire is like conducting a job interview—if you don't know a lot about computers or how to measure a computer professional's experience, use common sense. One thing I have noticed is that computer professionals are tolerated more so than other types of professionals. It's as if some businesses accept the notion that computer professionals as a group tend to be idiosyncratic. Don't fall for this line of thinking: if you find yourself discussing a job opportunity with someone you don't feel comfortable with, maybe it *really* says something about the kind of work that person will do.

Don't Pay Too Much

Professional computer services are in very high demand these days, and computer professionals know it. Allow me to tell you first-hand that we are among the most overpaid people on the planet considering the work we do is generally pretty simple.

Fair or unfair, the law of supply and demand is a fact of life. Fortunately, market forces are also a fact of life and you can benefit by shopping around and knowing what to look for.

If you want to hire a really good independent consultant or developer, you should expect to pay about $50 per hour and up; a really good consulting firm can cost twice that amount. Training services are *really* expensive: although I have seen them offered as low as $300 per day, it is more common to see them run about $1,200 per day and up plus assorted expenses (including catering or reimbursement for catering, courseware, hotel and travel, etc.).

If you are confronted with a good prospect who is asking for an amount significantly higher than these, and there doesn't seem to be anything that necessitates a higher rate, look elsewhere before committing.

WHERE TO FIND HELP

Amid all the talk about computer professionals, you might be asking yourself, "Where do all these people come from anyway? Do you find them under a rock somewhere? In an abandoned shack?" Actually, there are a number of sources you can turn to.

Below is a list of Access professionals all across the United States. The list includes information to help you make decisions based on the tips we've discussed. The list also includes contact information such as phone numbers, fax numbers and CompuServe numbers.

Another great place to find help is on the Microsoft Access forum on CompuServe (called MSACCESS). Section 15 of the forum is where Access third-party businesses and contractors hang out. If you post a request for service in this section, you'll probably get more than one response.

If you can't find someone in your immediate area, you still have plenty of options. Depending on the length of the project, many contractors and firms are willing to travel if you cover air fare, hotel stay and meals, and if the price is right. Also, don't forget that we are living in the age of the information superhighway: a lot of development work can be done off-site via an online service.

See below for information and addresses for Access professionals listed by state.

California

Name:	**Merriam-Leith Consulting**
Type:	**Independent Contractor**
Services:	**Consulting, Application Development and Training**
Address:	2600 Ponderosa Suite #76 Camarillo, CA 93010
Phone:	(805) 390-2856
Fax:	(805) 388-3061
CompuServe:	73354,567

Chris Merriam-Leith has several years of computing experience, including six years with mainframes and ten years experience with PC-based systems.

Chris specializes in integrating Access into IBM AS400 mainframe environments.

Contact Chris Merriam-Leith.

Name:	**Dan Madoni**
Type:	**Independent Contractor**
Services:	**Application Development, Consulting and Training**
Address:	9630 Stafford Street Rancho Cucamonga, CA 91730
Phone:	(909) 980-6967
CompuServe:	73201,533

Dan was employed by Microsoft as a FoxPro product manager, and by Borland and Ashton-Tate as a technical advisor. Most recently, Dan's clients include Jet Propulsion Laboratory and Microsoft.

Dan has developed widely distributed utilities and applications, such as Microsoft's Database Analyzer for Access, Paul Nielsen Computing's TeamAccess and others, including a forthcoming visual development tool for Windows (not related to Access), to be released by New Generation Development.

Dan is a published author, contributes articles to a number of trade magazines and gives seminars on a wide variety of subjects at conferences and trade shows.

The areas he serves include Orange, San Bernardino, Riverside and Los Angeles counties. Travel to other areas can be arranged.

Name:	**ACA, Inc.**
Type:	**Consulting Firm**
Services:	**Consulting and Application Development**
Address:	47000 Warm Springs Boulevard, Suite 451 Fremont, CA 94539
Phone:	(510) 490-2833
CompuServe:	76556,557

ACA's consultants average 12–15 years experience in distributed systems and client/server systems development and support. They have three consultants with over 10 years each of SQL experience, covering all major server and mainframe-level SQL products.

Contact ACA for client referrals.

ACA serves the United States and beyond, offering teleconsulting and limited onsite support for worldwide Access-related services.

They specialize in the following areas of Access:

❍ Resolving performance issues, including query and database restructuring, re-coding critical components and resolving multi-user issues.

❍ Porting single-user applications to SQL server-based applications.

❍ Integrating stand-alone Access applications into corporate or division level databases.

ACA also provides complete custom application development services in several business areas.

Contact Scott Alexander.

Name:	**Lauren Meyers**
Type:	**Independent Contractor**
Services:	**Application Development and Consulting**
Address:	1662 Chestnut Street San Francisco, CA 94123
Phone:	(415) 923-9848
CompuServe:	74031,2460

Lauren Meyers's clients include Visa International and Lamorte Burns.

Lauren serves the Northern California area and specializes in accounting and order entry systems.

Name:	**AccessAdvice**
Type:	**Independent Contractor**
Services:	**Consulting, Application Development and Training**
Address:	1798 Scenic Avenue #487 Berkeley, CA 94709
Phone:	(510) 849-0788
CompuServe:	72401,2743

AccessAdvice clients include the University of California and Hasting College of the Law. In addition, AccessAdvice clients can be found worldwide.

AccessAdvice provides application troubleshooting for people building their own business applications. Access tutoring is also provided.

Areas served include California, the Bay Area, Marin and the Central Valley from Modesto to Sacramento.

Contact Kenneth Tyler.

Name:	**OakLeaf Systems**
Type:	**Independent Contractor**
Services:	**Consulting and Application Development**
Address:	1030 Clarendon Crescent Oakland, CA 94610
Phone:	(510) 839-3937
Fax:	(510) 839-9422
CompuServe:	70233,2161

Roger Jennings has authored several books on Access and other Microsoft products. He is contributing editor of Pinnacle Publications' Smart Access newsletter and coauthor of *Creating Scalable Client-Server Applications* with Microsoft Access presented at Microsoft Tech Ed '94. He is also a contributing author to *Microsoft Developer Network News* and database-related periodicals.

Some of Roger's clients include Microsoft, National Semiconductor Corp. and other Fortune 500 firms.

OakLeaf Systems serve the San Francisco Bay Area and Silicon Valley.

Services offered include Access 2.0 database consulting services for client-server applications, with emphasis on the use of Access Basic code for creating server-specific SQL statements, SQL passthrough and transaction processing. Client-server RDBMSs supported include Microsoft and Sybase SQL Server for OS/2 and Windows NT, Sybase System 10 and IBM DB2 through a variety of gateways using NetBEUI and TCP/IP network protocols.

Contact Roger Jennings.

Colorado

Name:	**Nicholas Couch**
Type:	**Independent Contractor**
Services:	**Application Development, specializing in Microsoft Access**
Address:	Information Services City & County of Denver #10 Galapago Denver, CO 80223
Phone:	(303) 436-2000
CompuServe:	76436,2741

Nick Couch's current client is the City & County of Denver, where he develops government accounting software using Access.

Nick serves the Denver metropolitan area.

Indiana

Name:	**Michael Groh**
Type:	**Independent Contractor**
Services:	**Application Development, Consulting and Training**
Address:	1133 Aqueduct Way Indianapolis, IN 46280
Phone:	(317) 574-0594
CompuServe:	70031,2231

Michael Groh is an author and lecturer in Windows and database topics. He has over 15 years of application development experience.

Mike's clients include Prentice-Hall Computer Publishing.

Michigan

Name:	**CompuWorks, Inc.**
Type:	**Consulting Firm**
Services:	**Application Development, Consulting and Training**
Address:	1500 44th Street SE Grand Rapids, MI 49508
Phone:	(616) 249-3344
Fax:	(616) 538-3773
CompuServe:	76276,203

All CompuWorks associates are certified Microsoft professionals and have a minimum of 14 years business experience in applications development.

CompuWorks clients include many Fortune 500 clients and government agencies at both the federal and state level.

Contact Rich Wolf.

Minnesota

Name:	**Computer U, Ltd.**
Type:	**Consulting Firm**
Services:	**Training and Application Development**
Address:	668 Transfer Road St. Paul, MN 55114
Phone:	(612) 641-0744
Fax:	(612) 641-1208
CompuServe:	73061,1074

Computer U's clients include Carlson Travel Network, Northern States Power and Unisys. Carol Janetzke's experience includes over 15 years in all phases of application development. She has also taught a variety of computer classes at the college level in both Illinois and Minnesota.

Most recently Carol was a featured speaker at the 1994 Twin Cities PC Database Conference.

Computer U's associates are members of the Professional Association of Computer Trainers (PACT), and the International Computer Training Association (ICCA). They are also a Microsoft Solution Provider.

Contact Carol Janetzke.

New Jersey

Name:	**Sharing Enterprises**
Type:	**Consulting Firm**
Services:	**Training and Consulting**
Address:	208 Kinderkamack Road Oradell, NJ 07649
Phone:	(201) 261-3325
Fax:	(201) 599-0445
CompuServe:	75450,2253

Sharing Enterprises's clients include Amoco Oil, AT&T, ABC Television, Pharmaceutical Research Institute (a division of Ortho-MacNeil) and Prescriptives (a division of Estee Lauder).

Sharing Enterprises, a.k.a. Lauren Zenreich and Caitie Sher, specializes in training new users of Microsoft Access. They also provide consulting to "unstick" projects, and develop turnkey applications. They are staffed by professional trainers and developers who understand real-world concerns and can provide business solutions.

They also provide courses, which consist of training manuals and an accompaning disk. The series includes a unique Executive Overview, Introductory, Intermediate and Advanced courses. The curriculum is based on real-world concerns; all courses are interactive, hands-on, step-by-step exercises. Custom training is available to help design special courses that make optimal use of Access. They have training facilities in the New York and New Jersey areas, but will travel onsite if necessary.

New Mexico

Name:	**Techtryx Systems, Inc.**
Type:	**Independent Contractor**
Services:	**Consulting**
Address:	8220 Eddy Avenue NE Albuquerque, NM 87109-4958
Phone:	(505) 823-1932
CompuServe:	71250,563

Paul Cassel has been an independent consultant since 1987. He has taught at the University of New Mexico and Casper College (Wyoming), and has written two books about Microsoft Access both published by SAMS division of Prentice Hall. Paul regularly writes columns for various trade magazines.

Paul's clients include the University of New Mexico, Northern New Mexico college system, Public Service of New Mexico, University Hospital, AMREP International, Indian Health Service, Pacific Gas and Electric and Lovelace Health System (HMO).

Techtryx Systems provides complete PC software and hardware consulting, hardware design vending, networking and custom programming. They now specialize in Microsoft Office products. Techtryx Systems is a generalized consulting business, offering not only computer services, but legal, marketing and organizational consulting. Our noncomputing services specialize in not-for-profit organizations.

Contact Paul Cassel.

New York

Name:	**Micro Modeling**
Type:	**Independent Contractor**
Services:	**Consulting and Application Development**
Address:	111 Broadway, 18th Floor New York, NY 10006
Phone:	(212) 233-9890
Fax:	(212) 233-9897

Micro Modeling is a Microsoft Solutions Provider. Please contact Micro Modeling for client referrals.

Contact Lenore Michaels.

Name:	**MPSI, Limited**
Type:	**Independent Contractor**
Services:	**Application Development and Consulting**
Address:	35 DiRubbo Drive Peekskill, NY 10566
Phone:	(914) 739-4477
Fax:	(914) 739-5545
CompuServe:	73767,2326

Roger Grossman has been working in the computer business for seventeen years. His past and current clients include Citibank, New York Life, Bankers Trust and Mobil Oil.

MPSI provides nationwide service, in the area of programming—from design to support.

Contact Roger Grossman.

North Carolina

Name:	**The Bruce Group**
Type:	**Independent Contractor**
Services:	**Consulting, Training and Software Documentation**
Address:	109 Pebble Springs Road Chapel Hill, NC 27514
Phone:	(919) 408-0331
Fax:	(919) 408-0415
CompuServe:	72777,3132

Walter Bruce, Executive Editor of Ventana Press and principal in The Bruce Group, is author of more than a dozen internationally published books on microcomputer software products with more than 250,000 books in print. Walt's books cover a wide range of topics, including Access and many other familiar names. Walt also has led training seminars on these and other software products for government and private industry clients coast to coast.

Contact Walt Bruce.

Name:	**Paul Nielsen Computing**
Type:	**Independent Contractor**
Services:	**Consulting, Training and Application Development**
Address:	6011 Willow Bottom Drive Hickory, NC 28602
Phone:	(704) 294-2387
CompuServe:	76517,1162

Paul Nielsen is Technical Editor for *Access Advisor* magazine and has written an Access developer book and numerous articles for trade magazines. Paul appears often at conferences throughout the nation, and is even involved in organizing many of them.

Paul Nielsen Computing is in the forefront of Access training and consulting, having been with the Access project long before the first version was released. PNC has published two major Access add-on products: TeamAccess and PowerShell.

Name:	**Learning Network, Inc.**
Type:	**Consulting Firm**
Services:	**Training**
Address:	4421 Stuart Andrew Boulevard, Suite 202 Charlotte, NC 28217
Phone:	(704) 525-9330
Fax:	(704) 525-9539
CompuServe:	72114,3552

Learning Network's clients include AT&T, Law Engineering, City of Gastonia, USLan, Springs Industries, BASF and J.C. Penny.

Learning Network has two classrooms located in Charlotte, NC. However, they also provide training and development services anywhere their customers need them—from New York to California. Their staff develops custom Access database applications in response to customer needs. All applications are very user-friendly and powerful.

They also offer Access training for power users and for developers. The developers training consists of four hands-on courses. Beginning (1 day), Intermediate (2 days), Advanced (2 days) and Access Basic Code (3 days). Classes are limited to 10 students.

All students receive a copy of their easy-to-understand manuals as well as sample code and a copy of the Wizards and utilities developed by the staff at Learning Network.

Contact Tom Lucas, Barbara Lucas or Craig Moore

Name:	**VisualAccess Corporation**
Type:	**Independent Contractor**
Services:	**Consulting and Application Development**
Address:	6118 Cork Tree Court Charlotte, NC 28212
Phone:	(800) MDB-FILE
Fax:	(704) 568-0064
CompuServe:	73500,2572

Michael Harding is a coauthor of the Access portion of *Inside Microsoft Professional* (New Riders Publishing). VisualAccess Corporation is a Microsoft Solutions Provider whose clients include First Union Nation Bank, Global Water Systems, American Express, Nationwide Recruiters and Planned Parenthood.

VisualAccess Corporation offers these services:

○ Access Development & Consulting

○ Microsoft Office Customization & Integration

○ WFW & NT Installation and Consulting

Areas served include North Carolina, South Carolina, Virginia, Georgia and Tennessee.

Contact Michael Harding.

Tennessee

Name:	**CDM Associates**
Type:	**Independent Contractor**
Services:	**Consulting, Application Design and Development.**
Address:	114 Ledgerwood Lane, RR#4, #311B Rockwood, TN 37854
Phone:	(615) 354-1500
Fax:	(615) 354-3116
CompuServe:	73770,1501

Bliss Sloan, an MIT graduate, has over 15 years of successful experience in medical, nuclear, aerospace and business computing.

Her clients have included NASA, NIH, Quorum Litigation Services, Bartlett (Nuclear) Services, Vande Vere Publishing, Lufthansa Airlines, Mt. Sinai Hospital in NY, DOE/Martin Marietta, Clinical Data, Stanley Hardware, Scientific Ecology Group and many others.

Bliss has authored or coauthored papers for Clinical Research Practice and Drug Regulatory Affairs, Harvard Seminar in Medical Information Science, IEEE Proceedings of Computers in Cardiology, and Proceedings of the Association for the Advancement of Medical Instrumentation Annual Meetings.

CDM Associates provides consulting and systems development services worldwide. Past and current clients have been from the United States, Canada, Europe and Africa.

Services offered include offsite consulting and systems design, development, and documentation using Windows, Access and other Windows development tools.

CDM Associates creates business applications and databases, research reports, data acquisition and analysis systems for medical, nuclear and aerospace applications as well as offsite direction and resources for your technical staff.

Contact Bliss Sloan.

Texas

Name:	**Presley Computing**
Type:	**Independent Contractor**
Services:	**Consulting and Application Development**
Address:	29322 Mandetta Drive Boerne, TX 78006
Phone and Fax:	(210) 981-9554
CompuServe:	70700,166

Jack Presley has over 10 years experience building custom database applications. He has written several applications for various government agencies.

Contact Jack Presley.

Name:	**Advanced Computers**
Type:	**Independent Contractor**
Services:	**Application Development and Consulting**
Address:	20067 S. Pecos Valley Trail Katy, TX 77449
Phone:	(713) 579-9466
CompuServe:	71623,1470

Ken Golding has 15 years of experience in computer software development and computer hardware support.

Advanced Computers offers custom-built Access applications for enterprise-wide systems.

Contact Ken Golding.

Virginia

Name:	**FMS, Inc.**
Type:	**Consulting Firm**
Services:	**Application Development**
Address:	8027 Leesburg Pike, Suite 410 Vienna, VA 22182
Phone:	(703) 356-4700
Fax:	(703) 448-3861
CompuServe:	75160,3375

FMS, Inc. is a leading developer of database tools and custom application for a variety of clients. Their products include Total Access, the database documentor for Microsoft Access.

FMS is a Microsoft Solutions Provider and has a combined thirty years of database development experience.

Their staff includes a contributing editor to *Smart Access*, a Microsoft MVP and an author of technical documentation for Microsoft.

Washington

Name:	**LEX Software Systems, Inc.**
Type:	**Independent Contractor**
Services:	**Consulting, Training and Application Development**
Address:	9665 N.E. Timberlane Avenue Winslow, WA 98110
Phone:	(206) 528-6868
CompuServe:	71204,2625

LEX Software Systems's clients include Glaxo, Hewlett-Packard, Microsoft, National Semiconductor, San Diego Gas & Electric and Walt Disney Pictures.

Mark Nelson is the developer of Microsoft's EIS-Builder and author of *Mastering Excel 5* from Sybex.

LEX Software Systems provides consultation and training in the development of client-server, EIS (Executive Information Systems) and database systems. LEX is currently one of the leading providers of EIS solutions under Windows.

Contact Mark Nelson.

Name:	**Applications Plus**
Type:	**Independent Contractor**
Services:	**Application Development, Consulting and Training**
Address:	23820 50th Avenue, SE Woodinville, WA 98072
Phone:	(206) 485-5907
CompuServe:	71042,1073

F. Scott Barker has worked at Microsoft where he has been part of the Microsoft FoxPro and Access teams, both as an employee and currently as a contractor. Prior to Microsoft, Scott worked as an independent consultant for six years. He has been published in both *Access Advisor* and *Smart Access*.

Scott is now doing full-time contract development in various industries including the banking, medical and insurance fields.

Contact F. Scott Barker.

B

INSTALLATION

This appendix will give you an overview of the Microsoft Access installation process. It details both the minimum and recommended hardware requirements for Microsoft Access and discusses the three different types of installation.

HARDWARE REQUIREMENTS

With most Microsoft Windows applications, the performance of the software can be in direct relation to the speed of the processor, the amount of free space on your hard drive and the amount of memory. Microsoft Access is no exception. You will notice that this section has two parts; the first outlines the minimum requirements for running Microsoft Access and the second outlines the recommended requirements.

Minimum Requirements

In your manual, Microsoft states that Access can run on the following requirements:

○ IBM compatible 386SX processor.

○ 6mb RAM.

○ At least 5mb of free hard disk space for a minimum installation and 19mb for a typical installation.

○ EGA or VGA display.

○ Microsoft Mouse or compatible pointing device.

○ MS-DOS 3.1 or higher.

○ Microsoft Windows, Windows for Workgroups or Windows NT 3.1 or higher.

There is a difference between what is required and what is *recommended*, however. The following sentence puts that into perspective: If you wanted to visit Hawaii, you'd be required to cross a large body of water. You *could* swim, but going by ship or plane is recommended.

When working with the minimum requirements, Access may exhibit some undesirable behavior. The less memory you have, the slower Access will run. It is also possible that you will experience some memory errors when you try to run large queries or complex forms.

Recommended Requirements

Executing an application on the minimum requirements will take longer than on a recommended system. The actual amount of time differs depending on the processor, free hard disk space and memory. The following is a list of the recommended requirements to run Microsoft Access:

○ IBM compatible 486SX processor (486/66 desired).

○ 16mb RAM.

○ 19mb free hard disk space for a typical installation.

○ VGA (640 x 480 or greater) display.

○ Microsoft Mouse or compatible pointing device.

○ MS-DOS 3.1 or higher.

○ Microsoft Windows, Windows for Workgroups or Windows NT 3.1 or higher.

This list is based on the experience of most of the professional developers in the industry. Of course, to have a Pentium with a gig drive and 32mb RAM would not hurt you (though it may hurt your wallet).

 If it is not feasible for you to upgrade your entire system to meet the recommended hardware requirements, you can choose to upgrade components of your hardware. Memory should be the first component upgraded. If you purchase a new system later, you can re-use the memory. The processor is the next most important component.

INSTALLATION

There are three different kinds of Access installation. You can install Access on your local hard drive, on a network server or on a network workstation. Before you install Access, you need to know where you are going to install it. Most users install Access on their local hard drive. Once you know where you are installing Access, you will be ready to begin.

In your Microsoft Access box, there are a number of disks that you will use to install Access. After you have started Windows, take disk 1 and place it in your floppy drive. Double-click the Program Manager to open it, if it is not already open. From the File menu, select the Run menu item. A dialog box like the one in Figure B-1 appears. Type **A:\SETUP** on the Command Line. Then choose OK to begin the installation process.

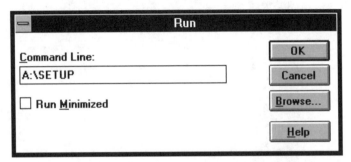

Figure B-1: Type **A:\SETUP** to begin the installation process.

 Keep in mind that you cannot start the Access installation process while a version of Access is running. You must close your Access applications before you begin the installation process.

Setup is a program that asks you a series of questions about how you want to install a Microsoft Windows product. Through Setup, you can determine where Access will be stored and which options will be installed.

Local Drive Installation

Most users will install Access on their local hard drive. After you have begun the installation process, Access will pop up a couple of dialog boxes. These boxes will let you know information such as your product identification number. In Figure B-2, you can see that

Access will install itself on the C: drive in the Access directory. If this directory does not exist on your hard drive, Access will create it.

If you have an earlier version of Access in the Access directory, you may want to consider installing Access 2.0 in a different directory from Access 1.x. Until you have had a chance to convert your database applications over to Access 2.0, you may need Access 1.x.

Also, if you are using security or workgroups, your settings will be renamed to the SYSTEM1X.MDA file. For information on how to rejoin your workgroup, refer to Appendix D, "Database Administration."

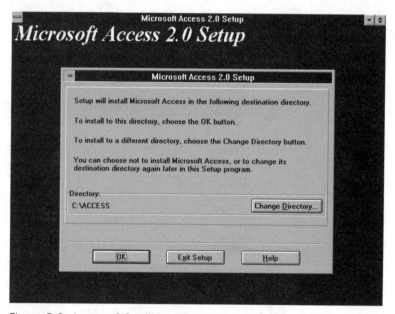

Figure B-2: Access 2.0 will install itself in the Access directory on your local drive.

Once you have decided where to install Access 2.0, you will be given three options. You can choose a Typical, Complete/Custom or Laptop installation.

Typical Installation

In the Typical installation, only the most commonly used features will be installed. After you select this installation process, you are prompted to choose a Program Group. The Program Group you select will house the Access 2.0 icons. This screen is visible in Figure B-4.

Custom Installation

The Complete/Custom installation allows you to select all or a combination of the features in Access. When you select Complete/Custom, a dialog box will appear, like the one in Figure B-3. Here you can pick and choose the features for Access 2.0.

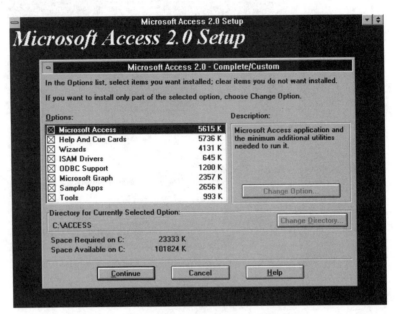

Figure B-3: The Options list for items to be installed.

In the lower-left corner of the box, Setup shows you the amount of space required for the installation of the options that you have selected. It also shows you the amount of free space on the hard drive. You can choose to install either all of the options or a combination of the options. This choice can be very helpful when you do not have a lot of hard drive space available.

Notice that each option has a small box to its left. The boxes with an X in them indicate the options that will be installed. You can turn off an option by clicking on that box to remove the X. These boxes are toggle switches. Either the X is in the box, or the box is empty. You can install a part of an option by highlighting that option and clicking on the Change Option button. Remove the X from the options that you do not wish to install and select OK to return to the main Options list. The amount of space required changes for every option that you remove.

Once you have decided what options to install, click on the Continue button to proceed with the installation. Choose a Program Group, as seen in Figure B-4, where you want the Access 2.0 icons to appear.

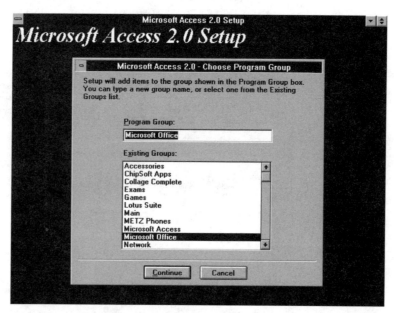

Figure B-4: Choose the Program Group in which you would like the Access 2.0 icon to appear.

Laptop Installation

A Laptop installation will install only the minimum features required to run Access 2.0. After you select this installation process, you are prompted to choose a Program Group. The Program Group you select will store the Access 2.0 icons.

Depending on the speed of your computer, Access 2.0 can be installed on your local drive in about 15 to 30 minutes. The icons associated with Access 2.0 are found in the Program Group specified during the setup process. Simply double-click on the Microsoft Access icon to launch Access 2.0.

Note: If you choose the Laptop or Custom installation to begin with and later find that a component is missing, you will have to go back into Access's Setup and choose Custom to reinstall just that component.

Network Server Installation

There are a number of different types of network operating systems on the market. Microsoft gives its blessing to five of them. Of course, Microsoft LAN Manager, Windows for Workgroups and Windows NT are the top three. Novell NetWare and Lantastic are the other two operating systems approved.

To install Access on a server, you must go through a workstation on the network. Why? For every workstation on a network, the server's hard drive does not appear as a local drive. To the user working on a non-dedicated server, its hard drive is not considered a network drive; it is considered local. Access can only install a server copy to a network drive. It cannot install a server copy to a local drive that is being used as a network drive for other workstations, because the local drive is not seen by Access as a server drive. In the case of a dedicated server, you cannot use the server at all. In the case of NetWare, there is no DOS prompt, hence you cannot run Windows.

Installing Access on a network server is similar to setting it up on a single machine:

1. Make sure that you are connected to the network server.

2. Launch Windows.

3. Close all applications except for Program Manager. Check your Task List to close all other applications.

 TIP   To check your Task List, shown in Figure B-5, press Ctrl & Esc.

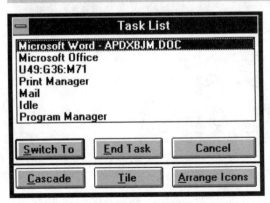

Figure B-5: The Task List shows all of the open programs. To close a program, highlight that program and click on End Task.

4. Take disk 1 and place it in your floppy drive.

5. From the Program Manager, select the Run menu item from the File pull-down menu.

6. On the Command Line, as seen in Figure B-6, type **A:\SETUP /A**.

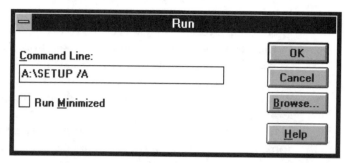

Figure B-6: This line uses the Access Administrator installation.

7. Click OK or press Enter.

During the installation process, Setup will ask you for a destination directory for Access. If you need to change the destination drive or directory, you can do so by clicking on the Change Directory button. A box like the one in Figure B-7 will pop up, allowing you to choose your desired drive and directory. Choose OK to return to the installation process.

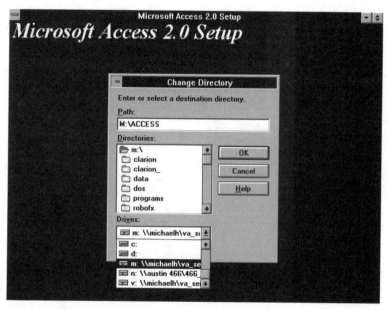

Figure B-7: Choose the correct network drive and directory of the server where Access is to be installed.

Access will prompt you to verify the destination of shared files. There will be files that are shared by users on the network. An example of a file that is shared by all users is Graph. Figure B-8 shows the screen where this information is visible. If you need to change the destination of the shared files, type in the correct server and path name. When you are satisfied with the location, choose Continue to proceed with the installation process.

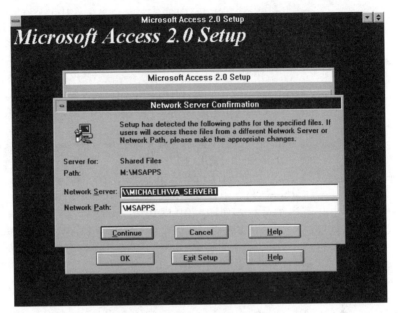

Figure B-8: Make sure that the server and path command lines are where you want the shared files to be located.

After you have completed installing all of the floppy disks, Setup will ask you where you would like to store your SYSTEM.MDA file. The SYSTEM.MDA file is one of the four kinds of Access files in the networking environment; the other three files are the program files, application databases and data databases. The SYSTEM.MDA file holds your user and security information as it pertains to your workgroup. This information is needed when joining a workgroup, and users within a workgroup share the same SYSTEM.MDA. When you are replacing an earlier version of Access, it may appear that Access has overwritten your SYSTEM.MDA file. Access simply renamed your old SYSTEM.MDA file to SYSTEM1X.MDA and gave you a new SYSTEM.MDA file. Any information needed to reconnect to a workgroup can be found in that file.

Network Workstation Installation

On the server, you should have installed a shared copy of Access 2.0. For a workstation installation, you choose whether you want to have access to the shared server copy, or whether you would like a full copy installed on your local hard drive from the shared server copy. On computers with small hard drives, it is recommended that you run from a shared copy.

The advantage of a shared copy is that most of the Access files remain on the server and leave more room on your hard drive. The disadvantage of a shared copy is that performance (speed) is slightly reduced because you are sharing the same copy of Access with all of the concurrent users on the network. The major disadvantage with a shared copy of Access is that if something were to happen to the server, it would not be possible for you to run Access.

If you choose to install a full version of Access from the server onto your local hard drive, you will have better performance, and you'll be able to remain productive when the server is non-operational. The major drawback is that you are required to have no less than 23.4mb free on your hard drive. You are probably wondering why would you want to install a full version from the server, as opposed to installing a local copy from the disks. The key word in that sentence is disks. For larger firms, like the Fortune 500 companies, it would be impractical for everyone to have his or her own copy of the Access floppy disks.

To get to this crossroads, you will need to access the network server drive. The easiest way to do this is to open up the Main program group from the Program Manager and double-click on File Manager. Select the drive icon for the server drive and locate the directory where the shared copy of Access is located. Highlight the file SETUP.EXE and choose the Run command from the File pull-down menu, as shown in Figure B-9.

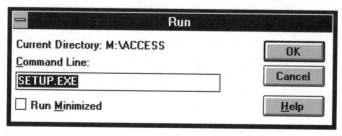

Figure B-9: Highlight SETUP.EXE and select Run from the File pull-down menu.

No matter which workstation installation you choose, the shared copy or the full copy, you will need to have some files installed on your workstation. Access asks you where to install your local copy of the user files, as seen in Figure B-10. If you want to change the destination of those files, click on the Change Directory button and select the desired destination.

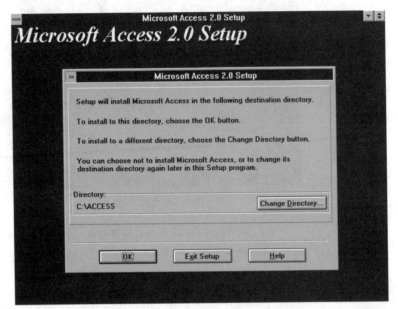

Figure B-10: This is where you want to install your local copy of the user files.

When you continue with the installation process, Access presents you with a screen like the one seen in Figure B-11. Notice that the first three icons are familiar; we discussed them earlier in this appendix. The last icon is the Workstation icon. When this is selected, only a few user files will be installed on the local workstation. The main core of Access remains on the server.

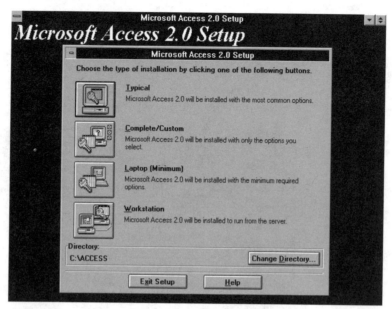

Figure B-11: Here the Workstation icon is visible.

The next step is to select the Program Group in which you want the Access workstation icon to be housed. The default location is in the Microsoft Office program group.

MANUAL FILE DECOMPRESSION

In the event of an accidental file deletion or corruption, you may need to restore a single file from the installations disks. Decompressing a single file is much less time-consuming than doing a full reinstall just to retrieve that file.

The Access installation files are compressed and stored on the floppy disks. The compressed files generally have an underscore (_) as the last character of the filename. This character needs to be replaced with the missing character. The file also needs to be decompressed to its original size.

Manual file decompression requires access to the file DECOMP.EXE. This file is stored on disk 1 of the installation set.

To manually decompress a file, follow these steps:

1. Copy DECOMP.EXE from disk 1 of the Access installation disks to a temporary location on your hard disk.

2. Copy the file you want to decompress from the disk on which it is located to the same temporary location as you copied DECOMP.EXE. The file you choose to decompress should end in an underscore (_).

3. At a DOS prompt, change to the temporary location on your hard disk (e.g., C:\TEMP).

4. Type **DECOMP C:\TEMP\MSACCESS.EX_ C:\ACCESS\MSACCESS.EXE.** Replace the path and filenames with the paths and files you are working with.

The new file will now be available in its original decompressed format.

C

SETTING UP MULTIUSER DATABASES

If you use Access on a stand-alone computer (i.e., a computer not connected to a network), you generally don't have to worry about making the tables in your databases accessible to other users. But when you are using Access files that are stored on a local area network (LAN)—often referred to as a *multiuser environment*—you do need to be aware that other users may at times need access to a database concurrently with your access. This appendix addresses steps you should take to get the best performance from your Access databases in a networked environment.

UNDERSTANDING EXCLUSIVE VS. SHARED MODES

By default, Access opens each database in *Exclusive* mode. This means that the user who opens the database is the only one who will be able to work on it. If you want other users to be able to use a database that you are about to open, you need to open in *Shared* mode.

When you are tuning for performance in a multiuser environment, there a couple of things to think about:

○ If only one person at time will access the database, by all means open it exclusively (in Exclusive mode), because performance will benefit greatly.

○ If more than one person needs to use the data concurrently, open the database in Shared Mode.

OPENING A DATABASE IN SHARED MODE

Following are the three methods you can use to open Access databases in Shared mode.

Unmarking the Exclusive Check Box

By default, when you open an Access database, the Exclusive check box in the Open Database dialog box is checked. To open a database in Shared mode, you have to unmark this check box (see Figure C-1).

Unmark this check box ———

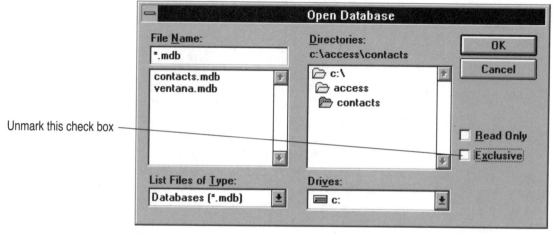

Figure C-1: To open a database in shared mode, unmark the Exclusive check box.

 When you display the File menu, Access lists the most recently opened databases at the bottom of the menu. If you open a database by choosing from this list, Access "remembers" whether you last opened it exclusively or shared.

Setting the Default Open Mode

If you are going to be opening most of your databases shared, you may want to set the Default Open Mode for Databases to shared so that you don't have to remember to unmark the Exclusive check box each time you open a database.

To change the default setting, first open any database. Then choose View, Options from the menu bar to display the Options dialog box. Scroll the Category list box and select the Multiuser/ODBC category. Finally, change the Default Open Mode for Databases setting to shared (see Figure C-2).

The next time you open a database, the Exclusive check box in the Open Database dialog box no longer will be marked. You can still open any database exclusively by remembering to mark the Exclusive check box when you open the database.

Change this setting to shared

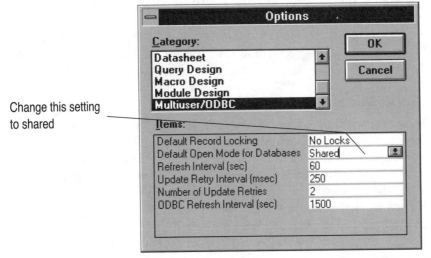

Figure C-2: The Options dialog box with the Default Open Mode for Databases setting changed to Shared.

Using the Startup Command

Adding a database name to Access's startup command enables you to bypass the Open Database dialog box completely, and it overrides the Default Open Mode for Databases setting.

To open the database in Shared mode, include the database name in the Access startup command. For example, to open the CONTACTS.MDB database (located in the C:\ACCESS\CONTACTS Directory) use the following command (from the File Manager or Program Manager):

```
c:\access\msaccess.exe  c:\access\contacts\contacts.mdb
```

To start Access and immediately open a database in Exclusive mode, add the database name to Access's startup command and follow it with the /excl switch. For example, to open the CONTACTS.MDB database, use the following command (from the File Manager or Program Manager):

```
c:\access\msaccess.exe  c:\access\contacts\contacts.mdb /excl
```

SELECTING A RECORD LOCKING SCHEME

When you are using Access in a multiuser environment and using tables in a shared database, there may be times when you are trying to use a table at the same instant that another user is working with the same table. To protect data in shared databases, Access enforces a record locking scheme.

Access has three record locking schemes that you can choose from. These can be set both at the global level and at the individual form level.

Global Record Locking

To set record locking at the global level, use the following procedure to change the Default Record Locking setting. Keep in mind, however, that changes to the Default Record Locking setting apply only to table and query datasheets and to forms created after you make the changes. Use the RecordLocks form property to set the record locking scheme for any forms that already exist when you change the Default Record Locking setting.

To change the Default Record Locking setting, follow these steps:

1. Open any database and choose View, Options to display the Options dialog box.

2. Choose the Multiuser/ODBC category from the Category list box.

3. Use the drop-down list to set Default Record Locking to one of the following schemes (see Figure C-3):

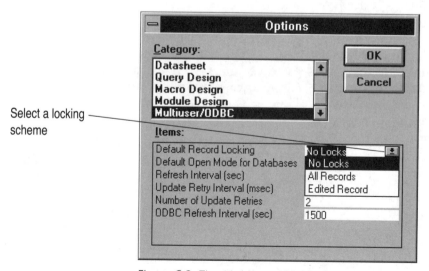

Select a locking scheme

Figure C-3: The Multiuser/ODBC category in the Options dialog box with the Default Record Locking drop-down list displayed.

○ *No Locks.* With the No Locks scheme (the default setting), records are not locked at all when a user begins to edit them. If another user makes changes to a record that you are editing and saves his or her changes before you have a chance to save your changes, Access displays the message shown in Figure C-4. This dialog box gives you the following options: 1) *Save Record*–the other person's changes are blown away; 2) *Copy To Clipboard*– the whole record is copied to the clipboard, which may later be appended at the end of the table so that your changes are not lost (which in turn can result in a problem of duplicate keys if the key field is not of counter data type); 3) *Drop Changes*–all the changes you made to the record are lost.

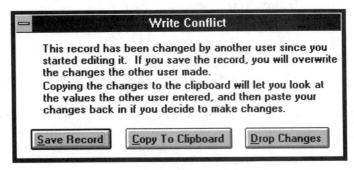

Figure C-4: The Write Conflict dialog box is displayed if another user has saved a record while you were editing the record.

○ *All Records.* Under the All Records locking scheme, if you open a table that another user already has opened, Access opens the table for you in Read Only mode. This means you can look but you can't "touch"–you can't make changes. This scheme is obviously not workable if multiple users need frequent access to the same data.

○ *Edited Record.* This is the most suitable locking scheme for most multiuser situations. The Edited Record locking scheme locks only the record that you are editing. You don't have to be concerned that another user may change the record while you are editing it (as would be the case under the No Locks scheme), and you are not locking all records in the table (as would be the case under the All Records locking scheme). Access informs other users that the record is locked by display- ing the international NOT symbol (a circle with a line through it) in the record selector column.

. . . .

Record Locking vs. Page Locking

Access does not have true record locking, but uses *page locking* instead. In this context, a page is a 2k chunk of data that may span a number of records—depending on the size of those records. Consequently, several records may be locked while you are editing a record. It is also possible that another user will be prevented from using the Append command if you are editing at the end of the table.

. . . .

Individual Record Locking

In addition to setting the record locking scheme globally, you can set the Record Locks Property for each form you create so that it will best reflect the record locking method needed for the form. The Default Record Locking setting determines the default setting for this form property. But you can change the property on a case-by-case basis when the particular form requires a different locking scheme.

The No Locks Default

In some cases, you may not have to worry about locking records at all. When record locking is not an issue, be sure to set the Default Record Locking setting to No Locks. This will relieve Access from the responsibility of locking and unlocking records and thus improve performance.

CHANGING THE REFRESH INTERVAL

Another way to fine-tune multiuser performance is to adjust the Refresh Interval—a setting in the Multiuser/ODBC category of the Options dialog box (see Figure C-2). The Refresh Interval tells Access how often (in seconds) it should refresh the current dataset in memory from its source located on the network. The lower the number, the more frequently the network is polled.

If you have many people making changes, then it may be a good idea to use a lower number in the Refresh Interval setting. It looks pretty "cool" to watch the data change practically instantaneously as users across the network make changes concurrently. But a low refresh interval takes its toll on Access's performance. If you have a subform that is updated frequently, other tasks in the form, assigned through controls and events, will not perform as fast as you would normally expect. The network traffic is also increased and will therefore slow down.

SEPARATING THE WHEAT FROM THE CHAFF

One way to optimize your application for multiuser performance is to keep the data on the network and keep the forms, queries, macros and Access Basic code in a database on the local machine. There are a number of advantages to using this method:

○ Performance is almost always enhanced. With all the application components local, they don't have to be transmitted over the network. The only time performance might not be improved is if you have an extremely slow workstation and a super-fast file server.

○ It is easier to update an application with no risk of affecting data. As your application matures, you will most likely be adding and modifying forms, reports, queries, macros and modules.

○ Temporary tables are no longer a problem. In a multiuser situation, temporary tables can become a problem if you have more than one person creating a temporary table for a report at the same time. This problem can cause some very interesting results, but it is eliminated by placing the temporary tables in the local database.

One complication that results from separating the data from the code is the need to attach tables contained in the database stored on the network to the local database. This is not really a problem, except that you need to use additional code when you are accessing the attached tables from Access Basic. Use the OpenDatabase function, supplying the path and name of the other database, where normally you would just use the CurrentDB function. The Attachment Manager add-in, included with Access 2.0, alleviates much of the tedium of reattaching tables when you update code.

OTHER MULTIUSER ITEMS OF INTEREST

When setting up Access for performance in a multiuser environment, it is a good practice to install Access on each workstation, rather than installing just one main copy on the file server.

For each Access database, the program maintains an .LDB file. This file keeps track of Access locks on various objects in the database. When you distribute a copy of a database, you don't need to include the .LDB file. Access will generate a new copy the first time the database is opened. Just be careful not to delete this file while a user has the corresponding database file open.

Note: There is a possibility that a user will be blown out of Access while editing records and will be left locked. If this occurs, have the user leave Access and delete the .LDB file associated with the database (.MDB). This will take care of the problem.

Database Administration

The maintenance of a database is as important as the maintenance of your computer hard disk or your car's engine. To keep it running at its optimal level of performance, you must spend some time with it every so often. As with any preventative maintenance schedule, the more frequent the checkups, the less likely you are to experience any data-damaging mishaps.

This appendix will discuss the steps that should be part of any preventative maintenance plan. We'll look at methods that organize your data for quicker access and at safeguard practices that help minimize losses in the event of damage or accidental deletion of critical information.

COMPACTING A DATABASE

If you have experience with hard disk defragmentation, you'll see that *compacting* a database is very similar. As time passes and the users of a database add, change and delete records, your actual data becomes scattered throughout your hard disk. Although you may be storing your database in a single .MDB file, Microsoft DOS actually controls how data is physically stored on the hard disk. As you add new records to your tables, the data is placed in the closest free area of the hard disk that DOS finds. When you delete records from your tables, DOS leaves the space used by those records empty. Eventually other unrelated records—or even unrelated data, such as spreadsheets and word processing files—may fill these gaps.

When you change data, the new changes sometimes require more space than the old data. DOS then puts part of your new record in the old location and the remainder in another location. This spread-out data splattering is known as *fragmentation*.

Some may ask why a hard disk has such a disorganized manner of storing data. Believe it or not, this is what makes the PC hard disk so fast. You don't have to wait for data to be rearranged in an organized fashion. DOS places pieces of data in the first open spaces it finds and returns the control of the computer back to you quicker. After all, that's what you are mainly concerned with– *response time.*

Over time this disorganized data placement may begin to affect the performance of your database. As a preventative measure you can reorganize the data in your database so it is contiguous. This method of *defragmentation* is known in Access as *compacting.*

You can compact a database using one of the following three methods, depending on your specific requirements:

○ Menu commands.

○ An Access Basic routine.

○ A macro.

Compacting Using Menu Commands

Using the menu commands is the most common and easiest method of compacting a database. As with all methods of compacting, the database must be closed in order to compact it.

To compact a database using menu commands, follow these steps:

1. Start Microsoft Access, but do not open any database.

2. Click on File, Compact Database. Access opens a dialog box that allows you to choose the database you wish to compact. Select your database and click on OK.

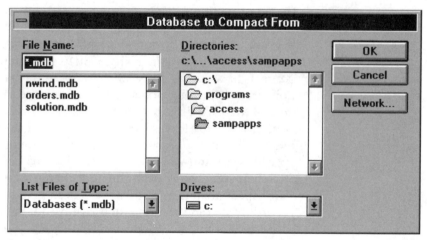

Figure D-1: Access asks for the database you want to compact.

3. Access now presents another dialog box, which asks for the name of the database you want to compact the database into. You can give the newly compacted database a new name, in which case you will have two copies—one uncompacted and one compacted. You can also specify the name of the original database to compact back into. If your database is very large, you may consider compacting your database into a new name so that in the event of a power loss or computer malfunction you will not risk the corruption of your original database. Upon completion you can copy the newly compacted database onto the old one. Click OK when you have selected a filename.

4. Access starts the compacting process, as you will notice by watching the status bar at the bottom of the screen.

5. When the compacting process is complete, Access clears the screen and returns you to a clean database window.

 You cannot compact a database that is in use. If you are using a database on a network, no other user may be using the database. If you attempt to compact an open database, an error will occur.

Things to remember about compacting:

○ The Compact program does not automatically convert Access 1.x databases to 2.x.

○ When you compact a database, you will need enough space on your hard disk to store two copies of it, even if you compact the database back into itself. If you *have* chosen to compact a database back into itself, Access will automatically delete the temporary one it used during the process. However, Access still needs enough space to store them both temporarily.

○ You can only compact a database from within the Database window. There is no Microsoft utility provided to compact a database without running Access. Some third-party developers do provide such utilities; however they are not endorsed or supported by Microsoft.

○ It may take a while to compact, depending on the size of the database and speed of the machine, so be patient.

Compacting With Access Basic

It is possible to compact an unopened database from within a different database already in use. One such method uses an Access Basic routine to accomplish this task. Using this technique, the user can be shielded from the dialog boxes and questions involved in using the menus. An Access Basic routine could start the compacting process, and provide the name of the original database and the database to compact into. You could use this to perform periodic maintenance with the single click of a button.

To use Access Basic to compact a database, you must use the CompactDatabase Method:

```
DBEngine.CompactDatabase "C:\OLD.MDB", "C:\NEW.MDB",
DB_LANG_GENERAL, DB_ENCRYPT
```

For more information on using the CompactDatabase Method, refer to the Access Help.

Compacting With a Macro

Similar to using Access Basic, you can also compact using a macro. The Access Basic routine is more direct, but if your knowledge of Access Basic is limited, this macro method will suffice. You can use the SendKeys Action to pass to the dialog boxes the original and new filenames. Use the SendKeys action with caution. If a future version of Access changes the structure of Access and its related functions, your SendKeys actions may not work. Fortunately, in the upgrade from Access 1.x to 2.0, no structural changes have affected the use of SendKeys. However there is always this possibility in future versions.

To use a macro to compact an unopened database, create a new macro as follows:

Action	Argument	Argument Value
SetWarnings	WarningsOn	No
DoMenuItem	Menu Bar	Startup
	Menu Name	File
	Command	Compact Database
	Sub Command	none
SetWarnings	Warnings On	Yes

REPAIRING DAMAGED DATABASES

One of the most terrifying sights a user can see is the dreaded "Database Corrupted" message.

Figure D-2: Access notifies you if it can't determine the format of a database due to corruption.

Access automatically offers you the option of repairing your database. In most cases clicking the OK button will do the trick and return the database to its original state.

To manually repair a database using the menu commands:

1. Start Microsoft Access, but do not open a database.

2. Click on File, Repair Database.

3. Access displays a dialog box and asks for the filename of the database you wish to repair.

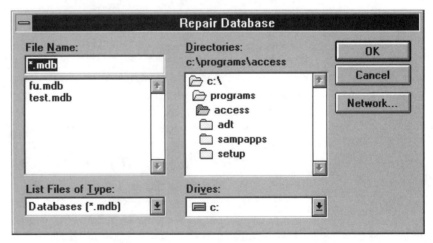

Figure D-3: Access asks for the filename of the database to repair.

4. Access acknowledges the database repair. Click OK to accept the repair. Access then returns you to the Database window.

Figure D-4: Access lets you know if the database repair was successful.

You can also use an Access Basic routine or a macro to repair a database, just as with compacting. Both are almost identical to the compact method.

To use the Access Basic routine, use the following:

```
DBEngine.RepairDatabase...
```

To use a macro, use the following:

Action	Arguments	Argument Values
SetWarnings	WarningsOn	No
DoMenuItem	Menu Bar	Startup
	Menu Name	File
	Command	Repair Database
	Sub Command	none
SetWarnings	Warnings On	Yes

If Access is unable to repair your database, there is not much else that can be done except hope that you have a backup copy. Currently there are no other utilities for repairing an Access database other than the Repair Database function.

ENCRYPTING/DECRYPTING A DATABASE

Encrypting an Access database scrambles the database in such a manner that it is impossible to use a utility such as a text editor or word processor to view its contents. During the encryption process Access also compacts the database.

To encrypt a database, follow these steps:

1. Start Microsoft Access, but do not open a database.
2. Click on File, Encrypt/Decrypt Database. Access displays a dialog box and asks for the filename of the database you want to encrypt/decrypt.
3. Enter the filename you want the database encrypted/ decrypted into. As with compacting, you can use a new filename or have Access encrypt/decrypt the original.

TIP Encrypted databases run about 10 to 15 percent more slowly than nonencrypted databases.

 TIP If a backquote (') character is used anywhere within an Access 1.x database, that database cannot be encrypted. Use Access 1.x to remove all references to the character, convert the database to Access 2.x and then encrypt it.

BACKING UP

Backing up your Access databases is no different from backing up any other information within your computer. In the development stages of a database, it is helpful to have backup copies in the event of corruption or accidental deletions.

To back up your Access database, follow these steps:

1. Close the database you want to back up. Database files in use by local or network users cannot be copied or backed up.

2. Using either DOS COPY, BACKUP or a third-party backup utility, such as PC Tools or Norton Backup, make a backup copy of your .MDB file(s). The .LDB files are record-locking storage files and will be created the first time you use your database. Therefore, there is no need to back up the .LDB files.

3. Make a backup of your SYSTEM.MDA file. This file is used by the Access security system. If your system is secured, and you lose the SYSTEM.MDA used when it was created, you run the risk of being locked out of that database FOREVER. You will have to start over from scratch.

4. Always back up your files to a removable media source, such as a floppy disk or tape.

5. Remove the media from the host computer and store a copy off-site if possible. Floods, fires, earthquakes, tornadoes and hurricanes are less likely to search around town for all of your backup copies.

SUMMARY

The proper care of a database takes only a few minutes every so often. However the re-creation of a lost or corrupted system will require much longer. Every administrator should set up a regular maintenance schedule for backing up and compacting databases.

INDEX

P

Colophon

The Visual Guide to Microsoft Access® was produced using PageMaker 5.0 on a Macintosh Quadra 650 computer with 20mb of RAM. The body copy is set in Garamond and headlines are Kabel and Bernhard Fashion, all from the Digital Typeface Corporation collection.

Pages were proofed on a LaserWriter Pro 630. Final output was produced on film using a Linotronic 330.

Ventana's
Visual Guide
Library

The Pictorial Companion to Windows™ Database Management & Programming

For Version 2.0

Walter R. Bruce, III
Dan Madoni
Rich Wolf

VENTANA PRESS

The Visual Guide to Visual Basic for Applications

A complete overview of all customs, features and uses—step-by-step examples for users with no previous programming experience.

The Visual Guide to Visual Basic for Windows, 2nd Edition

An A-to-Z encyclopedia of every command and technique—the classic reference!

The Visual Guide to Microsoft Access

This book/disk set takes you step-by-step from an overview of Access' features through detailed examples of each program element's use.

The Visual Guide to Paradox for Windows

AVAILABLE JULY '94

For DOS veterans and newcomers to Paradox! Covers all the new graphical capabilities of Windows as well as all the latest features of Paradox.

The Visual Guide to Visual C++

AVAILABLE JULY '94

A complete overview organized in an encyclopedic format, including AppWizard and the Foundation Class Library.

Call toll-free to order any Visual Guide, or the entire library!
(800) 743-5369 (U.S. orders only)

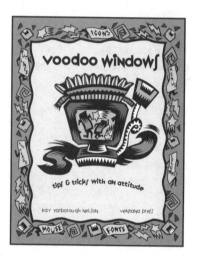

Ventana Companions

Design and Conquer!

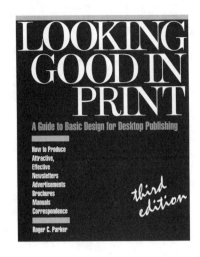

Looking Good in Print, Third Edition
$24.95
412 pages, illustrated
ISBN: 1-56604-047-7
For use with any software or hardware, this desktop design bible has become the standard among novice and experienced desktop publishers alike. With over 200,000 copies in print, *Looking Good in Print* is even better, with new sections on photography and scanning.

Advertising From the Desktop
$24.95
427 pages, illustrated
ISBN: 1-56604-064-7
Advertising From the Desktop offers unmatched design advice and helpful how-to instructions for creating persuasive ads. With tips on how to choose fonts, select illustrations, apply special effects and more, this book is an idea-packed resource for improving the looks and effects of your ads.

The Presentation Design Book, Second Edition
$24.95
320 pages, illustrated
ISBN: 1-56604-014-0
The Presentation Design Book is filled with thoughtful advice and instructive examples for creating business presentation visuals, including charts, overheads, type, etc., that help you communicate and persuade. The *Second Edition* adds advice on the use of multimedia. For use with any software or hardware.

Immediate shipment!
Full money-back guarantee!

To order any Ventana Press title, fill out this order form and mail it to us with your payment.

	Quantity		Price		Total
Advertising From the Desktop	_____	x	$24.95	=	$ _____
The Official America Online for Windows Membership Kit & Tour Guide	_____	x	34.95	=	$ _____
Desktop Publishing With Word for Windows, 2nd Edition	_____	x	$21.95	=	$ _____
Desktop Publishing With WordPerfect 6 for Windows	_____	x	$24.95	=	$ _____
The Gray Book, 2nd Edition	_____	x	$24.95	=	$ _____
Looking Good in Print, 3rd Edition	_____	x	$24.95	=	$ _____
The Makeover Book	_____	x	$17.95	=	$ _____
Newsletters From the Desktop, 2nd Edition	_____	x	$24.95	=	$ _____
The Presentation Design Book, 2nd Edition	_____	x	$24.95	=	$ _____
The Visual Guide to Microsoft Access	_____	x	$29.95	=	$ _____
The Visual Guide to Visual Basic for Applications	_____	x	$27.95	=	$ _____
The Visual Guide to Visual Basic for Windows, 2nd Edition	_____	x	$29.95	=	$ _____
Voodoo Windows	_____	x	$19.95	=	$ _____
The Windows Shareware 500	_____	x	$39.95	=	$ _____
Windows Internet Tour Guide	_____	x	$24.95	=	$ _____
Windows, Word & Excel Office Companion, 2nd Edition	_____	x	$21.95	=	$ _____
Word for Windows Design Companion, 2nd Edition	_____	x	$21.95	=	$ _____
			Subtotal	=	$ _____

SHIPPING:
For all regular orders, please <u>add</u> $4.50/first book, $1.35/each additional. = $ _____
For "two-day air," <u>add</u> $8.25/first book, $2.25/each additional. = $ _____
For orders to Canada, <u>add</u> $6.50/book. = $ _____
For orders sent C.O.D., <u>add</u> $4.50 to your shipping rate. = $ _____
North Carolina residents must <u>add</u> 6% sales tax. = $ _____
                                                                         TOTAL = $ _____

Name _____ Company _____
Address (No PO Box) _____
City _____ State _____ Zip _____
Daytime Telephone _____
___ Payment enclosed ___VISA ___MC Acc't # _____
Expiration Date _____ Interbank # _____
Signature _____

Mail or fax to: Ventana Press, PO Box 2468, Chapel Hill, NC 27515 ✈ 919/942-0220   Fax 919/942-1140

CAN'T WAIT? CALL TOLL-FREE ✈ 800/743-5369 (U.S. only)